"Better Living"

Media Topographies

General Editors

James Schwoch

Mimi White

Advertising,
Media,
and the
New Vocabulary
of
Business
Leadership,
1935–1955

William L. Bird, Jr.

Northwestern University Press
Evanston, Illinois

Northwestern University Press
Evanston, Illinois 60208-4210

Printed in the United States of America

ISBN 0-8101-1585-9 (cloth)

Library of Congress Cataloging-in-Publication Data

Bird, William L.
"Better living" : advertising, media, and the new vocabulary of business leadership, 1935–1955 / William L. Bird, Jr.
p. cm. — (Media topographies)
Includes bibliographical references and index.
ISBN 0-8101-1585-9 (cloth : alk. paper).
1. Advertising—United States—History. 2. Public Relations—United States—History. 3. Corporate culture—United States—History. I. Title. II. Series.
HF5813.U6B53 1999
659.1'0973—dc21 98-45398
CIP

The paper used in this publication meets the minimum requirements of the American National Standard for Information Sciences—Permanence of Paper for Printed Library Materials, ANSI Z39.48-1984.

for Mary, Emma, and Bill

	Acknowledgments	viii
	Introduction	2
Chapter One	The Politics of Better Living	10
Chapter Two	The Drama of Business Showmanship	24
Chapter Three	From Speeches to Stories	48
Chapter Four	The Notoriously Persuasive Voice	86
Chapter Five	The Return of the *Cavalcade*	96
Chapter Six	Talkers versus Doers: The Sponsored Motion Picture	120
Chapter Seven	Creative Discontent	144
Chapter Eight	Showmanship Triumphant	182
	Epilogue	206
	Abbreviations of Frequently Cited Collections	214
	Notes	215
	Select Bibliography	245
	Select Annotated Filmography and Videography	267
	Index	275

It is my pleasure to acknowledge the many obligations that I have incurred in the course of researching and writing this book. A Rockefeller Foundation Humanities Fellowship awarded by the Wisconsin Center for Film and Theater Research at the University of Wisconsin–Madison allowed me to explore at length the film and manuscript collections of the State Historical Society of Wisconsin. David Bordwell and Maxine Fleckner Ducey of the Wisconsin Center made my stay there as enjoyable as it was profitable; fellow Mark Vernet reminded me on occasion that sponsored motion pictures are mercifully short. Harold L. Miller guided me through the State Historical Society of Wisconsin's superb mass media manuscript collections, including most notably the papers of Bruce Barton and the National Broadcasting Company. A research grant from the FDR Four Freedoms Foundation supported my emerging history with materials gleaned from the manuscript collections of the Franklin D. Roosevelt Library. Grants from the National Museum of American History Research Opportunity Fund allowed for timely travel to collections in New York; Wilmington, Delaware; and Detroit and Flint, Michigan.

At the Hagley Museum and Library, John Rumm provided access to recently acquired DuPont Company papers describing the corporation's institutional television activities in the early 1950s. Michael Nash and Marjorie McNinch helped me navigate Hagley's extensive National Association of Manufacturers papers. Jon M. Williams entertained what perhaps seemed to be endless requests to listen to *Cavalcade of America* tapes. Barbara D. Hall provided access to collections of company photographs picturing key *Cavalcade* personnel and publicity. At the Library of

Congress, David Parker, Paul Spehr, Barbara Humphrys, Kathy Loughney, and Joe Balian generously imparted their special expertise and expedited access to collections of sponsored films, and scripts and synopses held in the motion picture copyright deposit file. Rick Prelinger of Prelinger Associates graciously provided viewing copies, frame stills, and thoughtful analyses of films that I had come to know only through scripts and synopses. Without his foresight, they would have been inaccessible or presumed to have vanished. Pierce Rafferty of Petrified Films kindly provided frame stills and a prized videocassette viewing copy of the *Middleton Family*.

Individuals and institutions that made this book more richly documented and illustrated than it might have been include Stanley Yates of the American Archives of the Factual Film at Iowa State University; Catherine Heinz of the Broadcast Pioneers Historical Library; J. Fred MacDonald, who kindly provided tape copies of radio's *American Family Robinson*; Peter Lyon; Charles Ruch of the Westinghouse Historical Center; Cynthia G. Swank of J. Walter Thompson; Jeff Williams and Mary Muenkel of Batten, Barton, Durstine & Osborn; George Wise of General Electric; Bob Finehout of Modern Talking Picture; Herbert Rolfes, who shared stills of the Century of Progress and the New York World's Fair; Arthur M. Schlesinger, Jr., who kindly granted access to his father's papers, and called my attention to the popular theatrical film *Cavalcade*; Patrice Donoghue and David Ware of the Harvard University Archives; Robert Burk, who shared his research on The Crusaders, Inc.; Jennifer Klein, who shared her research on automotive industry health plan policies; Bill Holleran of the General Motors Institute Alumni Historical Collection; the Walter P. Reuther Library, Archives of Labor and Urban Affairs, Wayne State University; Tom Hope of Hope Reports, Inc.; David Warrington of the Lilly Library, Indiana University; Mark A. Greene of the Bentley Library, University of Michigan; the manuscript and audiovisual sections of the National Archives and Records Administration; the Music Reading Room and the Manuscript Reading Room, Library of Congress; the UCLA Film and Television Archive, especially Dan Einstein; the Ronald Reagan Library, especially audiovisual archivist Steve Branch; the manuscript division of the New York Public Library, especially Christopher Alksnis; the Labor-Management Documentation Center, Cornell University; John Fleckner, Robert Harding, Fath Davis Ruffins, and Wendy Shay of the Archives Center, National Museum of American History; and Lisa Kathleen Graddy, Sandra Matthews, and Marilyn Higgins of the Political History Collection, National Museum of American History. I am further indebted to the staff of the Smithsonian Institution Libraries, especially Rhoda Ratner, Jim Roan, Helen Holley, Amy Begg, and Stephanie Thomas; and to the photographers of the Smithsonian's Office of Printing and Photographic Services, especially Dane Penland, Joe A. Goulait, Larry Gates, Terry McCrea, Hugh Tolman, Alan Hart, and John Dillaber.

This book came about as a consequence of my dissertation research on the history of political "spot" advertising. My primary advisers at Georgetown University, Father Emmett Curran, S. J., and Dorothy Brown, provided spirited comment, criticism, and direction that has led to the present work. From the start of my project the late Roland Marchand proved an invaluable source of inspiration, and he applied a critical eye to the manuscript in its entirety at crucial stages of development. Paul Boyer and Erik Barnouw read early versions of the *Cavalcade of America* material. Sally F. Griffith, Erika Doss, George H. Roeder, Jr., Victoria O'Donnell, Gerry K. Veeder, James Schwoch, and Mimi White commented on portions of the work presented in seminars and symposia. T. J. Jackson Lears, Leo P. Ribuffo, Harry Rubenstein, Keith E. Melder, Charles F. McGovern, John Rumm, Michael Nash, Peter Liebhold, Anna McCarthy, and Andrew Shanken provided thoughtful criticism and comment as the manuscript took final form. Sue Betz, my editor at Northwestern University Press, applied a critical eye to the crucial details of copyediting and production. Though my readers and editor saved me from interpretive errors, omissions, and lapses of judgment (so goes the usual product disclaimer), I accept responsibility for the work within these pages.

It is my privilege to be able to combine research interests in radio, film, and television with the demands of a museum career of collecting and exhibit projects that however much postponed the completion of the manuscript always made it better. In this endeavor Roger Kennedy, Gary Kulik, Tom Crouch, Spencer Crew, Lonnie Bunch, Art Molella, Edith P. Mayo, Rodris Roth, Susan Myers, Barbara Clark Smith, Pete Daniel, Mark Hirsch, and Bob Selim offered me invaluable advice and encouragement.

I am further indebted to Gordon Marsden, editor of *History Today*; to Matthew Geller, the curator of the New Museum of Contemporary Art exhibit and catalogue *From Receiver to Remote Control: The TV Set*; and to Horace Newcomb, editor of the *Encyclopedia of Television*, in whose publications portions of the manuscript first appeared.

I wish to thank my parents, William L. Bird and Lois Ann Bird, for their steadfast love and encouragement. My wife, Mary Dillon Bird, and our children, Emma and Bill, have shown me the true meaning of better living, and it is to them that I dedicate this book.

Washington, D.C.

"Better Living"

Introduction

"Better Living": Advertising, Media, and the New Vocabulary of Business Leadership, 1935–1955 describes the aspiring drama of a political claim. Beginning with the changes in business-government relations occurring under the New Deal, the work focuses upon the creation of radio, sponsored-motion-picture, and television entertainment that played a transitional role in moderating business discourse from the dark days of the Depression to the restored hegemony of the corporate commonwealth of the early 1950s. By "business" I mean an industrial organization or trade association that is able to produce—or cause to have produced—an entertainment for the primary purpose of sustaining a political point of view. This definition includes advertising, public relations, and media specialists, as well as a core group of network and advertising agency program builders, sponsored-motion-picture producers, and public and employee opinion survey specialists. *Better Living* pays particular attention to the business leaders who underwrote anti-administration talks during the New Deal, and to the specialists who turned those speeches into stories of selfless corporate social purpose. Among business leaders, the du Ponts and their associates in the General Motors group come to mind, as does the overlapping constituency of the National Association of Manufacturers (NAM), the American Liberty League, and other representatives of an entrepreneurial right, who came late to a broadcast strategy of entertainment and ingratiation of the American public.

The reclamation of lost leadership under the New Deal animated business discourse for a generation. Arguing that President Franklin Delano Roosevelt's political popularity stemmed from the promise of personal and specific benefits in the form of jobs and ever-higher standards of living, public relations and advertising specialists proposed that business learn to dramatize a rival promise of *better* living. Capitalizing on the commercial formulas of the mass media and projecting this competitive claim of "more," "new," and "better," they ushered in a shift from the rhetorical to the dramatic that looked beyond news and public affairs to culture.[1] The emerging drama of "leadership" was exercised diffusely by specialists who viewed elective politics as but an indicator of larger social and economic trends, irrespective of the party in power. Public relations counselor Edward L. Bernays, for example, devised a strategy of "action," featuring dedications and ceremonies reported by a compliant press that captured the attention and interest of "thought leaders."[2] Bruce Fairchild Barton, founding partner of the Madison Avenue advertising agency Batten, Barton, Durstine & Osborn (BBDO), urged businessmen to "spend half as much time with our lawyers trying to circumvent the politicians, and twice as much time with our sales managers and our advertising agents seeking to make ourselves popular with the Boss of the politicians, the public."[3] In the workplace, business discovered that leadership was an asset of industrial human relations. The guarantees to labor in section 7(a) of the National Industrial Recovery Act, for example, required that employers deal with workers in groups, rather than as individuals. Leadership meant discovering public and employee opinion, and modeling predictive communications techniques based on it.[4]

A merchandising proposition rather than a historical concept, the "New Vocabulary" traded in promotional language that had become the mainstay of American political culture. One recalls the New Nationalism of Theodore Roosevelt, the New Freedom of Woodrow Wilson, the New Era of Herbert Hoover, and, most immediately, the New Deal of Franklin D. Roosevelt.[5] The New Vocabulary's iconography of home and family life can be traced to nineteenth-century political campaign posters and handbills picturing, for example, the trickle-down munificence of tariff protection (fig. 1). Closer to the period, its antecedent personal and domestic focus may be seen in the 1920s institutional advertisements of General Electric, General Motors, and other center firms.[6]

What, then, was new about the New Vocabulary? The New Vocabulary allowed alternative and oppositional values into business discourse.[7] The most alternative idea was that of entertainment itself. Promoted as a preemptive strategy of business "showmanship" and a "psychology of business leadership," the New Vocabulary shifted the ground of the New Deal's rhetorically prone opponents to what many regarded as the equally dubious footing of popular culture. Network and ad-

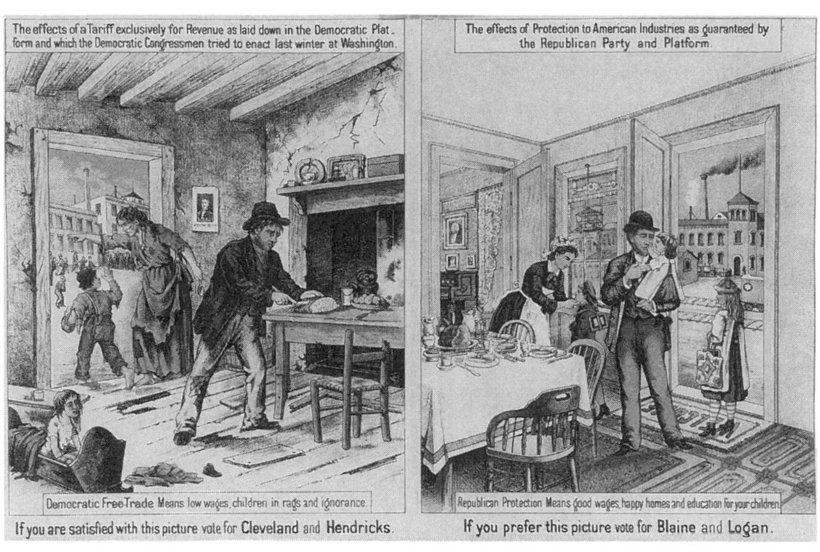

FIGURE 1.

Handbill, "The effects of a Tariff. . .The effects of Protection. . ." (1884).

Ralph E. Becker Collection, Smithsonian Institution.

vertising agency program builders countered that a carefully-thought-out plan of entertainment would pay political dividends in the long term. Channeling politically active clients into such a strategy, however, increased production costs and raised expectations of immediate effect. More often than not, the process of building radio programs and sponsored motion pictures for politically active clients faltered upon the remedial condition of sponsorship: the schooling of the upstart New Deal–Fair Deal coalition in conservativism's time-tested truths, principles, and economics.

Beginning with radio, I will argue, the dramatic anthology program formula represented a political compromise between an increasingly shrill and troublesome chorus of American business leaders and their public relations, advertising, and network specialists.[8] The process of radio program-building, played out for the officers of the NAM and the executives of the DuPont Company, brings political perspective to the economic "risk theory" of program formula.[9] Dramatic radio technique allowed specialists to adjust the distinctions of education and entertainment. Pliable drama with multiple meanings for multiple audiences explored the new social history (which by now included business), developed a flair for documentary expression, and synthesized the progress talk of science and invention. No subject was thought averse to play and fun.

The work proceeded by fits and starts. At BBDO, Bruce Barton declared that politics could be made appealing if conceived as a "show." During the 1932 presidential campaign Barton himself took to the air to introduce a series of pro-Hoover radio talks sponsored by the Republican National Committee. Barton decribed the talks as "something new in American politics . . . a series of political programs without a single politician. Instead of talks by politicians," Barton told listeners, "we are to have talks from famous writers, artists, singers, actors and motion picture and radio stars, and men who are doing interesting things in business."[10]

By 1937, this envelopment of "men who are doing interesting things in business" with "famous writers, artists, singers, actors and motion picture and radio stars" had become the basis of what Barton's fellow founding partner (and BBDO radio department head) Roy Sarles Durstine described as a "new vocabulary" of business showmanship. Durstine first used the expression to describe the mediated products of the "quickened tempo of today" conditioned by a public" influenced only by the dramatic, the exciting, the graphic, the simple smash." Durstine explained, "Big business has learned a new vocabulary. It has grabbed a new sales tool, absorbed a new technique, adopted a new medium. It's now in showbusiness."[11] Business showmanship, however, remained problematic. It was difficult to reduce a program's emotional impact to the quantifiable standards with which business rationalized choices and decisions. Acknowledging the problem, BBDO's house organ *The Wedge* described showmanship as "a spontaneous appeal to an emotion common to all. It isn't reasonable or logical. It has nothing to do with studied technique. It need not be relevant to the product. Very likely it has no sales appeal . . . . In the welter of economic facts and fantasies which bewilder business, there is still this solid ground of showmanship. Any business with the courage and imagination to put on a good show has as promising a chance to win out as it ever had."[12]

Quantification and elaboration of the New Vocabulary concept later came from the chart readers of the Psychological Corporation. A public opinion research firm alternately known as the PSC, the Psychological Corporation took up the new vocabulary in 1941 in promoting its interpretive social survey data, which were used to model a relaxed, corporate-cool "psychology for effective leadership." An organization of affiliated social scientists founded in 1921 by James McKeen Cattell, Robert S. Woodworth, and Edward Lee Thorndike, the PSC demonstrated the commercial value of applied social science with consumer surveys of brand awareness marketed as the "Psychological Brand Barometer."[13] Under the leadership of Paul S. Achilles, Matthew N. Chappell, and Henry C. Link in the 1930s, the PSC extended its reach with various survey tasks for corporate clients, including a 1934 survey of listener preferences for the National Broadcasting Company. Seeking to attract a lucrative client base, in 1937 the PSC began tracking public opinion toward the DuPont Company, General Electric, Westinghouse, General Motors, United States Rubber, Ford, United States Steel, and Bethlehem Steel.[14] The firm simultaneously embarked upon a program of "developmental research" to test survey techniques that were designed to provide data "of current importance" to corporate clients. *The Perils of*

Peace, the seventh in a series of reports published in October 1941, sought "to discover some of the forces influencing the present morale of the American people." The report looked beyond the present national defense emergency to identify a greater, more insidious threat: Americans' ambivalence toward their private enterprise system, its business leaders, and the anti-corporate features of the New Deal. Alarmingly, the PSC's survey questions, designed to probe the public's awareness of socialistic trends, had "proved impractical." "Questions aimed at this very point, namely, to discover the extent to which the public thought our present system was threatened" fell flat. "Quickly it became obvious that very few people feared state socialism, or even knew what it really meant." Armed with data demonstrating the public's indifference to the business system, the PSC charged that the anti-administration publicity typically spread by the NAM and other business groups had become clichéd and ineffective. "The public," warned the report, "cannot easily be stirred or influenced by speeches and pamphlets in defense of our present economic system as such. Broad generalities and statistics about the Merits of the American Way, Free Enterprise, the Merits of Advertising, the Partnership of Capital and Labor, leave the people cold."[15]

Arguing that business's prevalent rhetorical pattern of reaction and attack had failed to arouse, much less interest, the public, the PSC proposed a forward-looking "new vocabulary" of business leadership. It emphasized the specific and personal benefits that American business enterprise conferred, "and which people understand." The challenge remained for business to fashion a personally meaningful platform from which to "protest effectively against restrictions, such as unfair taxation and government interference" in the years ahead. To this end, the PSC awarded high marks to General Electric's institutional advertisements highlighting research, product development, and the preparation of new jobs for the future; General Motors' *GM Folks*, a *Life*-like employee picture magazine; and DuPont's dramatic radio anthology, *Cavalcade of America*.[16]

Public relations and advertising specialists might assimilate anything to meet their communicative challenge. Had not their counsel fallen on deaf ears, this would be the end of our story, yet it is the beginning. Chapter 1 shows how the politics of personal meaning, represented by the FDR fireside chat, acted as the starting-over point for modeling an intimate stage craft of "better living." Chapter 2 introduces the Madison Avenue and network program builders who drew upon the historical past and the world of letters to fashion reassuring radio salutes and tributes to American cities, states, and industries in the depth of the Depression. Here, a recurring paradox appears: a crisis necessitates a statement from business, but the proliferation of mass communication's popular possibilities poses dilemmas of its own. The dilemma in this case involves sacrificing the emergent, and popular, technique of dramatic radio production for verbatim broadcasts of the empty rhetoric of dinner and intermission talk.

The technique of dramatic radio production challenged the assumptions of businessmen, who preferred their culture whole and coherent. Chapter 3 examines the effort of the National Broadcasting Company to channel its largest commercial sponsors' escalating demands for anti-administration talk into the form of oblique dramatic programs. The program-building process begun by NBC and brought to fruition on CBS in 1935 by Roy Durstine and the BBDO radio department resulted in DuPont's *Cavalcade of America*. The *Cavalcade* established anthology drama as the broadcast formula of choice among specialists, if not their politically active clients, who persisted in launching indiscriminate efforts to unseat FDR and turn out the New Deal. Chapter 4 treats the specialists who joined the Republican presidential campaign of Alfred M. Landon to demonstrate the efficacy of commercial radio techniques such as time buying, the organization of regional spot networks, and broadcast merchandising. Roosevelt's resounding 1936 victory swept away the hubris of specialists and advertising generally, called into question the pursuit of short-term campaigns and short-term effects, and laid the groundwork for long-term strategies by business that focused upon "better living." Chapter 5 concludes the discussion of radio in the 1930s by looking at the *Cavalcade of America*'s endorsement by the du Ponts and their associates. The story touches on the role played by survey research in supporting the anthology formula, its assimilation of democratic values at odds with those of its sponsors, and its relaxation of educational values in merchandising stars and stories.

Chapter 6 shifts to a discussion of the sponsored motion picture. Specialists posed film as an alternative to radio when business most needed to speak. As in radio, entertainment complicated business discourse. Sponsored pictures abandoned the voice-over narration and the static demonstrations of manufacturing processes that had long defined what industrial films looked like and talked about. At the New York World's Fair 1939/40, for example, films played a central role in corporate exhibits, and they extended the life and meaning of exhibits for audiences otherwise unable to attend. Sponsored films that were made for theatrical release and circulation on the club and school circuit included Westinghouse Electric's *The Middleton Family at the World's Fair*, a lavish Technicolor production that blended industrial exhibitry, consumer stage shows, and the comedy-drama of pleasant suburban home life.

Chapter 7 views the sponsored screen's picture of community life as a successful strategy of corporate public and employee relations. Idealized pictures of home and family life successfully promoted private sacrifice and national purpose during the Second World War. After the war, however, contentious labor-management relations contributed to a resurgence of ill-conceived public and employee economic education campaigns touting the sanctity of private enterprise. The Taft-Hartley Act relaxed restrictions on top-down management communication, emphasizing letters and written argument. Campaigns imbued with this idea included the American Heritage Foundation's "Freedom Train" exhibit, the advertising industry's "Miracle of America" economic education campaign, and General Motors' employee contest, "My Job and Why I Like It." Displaying little patience with entertainment, advertisers backslid. The discourse of reaction and attack pervaded the short subject films of the NAM, allied industry groups, and corporate sponsors, who acted out the pedagogical urge "to write something serious," as the protagonist of the NAM's *Price of Freedom* put it.

Chapter 8 concludes with business's acceptance of entertainment as a strategy. Anticipating the home as the setting and location for the drama of business leadership, education was no longer the prerequisite for an evening's entertainment. By 1955 the dramatic anthology telefilm had become the medium and formula of choice among the nation's largest industrial corporations and institutional advertisers. This was particularly true of the institutional clients of BBDO, the advertising agency and program producer of television's *Cavalcade of America, U.S. Steel Hour,* and *General Electric Theater*, the latter a top-rated showcase of entertainment conceived to attract the largest television audience.

While we know a great deal about the public culture of the New Deal, relatively little has been written about the private culture of "more," "new," and "better" that was created to contain and combat the New Deal. Though we have no dearth of comment upon the documentary photography projects of the Farm Security Administration, the films of the Left, and FDR's radio style, until recently historians have paid little attention to the aesthetics of business's consciousness-shaping operations in quite the way that its creators did.[17] While others characterize the 1930s as the Red Decade, business efforts to infuse popular radio, industrial filmmaking, and television production with the personally meaningful drama of home and family life instead recommend the period as the conservative seedtime of modern entertainment.

The Politics of Better Living

By his newsreel and radio appearances he has planted himself in the spotlight, drawn attention to his personal qualities, and in effect invited a personal approval or disapproval of his acts. He is by all odds the best actor in talking pictures and the best voice in radio: until Mr. Roosevelt taught the world how that titanic trombone of tubes and antennas could be played no one had any idea of the possible range of virtuosity. The Republicans have no sweet singers to put up against him: none who would not be switched off at the second sentence in a public competition.

— "The Case against Roosevelt,"
Fortune, December 1935

Historians have noted advertising's cultivation of a personal voice. The personal voice and its use in fending off the intrusions of an impersonal world are, in part, advertising's own.[1] Conveying an impression of intimacy and confidence, the approach could be powerful indeed. Perhaps its most able practitioner was President Franklin Delano Roosevelt, whose inimitable style of address, the "fireside chat," built an audience for radio talk. A master of timing and tone, FDR, according to H. G. Wells, embodied "the most effective transmitting instrument possible."[2] The characterization of the FDR talk as a fireside chat fit radio's newly won position as the focus of family attention in the home. Seated before the microphone, FDR imagined his audience individually. His audience in turn believed him to be responsible for their personal well-being and improvement. The superintendent of the White House mail room recalled that when FDR asked listeners to "'tell me your troubles,' most of them believed implicitly that he was speaking to them personally and immediately wrote him a letter."[3] Leila A. Sussmann, in a sample of listener correspondence in the Roosevelt Library, found that "several writers treated these broadcasts literally as a conversation, listening and writing to 'Dear FDR' at the same time. Listeners interspersed their paragraphs with responsive comments such as, 'Excuse me while I laugh at that remark you just made.'"[4] Harold Ickes, traveling with FDR in 1936, noted the snatches of conversation he overheard from campaign crowds—on the order of "He saved my home"—which confirmed the effect. Republicans alike acknowledged FDR's semantic gift. Republican congressional campaign pollster Claude E. Robinson, for example, noted FDR's "marvelous sense of showmanship—use of words like 'social security,' use of channels of publicity, use of events to make the common man feel that at last he had a friend in the White House." Others read into "New Deal" the qualities of sportsmanship and fair play. Adman and Republican presidential campaign adviser Bruce Barton, no friend of Roosevelt's, though a dedicated practitioner of the personal technique, recommended the president's intimate method and heartfelt manner of expression to his clients. The New Deal's cumulative effect, Barton conceded after the 1936 plebiscite returned FDR to the presidency for a second term, was to impress upon the mind of the average man and woman that "*He is trying to do something for me.*"[5]

FDR's personal touch eluded those whom it infuriated most. If, as Barton claimed, the average American voter felt that FDR was "*trying to do something for me,*" an increasingly shrill chorus of American business leaders felt that FDR was trying to do something to *them*. This idea took hold among the leaders of the National Association of Manufacturers (NAM) and the American Liberty League. By 1936 the "Roosevelt Haters" had developed into a well-defined cult among the nation's business elite.[6] *Fortune* magazine intoned:

> The discussion of personalities is open, public, and confessed. Conversation turns not upon the national government but upon the person of the President. . . . It is His smiles, His phrases, His tricks of speech, His habits of mind, which the country discusses when it discusses politics. Matters which would appear as general issues in another campaign here appear in their reflection upon the character of the President. . . . For one criticism of a New Deal measure you will hear ten criticisms of the presidential voice, the presidential enthusiasm, the cocksure manner, the gladsome face, the cheerful elusiveness, the happy heart. There is nothing about the man which may not be made a cause for dislike.[7]

A measure of the depth of business's enmity toward Roosevelt could be heard in the corridors of power in New York, where it was whispered aloud that yes, the president was in fact insane.[8]

The "character of the President" inspired the NAM's and the Liberty League's top-down merchandising of Republicanism. Business complained that the New Deal had substituted political judgment for the workings of the market. Conservatives blasted the New Deal for violating economic law, for harassing businesses with labor legislation, for state competition, for congressional committee investigations, for expansion of constitutional processes, and for the illusory but ever-potent symbol of redistributive taxation.[9] In December 1935 the NAM announced publicly that the discomfiting trend of current events had forced it into "politics."[10] This announcement, issued from a business association established for the express purpose of tariff protection in the era of William McKinley, seemed preposterous. Howls of incredulity greeted it. The *New Republic,* applying a show business metaphor, compared NAM to the "Hollywood maiden who was studying to become a virgin, presumably for the purpose of being seduced."[11] In turn, Strother Holland Walker and Paul Sklar, former associate editors of *Tide*, a journal of advertising and marketing, noted the increasing expenditures for show business by business groups that desired to "turn out" the New Deal. Walker and Sklar were among the first to detect a trend toward "unit thinking" and "unit action" by the New Deal's business opponents.[12] Unit thinking proposed that business consider an attack upon one business or industry as an attack upon all; unit action proposed a consistent and concerted response in defense of capitalism. Culling through the radio programs, sponsored motion pictures, exhibits, and advertisements accruing to "unit thinking" and "unit action," Walker and Sklar concluded that business, in finding its voice, had become a faction: "lectures come with automobiles, confidence is sold with facial creme, along with electricity you get a philosophy of government and perhaps a tip on how to vote."[13] Other contemporary observers questioned business's errant sense of timing. The richer business leaders became, the louder they complained. The stock market appeared to be on the rebound. Could not the rising rate of return on investment be attributed to Roosevelt's New Deal reforms? Noting these "strange times," one reporter wondered that "a great many people who have done very well indeed under the New Deal are so bitterly opposed to it that they are backing their protests with their own money." For example, among the prominent backers of the Liberty League were the owners of the Phillips Petroleum Company, "whose common stock on March 3, 1933, the day before President Roosevelt's inauguration, was quoted at $5\frac{1}{8}$, and yesterday, was quoted at $44\frac{1}{8}$." Among the league's other backers, E. T. Wier of the National Steel Company saw his stock advance from 16 to $72\frac{3}{4}$; Alfred P. Sloan, John J. Raskob, and various members of the du Pont family saw their General Motors stock rise from $10\frac{3}{4}$ to $59\frac{3}{4}$ and DuPont Company stock advance from $33\frac{3}{4}$ to 148. "Of course," the reporter concluded, "Roosevelt may not have had anything to do with all this, but at least, like Lincoln when the Emancipation Proclamation was signed, he was there."[14]

Today the disparity between institutional appearance and reality is as great as ever, but at the Depression's outset, little distinguished the private discussion of business's so-called philosophy from the cruder manifestations of its interpretation to the public. In 1931, setting an early and unapologetic tone, NAM president John E. Edgerton described the Depression as "psychological" and stated that "anyone who used the term 'revolution' should be put in jail."[15] S. Wells Utley, the president of the Detroit Steel Castings Company and the National Founders Association, indulged the conservative assumptions of a usable past. If the American people supported the administration in the 1934 congressional elections, warned Utley, the consequence would be "retreading all the steps of progress taken by the English-speaking race since that day seven centuries ago when Englishmen forced the great charter from King John." Three years earlier Utley had attracted attention by stating that demands for the "dole, unemployment insurance and old age pensions should be met with the motto of Captain John Smith, 'he who does not work shall not eat.'"[16] The same forbidding tone echoed through the 1930s, in reaction to the ascendant Keynesian thesis of scarcity and diminishing expectation. A usable past of examples to the contrary animated business leaders' talks to the public, talks laced with a self-interested Americanism that lent a certain transparency to the proceedings. In 1935 General Foods' Colby M. Chester, NAM's newly elected president, likened the partnership of labor, the investor, and the consuming public to the "adventurous pioneers" of Jamestown and Plymouth, who wrested civilization from the wilderness and built institutions to match. "They came," Chester explained, "in search of liberty, of freedom from intolerable restrictions." The story of business, Chester concluded, was the story of America, "the story of continued resistance to arbitrary restrictions of all kinds."[17] Revolutionary-era parables of liberty and freedom animated business discourse through the Second World War and beyond. Writing in 1944, Edgar M. Queeny, the president of Monsanto Chemical, found it "fortunate that our colonists had endured a long era of oppressive government, which attempted to impose monopolies and restrictions on their freedom to engage in production and commerce." Fumbling his way toward a bid for audience participation, Queeny invited business's critics to imagine spending "the day at Mr. Wealthy's desk. They should have been given a chance to understand his problems!"[18]

The problems of Mr. Wealthy included the erosion of a native culture of value once affirmed by traditional texts. "For most of the 150 years of our existence as a nation," General Motors' Paul Willard Garrett explained, "our songs and poetry, our school books, our popular literature were written in a vein reminding people that they lived in the best of all lands. Ambition was generally taught as an admirable trait." "Successful men were objects of popular regard. To call a man a captain of industry was to praise him. So it is only in recent years that we have begun to talk about public relations."[19] The advent of new media in business's hour of need had only compounded the problems of ideological reproduction. Garrett's reminiscence figured as an apologia for GM's on-again, off-again sponsorships of radio's *Parade of the States* and *General Motors Symphony Concerts*. The latter, a tony showcase of intermission talks on subjects such as consumer research and auto safety, had rumbled into the defensive ditch of property rights during the United Auto Workers sit-down strike of 1936–1937. Jonathan A. Senneff, Jr., a correspondent of DuPont Company president Lammot du Pont, suggested, "Plain, old-fashioned visiting, which was a pretty good stimulus for the exercise of common sense, has been crowded out by progress in the form of entertainment via radio and the picture show." Determined to exploit "our greed for radio entertainment," Senneff's remedy was typical: "A gigantic weekly broadcast of the most acceptable radio talent in the county . . . broken so as to permit three three-minute talks on vital social and economic problems of national importance by commentators who could get the message across."[20]

The large corporation, much less the textbook of yesteryear, had lost what Stuart Hall has described as "the symbolic power to map or classify the world for others." Such power, Hall explains, accrues to "the inertial authority of habit and instinct" as well as the commonsensical "horizon of the taken-for-granted: what the world is and how it works, for all practical purposes."[21] The yielding of the direct prescription of "mental content" to indirect and cumulative effects was among the New Vocabulary's lasting lessons. Yet businessmen, who preferred their discourse whole, coherent, and without the apparent contradictions of education and entertainment, learned with difficulty, when at all.

The manner and bearing of business leaders, who were used to command from the dais, grated upon the sensibilities of listening audiences. "Leaders in business with few exceptions," a Republican National Committee publicist complained after FDR swept the opposition in 1936, "are unskilled in the more subtle aspects of symbol management. Verbal bludgeoning—vitriolic charges and vituperative denial—are almost the only tools they know how to use, and these can hardly be called the instruments of finesse."[22] Lack of skill in applying the instruments of finesse proved little impediment to the proliferation of radio talks by business spokesmen. Network schedules of business talks from the National Industrial Recovery Act in 1933 to the election of 1936 offer an index of the unsettling conditions of the Depression and the changes in business-government relations occurring under the New Deal. Both CBS and NBC broadcast business talks on a "sustaining basis" (free) whenever network officials judged the speaker, the sponsoring organization, or the occasion prominent enough. Flexible network policies regarding such broadcasts resulted in generous grants of sustaining time to businessmen, many who counted among the networks' largest sponsors of commercial entertainment. Carrying out the radio campaign of the entrepreneurial right, groups such as the NAM, American Liberty League, and The Crusaders, Inc., built or sustained national organizations with awards of network time. When it was denied, they attempted to purchase the time, desiring to appear as frequently as the physiological limits of listener fatigue and the deep pockets of their backers allowed. Between the congressional elections of 1934 and the presidential election of 1936, the Liberty League, for example, mounted a broadcast campaign costing in excess of $200,000 subscribed largely by individuals in the DuPont and General Motors groups. The Crusaders, Inc., the creation of Cleveland oil man Fred G. Clark, and whose prominent subscribers included Lord & Thomas advertising agency owner Albert Lasker, General Mills president Donald D. Davis, and General Foods chairman Colby M. Chester, successfully placed sustaining talks on NBC and CBS. The group later spent upwards of $160,000 for broadcasts on Chicago and Ohio stations, the Mutual network, and New England's Yankee network.[23]

The negligible cost and relative ease of production made sustaining talk a staple of business discourse. In an earlier time, network awards of sustaining time played a decisive role in shaping the politics of network "cooperation" with educators, who claimed a portion of the broadcast spectrum.[24] As Robert W. McChesney notes, the networks used sustaining time for demonstrations of "high grade" cultural programs deemed educational, good for radio, and available for sponsorship.[25] Beginning in 1934, NBC deployed this strategy against its politically active sponsors, whose talk requests made through the NAM, the Liberty League, and the Crusaders were becoming increasingly problematic. Specialists' experience at the hands of their politically active sponsors and clients was long, tortuous, and understandable. Soliciting NBC for sustaining time in 1934, for example, the Crusaders justified their proposal for a lengthy schedule of anti-administration talks with the disingenuous explanation that FDR had "ably succeeded in getting the public into the habit of looking for and listening to radio talks which five years ago did not approach public interest as such talks do today." The Crusaders' list of proposed speakers implied that the public's new habit included, in addition, looking for and listening to fireside chats underwritten by American business.[26]

The problem of network access became all the more apparent in early 1935. Noting Senator Huey Long's and Father Charles E. Coughlin's use of radio to turn public opinion against U.S. participation in the World Court, NBC's Washington liaison, Frank M. Russell, wrote, "Washington today has a very exaggerated case of 'jitters' on the effectiveness of radio in a determination of public policies."[27] NBC vice president for programming, John F. Royal, confirmed, "Our business is changing weekly."[28] Earlier Royal had decided not to sell time to Coughlin, who later succeeded in purchasing it on the Mutual network. Senator Huey Long was another matter; until removed from the scene by an assassin's bullet in October 1935, he ably exploited NBC's stated policy of making its network facilities available to any U.S. Senator or Congressman who requested them. As the jockeying for position between Republicans and Democrats became more heated, Royal determined to treat "politics" like "religion," that is, to award set amounts of sustaining time to organizations, to be parceled out among their designated speakers, rather than to individuals.[29] The comparison of politics and religion was apt, for each was freighted with controversy, something the networks wished to avoid at all costs. The practice of giving offense to no one had been instilled in Royal, who before joining NBC had risen through the ranks of the B. F. Keith vaudeville chain to the position of Midwest regional manager. When the Keith chains collapsed in 1930, Royal joined Cleveland's WTAM, where his showmanship and skill in developing talent for radio came to the attention of NBC President Merlin H. Aylesworth. Brought to New York in 1931 to take charge of network programming, Royal brought with him the sensibilities mindful of even the smallest of minorities. The practice of giving offense to no one would be judiciously enforced as a matter of network policy, Royal explained, because of radio's unique position as the focus of family attention in the home and the oversight of the public airways from Washington. The Federal bureaucracy, Royal quipped, contained no shortage of individuals who thought themselves expert in putting on a show.[30] That observation, made in an interview in the mid-1940s, applied to the New Deal's opponents as well. Many of them were among NBC's most politically active sponsors of commercial entertainment, whose determined effort to launch an expansive schedule of anti-administration talks showed no sign of abating in 1935. NBC officials noted that while administrations preceding Roosevelt's had used network facilities more than the opposition, by October 1935 the opposite was true. NBC president Aylesworth noted, "[It] is not due to the fact that we have offered more time to the opposition than heretofore. We have many more requests for radio time from the opposition than during the first two years of the present Administration."[31]

Business leaders demonstrated neither patience nor skill, other than in the scheduling of talks. It was left to their advertising, public relations, and network program builders to channel business's inclination to react into a drama of substitution. The popularity of New Deal liberalism, they patiently explained, required that business abandon rhetorical one-upsmanship for a selfless expression of social purpose. The New Deal's promise of a better life became both a stumbling block and a starting point for clients who persisted with attacks that neither advanced a meaningful claim of social leadership nor improved the condition of broadcast address.

Dedicated to drama in the largest sense of the word, "better living" became the uppermost objective of corporate enterprise, at least in its interpretation to the public. Bruce Barton, founding partner of Batten, Barton, Durstine & Osborn, whose clients included DuPont, General Electric, and lesser concerns, called on business to roll up its sleeves and start selling. Barton's contribution to the politics of better living lay in removing it wholesale from the legislative and policy-setting agenda of the politician, and putting it into the homespun domain of the consumer. Business and government, Barton explained, had become locked in a competition for public favor. Though government knew it, business operated as if it did not.

Businessmen talked too much to themselves and too long at Washington, with little to show for their efforts save their Pullman stubs. Insularity and self-interest undermined business's attack upon the anti-corporate features of the New Deal, an attack that Barton believed to be deserved but misconceived, because it failed to frame business's interests and activities in terms of the hopes and aspirations of the American people. "Fundamentally," explained Barton, "the people of the United States *think* they should have a better life, more comfort, more security, more opportunity, more hope. What they are likely to *do* is to make a choice between industry and politics as to the easiest method of achieving all these benefits."[32]

Bruce Barton was the son of a Congregationalist minister and historian, the Reverend William E. Barton. He was born in 1886 in Robbins, Tennessee, where his father had been temporarily assigned as a circuit rider. Barton grew up in the comparative comfort of Boston and Oak Park, Illinois. Graduating from Amherst College in 1907, Barton was accepted into the graduate school of the University of Wisconsin, where he planned to pursue an advanced degree in history, but for reasons that cannot now be determined, he never matriculated. Ineligible for active service in the First World War, Barton joined the United War Work Campaign, a fund-raising consortium of charities including the Salvation Army, YMCA, and Knights of Columbus. An early indication of Barton's gifted turn of phrase appeared with a slogan scribbled on a piece of paper for the Salvation Army's Evangeline Booth. Barton believed it would become "my most lasting words": "A man may be down but he is never out."[33]

In New York during the war, Barton met Roy S. Durstine and Alex F. Osborn. The three formed the advertising agency Barton, Durstine and Osborn (BDO) on the first day of 1919. Nine years later they merged with the George Batten Agency, forming Batten, Barton, Durstine & Osborn, Inc. (BBDO). The merger came about on the strength of the BDO radio department and the proximity of the two agencies in the same Madison Avenue building. Barton, the "word man," wrote advertising copy. Durstine, a Princeton graduate and Triangle Club thespian, supervised the radio department, while Osborn occupied himself with an agency field office in Buffalo.[34]

Initially Barton regarded his advertising career as a default for the less remunerative, though more fulfilling, service of the amateur historian or the professional politician. Behind the scenes, Barton advised every Republican presidential candidate from Calvin Coolidge to Richard Nixon and played a unifying role among congressional Republicans during the long night of Herbert Hoover, Alfred M. Landon, Wendell Willkie, and Thomas E. Dewey. In 1937 a seat in New York's Seventeenth Congressional District became vacant, and Barton ran for Congress. Winning the special election called to fill the vacancy, Barton went on to run successfully for a full term in 1938. Barton's prospects as Republican presidential timber enjoyed a boomlet of editorial support in early 1940. Importuned by Wendell Willkie to run for the U.S. Senate that year, Barton lost the election. Though humbled by the experience, Barton returned to BBDO with a renewed sense of social purpose. "The enthusiastic welcome which greeted my return was heart warming," he wrote. "I want to do in the next few years the best advertising work I have ever done and I want some of it at least to be beyond and above the mere garnering of box tops."[35]

Identifying the formative influences upon his philosophy of advertising, Barton's biographers emphasize his Protestant ideals and understanding of the use of the past that combined to inform the construction of a "historical Jesus" and served as a source of biblical parables on the importance of incessant advertisement. Barton was best known outside the field of advertising as the author of *The Man Nobody Knows* (1925), an interpretation of the New Testament that cast Jesus as an organization man and super-salesman. If only for this reason, Barton might have become a lightning rod in the historiography of consumption. Barton's philosophy of advertising, notes Warren Susman, not merely defended capitalism, but reconciled salvation with the emerging business order, thus helping transform a producer-oriented culture of thrift, savings, and self-denial into a modern consumer culture of spend, enjoy, and use up.[36] According to his own carefully cultivated press image, Barton continually studied the tastes and habits of the public. In the 1950s his office featured a large photo mural of the Atlantic City boardwalk that filled the wall behind his desk (fig. 2). A BBDO press release explained that the mural "was a clue to his constant interest in and curiosity about human beings and their doings."[37] In the 1930s Barton's office featured a framed quotation from the "gifted French gentleman" Talleyrand: "There is one person wiser than Anybody and that is Everybody." Barton explained that Talleyrand "so shaped his conduct that he was able to survive and exercise influence under a monarchy, through a revolution, under a consulship, under an empire, and finally under a monarchy again. An achievement that would seem to be worthy of respectful attention amid the tumultuous changes of today."[38]

Barton retained a lifelong interest in history and its uses, as well as in promoting the cause of corporate social leadership. Not unlike his "young man's Jesus," Barton detached himself from the day-to-day sale of goods, preferring instead overarching sales of service. This theme pervaded institutional advertising copy in the 1920s for General Motors and General Electric. General Motors advertisements promoted the "GM Family." General Electric advertisements promoted the company monogram as "more than a trademark . . . an emblem of service—the initials of a friend."[39] In later years Barton told a young BBDO staffer how he had won the General Electric account from corporation president Owen D. Young. Barton recalled paging through *Popular Mechanics* and other papers, "cut[ting] out everything that looked interesting in the way of new inventions or devices." Pasting it to cardboard

Figure 2.

Bruce Barton with office photo enlargement of the Atlantic City boardwalk (1956). Courtesy of BBDO.

with descriptive copy in the manner of a double-page spread in the *Saturday Evening Post*, he created a "very crude layout" that made GE "synonymous in the public mind with research, invention, progress." He told Young that each ad would feature some GE research accomplishment but would also "report dramatically progress from any and all sources, including competitors." "G.E. would not claim that it alone was making American civilization, but by sponsoring this report to the nation it would create in people's minds the belief that it is the headquarters of progress."[40]

When thinking out the possibilities of mass communication, Barton glided effortlessly from the corporate stewardship of science and invention to the personal touch needed to put on a show. Almost instinctively, Barton acknowledged that the products of science and technology—the telegraph, the motion picture, and radio—had changed business discourse more than the scientific methods and techniques that brought them to fruition ever had.[41] Pausing to contemplate the "magic of radio" during a 1922 broadcast performance of Ed Wynn's *The Perfect Fool*, Barton slipped out of the studio to inspect the transmitter atop the building. As he looked up at the stars, Barton's thoughts drifted from the "machinery" out into the night. Thinking not of transmitters, antennas, receivers, or the comedian's difficulty warming to the microphone, Barton contemplated the program's place in the lives of listeners.

> At that very hour, a gray-haired woman, in a little house up the Hudson, sat at her desk and, reaching across to a wooden cabinet, turned a round black knob. . . . In Pittsburgh, the rector of a fashionable church stepped up to the pulpit and touched an electric switch. . . . In a certain Western [*sic*] city a man excitedly pressed a telephone receiver to his ear. . . . In a far-off camp in northern Ontario a group of lumbermen's wives crowded eagerly, almost fearfully, around a table on which was a queer-looking square box. . . . Human atoms, separated by hundreds of miles, yet acting at that hour as if some invisible bond united them with a common expectation. What seeming madness![42]

Barton acknowledged that much of radio's progress had come "from the individual efforts of inventors," but "a very great deal of it has grown out of the organized research carried on in the laboratories of such great corporations as the General Electric, the American Telephone, the Westinghouse, the Western Electric, and others." "In a word, the companies that are greatest in this country have attained and hold that position because they make a systematic business of *looking ahead*. All of which," Barton concluded, "leads naturally to this last little personal question: How many people have a department of dreams, in their own minds? A research laboratory where the results that they expect to bring to pass, ten years from now, are being dreamed out and planned out today?"[43]

This vision became problematic with the onset of the Depression. Having used institutional advertising to claim responsibility for the progress and prosperity of the 1920s, business could not now escape responsibility for the dislocations of the 1930s. What Barton contributed to the reassertion of business leadership was a timely intensification of the progress theme that had sanctified the unbridled expansion of corporate enterprise in a more prosperous time. Business, Barton proposed, could reclaim its rightful position of social and political leadership by affirming that its products were the personal benefits of a uniquely productive business system. Barton provided an unapologetic defense of what by then had become roundly criticized as the "whig theory" of history. The central tenet of whig theory was the inevitability of progress. Described as a fallacious concept by historian Herbert Butterfield, whose *The Whig Interpretation of History* appeared in 1931, the unswerving delineation of progress figured as the mainstay of the English historiography in which Butterfield specialized. Butterfield criticized the whig method as an "abridgment" that made easy and irresistible the classification of "historical personages . . . into the men who furthered progress and the men who tried to hinder it." The collapse of past into present (which Butterfield described as "this system of immediate reference to the present-day") was remarkably like the method of Barton and the friends of business, whose particular brand of "progress talk" made comparable claims of abridgment and division. By 1935, these had delimited social and economic history to the status quo ante 1929 and ranked the leaders of the New Deal preeminent among the modern enemies of progress.[44] Addressing the self-styled Congress of American Industry, held in conjunction with the annual convention of the National Association of Manufacturers in 1935 (where Colby Chester set forth the association's opposition to "arbitrary restrictions" consistent with the "adventurous pioneers" of Plymouth and Jamestown), Barton elaborated upon the centrality of the product to the reclamation of social leadership. Engaging in a bit of historical revision of his own, Barton recalled the flush times ushered in with the growth of new industries in the 1920s. Worth quoting for their us-versus-them confidence in the uplifting attributes of consumption, Barton's remarks launched the notion of a usable past of consumer convenience and well-being in which the New Deal counted for little more than a brake upon the expansion of future prosperity.

> We say that the automobile business found the poor man chained to his own door-yard, with no horizon but the borders of his own little hamlet, and it has made him the monarch of time and distance. We say that the farm implement industry found man only a little higher than the animals—a valet to horses and chickens and cows; and it leaves him riding like a conqueror over his fields, doing the work of ten men, and yet not too tired for the radio or the movies at night. The electrical industry, the steel industry, the chemical industry, the food industry—dozens of industries—have similar records of achievement in adding to the comfort, healthfulness, and satisfaction of life. The politician says to the people: "Give us your dollars in taxes, and we will redistribute them." Industry says: "Give us your money in exchange for goods, and we will use it to produce more and better and lower-priced goods." On this issue the competition is joined.[45]

Thus for a generation of advertising and public relations specialists, Barton established a contest pitting personal well-being and improvement against the New Deal and all its work.

Distinguished by Barton's appreciation of the use of the past, American history became a marketable commodity that eased reluctant clients into ingratiating and ultimately entertaining expressions of corporate social leadership. At BBDO the polity of consumption that Barton envisioned inspired a stage craft of intimate proportion. Client slogans contained the kernel of the idea. The earliest and most widely imitated—"Better Things for Better Living . . . through Chemistry"—appeared in the fall of 1935 in DuPont's first institutional magazine advertisements and the broadcast debut of the *Cavalcade of America*. The slogan originated in BBDO's Madison Avenue offices, where DuPont account executive Maurice Collette and copywriter Les Pearl collated slogan suggestions solicited from agency staff. Collette put "better things for better living" at the top of a list of phrases sent to DuPont Company advertising director William A. Hart. Hart selected the first, adding the words "through chemistry."[46]

DuPont's succinct expression of the personal meaning of corporate enterprise inspired a glut of similar mottoes, notably, client General Electric's "More Goods for More People at Less Cost" and "More and Better Jobs at Higher Wages."[47] BBDO became the concept's command central, and Barton its arbiter and clearing house. General Motors' Paul Garrett, for example, forwarded several prospects for Barton's consideration. Garrett implicitly acknowledged Barton as the author of the ideal. Though BBDO had not handled the General Motors institutional advertising since the 1920s, nevertheless, Garrett asked Barton to select a company slogan for General Motors as a personal favor. He wrote:

> Give me your instinctive judgement and check off which of the following you like best to express the philosophy and character of General Motors:
>
> MORE THINGS FOR MORE PEOPLE
>
> BETTER THINGS FOR MORE PEOPLE
>
> MORE AND BETTER THINGS FOR MORE PEOPLE

Somewhat perturbed, Barton replied, "I think any one of those three lines is good, but they all sort of border on what we have been doing for years for du Pont [*sic*] . . . and more recently for General Mills, 'New Foods, New Ideas for a Better World.'"[48]

It remained for other specialists to devise a technique of dramatic production joining the imperatives of showmanship to the dramatization of a meaningful leadership of "better living." Showmanship was not merely incidental. It was essential. In this discourse, radio, by virtue of its newly won position as the focus of family attention in the home, occupied the seat of personal meaning. The drama of building and selling unfolded as America's largest industrial corporations entered the entertainment business, and entered to stay as the most expeditious way of asserting their leadership to an indifferent public.

The Drama of Business Showmanship

The Depression set in motion a review of institutional advertising accounts on all fronts. Budgets that met with scrutiny even in the best of times became subjects of skepticism, retrenchment, and cancellation. As outwardly business struggled to regain the public's confidence, an inner contest of wills developed between specialist and client. At issue were strategies of short- and long-term effect, of direct and indirect action, and of the relative value of education and entertainment. The contest often turned on the personality of the client. Many a campaign presented the unvarnished philosophy of its sponsor when the desired effect was short, remedial, and direct. Prominent examples included radio's *General Motors Symphony Concert* intermission talk by the "Voice of General Motors," the *Ford Sunday Evening Hour* intermission talk by Ford spokesman William J. Cameron, and the National Association of Manufacturers' serial adventure *American Family Robinson*. Many of the same sponsors had recently stepped up their investments in sponsored motion pictures and traveling exhibits. General Motors, a leading packager of exhibits for world's fairs and expositions, mounted Barnum-like motor caravans of scientific and technological displays.[1] The NAM took on the burden of film distribution in 1937 to place its message before the theater-going public more quickly. By 1935 such entertainments could hardly be made without an acknowledgment of political intent. A sponsored motion picture that promoted Chevrolet's sponsorship of the annual Soap Box Derby in Akron, Ohio, for example, idealized "red-blooded American boys, full of that grit and determination that makes winners and champions . . . hard at work inventing, creating, building something."[2] More to the point, Chevrolet advertising director C. P. Fiske quipped, "It's the Soap Box Derby against the soap-box orators. How can you have soap-box orators when thousands and thousands of boys are looking for soap boxes?"[3]

While specialists discovered new reasons to invest in motion pictures and special exhibits, along Madison Avenue the runaway success of commercial radio epitomized "the change in the agency business," as BBDO's Roy S. Durstine put it, "since Drama came knocking on our doors."[4] Production of programs for a new home-based audience, as Simon Frith suggests in the context of the BBC, traded in light, middlebrow entertainment shorn of theatrical speech and the rough edges of the music hall.[5] In America the smoothing of rough edges faltered upon rival conceptions of the listening audience. "One thing that makes radio programmes hard to plan," Durstine explained, "is that the sponsor usually has ideas." Durstine's favorite attention-getting technique when appearing before his fellow specialists was to parody clients critiquing a program—tellingly, the company "treasurer," "head chemist," "chairman of the board," "head of the research laboratory," "comptroller," "president," "advertising manager," and "export manager."[6]

Radio's growth, as well as its sale to clients with ideas, tapped established cultural forms.[7] By the early 1930s, radio's program formulas and conventions had begun to emerge from a decade of haphazard and chaotic development.[8] Ongoing experimentation with production techniques distinguished the work of the in-house radio departments of advertising agencies and the programming staffs of the National Broadcasting Company and the Columbia Broadcasting System.[9] In 1927 Barton, Durstine & Osborn established the first self-contained radio program production department in an advertising agency. By 1933 the trade press described the agency's radio department as the "ablest" in America and its leader Durstine as the "father of commercial broadcasting."[10] Born in Jamestown, Dakota Territory (North Dakota), in 1886, Durstine entered Princeton University in 1904, where he edited the student humor magazine *Tiger* and performed in the productions of the campus Triangle Club. Durstine later described these activities as the defining experiences of his career. After college Durstine began work as a reporter for the New York *Sun*. In 1912 he left the paper to do publicity work for Theodore Roosevelt's Bull Moose campaign, an experience that led to a career in advertising. Durstine's published work included *Making Advertisements and Making Them Pay* (1920), *This Advertising Business* (1928), and *Red Thunder* (1934), an account of his travels in Soviet Russia and Nazi Germany.[11] Taking life's lessons where he found them, Durstine ranked the popularity of tabloid journalism with that of the totalitarian spectacles of Stalin, Hitler, and Mussolini. Durstine wrote, "There are those who may feel that showmanship was even known in this country in our last presidential campaign when a gentleman asked for a glass of water in the midst of a fire-side chat with his one hundred and thirty million neighbors. Is it any wonder that American industry realizes that it, too, must be interesting?" According to BBDO agency lore, Durstine first learned about radio from Bruce Barton, who had attended Ed Wynn's 1922 broadcast of *The Perfect Fool*. It was Durstine, however, who schooled Barton and BBDO's "stalwart" institutional clients in showmanship conditioned by "the stepped-up pace of life today."[12]

The production of radio culture began at BDO when Durstine brought radio manufacturer Arthur Atwater Kent to the air. The *Atwater Kent Hour* (1925), on which many of the stars of the Metropolitan Opera made their broadcast debuts, built an audience for radio among listeners most able to afford Kent's high-end receivers.[13] Institutional accounts followed. The "all-star variety" show *General Motors Family Party* inaugurated NBC's 24-hour, coast-to-coast network operation on Christmas Eve 1928. Conceived as a symbol of corporate scientific and technological mastery, the Carnegie Hall broadcast featured soprano Maria Kurenko, baritone Marshall Everett, and a talk by General Motors president Alfred P. Sloan, Jr.[14] The broadcast's integration of institutional salesmanship with the festive holiday spirit soon became a commonplace.

Carrying out the production of the broadcasts brought Durstine into contact with the "far sighted people" of the networks, particularly NBC, who "realized the responsibility involved in radio's intimate touch with the family circle," and who had "invested in the training of talent for the unique purposes of radio." Endeavoring to discover a production "technic," Durstine claimed that there were no precedents, only "people of imagination." "They believe that a technic will be found which is not an adaptation of musical comedy, nor of the legitimate stage, nor of the opera nor the concert platform. They believe that a technic will be found that is not an adaptation of anything—that is all radio."[15] Developing an all radio technique and an agency staff, Durstine hired Arthur Pryor, Jr., the son of the celebrated Sousa trombonist and band leader. The junior Pryor became the link between the emergent technique of dramatic radio production and the music of Sousa, Gilmore, and others of his father's generation, whose performance in an earlier day expressed values that heretofore could only have been expressed verbally.[16] Hired to head the BDO radio department in 1927, Pryor either directed or oversaw the development of the *General Motors Family Party*, Standard Oil of New York's *Soconyland Sketches* (1928), GM's *Parade of the States* (1931), DuPont's *Cavalcade of America* (1935), and other culturally reassuring entertainments.

Program builders discovered positive qualities in radio's limitations as a medium, not the least radio's apparent capacity to focus listener attention and engender a sense of confidence and participation. Radio's dramatization of the historical past, for example, capitalized on willing listeners already familiar with national figures and events. In short order, program builders appropriated the historical reputations of Washington and Lincoln with the same relish that they adapted the plays of Shakespeare and the short stories of O. Henry.[17] They capitalized upon the vast market for biographies and the narratives of popular amateur historians like poet and Lincoln authority Carl Sandburg and independent scholars like James Truslow Adams.[18] The discovery of the historical past as an asset to be mined in the mind of the listener held advantages for the adventurous advertiser. Dramatic radio production visited the preindustrial past popularized by the Colonial Revival and the dawning state and local history movement, whose enthusiasms ranged from displaying early American decorative arts to putting up roadside historical markers.[19] Under the watch of Barton, Durstine, and Pryor, BBDO, too, discovered a "treasure house of Americana." In keeping with vehicular notions of tourism and travel, client Standard Oil of New York's *Soconyland Sketches* focused radio's transporting qualities upon the discovery of regional historical shrines and manufacturing centers. Said by a BBDO company history to be the first commercial sponsorship of dramatic "sketches" on the air, *Soconyland Sketches* debuted little over a year after Standard Oil's John D. Rockefeller, Jr., announced the restoration of Colonial Williamsburg.[20] The program, presented on an eight-station network of NBC affiliates covering New York and New England, was heavily merchandised using traditional media. Program director Arthur Pryor explained that radio "is a whole lot more effective . . . when it is supplemented with, or is supplementing a swell copy job."[21] Though little remains today in the way of scripts and synopses, contemporary advertisements in the *Saturday Evening Post* suggest something of the broadcast's regional and civic appeal. Each described the "lore and legend" of "Soconyland," "a glorious playground where history was made," a "storied" country of "rugged mountains," "noble rivers," "fertile valleys," and "thriving hamlets." The first advertisement, entitled "Come to New England," exclaimed,

> Here five Presidents were born. Four of the houses still stand. Here Paul Revere made his midnight ride and the tea was tossed into Boston Harbor. Here lived Emerson and Longfellow, Whittier and Hawthorne. Stand in the rooms where their great works were produced. Toss a stone on the ever-growing pile which pilgrims have built on the site of Thoreau's cabin. . . .
>
> And, while you are making history live again, visit the industries of modern New England. Their products go all over the civilized world. The men who make them are friendly and glad to welcome visitors.[22]

Depositing the reader at the scene of production, the series' last advertisement, subtitled "See the Workshop of the Nation," suggested:

> There is no better education in Americanism for your children than a tour through this lovely and friendly land. Many of the industries are open to visitors. All the historic shrines are open. And everywhere you will find clean, inexpensive inns, and hospitable people eager to make you welcome.
>
> Bundle the children into the car, put in the luggage too, start your good motor, and come.[23]

In addition to advertisements in the *Saturday Evening Post*, the campaign produced broadcast talks and magazine advertisements that featured the governors of the New England states and New York, and New York City mayor Jimmie Walker. BBDO calculated that the "job" involved taking eight pages in the *Post*, arranging for the on-air appearance of seven governors and Mayor Walker, printing and distributing 25,850 16-page portfolios and 245,000 enlargements of the *Post* advertisements, and producing eight special radio shows, eight radio talks, and countless spin-off publicity stories. Behind-the-scenes activities included keeping governors William Tudor Gardiner of Maine and Frank G. Allen of Massachusetts "in line." A copywriter had to make a special trip to get New York governor Franklin D. Roosevelt's "approval on final proof."[24]

The use of the historical past to point up the prospects for industrial progress became a mainstay of dramatic radio production. Notable examples included *Westinghouse Salutes* (1929) and the derivative General Motors' *Parade of the States* (1931), which offered "tributes" and "salutes" to states, cities, and industries. *Westinghouse Salutes* debuted nationwide over the forty-station NBC Blue network on a Wednesday evening, November 6, 1929. Billed as "a distinct departure from the usual type of radio entertainment," it presented the first in a series of weekly half-hour industry salutes, "a tribute to the world's workers in iron and steel." Featuring "dramatic sketches" and "musical numbers," the program took as its theme "dramatic moments in the history of this industry." Other broadcasts in the series celebrated the aviation, paper, and food industries, the last "in keeping with the Thanksgiving spirit."[25] A second schedule of salutes announced for 1930 celebrated the petroleum, farm, cement, motion picture, newspaper publishing, rubber, lumber, glass, metal mining, and radio industries.[26] Depleting the supply of industries by 1931, *Westinghouse Salutes* turned the spotlight to cities, rendering "musical scores and vocal descriptions . . . to interpret to the American Radio public the spirit, the 'tone' of each city's flourishing industry, commerce and culture."[27] "Under industrial guidance, science conquers time and space . . . cities rise overnight . . . great business groups work miracles in manufacture, research, transportation and civic development. In *Westinghouse Salutes* these threads of modern magic are woven into the fabric of a novel series of radio programs."[28] The merchandising campaign never presented a program as an entertainment without acknowledging its educational value ("Westinghouse . . . in paying tribute to forward steps taken by industry and culture, combines educational features with entertainment")[29] and objectifying its choice of dramatic technique ("Music was chosen as the medium for a very obvious and sound reason: music will do more to heighten the dramatic quality of each broadcast than any mere dull recital of statistical facts could do").[30]

General Motors' *Parade of the States* carried on the reassuringly rich admixture of education and entertainment as the Depression deepened from 1931 to 1932. Proposed by NBC president Merlin H. Aylesworth and developed by Barton, Durstine, and Pryor, *Parade of the States* aimed "to sell America to Americans" in a "salute to the states," one a week for a year. General Motors president Alfred P. Sloan, Jr., explained the goal: to unite the two great forces—transportation and communication—that bound the people of North America together in a "homogeneous whole." From the days before the Pony Express to the current "instantaneous transmission of intelligence by means of the radio," the "catalytic agent . . . Transportation," had built a continent—and in Barton's words, "knit [it] into a neighborhood."[31] Continuing this tradition, the *Parade of the States* proposed to "use radio to bring the country together, to go even further towards proving that radio can, and does, break down sectional barriers and laugh at distances."[32]

On a grander scale than *Soconyland Sketches*, and with more substantial backing than *Westinghouse Salutes*, *Parade of States* coupled Barton's idea of the usable past and Durstine's dramatic radio technic with Sloan's emphasis of the role of advertising in shaping corporate identities. Sloan's insight into the administrative problems of large-scale corporate enterprise had propelled him to the presidency of the world's largest automaker. Born in 1875, Sloan's formative experience included a visit to the World's Columbian Exposition of 1893 and education at the Massachusetts Institute of Technology, from which he graduated with a bachelor's degree in electrical engineering in 1895.[33] He gained early experience in the automobile industry as a managing partner of the Hyatt Roller Bearing Company, a manufacturer of anti-friction bearings. In 1916 Sloan sold the company to William C. Durant, the founder of General Motors. Brought into the GM fold, Sloan resumed the management of Hyatt as the president of United Motors Corporation, a Durant holding company of automotive parts suppliers that included Dayton Engineering Laboratories (Delco), New Departure Manufacturing, Remy Electric, Perlman Rim, Klaxon, and Harrison Radiator.[34]

Fast becoming a modern necessity, the automobile attracted the capital of investors predicting a healthy rate of return on investment. John J. Raskob, the treasurer of the DuPont Company, invested in General Motors stock and soon convinced DuPont Company president Pierre du Pont to do the same. In 1918 the DuPont Company became involved in GM's capital expansion and financial control, investing 25 million of its 90 million dollar profit from First World War munitions contracts. Having already allocated 40 million dollars of the surplus to fund post-war diversification, DuPont's directors hesitantly agreed to invest 25 million dollars, or roughly half of the remaining surplus, in General Motors stock. Raskob actively promoted the deal, stressing that "our interest in General Motors will undoubtedly secure for us the entire Fabrikoid, Pyralin, paint and varnish business" of GM's car divisions. His prophecy was brought full circle with joint ventures managed by Sloan and GM research director Charles F. Kettering—Ethyl "knockless" motor fuel and quick-drying Duco paint, which reduced the time needed to manufacture an automobile, and whose possibilities provided consumers with a colorful alternative to the "any color as long as it's black" utilitarianism of Henry Ford.[35]

The key concept of Sloan's administration, "decentralized operations and responsibilities, with coordinated control," deployed accounting techniques and statistical controls to evaluate the profitability of the corporation's car divisions, and the firm allocated resources accordingly.[36] Applying his modern understanding of advertising to the redundant products of GM's car divisions, Sloan put in place a pricing scheme that encouraged consumers to trade up to the next level of automobile. Developed in response to the saturation of the primary market for basic transportation in the 1920s, GM offered "A Car for Every Purse and Purpose" in an overlapping hierarchy ascending from Chevrolet through Pontiac, Oldsmobile, Buick, and Cadillac. Increasing outlays for advertising emphasized style and design features, and by the mid-1930s centered on the annual "model change" and unique selling propositions such as "knee action" front suspension and "turret top" roof construction.[37]

The pricing scheme played to a similarly conceived hierarchy of radio entertainments ranging from comedy, light music, and variety programs to broadcasts of semiclassical and classical concerts. Each division's program reflected the scheme's assumptions about the listening tastes and preferences of the targeted consumer. Chevrolet and Pontiac, for example, sponsored comedy-variety programs—notably, Chevrolet's *Al Jolson* (1933) and *Jack Benny* shows (1934) and Pontiac's *Stoopnagle and Budd* (1934). Up the ladder, Pontiac, Oldsmobile, and Buick sponsored variety and light orchestral music. Pontiac sponsored the *Paul Whiteman* program (1932), later sponsored by Buick (1933). Climbing to the top, Buick and Cadillac sponsored semiclassical and classical concerts, the *Buick Concert* (1932–1933) and the *Cadillac Symphony Concert* (1934).[38]

Sloan chaired the corporation's first institutional advertising committee in 1922. Contracting with Barton, Durstine & Osborn, the following year a campaign that was directed to the attention of GM employees, dealers, suppliers, and the two million "families who own one or more of its products," began with magazine advertisements headlined "What Is General Motors?" and "Why Is General Motors?" The campaign, Pierre du Pont explained to stockholders, sought to acquaint the public with General Motors and its products, "just as a family might seek to introduce itself by capitalizing upon the goodwill of its well-known members." Though du Pont generally questioned the value of advertising, he acknowledged that Sloan's institutional advertising committee, having brought together individuals from the corporation's far-flung manufacturing divisions, had fostered a "General Motors atmosphere" and a "working together spirit." For Sloan, the campaign confirmed advertising's value as a management tool. Moreover, it underlined the unifying effect that even the largest of industrial corporations might achieve by adopting the manner and speech of a "family."[39] The concept extended to the corporation's earliest radio programs, the *General Motors Family Party* and the *Parade of the States*.

Publicity for *Parade of the States* announced that "the treasure house of Americana has opened its rich stores to radio." The "assets, resources and romance" of each state provided the basis for musical interpretation composed and conducted by Erno Rapee, the right-hand man of impresario S. L. "Roxy" Rothafel. Over the course of its year-long run, *Parade of the States* employed a cast of several hundred musicians, actors, and actresses. The program debuted nationwide on the NBC Red network on October 10, 1931. Coinciding with the celebration of the Yorktowne Sesquicentennial, the first broadcast saluted Virginia. The program opened with a "symphonic poem" written by Rapee that transposed Stephen Foster's "Carry Me Back to Old Virginia," followed by a selection of Virginia reels. Next, the *Parade* transported listeners "by music to an Indian wedding festival, followed by a musical interpretation of the legend of Pocahontas." Then, a "hunting scene . . . was pictured in music, with lords and ladies of the manor house gathered together on New Year's Day for the hunt." The broadcast concluded with the "Negro Rhapsody" *(Rhapsodie Negre)* by composer John Powell, who accompanied on piano, followed by a medley of "patriotic airs associated with the state."[40] This disarming "priceless treasure" from "Uncle Sam's song chest" bracketed a three-minute tribute written by Barton, who prepared each week's talk after traveling "in my library."[41] It was left for Sloan to explain that General Motors' venture in institutional programming culminated a search for a program type. It combined "national interest" and "education presented in so romantic a way as to be entertainment as well," and was "one step nearer solution to the problem of giving a real theatrical performance on the air instead of a straight musical program."[42]

During the course of *Parade of the States'* year-long run, NBC's Merlin Aylesworth attempted to interest President Herbert Hoover in appearing on the program. Aylesworth asked that "the Chief" consider making a brief talk on the "stability, progressiveness and firm foundation of our country." Apparently concerned about the propriety of Aylesworth's request, Hoover declined.[43]

Like Aylesworth's suggestion, Barton's state tributes spoke to the series' inherently civic design, and the packaging of an influential audience of government officials, educators, religious leaders, and members of fraternal organizations and women's clubs. The merchandising plan included presentations of Barton's tributes, elaborately framed, to state and local historical societies. Specialists were able to quantify the program's success: each broadcast brought on an outpouring of listener requests for printed tributes in scroll form suitable for framing (figs. 3 and 4). After forty-eight states, the District of Columbia, the U.S. Territories, and a special finale, General Motors compiled Barton's tributes for similar coverage. In the spirit of the broadcast, the dust jacket exclaimed, "We know of no man more fitted to rediscover America, and to re-sell it to Americans than BRUCE BARTON as he has done in this Epic of America." The foreword, signed by Sloan, gushed, "Only the spirit of the pioneer, battling new frontiers, could have created such a nation." The *Parade of the States* provided "the answer of the General Motors Corporation, its sponsors, to

FIGURE 3.

Bruce Barton and Alfred P. Sloan, Jr., with a day's mailing of scroll-tributes sent in response to listeners' requests, *Parade of the States* (1932). Courtesy of NBC Collection, State Historical Society of Wisconsin.

LAPPING waters under the prow of the birch canoe, silent sweep of glistening paddle, soft padding of moccasined feet over the brown cedar needles—all the way from Quebec came the intrepid Jean Nicolet to beach his canoe on the shores of Green Bay—first white man to gaze upon the green hills and azure lakes of WISCONSIN, happy hunting ground of the Winnebago Indians. That was three centuries ago. ℂ Spirit of Nicolet and those other valiant pioneers who followed your moccasin tracks—what a heritage of constancy and courage you have passed on to WISCONSIN and her people! Over the green wooded landscapes where Black Hawk led his red warriors in a hopeless cause against the intruding whites, now rise shining cities. The hidden trails that echoed only to moccasins and unshod hoofs now are thousands of miles of modern motor highways. And in between sweep the fertile, generous, rolling acres of farmland, golden with grain or green with pasture, dotted with cattle, the aristocrats of the dairy world. ℂ Wherever we live we dine on WISCONSIN'S food products, prepared in WISCONSIN'S utensils. We wear WISCONSIN'S fabrics at work and at play; we sleep in WISCONSIN'S beds. And the fruitful acres of all the earth yield their bounty through WISCONSIN'S ploughs and threshers. ℂ "Forward" is her motto, and well she deserves it. In Watertown America's first kindergarten was born. At Madison, the capital, on beautiful Lake Mendota, rises the magnificent State University, a pioneer and a power. ℂ At Milwaukee, John Comfort Fillmore made transcriptions of native Indian melodies. Literature has been enriched by Hamlin Garland, Edna Ferber, Zona Gale, and Thornton Wilder. And on the honor roll of statesmanship WISCONSIN has written the name—LaFollette. ℂ With all WISCONSIN'S growth, her initiative, her development, here you will still find the WISCONSIN of three centuries ago, the happy hunting ground, an unrivalled vacation land where the trout, the black bass and the muskellunge lure and reward the eager sportsman. ℂ Gleaming lakes, tranquil rivers, laughing brooks, flowering hillsides, and two great inland seas—all these call you. ℂ Answer the call, for WISCONSIN will welcome you. On her behalf General Motors extends an invitation to the nation. And to her, in turn, for what she is through nature's generosity, for what she has become by the courage and effort of her people, for what her golden future holds—General Motors pays tribute tonight.

As broadcast by General Motors
to the Nation — August 1st 1932

Figure 4.

General Motors' *Parade of the States* tribute to Wisconsin. Smithsonian Institution.

the assertion that there can be nothing new in radio."[44] Yet Sloan had by no means entered the entertainment business. The number of states unsaluted by the *Parade of the States* had dwindled to a handful by the summer of 1932, and it became apparent to NBC officials that Sloan would allow General Motors the institution to leave the air, much as Westinghouse officials had, after exhausting their programs' available supply of state, industry, and city salutes. NBC officials desired that Sloan and General Motors maintain a continuous institutional presence on radio, beyond the corporation's commitments to the popular music programs of its manufacturing divisions. General Motors went on the air institutionally, explained Sloan, only when it had a good idea.[45]

As the final broadcast of *Parade of the States* neared, NBC executives anxiously solicited ideas for its replacement. A synopsis entitled "Problems of the States," for example, proposed a schedule of panel discussions on public affairs broadcast from state capitals. Network officials apparently rejected the idea out of hand.[46] A proposal presented by NBC continuity editor Burke Boyce sustained the series' civic premise. "The program I have in mind," wrote Boyce, "would do for radio what 'The Covered Wagon' did for the movies; it would show in fiction form the growth and development of a nation." Entitled "The American Cavalcade," the program "would really be a historical novel" on the order of James Galsworthy's *Forsyte Saga*. Boyce wrote:

> [The] first setting might perhaps be at a tavern and at the house of a wealthy land owner somewhere on the road between Virginia and Philadelphia. A plot would be developed which would focus interest around the family living on this plantation and the people living in and near the roadside tavern. And through their eyes and through what happens to them we would following [*sic*] the developments of American independence.
>
> The famous figures of the age such as Washington, Franklin, Jefferson and so on would pass along the road so that we would see them as the average person of the day really saw them—as rather distinct and mysterious figures. I know from my radio writing experience that this point of view is often the most dramatic and the most interesting—and it is a new way of treating history on the radio. . . . a most unusual show could be presented on a very large, dignified and intensely interesting canvas.

Beginning with the revolutionary generation, listeners would follow the fortunes of the family through its descendants, leading to "the real development and settlement of the Ohio and Mississippi valleys—the growth of trade—the opening of the Great Lakes and the river waterways—and in brief follow the whole general history of the building up of our country."[47]

Though Boyce's program synopsis for "American Cavalcade" failed to attract Sloan's interest, it nevertheless anticipated the historical anthology drama as a program type. Boyce's proposal exhibited features that would later endear the form to a generation of specialists: a personal focus, figures and events already familiar to listeners, and the recovery of a usable past that had everything to do with the deadening reality of the deepening Depression, by having nothing to do with it at all.

Others would add to the malleable store of broadcast Americana; however, Sloan's managerial competence had little use for multiple meanings and audiences less in search of an education than an evening's entertainment. While business leaders expressed little doubt that the progress of the machine age would end the Depression, the progress of dramatic radio production did come to a standstill among the largest industrial producers. Radio showmanship involved significant expense, which few pursued without pause. *Soconyland Sketches* continued its regional run until 1934; *Westinghouse Salutes*, having expended its supply of city, state, and industry tributes, left the air in 1931, the apparent victim of a cutback in corporate advertising and public relations activities. After General Motors' *Parade of the States* expired without replacement in October 1932, Sloan confided to Fisher Body's Charles T. Fisher that although the corporation's car and institutional advertising would continue, "we can ill afford to do it." Sloan justified reduced expenditures for advertising, institutional or otherwise, with the statement that one-tenth of the savings applied to "proper public relations work" would provide GM with "a better balance and a more effective position."[48]

Sloan's quest for value did not reflect a desire to roll back the promotion of GM's products or philosophy; rather the opposite. In the deepening Depression there was work to be done. Complaints about corporate size, for example, resonated through the early Depression in the often-expressed suspicion that large corporations were poorly managed, as evinced by the capacity for overproduction and technological unemployment. The issue of corporate size crystallized in the "production for use" theories advanced by the Technocracy movement of the early 1930s. Though the movement had collapsed by 1933, the "menace of the machine" perceptions that had sustained it lingered.[49] Additionally, with the coming of the New Deal, uncertainties about federal and state tax policies toward the auto industry and about the growing power of labor preoccupied General Motors' managers.[50]

Day-to-day supervision of General Motors' response to the Depression's dislocations proceeded under the management of Paul Willard Garrett. A Wharton Business School graduate and former financial page editor of the New York *Evening Post*, Garrett joined the GM public relations department in 1931. Setting out to combat the public's apprehension of "bigness," Garrett proposed "A Bigger and Better General Motors." Garrett conceived two distinct yet overlapping publics—consumers and opinion leaders. Important to consumers, Garrett noted, was GM's competitive position with Ford and Chrysler, and the auto industry's unique position among smokestack industries. The consuming public—"Mr. and Mrs. Jones"—directly touched its products, unlike, for example, those produced by the steel industry. For GM's opinion-leading public of "conservative students of finance," "the upper ten or twenty per cent of intelligent observers whose views in turn influence public opinion," Garrett proposed to release "accurate figures" and "scientific data on the auto industry and its own operations." Public relations activities would "impress General Motors on the minds of the thinking classes as a great and unique industrial enterprise." To this end, Garrett proposed to publish a company history and investigate sponsored motion pictures, "among the most effective media for building good relations internal and external." Garrett mentioned nothing of radio.[51]

As a further measure of Sloan's drive for economical promotion, in December 1932 Garrett contracted with public relations counselor Edward L. Bernays for the specific purpose of conducting a "propaganda" campaign around the annual auto shows held in New York and Chicago. A publicist with the Committee on Public Information during the First World War, Bernays specialized in the modeling of "two-step" communications effects that caromed from opinion-leading elites to the general public. The technique remained unchanged since the promulgation of Woodrow Wilson's Fourteen Points: the framing of an appeal in terms of the "self-interest" of thought and opinion leaders, the roundup of approving statements from "disinterested authorities," and the use of personalities to promote the news value of an "action"—typically, a dedication, celebration, or commemoration. The technique capitalized upon the instrumentalities of the mass media, particularly the press, but included radio inasmuch as it played a reportorial role.

Bernays did not limit his considerable energies to the promotion of a mere auto show. Rather, he conceived a campaign to promote the automobile's contribution to social and economic progress, with General Motors' products as its leading examples. Compared to a double-page spread in the *Saturday Evening Post* or production of the *Parade of the States*, the cost of the campaign was modest. Bernays wrote a telegram that, under Sloan's signature, went out to 200 industry, finance, and education leaders, requesting an affirmation of scientific and technical progress. The campaign's first "action" became a dinner to honor automobile pioneers featuring General Motors vice president for research Charles F. Kettering. The following day GM released the telegrams to the press. Though neither dinner orators nor telegrams mentioned Technocracy, the press made the connection, reporting that the telegrams lauded General Motors as a public-spirited institution pressing ahead with research and invention. Bernays's campaign did not circumvent Technocracy so much as co-opt the Technocracy movement's machine-tooled rationalization of progress and abundance for all.[52] The reportage impressed Sloan, who thereafter endorsed public relations actions as a needed corrective to GM's outlays for advertising.[53]

Thereafter, the action, which Bernays in a moment of self-deprecation described as the "dinner plan," became the operating feature of General Motors' institutional promotion. Dinner plans celebrated the opening of the Century of Progress exhibition (1933–1939) and General Motors' exhibit building, the dedication of an exhibit section entitled the "Gallery of the States" (celebrated on the Fourth of July, America's "natal day," Bernays explained), and the publication of *The Turning Wheel* (1933), Arthur Pound's company history. A dinner arranged by Bernays at the Columbia University Faculty Club hailed Pound's work as a "new approach to the writing of history." History department chairman Dixon Ryan Fox, who later played an instrumental role in merchandising DuPont's *Cavalcade of America*, noted that "one of the best ways to learn how the present world came about during the last fifty years is studying the history of a single great corporation." At times the success of such events caused even Bernays to wonder at the limit, if any, of his suggestive powers. In a note to himself, Bernays recorded that *The Turning Wheel*'s real value lay in its reception as the history "around which future histories would be written and the Columbia faculty had delightedly accepted the idea."[54]

Though Bernays fell out of favor with GM's managers by 1934, the public relations "action," amplified by after-dinner oratory, established the promotional economy in which NBC executives determined to win back Sloan's institutional business. NBC executives pursued Sloan, hoping to interest him in returning to the network as a regular sponsor of a prestigious institutional entertainment. In the year following the conclusion of the *Parade of the States*, network officials courted Sloan with generous awards of sustaining time for the broadcast of "dinner plan" events. Especially anxious for the return of GM's institutional business, NBC president Merlin H. Aylesworth traveled to Chicago in May 1934 at Sloan's invitation to take part in a dinner celebrating the reopening of the Century of Progress. Broadcast on NBC, the celebration featured talks on the future of American industry. These talks, delivered by Aylesworth, Sloan, Kettering, and other "top men," discussed new developments in their respective industries and "what these might lead to in the next hundred years."[55] Aylesworth, widely acquainted with business leaders as the former president of the National Electric Light Association, usually distanced himself from his friends' discussions of controversial matters, especially those likely to result in a troublesome request for time on the network. Sloan's invitation to speak at the Century of Progress on the future of the radio industry, however, offered as safe and comfortable a venue as any, and Aylesworth, not wishing to refuse Sloan, consented to appear.[56]

The Century of Progress had enjoyed a remarkably successful first season. The fair commemorated the centennial of the settlement of Chicago near Fort Dearborn in 1833. A log-hewn replica of the fort, erected close to the original site, served as the fair's icon. In sharp relief to displays of rustic simplicity, major corporations mounted ambitious exhibits, the largest being General Motors' demonstration of the final stages of "the making of a motor car" (fig. 5). From a gallery encircling a facsimile assembly line that was powered by Kettering's experimental Diesel engines, visitors could witness a demonstration of "manufacturing science," tended by Chevrolet and Fisher Body workers in white lab coats.

While the first season of the Century of Progress celebrated the progress of the past, the second, Sloan noted, would celebrate the promise of the future. In his telegram to Aylesworth, Sloan stated that the progress of scientific research and invention was fast becoming GM's institutional hallmark and banished the idea that the Depression had become a permanent condition. "For sometime past," he cabled Aylesworth, "I have been concerned with the thinking of many who believe that our progress in this world is finished. That we must retrogress. That there are no worth-

FIGURE 5.

General Motors exhibit building, with Indian village exhibit in foreground, at the Century of Progress. Courtesy of Herbert Rolfes.

while possibilities ahead." The theme of the broadcast, Sloan explained, would be "a preview of progress and benefits yet to come. The Century of Progress Exposition last year celebrated accomplishments of the past. We want at this conference to look into the future. We feel positively that industry is on the threshold of great achievements. . . . there could be no better vindication of the role of industry in the years ahead."[57] Later Sloan thanked Aylesworth for broadcasting the event, "adding, therefore, tremendously to its importance and sphere of influence." "Let us hope," Sloan wrote, "that there will not be such a complete interference, in the natural order of things, to prevent our experience in enjoying the wonders that are ahead."[58]

Though network specialists preferred that Sloan sponsor an institutional program on a commercial basis, NBC executives nevertheless accommodated his request for time. When he did decide to return to the air, the model of the public relations "action" that emphasized the verbatim transmission of available events, rather than the modeling of a production technique unique to radio, informed his decision. In 1934 Sloan consented to make the *Cadillac Symphony Concerts* "the base for a year-round institutional program."[59] The program, retitled the *General Motors Symphony Concerts*, featured the New York Philharmonic Symphony, guest conductors and solo artists, and an "intermission talk" delivered by the "Voice of General Motors" (fig. 6). The program concept necessarily reflected "leadership," a quality impressed upon NBC by GM's Paul Garrett. With characteristic dispatch, Garrett informed NBC's Roy C. Witmer, "We would not want to be on the air institutionally unless we occupied a dominant radio position and a time that would reflect leadership. You, better even than we perhaps, can say what are the best hours in radio. Whatever those best hours in radio are, we should have." Garrett soon agreed to a time slot Sunday evenings from 8 to 9 P.M. on NBC Blue, a secondary lineup of network affiliates that offered less coverage than the flagship NBC Red. Though limited to seventeen stations from Boston to Kansas City, NBC Blue covered 60 percent of GM's sales territory, estimated to include 11,820,000 radios.[60]

Press releases announcing the renewal of the Cadillac concert series under the General Motors banner pitched the program's return as a concession to popular demand. The decision, however, was Sloan's to make, though it was not endorsed unanimously by the corporation's directors and high executives, who questioned the value of radio in institutional promotion.[61] Nevertheless, a press release announcing the *General Motors Symphony Concerts* attributed the renewal to "the magnificent success of the *Cadillac Concerts* last season . . . positive proof of the wishes of the great radio audience to hear the best of symphonic music as interpreted by the foremost conductors and soloists. Insistent demands have been received from every section of this country and Canada for the opportunity of hearing

Figure 6.
Program cover,
***General Motors Symphony Concerts* (1935).**
Courtesy of NBC Collection, State Historical Society of Wisconsin.

again, in one connected series of broadcasts, the world's greatest musical talent. The requests to renew the series have been irresistible. We are happy to be privileged to comply." The first concert broadcast, on October 7, 1934, featured conductor Leopold Stokowski of the Philadelphia Orchestra and American tenor Richard Crooks.[62] NBC officials concurred with General Motors' happy announcement and declared that Sloan's decision for institutional promotion by radio was a significant development in modern public relations.

The *General Motors Symphony Concerts* resembled CBS's *Ford Sunday Evening Hour*, an outgrowth of Ford's Detroit Symphony broadcasts, made from the Century of Progress during the summer of 1934. Ford's light and semiclassical music seemed less stilted than GM's classical and semiclassical fare, attracting an estimated 13 million listeners a week. *General Motors Symphony Concerts*, in contrast, attracted a weekly audience estimated at 7 million, though observers noted that in all fairness the program went head to head with CBS's excessively popular Charlie McCarthy. Contemporary comparisons of the programs focused instead upon the differences in the temper and tone of the intermission talks delivered by the anonymous "Voice of General Motors" and by Ford spokesman William J. Cameron. Whereas the Voice delivered driving tips and discussed product improvements such as "venti-pane" no-draft window ventilation, Cameron interpreted the "philosophy" of Henry Ford. The major expression of the corporation to the public from 1934 to 1942, Cameron's weekly talks explained the obligations of Ford to society, and of society to Ford, with the religious conviction and "folksy style reminiscent of an earnest village parson."[63]

The symphonic soundtracks of the *Ford Sunday Evening Hour* and the *General Motors Symphony Concerts* held understandable appeal as metaphors of administration and that "working together spirit." The *General Motors Symphony Concerts*, however, bedeviled Sloan, who found himself caught between General Motors' dealers, who wanted popular selections, and the corporation's policy committee, whose members criticized the broadcast as an extravagance and a waste. NBC's R. H. White reported that "Mr. Sloan, personally, is sold on radio for General Motors, but it so happens that a number of the directors and high executives are not, and you know how they keep 'pot shotting' at whatever program is on the air. As Paul Garrett expressed it, Mr. Sloan fights for the program for a certain length of time and then gets tired of arguing and vindicating the thing and then just lets it go. Whether General Motors continues or not is in the lap of the gods."[64]

Sloan remained the program's sole defender on the General Motors policy committee, though he never reconciled his defense of the program with his own musical taste. "The programs were good," Sloan complained to Aylesworth, but "too technical." "It would be better if we could have the music more tuneful, at the same time preserve its fundamental character, which I think is possible, but whether it could be done or not, I do not know." "By saying, I do not know whether it could be done or not," wrote Sloan, "is because of the impossibility of getting into the minds of musicians that people are interested in music not from the standpoint of the difficulty of its rendition, but rather from the effect that it has on the ears. Musicians are too much concerned with playing those things that are difficult to play, simply to show how much skill they have, in which, of course, the public is not concerned, only in a negative sense." "There are certain things in music," Sloan explained, "especially if it is rendered in the way which is possible with a set up such as we have, that gives one a thrill, making a profound impression, but that impression does not come from seeing how many notes, over the widest range, the musician can cover in a certain number of seconds—quite the contrary—and it is that kind of thing that, in my humble judgement, there is too much of in the selections that have been played up to the present."[65]

A second season of concerts, marking the radio debuts of Myra Hess, Igor Stravinsky, and Artur Schnabel, brought Sloan no relief. "I understand that some Conductor—whoever he may be, is inconsequential—was permitted to perpetrate, on the radio audience, a composition of his own, which is a very sore point with me. I have given instructions, time and again, that this should not be done. . . ." "I am informed further, that the concert was far from tuneful—another point which I have urged," Sloan complained. "Now please understand, Mr. Aylesworth, that I do not believe in jazz. Nobody hates it more than I do, but I contend that there is plenty of music available, if one will adjust their thinking to its importance, that has some melody in it, and at the same time is not of the jazz order." Sloan continued: "I am going to have the programs reasonably tuneful, at the same time not of the jazz order, and I am going to prevent Conductors from perpetrating their own compositions on an unsuspecting public, at the expense of General Motors stockholders, or else there is not going to be any program at all." Sloan ordered Garrett to cancel GM's longtime advertising agency, Campbell-Ewald, and find another capable of delivering music in line with his ideas on the subject. "If that fails," Sloan wrote in exasperation, "then the next thing I am going to do is not to support the programs any further, on the assumption that I personally, with all the other things I have to do, can not contend against the odds that apparently are stacked against me."[66]

Having brought Sloan and the General Motors account this far, Aylesworth prevailed. So did Campbell-Ewald's Henry Souvaine, who continued to produce the concerts on NBC. "We are all in hearty accord with your view that conductors, as a general rule, should not play their own compositions when they are appearing on your General Motors program," replied Aylesworth to Sloan. Program personnel had enforced Sloan's wishes, inasmuch as "the public expects the more famous of these conductors to play their better known compositions." "This will be true in the case of Stravinsky," Aylesworth explained, as it had been with Leopold Stokowski, who "played his arrangement of a Bach number" on the opening program, and guest conductor Eugene Goossens, who had played one of his own compositions the previous Sunday. Aylesworth assured Sloan that NBC would immediately confer with the agency "to popularize the program still more, providing melody and lilting tunes the people know." "It is our desire," Aylesworth concluded, "to keep this wonderful program just the way you would like to have it."[67] In reply, Sloan reiterated his preferences. "The fundamental thing I am contending for is music with a reasonable amount of harmony. The reason I want a ban placed on conductors playing their own compositions, is because, while they may be very high in technique, they are very low in melody and appeal to the masses."[68]

The *General Motors Symphony Concerts* continued until 1937, though in the end the program failed to become the long-term commitment to radio for which its specialists and network executives had worked. From its inception in 1934 the program had featured an intermission talk by the anonymous Voice of General Motors. The talks had begun innocently enough with a series entitled "We Drivers," which sought "to exchange ideas we come across, in the hope that here and there we will pick up something that may actually *help us* to get the most out of our cars." A talk from the fall of 1935 entitled "When Our Young Folks Learn to Drive," for example, offered advice and empathy to the concerned parents of teenage drivers.[69]

The favorable long-term effect of presenting General Motors as a public-spirited institution—through both music and helpful talks—was sacrificed in pursuit of short-term effects during the great sit-down strike of 1936–1937 at GM's Flint, Michigan, Fisher Body Plant No. 2. As the strike wore on, the title "We Drivers" became the belligerent "American Way of Doing Things." While workers occupied the strategic Fisher Body Plant at Flint, thereby idling approximately 136,000 workers, the Voice of General Motors boomed an intermission talk entitled "The Right to Work," which was widely interpreted as an intimation that the corporation would soon take forcible action to reopen the plant.[70] The Voice expounded at length that "there are certain fundamental principles contended for by all peoples, in all places, in all times. Certain objectives which are recognized as the ultimate goals of humanity everywhere. Opinions may differ as to how these goals may be reached, but there is no difference of opinion as to the goals themselves." Tracing the "native desires" and "aspirations" of human beings through the Magna Carta and the Bill of Rights, the Voice explained that

> In these utterances the words may differ, but the meaning is the same. . . .
>
> It is found in our Declaration of Independence . . . the very fountainhead of all that we believe in, all that we hold dear. It is contained in those few words which claim man's inalienable right to "Life, Liberty and the Pursuit of Happiness."
>
> *Life* is the instinctive, primary desire of all conscious living things.
>
> The longing for *Liberty* is one we share even with beasts and birds.
>
> *Happiness* is—undeniably—the ultimate objective of all human effort.
>
> Many things go to make up Happiness. Some of them are essential. And among these essentials, surely, are the security, the independence and the welfare of self and family.
>
> And since, under every social order, every economic system and every political form on earth, the only way to acquire security, independence and well-being is to *earn* them, men therefore possess the inalienable right to *earn* . . . *which is to say, the inalienable right to work!* . . .
>
> We honor those who work. We deplore idleness. Our praise—our rewards—are reserved for honest effort and useful accomplishment.
>
> Work is the cornerstone of our existence. We *want* to work—that we may win through to that goal of happiness—and we proclaim our right to do so. . . .[71]

Approving the statement for broadcast, NBC vice president for programming John F. Royal explained to David Sarnoff that "we do not usually permit controversial matter on commercial programs, but this is so cleverly done that I think we can take a chance on it."[72]

The talk scheduled for the following week also proved troublesome, and Campbell-Ewald withdrew it at Royal's request. It expressed concern for GM employees "in the plants affected by the present strike, but not actually on strike themselves." The text went on to note that "we have been able during the past week to put over 50,000 people back to work. While their occupation must be, of necessity, mostly on a part-time basis . . . in some cases, perhaps, only a day or so of the week . . . it does furnish them some work, and hence some income for themselves and their families, who would otherwise be deprived entirely of income."[73]

The settlement of the strike on February 11, 1937, constituted a victory for the United Automobile Workers and a signal event in the history of industrial labor relations. For the first time in its history General Motors had been compelled to sign a union agreement.[74] Three days later, unbowed and unrepentant, the Voice of General Motors boomed a parting talk, "Human Rights and Property Rights—Inseparably Bound."[75]

Perhaps Sloan wondered if the talks might be broadcast without the expense of a symphony. A drop in expenditures for institutional promotion in all media followed the strike settlement in 1937, the last year of *General Motors Symphony Concerts*. GM's estimated total expenditures for institutional advertising in all media declined sharply, from $1,320,254 in 1937 to $119,285 in 1938. From 1938 through 1941 General Motors made no allocation for institutional radio.[76] NBC's attempts to entice Sloan to return to the air with Arturo Toscanini in 1939 met with refusal, the corporation having decided against expenditures for purely institutional promotion. NBC's Roy Witmer consoled his colleagues, stating that GM's expenditures at the New York World's Fair of 1939 "cannot be construed as being 100% [institutional]. That is a glorified General Motors Divisions automobile show."[77] The corporation that went on the air only when it had a good idea had left the air entirely.

In the end, the corporation's lack of commitment to institutional radio reflected its leaders' doubts about advertising, to which now might be added public relations "action." The technical background and administrative insight required to solve the problems of corporate expansion counted for little when it came to building and sustaining an audience. That kind of progress, Paul Garrett suggested, demanded sensibilities inspired by "consumer dreams and desires" rather than the production ethic of the "captain of industry." Important work remained in promoting a "philosophy of management" that counseled the "broader opportunities" of individuals as consumers, rather than the "narrower outlook" circumscribed by the occupational identities of workers and managers.[78]

In the strike's aftermath, radio remained a challenge. Labor economist Robert R. R. Brooks, a prescient critic of GM's strike advertising, suggested that while the "American way" theme of the *General Motors Symphony Concerts'* intermission talks seemed to be something new, its presentation was hopelessly static. The Voice of General Motors merely amplified the corporation's anti-strike newspaper advertisements, "dignified in language, reasonable in demands and long-suffering in tone."[79] Surveying the anti-labor advertising of 1937, Brooks detected a pronounced shift from discussions of abstract principles, rights, and the American way toward a propaganda imbued with personal meaning. Concurrent with the *General Motors Symphony Concerts*, for example, a National Association of Manufacturers billboard campaign prepared by Campbell-Ewald pictured home and family scenes beneath the headlines "World's Shortest Working Hours," "World's Highest Standard of Living," and "World's Highest Wages" (fig. 7). Posted on 60,000 billboards throughout the country, the initial series ran until superseded by a second headlined "What is good for industry is good for your family," "You prosper when factories prosper," and "Good times for industry mean good times for you."[80] The NAM's idealized picture of home and family life perhaps highlighted the subtleties that GM's strike advertising lacked, and ironically it was the billboard rather than the radio that ultimately elevated the American way of doing things to the proposition of a passing show, whose hero, Brooks explained, "is married to a beautiful wife and has two children, a dog and a car."[81]

Sloan's reason for sponsoring the *General Motors Symphony Concerts* brought to mind the unifying impulse of radio's earliest promotion as a cultural form. The lilt and lift of "tuneful" reassurance supplied the soundtrack for decentralized managerial and production processes, a metaphor of the "working-together spirit" that animated the period's sponsored films as well. Verbatim transmission of after-dinner oratory and classical music performances, however, did little to advance the technique of dramatic radio production. In the press of events under the New Deal, network and advertising agency program builders set out to create dramatic programs that would express what their most politically active sponsors and clients could no longer say.

FIGURE 7.

Outdoor advertising campaign, NAM (1937). Courtesy of Hagley Museum and Library.

Chapter Three

From Speeches to Stories

By successfully channeling troublesome political talk into inoffensive institutional entertainment, network executives could both generate a new and heretofore untapped class of revenue and relieve themselves of further broadcast obligations to the entrepreneurial right. However, at the same time that NBC officials felt encouraged by the development of the *General Motors Symphony Concerts* in the summer of 1934, talk requests by The Crusaders, Inc., the American Liberty League, and the National Association of Manufacturers had become more frequent and increasingly problematic. As a result, network officials were determined to build a popular program demonstrating the alternative technique of dramatic radio production. The culmination of the process, DuPont's *Cavalcade of America*, established the anthology drama as the formula of choice for broadcasting among institutional advertising, public relations, and network specialists, if not among their reluctant clients and sponsors.

Conservative business leaders coalescing around The Crusaders, Inc., presaged the organization of the American Liberty League and the revitalization of the NAM in 1934.[1] The Crusaders, led by "National Commander" Fred G. Clark, a Cleveland oilman, had organized in Ohio in 1929 to agitate for the repeal of Prohibition. In the early 1930s the group opened a New York office and proceeded to attract business leaders to its repeal campaign. Following the repeal of Prohibition in 1933, The Crusaders, Inc., shifted its attack to what its officers believed would be an equally lucrative campaign against the anti-corporate features of the New Deal. A 1934 prospectus entitled "Which Way America?" was tailored to win the support of the conservative business community. Vowing loyalty to the Constitution, The Crusaders, Inc., proposed "to fight vigorously any attempts to have the majority of Americans ruled by organized minorities seeking special advantages" and to "resist any so-called 'planned economy' which involves complete control of industry by Government and regimentation of the American people." The group promised to curb "any drift or drive toward Fascism, Communism or Socialism," fight for a balanced budget, and "insist that Government enterprise stimulate and not supplant private enterprise." Organized on the model of the American Legion, the Crusaders called for the creation of "battalions" in every state to "investigate the beliefs and qualifications of all candidates, particularly for Congress," and to support those "in agreement with The Crusaders' American principles." By "continuous discussion and publicity," the Crusaders would "stimulate a constant oversight of all public affairs."[2]

Endeavoring to build a national organization through radio, the Crusaders arranged sustaining broadcasts on NBC and CBS in 1934; from 1935 to 1936 they paid for regularly scheduled "Voice of the Crusaders" talks featuring Clark on the Mutual and Yankee (New England) networks.[3] Prior to its first sustaining talk on NBC in June 1934, the Crusaders acquired the services of L. A. Van Patten, formerly with the American Legion, where he promoted membership campaigns. In May 1934 Van Patten approached NBC with a list of speakers that the Crusaders hoped to sponsor in an effort to create a national following and stimulate contributions. NBC officials accepted a number of the speakers on the condition that the broadcasts not identify the Crusaders as the sponsor, effectively denying the group the promotional opportunities sure to arise from such an identification.[4]

Despite NBC's policy, the group nevertheless secured significant business support during the summer of 1934. A U.S. Senate investigation of lobbying activities chaired by Hugo Black later revealed The Crusaders, Inc., to be the most active group in radio among myriad business-backed right-wing groups, including the American Liberty League, the Southern Committee to Uphold the Constitution, and the Sentinels of the Republic. The Black committee also noted Fred Clark's enthusiasm for discussions of controversial topics tailored to attract contributors to the fold.[5]

The prominent business leaders that gathered around Colby M. Chester and E. F. Hutton in the board room of General Foods' Park Avenue headquarters in July 1934 unanimously endorsed the Crusaders, Inc., plan as outlined by Clark. Led by Chester, the assembled throng agreed "that the time had come for industry to stand up and fight." "In the last few years particularly," explained a privately circulated memorandum of the meeting, "industry had failed to present a coordinated and unified statement of its point of view on governmental actions affecting the country as a whole." The executives authorized the meeting's chair "to appoint a Steering Committee from amongst those present to work with The Crusaders and to start an active organization of industrial leaders through which the country could be organized, and through which the necessary funds could be secured." The executives authorized the creation of a second committee "to assist The Crusaders in perfecting its economic platform, and reducing this to 2, 3 or 5 major issues on which the national educational campaign would be focussed [*sic*]." Additionally, the group authorized the creation of a National Advisory Council, whose members would publicly support the Crusaders and actively participate in organization and fundraising work. Although subscriptions to the estimated $250,000 fund required to launch the national campaign had not been solicited at the meeting, five individuals volunteered a total of $10,500 on the spot.[6]

Despite the "big men" ready to adopt the Clark group "and give it a new coat of paint," NBC executives regarded the Crusaders as little more than a promotional front. Additional participants desiring to sponsor Crusaders talks appeared at NBC's Rockefeller Center offices in the fall of 1934 led by Donald D. Davis, president of General Mills, Albert D. Lasker of Lord & Thomas, Douglas Stuart of Quaker Oats, Howard Heinz of H. J. Heinz, and Edward Ryerson of U.S. Steel. They proposed a three-night-a-week schedule of talks to be delivered by Dr. Preston Bradley on "such subjects as Anti-Socialism, Anti-New Dealism and Anti-Communism." "The program," NBC president Niles Trammell later explained, "really was designed to attack the New Deal."[7]

Like the leaders of General Foods, the leaders of Minneapolis-based General Mills were taken with the Crusaders. General Mills president Donald Davis and chairman of the board James F. Bell figured prominently in raising a radio fund of $148,000 for Clark's "Voice of the Crusaders" broadcasts.[8] As early investors in commercial radio, Davis and Bell had been among the first to recognize the role that radio could play in the merchandising of products and politics. As executives of the Washburn Crosby Company, each had helped bring about Crosby's acquisition of milling operations to form General Mills in 1929. In similar fashion, Davis had brokered the Crosby Company's purchase of Minneapolis station WLAG in 1924. Changing its call letters to reflect its new owner, station WCCO returned to the air under Davis's leadership and later began taking programs from NBC. In 1929 Davis sold the station to William Paley.[9]

Donald Davis had definite ideas about merchandising General Mills programs and running a network. In 1933 Davis sought to schedule simultaneous network broadcasts on NBC Red, NBC Blue, and Columbia. At a dinner meeting with William Paley, George B. McClellan of NBC, Federal Radio Commissioner Thad Brown, and Glenn Sample and Frank Hummert of the advertising agency Blackett, Sample & Hummert,

Davis complained that competing programs denied him the total audience available to radio. To illustrate Davis's complaint, Sample and Hummert explained that they had aired a program on Sunday nights for Dr. Lyons Toothpowder and found themselves in competition on the opposite network with Will Rogers. Though Commissioner Brown seemed sympathetic to Davis's plight, a flabbergasted Paley and McClellan objected that the simultaneous transmission of programs would not be good for radio, and Davis's proposal ended at that. Earlier that year, Davis had urged NBC executives to take a definite position in molding public opinion. Niles Trammell recalled that Davis wanted NBC to obtain the "approval of the administration and have an editor on the air every evening, who would put on a program similar to an editorial column in a newspaper." On other occasions Davis had wanted to sponsor news, a sponsorship that NBC refused outright and that Davis later arranged on CBS.[10]

Investing early and often in radio, Davis and General Mills claimed to have broadcast the first singing commercial (by the Wheaties Quartette). General Mills developed a stock of radio characters to merchandise its line of packaged goods, with programs including the juvenile thriller drama *Jack Armstrong the All-American Boy*, the soap opera *Betty and Bob*, and the *Betty Crocker School of the Air*. The *Betty Crocker* program became a certifiable phenomenon, with thirteen women appearing as "Betty" on regional networks. Specialists marveled at the program's "chatty" conveyance of intimacy and confidence, an impression confirmed in letters received from listeners at the rate of some 4,000 a day.[11] Perhaps inevitably Davis, who had gained a foothold in radio with "home service personality" merchandising, opted for politics in the guise of fictional entertainment. The thought occurred to others as well. Crackerbarrel characters and "common sense" personalities kept network continuity officers busy policing the edge of commercial entertainment for facetious remarks about the "Raw Deal," Supreme Court decisions, taxes, and government officials and organizations.[12]

At the local level, Davis himself took to the air on WCCO Minneapolis to dispense advice as "Si Perkins." According to NBC vice president for programming John F. Royal, these performances began shortly after the network appearance of former vaudevillian Andrew Kelley on NBC's *Horse Sense Philosophy*. Kelley, explained Royal, had "a great knack of doing a fine Irish character . . . a la 'Mr. Dooley.'" The idea "was to tell the people in an entertaining way some common sense facts." First broadcast on WGY Schenectady, *Horse Sense Philosophy* won a local following including General Electric president Owen D. Young, banker George Baker, and several of his friends, who wrote to Kelley "telling him how much good they thought the program was doing." Kelley's Irish brogue and the use of a "stooge questioner," a reviewer noted, helped explain the "moves and maneuvers" of the nation's economic and political life that began with the election of FDR and carried through the first year of the New Deal. Royal scheduled *Horse Sense Philosophy* on the network, and soon afterward Davis began "Si Perkins." Whereas Kelley had imparted "common sense advice," Royal noted, "'Si Perkins' became more militant. . . . Davis took great delight in going on the air behind the cloak of 'Si Perkins' and putting over his bombasts. So much for that." A calling card in NBC's General Mills file suggests the just-folks demeanor of what may have been an earlier radio role played by Davis, "Hiram Jones of Friendlyville." His motto: "For the sake of all us taxpayers, keep the Guvment outta business. The greatest good for the greatest number."[13]

The National Association of Manufacturers raised the character concept to an art with the soap opera adventure *American Family Robinson* (1934). Much as Davis, Lasker, and others had adopted the Crusaders and given the organization a "fresh coat of paint," an overlapping constituency of leading industrialists seeking "business salvation" undertook the renovation of the National Association of Manufacturers in 1934. Organized in 1895 to promote protective tariffs and the construction of the Panama Canal, the NAM shifted its focus in the early 1900s to belligerent promotion of the open shop. From its incorporation in 1905 until the enactment of the Taft-Hartley Act in 1947, the association in its politics, as in its print-oriented publicity techniques, remained largely unchanged.[14] In the early Depression, membership dropped precipitously. The NAM returned to action after a 1932 fundraising drive, subscribed by metal trades industrialists (the so-called Brass Hats) led by Charles R. Hook, president of American Rolling Mill Co.; Tom M. Girdler of the Republic Steel Corporation; and Frank Purnell, president of the Youngstown Sheet and Tube Co. The association began anew under chairman of the board Robert L. Lund, the president of Lambert Pharmacal Company; president C. L. Bardo, also president of the New York Shipbuilding Company; and executive vice president Walter B. Weisenburger, the former president of the St. Louis Chamber of Commerce.[15] After Lund assumed the NAM chairmanship upon the retirement of John E. Edgerton in late 1931, the NAM executive committee attracted the support of the nation's largest industrial corporations. From 1933 to 1937, leading member-contributors included E. I. du Pont de Nemours and Company, General Motors, National Steel, United States Steel, Monsanto Chemical, Westinghouse Electric and Manufacturing, Chrysler, Bethlehem Steel, Texas Corporation, Borg-Warner, Republic Steel, Socony-Vacuum Oil, Swift & Co., Standard Oil of New Jersey, and Eastman Kodak.[16]

Provoked by the pro-labor clauses of the National Industrial Recovery Act, the NAM embarked upon a campaign of "employer opposition" to forestall the imposition of collective bargaining in the steel, chemical, and auto industries.[17] Projecting an "active campaign of education," in September 1933 Lund explained that NIRA section 7(a) posed a special threat to employers, given the "untruthful or misleading statements about the law" made by the American Federation of Labor and "communistic groups promoting union organization." "Selfish groups, including labor, the socialistic-minded and the radical, have constantly and continuously misrepresented industry to the people." Lund concluded that the same people would become favorably disposed toward business's traditional prerogatives and institutional choices if only its leaders would "tell its story."[18]

Drawing upon the "home service personality" expertise of its package goods producer-members, the newly reorganized NAM led the way in radio with the episodic adventures of the *American Family Robinson*. The program appears to have been the inspiration of Harry A. Bullis, General Mills vice president and the chairman of the NAM's newly constituted public relations committee. Syndicated by the World Broadcasting System from late 1934 to 1940, the 15-minute episodic drama was an anomaly. The NAM had a nearly exclusive investment in printed material overseen by James P. Selvage, a former Washington newspaperman, who, with Walter B. Weisenburger, shared editorial responsibility for the larger campaign.[19] By 1936 the NAM's publicity operation rivaled any in America, including those of the major parties, in mass mailings of press releases, bulletins, feature stories, and booklets. In 1940 the NAM's industrial press service reached 6,000 weeklies and small-town dailies; its *Industrial Information Bulletin* supplied facts and figures for editorials on a monthly basis to the chief writer of every daily newspaper and to a select list of radio commentators. It also distributed 1,750,000 "You and Industry" booklets to schools, YMCAs, and club groups. Additional activities included the distribution of spot news releases and feature articles based upon NAM surveys; a plant publication service for 1,200 editors; a poster campaign of 12,000 billboards with a daily estimated audience of 50 million; an "Industrial Facts" sheet with a monthly circulation of 35,000; a speakers division with an estimated annual audience of over 300,000; several motion pictures; a traveling window display entitled "Yardsticks of American Progress" booked in 42 cities; a "Fashions out of Test Tubes" stage show; a transcribed weekly commentary on current economic questions by George E. Sokolsky distributed to 186 radio stations; and finally the *American Family Robinson*, broadcast twice a week on 255 stations (fig. 8).[20]

The *American Family Robinson*'s drop-dead attacks on the New Deal reflected the print orientation of NAM publicity and the politics of the commercial newspaper, which, despite the inroads of radio, remained "the core of the apparatus of public opinion formation."[21] The continuous interjection of editorial comment into the series' soap opera plot reduced protagonist Luke Robinson, "the sanely philosophical editor of the *Centerville Herald*," to a caricature of the factory town editors that the NAM assiduously cultivated with an open-ended supply of preprinted mats, columns, and tracts. Like Centerville's Luke Robinson, they too might counsel a principled conservativism.

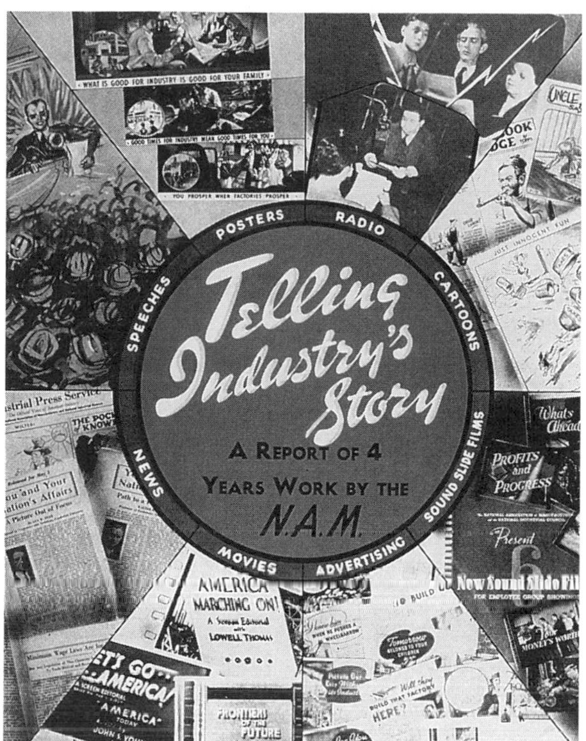

Figure 8. **Pamphlet cover, "Telling Industry's Story," NAM (1939). Courtesy of Hagley Museum and Library.**

Awash in the perilous waters of confiscatory taxation, deficit spending, and collective bargaining, the *American Family Robinson* reduced the New Deal to absurdity by kidding it along with everything else. Editor Robinson, the program's repository of sound thinking and common sense, is beset by social schemers and panacea peddlers. Some are threatening and even criminal, though most are simply misguided. Among the latter is Robinson's brother-in-law, William Winkle, a.k.a. "Windy" Bill, the itinerate promoter and inventor of the "housecar." Bill's meddlesome and uninformed political ideas are as unexpected as his unannounced visit with the Robinsons. More menacing is Professor Monroe Broadbelt, the "professional organizer of the Arcadians, a group using the depression as a lever to pry money from converts to radical economic theories."[22]

The story line of the *American Family Robinson* revolves around the notion that political conflict can be resolved in the home and immediate community through the application of "time tested principles." The catalyst of dramatic action on these fronts is Luke's wife, Myra, who founds a women's radio club, presumably for the sponsorship of talks, and soon organizes a counter-demonstration against the Arcadians'. The opening scene of an early episode finds the Robinsons pondering names for Myra Robinson's radio club. "With so many good name suggestions, I hardly know which to choose," Myra enthuses. "The 'Save America Club,' the 'Sound Recovery Club,' the 'Economic Freedom Club.'" "Why not," interrupts husband Luke, "call it the 'Women's Forum for the Promotion of Constructive Thinking as Contrasted with Radical Theories in Government and Business?'" The name they decide upon is typical: "Ladies Who Are Aiding in the Preservation of American Principles," or the "Ladies' Aid for America."[23] Warming to the idea of an anti-Arcadian demonstration organized by the Ladies' Aid, the Robinsons deliver one of the program's recurring attacks on organized minorities, alien "isms," and official regimentation.

> *Luke Robinson*: You know, the more I think about this counter-parade to the Arcadian demonstration the more I like it. The dissatisfied minority of society have always done the shouting, and that's why everyone gets the idea there are great numbers of people who want to change. It's about time that the people who know they're living under the best economic system there is had a chance to speak their piece, too. Imagine what a demonstration that would be. It would stretch from coast to coast and from Maine to California. A solid phalanx to true Americans—independent—self-reliant. Believing their country is the land of opportunity, and believing that sticking to sound principles and avoiding foreign doctrines is the quickest way of putting those who are out of jobs back to work. That's the kind of a parade I'd like to see.
>
> *Myra Robinson*: Bravo! Well, why not?
>
> *Luke Robinson*: Why not?
>
> *Myra Robinson*: Of course why not. Right here in Centerville we have men who do their jobs. Fight their battles. Make their own way. And they're proud of it. They won't ever accept regimentation. Why not get them to come out in public and say so. The Ladies' Aid would be delighted to have their ranks swelled with some good examples. I imagine the contrast between the discontented workers and the contented ones, for instance, ah, would be interesting. . . . You might even make a speech! I'm sure Broadbelt is planning to.
>
> *Luke Robinson*: Well, judging from past experience it might be better for you to make the speech.[24]

Myra Robinson's organizational and executive skills come into full play, revealing her as her husband's perfect ideological helpmate. The couple is shocked when their daughter Betty falls under the oratorical spell of the charismatic Professor Broadbelt, a common criminal whose turn of phrase suggests a certain Hyde Park, New York, upbringing. Complications attend Betty's engagement to the Arcadian leader, whose first consideration is his chosen mission, "the upliftment of mankind." Broadbelt's motives, however, are neither ideological nor romantic. In the next episode Luke Robinson helps apprehend Broadbelt, who has skipped town with the Arcadians' treasury. Returning to Centerville, Robinson presides over the liquidation of the Arcadian movement by publicly refunding the contributions of its confused and misguided members, including his daughter's.[25]

The plot weaves in and out of this messy business while enlarging upon opportunities for further editorializing. When the Robinsons are not discussing the organization of radio clubs or their opposition to organized minorities, they are kept busy exploiting the numerous devices introduced to hammer the NAM line. One episode, for example, finds editor Robinson and his young reporter, Dick Collins, poring over responses to a questionnaire sent out by the *Herald*. Collins's "Here's another interesting answer . . ." segues to the familiar drill. A radio letter-writing contest sponsored by Myra Robinson on the question "What will speed recovery" (in 250 words or less) yields an incessant supply of topics for future discussion. Contestants needing inspiration could write for a picture of the Robinson family and a free booklet entitled "The Road to Recovery." Subsequent episodes of *The American Family Robinson* never made clear whether the letters read on the air were received from the program's actual audience or the Centerville audience of Mrs. Robinson's women's radio club. Nevertheless, the intimation of a correspondence between the listening audience, fictitious or real, and the program's characters presumed a personal involvement in the lives of listeners. "Our household has a real live interest in the progress of national affairs and their relation to our own situation," Myra Robinson explains, "and I'm sure the interest is just as great in yours."[26]

In certain households, interest in the *American Family Robinson* undoubtedly did exist. The program attracted an articulate audience that appreciated and responded to the NAM's send-ups of the New Deal. From fan mail the NAM learned that listeners responded enthusiastically to editor Luke's brother-in-law and comedic foil "Windy" Bill. Written into the script as an incidental character, "Windy" soon returned to Centerville, his role expanded to include yet more meddlesome and annoying business. Other changes occurred as characters changed careers and took on new responsibilities. In 1935 Luke Robinson left the editorship of the *Centerville Herald* to become the assistant manager of the local furniture factory. While Robinson remained the series' protagonist, a new character, Gus Olsen, a janitor who had made the best of his lot in life, assumed Robinson's place as the managing editor and owner of the *Herald*. A tabloid "Herald" mailed to listeners from "Centerville" announced the changes and included photographs of the "Robinsons" reading their fan mail along with the paper's articles, editorials, cartoon, and crossword puzzle (fig. 9).[27]

When introduced to New York City listeners in 1935, *American Family Robinson* appeared five days a week until the show caught up to its regular twice-a-week schedule. NAM specialists considered mid-afternoon the optimum time for broadcasts. According to NAM vice president for public relations James P. Selvage,

CENTERVILLE HERALD

Published in Combination with the Radio Broadcast Program
'AMERICAN FAMILY ROBINSON'

Volume 1 | Centerville, U. S. A. | Number 1

COLLINS ESTATE 'COUNSEL' EXPOSED

Flotsam No Lawyer—Has Long Police Record

Fearlessly carrying on its fight for law enforcement, the CENTERVILLE HERALD has just uncovered one of the smoothest racketeers and confidence men in the history of its battle for law enforcement and good government. This latest recruit to the HERALD "public enemy" ranks is none other than Lemuel B. Flotsam, self-styled "lawyer and member of the bar," whose activities have recently caused so much trouble for our Feature Editor, Richard Collins.

Flotsam (or Samuel X. Gullton, as he is known to police in Chicago, New York and London), has a rec[illegible] as a jail-bird and public menace [illegible]h forms a new page in the an[illegible] of crime. The CENTERVILLE HERALD, true to its responsibility as a public servant and militant protector of decent American standards, finds that not only has this criminal genius mulcted thousands of dollars from his supposed "clients," without their ever recovering a penny, but that he has spent, at various times of his life, at least seven years in the nation's best jails.

Bankrupt Victims

Flotsam's (or Gullton's) favorite racket is that of advertising for people of a certain name, and then leading them to believe they have claim to a landed title in England or on the Continent. He charges them whatever fees he can get (payable always in advance), and without further ado moves to another town, leaving his victims often practically bankrupt and helpless to pursue and bring to justice this heartless monster. As a variation of the estate racket, Flotsam draws up fake wills for large fortunes, advertises for the would-be "heirs," and has them pay him fees in advance to prove their claims. [illegible] may be added that neither the [illegible]ments nor Flotsam ever appear [illegible] any court—except when the latter may be facing criminal prosecution.

It is on the "title" racket that Flotsam involved Collins, the amazing part of his work in this case being that he has left no opening for criminal action. Collins' sojourn in the town jail was brought about through the attempts of William (Windy Hill) Winkle to capitalize on the Chicago "con" man's pipe-dream, and it is interesting to note, incidentally, that the Collins affair is the first case in Flotsam's history in which the client has gone to jail instead of the "law[illegible]" [illegible] part

SHOWS CONSTITUTION NOT OUTMODED; CALLS IT GREATEST DEFENSE OF LIBERTY

FAN MAIL THRILLS ROBINSONS

Bob, Myra, Luke and Betty are having a grand time over the day's requests for the souvenir "Herald".

Editor Says Document More Modern Than All "Isms"

FORBIDS ENSLAVEMENT

By RICHARD COLLINS, Feature Editor

Speaking before a brilliant gathering of Centerville's leading citizens in the Town Hall Auditorium last night, Luke Robinson, editor and publisher of the CENTERVILLE HERALD, brought to a close the recent series of open forum discussions on various phases of the "American System" so violently attacked of late by would-be reformers, "share-the-wealth" enthusiasts, and others. The subject of this final meeting was "The Constitution of the United States." Mr. Robinson issued a stern warning to those who have tended to think, or claim, that the Constitution is outmoded or in any way a limiting or hampering document.

"Let me analyze, point by point, what the Constitution means to the average American," said Mr. [illegible]inson. "The Constitution [illegible] tees for all time the individual [illegible]erties of the people of the United States, and while it stands the government is required to recognize the following rights of the individual;

Constitutional Protection

1. The Writ of Habeas Corpus safeguards the individual against false arrest and imprisonment.
2. A man cannot be jailed for some offense which was committed before the law made his act something wrong to do.
3. Trial by jury for every individual.
4. Limits upon what can be called treason. This protects the individual from being shot for disagreeing with those in power.

Constitutional Freedom

5. Religious freedom.
6. Freedom of speech.
7. Freedom of the press.
8. Freedom of Assembly.
9. The right to petition the government to right wrongs.
10. The right of a person to the security of his own house, which can only be searched on a court warrant.
11. The right to an indictment, so that if a man is arrested, he can know the nature of the crime of which he is accused.

(Continued on Page 4, Col. 4)

SOVIET ROADS BUILT WITH DRAFTED LABOR

(Wireless to the HERALD.)

The ways of dictators were once more sharply brought out in the recent order of the Russian Government that obligatory highway labor for all farm employees will be instituted in order to build up the national road system more rapidly. Six days labor per year must be contributed by each farm worker, the workers to receive no pay or other consideration from the state for their labors. Workers of disenfranchised classes are to give twelve days per year at no pay and all those of any class failing to give the required time when and where demanded will be compelled to contribute double the time and work as a form of "fine" for their delinquency.

The Commissar of Domestic Affairs (similar to our Secretary of the Interior) will be empowered to draft this compulsory labor at will, thus enabling him to force all farmers to give up at least six of their nominal days of rest during any one year, without any choice in the pr[illegible]

POTATOES, CORN ONLY NICKNAMES

Sugar is much more useful as a building material than as a food, according to a report just issued by the Farm Cooperation Committee of Center County, of which T. P. Scoggins, farm implement manufacturer of Middletown, is the Chairman. Wood flour is discussed more enthusiastically than wheat flour, but for different purposes; and the chemists now say that "potatoes," "straw," "wheat," and such names are prehistoric—nicknames, in fact, for materials which have a far wider commercial value than the old-fashioned use as food to which they have been put these many centuries.

"Chemurgy" is the name by which this new science of adapting farm waste products (and over-production) to new industrial needs is known. The impregnation of wood flour with phenol-formaldehyde condensation makes a plastic material to be laid over metal sheet, to make a sheeting of unusual strength, good for auto bodies and other such uses. From sugar, either beet or grape, we shall soon

(Continued on Page 4, Col. 3)

Figure 9. Pamphlet, "Centerville Herald," vol. 1, no. 1, NAM (n.d.). Courtesy of Hagley Museum and Library.

tests showed that when scheduled between two and three P.M. the program had an excellent chance "to reach not only housewives but other members of the family." The *American Family Robinson*, Selvage wrote, presented "Industry's effective answer to the Utopian promises of theorists and demagogues at present reaching such vast audiences via radio."[28]

From the outset, Selvage had hoped to interest NBC or CBS in broadcasting the *American Family Robinson* on a sustaining basis. Neither did, and the series ended up in transcription, recorded and circulated to individual stations by the World Broadcasting System. A review of scripts submitted to NBC in October 1934 resulted in the program's banishment from the network's owned and operated stations as well. Reviewing the series' first three episodes, NBC script editor L. H. Titterton hardly knew what to make of the Robinsons, or the direction the story might take. "These three scripts," Titterton wrote to NBC vice president for programming John F. Royal, "indicate that the author desires to discuss economic and political ideas under the guise of giving entertainment of the familiar family script order. It is extremely hard to learn just what his point of view is. At one time you think he is all for the New Deal; at another you think he is all for the conservative point of view." "We might find ourselves with a definitely anti-administration series on our hands which would have to be ended suddenly." An outline for the rest of the series and a script of the last episode, received three days later, confirmed Titterton's suspicion. After meeting with Selvage and series scriptwriter Douglas Silver, Titterton reported that the *American Family Robinson* proposed "to take on a definitely anti-Rooseveltian tendency." Selvage and Silver, however, "minimized this and merely said that it was to indicate the enlightened conservative point of view held by intelligent business men." "You would probably not find in the entire series any specific sentence that could be censored," Titterton cautioned, "but the definite intention and implication of each episode is to conduct certain propaganda against the New Deal and all its work."[29]

NBC's rejection of the *American Family Robinson* only led to further requests for network time by the NAM. By February 1935 the situation had become tiresome for Royal and his staff. "Some members of the manufacturers' group have a feeling that we are going to give them unlimited time," Royal complained to NBC vice president Richard C. Patterson. When asked how frequently they wished to appear, "One of the members suggested five times a week . . . others suggested three periods a week, while others suggested twice a week." Only the NAM's inability to agree on a program forestalled further demands for time. NBC had already aired a number of the NAM's speakers, added Royal, and then a few more in late 1934.[30]

A flurry of program proposals passed between the executive offices of NBC and the NAM in early 1935. Negotiations opened with a proposal by New York Shipbuilding president F. N. Bard, forwarded by NAM executive vice president for public relations Walter B. Weisenburger. "Industry has never been adequately publicized in any way and, this to be effective must not only be well done but over a long period of time," wrote Bard. "It took us a long time to get into our present difficulties and we cannot assure our future without a long period of education." The program features that Bard enumerated reflected the thought of the NAM inasmuch as they evinced its leaders' unformed ideas of a program.

> There can be no success without a good program and adequate leadership.
>
> It must be volatile, newsy [*sic*], accurate in data, with simple statements tersely stated.
>
> It must vary from humor to ridicule and offensive argument as the occasion requires.
>
> It must carry news items, current interviews by the announcer of prominent men on current topics and up-to-the-minute items.
>
> The use of wise cracks of the Will Rogers type, from time to time, might be helpful.
>
> The program must not be loaded with too many things.
>
> The question of incidental music is a matter for professional opinion to settle.
>
> . . . We should get some man who, as an announcer or broadcaster, has already demonstrated his brilliancy and appeal and who is not too prominent—he must not have other affiliations or try to build up other pictures. He must be a man who wants to make a success of this program on its merits, and a success of himself by the same token.[31]

Royal considered the NAM ill advised and privately wished that it not pursue a program at all. "I am sure that anyone giving the matter thought would advise the group not to go on the radio at this time and do the thing they are contemplating," Royal confided to Patterson. But, "I don't think it is for the National Broadcasting Company to tell them that they are making a mistake, because they might question our motives."[32] Royal and other top network executives continued to meet with NAM officials and suggested the names of sympathetic journalists who might help the manufacturers sort out their ideas and come up with a satisfactory program. Possible candidates included Lewis Douglas, columnist David Lawrence, and editor Stanley Hoflund High. NAM executives ruled out Douglas and objected to Lawrence. This left High, the candidate they knew least.

Though High fit Bard's requirement for a "not too prominent" broadcast personality, he was a known quantity of proven value at NBC. Prior to 1935 he had appeared on the network as an occasional current events commentator, a broadcast extension of his work as a journalist and editor. High's network peers coveted his wide-ranging contacts and acquaintances, who cut across the fields of politics, religion, and international affairs. Born in Chicago in 1895, High had attended Nebraska Wesleyan University and Boston University, graduating with a bachelor's degree in Sacred Theology. Never ordained, he instead embarked on a career in journalism. Following the First World War, in which he served as an American Expeditionary Force aviator, High worked for the European Recovery Commission and later went to China with the Methodist Commission. While in China he became special correspondent to the *Christian Science Monitor*. Returning to the United States in 1928, High became editor of the *Christian Herald* and a contributing editor to the *Literary Digest*. An outspoken opponent of Prohibition repeal, High worked and spoke on behalf of Herbert Hoover in 1928 and 1932.[33]

High's broadcast career was perhaps assisted in no small way by his reports on the radio industry, published in the *Literary Digest* in 1934. For example, an article entitled "Radio's Policy Disarms Its Critics" dismissed conservative charges that the regulatory apparatus established by the Communications Act of 1934 had placed radio under the administration's control. High concluded that network officials, anticipating such criticism, had gone out of their way to open their Washington studios to speakers regardless of party affiliation. "Radio," explained High, "as a matter of survival, if for no other reason, has developed an amazing facility for placating its potential critics in high places." Citing the example of NBC, High noted the network's "standing rule" that its facilities "are at the disposal of any Congressman at any time to speak on any subject." Though NBC studios had not "been swamped," High nevertheless noted a statistical disparity between Democratic and Republican broadcasts. In the first three months of the 1934 legislative session, for example,

Democratic speakers had appeared 89 times and Republican speakers, 48 times. In a comparable period during 1932 in the waning days of the Hoover administration, NBC had carried 50 broadcasts by Republican members and 20 by Democratic members. High concluded, "No one in radio has ever sought to deny that, in the course of a year, the party in power would have more time on the air than the party in opposition. This has been and always will be the case, but it is a long jump from that premise to the conclusion that this or any preceding Administration has sought to exert a partizan [*sic*] control over radio."[34]

Whatever High's skill with a microphone, his influence in the netherworld of politics and prose seldom failed to impress his network superiors. A High tour of network affiliates and editorial centers in Seattle, Portland, San Francisco, Los Angeles, and Kansas City during August and September 1935 convinced John Patterson that "High is doing a real job for NBC." Returning east, High privately reported conversations on the "political scene" with social psychologist Hadley Cantril, who had recently published *The Psychology of Radio;* President Herbert Hoover; banker A. P. Gianinni; radical labor leader Harry Bridges; organizer Charles Francis Townshend; gubernatorial candidate Upton Sinclair; Governor Alfred M. Landon; and William Allen White, Henry J. Allen, and Roy Roberts of the *Kansas City Star.*[35]

Within two months of his return home, High became NBC's director of talks. A network press release announcing the appointment noted High's "broad background of intimate acquaintance with the world's great figures and problems as well as those of this country." High's new responsibilities included the development of sustaining programs under vice president for programming John F. Royal.[36] The appointment formalized High's promotion of the network's political interests. Charged with executive responsibility for allotting time among an increasingly vociferous clientele, High remained a sensitive student of NBC's political affairs. Whereas in the past the network had used sustaining time to satisfy obligations measured in talks, High determined to use sustaining time to test program ideas, develop malleable formulas, and present them in a form ready for sponsorship.

Despite the troubling transparency of *American Family Robinson*, the NAM's willingness to dramatize their deepest fears and concerns suggested an out. In the process of building a dramatic program for the manufacturers, the specialist could play a mediating role, negotiating a formula, and, conversely, the formula itself could play a mediating role, sustaining a "multiplicity of meanings rather than a monolithic dominant point of view."[37]

Faced with demands by their largest sponsors for a program through the NAM, Royal and High encouraged the NAM to consider dramatic fare that was capable of meeting both the network's and the manufacturers' requirements. Brought into the confidence of the NAM in early 1935, High expressed reservations about the timing and tone of a NAM program proposal entitled *The Men Who Made American Industry*. "The public," High wrote Royal, "rightly or wrongly, doesn't give a damn about the M.W.M.A.I. Their only interest in them is to condemn them. In that they're at least partly right. Its [*sic*] the sensing of this feeling that accounts for the fact that the *American Magazine* has laid off its Horatio Alger stuff and for the further fact that every popular businessman's biography of late has been of the debunking sort." High concluded that such a program "would be a boomerang, both for the businessman and for N.B.C." Instead, High proposed that the *Men Who Made American Industry* be made palatable in a larger package with a higher purpose. "If you're going ahead with a series of this sort," High wondered to Royal, "why not make it an 'Epic of America' sort of thing. Dramatize the lives of the men who gave us what we've got: in education, politics, science, religion—as well as in business. You've got just as good a chance there for propaganda and a whale of a lot better chance that the public will swallow it."[38]

Uppermost in the minds of NBC executives was the need to demonstrate a program able to assimilate conflict, and even definitions of reality conflicting with its own. Consulting with the NAM's Bayard Colgate, the toothpaste magnate, and later with DuPont Company president Lammot du Pont, High elaborated upon the concept. In a conference with Colgate, NBC president Alfred H. Morton, and NBC vice president Edgar Kobak, High framed the program's goals. First, the program would "make an appraisal—in human terms—of American civilization." Likewise, it would "dramatize the ways and means by which American civilization—so favorable to the average person—was produced." The program would not "white-wash" the country's shortcomings. It would "give a dramatic picture of just why the depression came to pass" and "spot-light the virtues and seek to restore confidence in those qualities—honesty, prudence, initiative, hard work—by which American achievements were brought to pass." "By presenting an adequate background of the rise of our civilization and the causes that gave us our present set-back we would be in a position to italicize those elements in our past success which need to be included in any plan for the future and those pitfalls which—as demonstrated in the 1914 to 1929 period—we need to avoid." This "background should be so presented as to indicate that we have been living in the period of 'American Cavalcade,' i.e. that we have been a nation on the march."[39]

"American Cavalcade" would not dwell upon the manufacturers' opposition to the New Deal, High explained, because

> the material will be historical. But the broadcast will not be a history of America. It will use the historical material not to dramatize events, as such, but to dramatize those American qualities which dominated the events. Having determined the qualities which are most characteristically American,

the program will begin with Colonial times and trace down to the present the way in which those qualities have operated—in all types of men and under all manner of conditions—to make America.

The broadcast will not make a direct tie-up with current events or problems. It is assumed that the qualities which have made America are as important now as they ever were; and that their employment now would work as well for the solving of the nation's difficulties as they ever did. The program ought to be designed to lead the listener to a belief in the current validity of the American spirit. But this leading will be done by inference, not by direct association.

As for a specific motif the series will present America as the Answer to the Age-long Search of the Common Man for a Place in the Sun.

It will tell how—not by chance—but by dint of hard work, resourcefulness, self-reliance, strenuous tugging at his own boot-straps, a confidence in himself, a respect for his neighbor and a faith in God he gained in America, in fuller measure than ever before in human history, the materials and the privileges of the abundant life.

"At the end," High wrote, "the National Broadcasting Company ought to be able to say that it has helped to create an appreciation of what Americans have in America; an understanding of how they got it; a conviction as to how it can and why it ought to be preserved."[40]

High's differences with the manufacturers, however, precluded his further involvement with the program. After meeting with the NAM's James Ford Bell, the General Mills executive then raising a radio fund for the Crusaders, High criticized the association's intractable opposition to even the most minor adjustment of capitalism under the New Deal. "In my opinion," High explained, "a vast majority of the American people believe in our economic system" and "overwhelmingly favor it to socialism or fascism." Most Americans, he continued, were (1) aware of capitalism's achievements and (2) "would not scrap the system, ultra-conscious of its faults though they are, until an attempt had been made to remodel it." The NAM, as High charitably put it, had misread the public's thirst for reform.

The whole of the present and, in some instances, perilous devotion to divers and sundry economic panaceas must be understood in the light of that second point. Nowhere in this country, so far as I have been able to discover, is there any significantly supported movement for the scrapping of capitalism. Everywhere, however, there are significantly supported movements for its remodeling. Roosevelt, Long and Coughlin are not preaching against capitalism. They are preaching against capitalism as it has been and, in general, still is. Their policies cannot, accurately, be described as offering substitutes for capitalism; but as prescribing changes in it. And so far as the country is concerned the issue—up to now—is not whether we will go forward under capitalism; but, rather, under what sort of capitalism shall we go forward?[41]

Though "the actual changes insisted on may be ill advised," High continued, "to argue that the desire to change is a sign of communistic or unAmerican tendencies will neither frighten nor fool anyone." While the NAM acknowledged the need for relief in the abstract, without a positive proposal of its own the association had become an obstacle to relief. Choosing examples from his conversations with Bell and other officials, High explained,

> There is a great outcry against federal expenditures, the unbalanced state of our budget, the increase of taxation. To date, however, I have not heard it said how we would care for the needy without some such financial dislocation. In other words, the attack upon the relief policies—in the absence of any proposals of a better sort—simply contradicts the conclusion that there must be relief.
>
> . . . As I understand it, a majority of the members of the National Association of Manufacturers might believe in unemployment insurance—as an abstract principle. But when it comes to the question of specific unemployment insurance measures most of them—on various grounds—are opposed. And opposition to each specific measure—since no better one is suggested—simply nullifies approval of the principle.[42]

Declaring his future with the program "somewhat indefinite," High excused himself from further discussions, leaving negotiations with the association to NBC vice president Edgar Kobak and network continuity editor Burke Boyce.

Anxious to develop this business, NBC's Edgar Kobak used the program's development to maintain correspondence and personal contact with NAM leaders, whom he regarded as commercial prospects for institutional entertainments. Kobak fancied the manufacturers as the program's "directors," kept them abreast of its progress and flattered them with requests for suggestions for a title. Earlier, after a presentation of High's "American Cavalcade" idea to DuPont president Lammot du Pont, du Pont declared the title unsuitable. Du Pont wrote, "My feeling that the name is inappropriate is based on the fact that the name does not give any indication of the character of the program. Since the meeting, I have thought a number of times about the matter, but have been unable to think of a more appropriate name." The NAM's Walter Weisenburger concurred. "I have the same feeling that the term 'Cavalcade' is not truly indicative of the nature of the program. I don't mean to infer by this, that the term 'industrial' should be in it, but I do believe that the name might be a little more indicative of the material that is being prepared for the public's ear, so that by name the public might identify the type of material it is interested in." After that, Kobak proposed "The American Scene"; Lammot du Pont considered this title "much better than 'The American Cavalcade,' but [I] do not feel that it is any too good at that." Never questioning du Pont's or Weisenburger's grasp of the program's significance, Kobak continued to solicit ideas for improving it and to pass along titles for reaction.[43]

The term "cavalcade" best described the concept of its network developers, if not its eventual sponsors. Though the word had yet to appear in the title of an American radio program, *Cavalcade* had become widely known on both sides of the Atlantic as a Noel Coward play. The word, Coward explained, had not been used much before 1932. Serialized in the English papers and dramatized by the BBC, the play gave the word "artificial respiration." Not unlike High's prospectus for "American Cavalcade," Coward's *Cavalcade* blended "domesticity, drama and patriotism," BBC historian Susan Briggs notes. In America, *Cavalcade* enjoyed a run on Broadway. It became the basis of a critically acclaimed American-made theatrical film, winning the Academy Award for best picture of 1932–1933.[44] The concept traveled well and apparently informed specialists' thought about the kind and type of program that might further the institutional goals of NBC and its sponsors.

The resulting NBC program was entitled *American Adventure*, however. Three months before the series' debut Burke Boyce described the concept. It grafted High's affirmation of capitalism's "abundant life" to the personal and domestic focus of the "radio historical novel" which Boyce himself had proposed in 1932 as a replacement for General Motors' *Parade of the States*. Boyce explained,

> As it is planned at present, it is the intention of the series to treat, in the form of a radio historical novel, a typical American family from generation to generation—showing that the people who laid the foundation of this country had their problems then just as we have them today; and showing how their spirit of individual courage and their American ideals carried them, and our nation, safely through every crisis. Dealing with an imaginary family in this fiction form, we feel that we can in this way cover a larger ground and bring into consideration a wider range of varied problems appealing more directly to the average listeners than would be otherwise possible.
>
> Naturally in the course of our series, some of our stories will deal directly with industrial development of our country.[45]

Neither scripts nor descriptions of *American Adventure* in broadcast form appear to have survived. The program escaped the reviewers of *Variety*, who acclaimed NBC's other sustaining entry that summer, *Town Hall of the Air*.[46] Fragmentary memoranda indicate that George Ludlam scripted the first installment of *American Adventure*, that NAM publications highlighted it, and that the weekly program ran from May 1 to July 22, 1935, costing $4,629 for orchestra and cast.[47] NBC officials considered the program a success; it relieved them of their immediate obligation to the NAM while demonstrating a program formula available for long-term institutional sponsorship.

American Adventure, however, bore bitter fruit. The commercial program that came about as a result of NBC's careful cultivation of the NAM debuted that fall on CBS. Inverting the wording of the title of High's "American Cavalcade" prospectus, the *Cavalcade of America* debuted under the sponsorship of the DuPont Company. The change of venue was more than a technicality for the program's producer, Roy S. Durstine of Batten, Barton, Durstine & Osborn. Later Durstine explained to RCA's David Sarnoff that BBDO's placement of programs on CBS had turned on the availability of a satisfactory network underwritten by the liberal terms of CBS's affiliate contracts, and on the network's willingness to broadcast programs developed by advertising agencies.[48] The DuPont Company's investment in institutional radio represented a prestigious windfall for CBS, and a significant victory for Bruce Barton, who had prevailed over the vigorous opposition of Lammot du Pont to convince the DuPont executive committee of the venture's soundness and necessity. What became the longest running radio program of its kind debuted October 9, 1935; it ran with but two brief lapses until 1953. In 1952 it moved to television, where it remained until 1955.[49]

Dedicated to the institutional rehabilitation of DuPont, the *Cavalcade of America* helped rescue the company's public image, rocked by the Senate munitions investigation, tax suits, and the du Ponts' unseemly association with the politics of the NAM and the newly organized American Liberty League. Its dramatization of the past provided a fitting program formula for a company whose own history dated to the early American republic. Incorporated by chemist Eleuthère Irénée du Pont in France in 1801, the company flowered on the banks of Delaware's Brandywine River, where Eleuthère Irénée located to produce black powder in 1802. The valley's most successful powder maker, the DuPont Company supplied the munitions and powder that opened the West and fought the Civil War. The company's purchase in 1903 by du Pont cousins Coleman, Alfred, and Pierre introduced modern management concepts and forward-looking product diversification. Under Pierre S. du Pont, the company's executive leadership looked past the lucrative government munitions contracts of the First World War to lay the basis of a broad-based chemical manufacturing concern. Pierre's younger brother Lammot, then vice president in charge of black powder, soon moved to the Miscellaneous Manufacturing Department to direct successful company ventures in paint and varnish, dyes, Fabrikoid artificial leather, and pyralin-based celluloid.[50]

In the mid-1930s the DuPont Company came under attack for alleged munitions privateering during the world war. If only because of its enormous scale, DuPont attracted attention in a book-length indictment of the international arms industry entitled *Merchants of Death*. The book achieved notoriety as a Book-of-the-Month Club selection in April 1934. An article of similar bent appearing that March in *Fortune* achieved wide circulation in *Reader's Digest*. Testifying before the Nye Committee, DuPont executives successfully refuted allegations of war profiteering;

even so, the "merchants of death" moniker tarred the industry.[51] Additional embarrassments beset the company's leadership when the U.S. Department of the Treasury reopened a lawsuit initiated in 1932 by the Hoover administration against Pierre du Pont and John J. Raskob, who in 1929–30 had exchanged 14 million dollars of stock to create fictitious losses for tax purposes.[52]

And still there was the organization of the American Liberty League. Announced in August 1934, the league's public association with the du Ponts linked the munitions industry investigation to the politics of wealth and reaction. Roy Norr, a publicist with ties to the Roosevelt administration, privately suggested that the league's "back-fire publicity" had cemented DuPont's reputation as a munitions maker in the public mind. "Rightly or wrongly," wrote Norr, "what name more than 'DuPont' suggests 'munitions' to the American public?" "Poor League! If it ever shows its head in the heat of a political campaign, what taunt is likely to be flung at it? That the slogan at its masthead should read not 'Give Us Liberty' but *'Give Us Death.'*"[53]

The du Ponts and their associates often acted upon personal political concerns with little regard for corporate consequence. The issue had come up before, when in 1928 DuPont Company treasurer and General Motors finance committee chairman John J. Raskob had become the manager of Democrat Al Smith's presidential campaign and, soon after, became the chairman of the Democratic National Committee. Raskob had come in contact with Governor Smith while helping Pierre S. du Pont organize a campaign for the Association Against the Prohibition Amendment. Raskob's high-profile activities on behalf of Smith and the Democratic Party led General Motors president Alfred P. Sloan to demand that Raskob resign the chairmanship of the GM finance committee. Challenged by Sloan's drive to project a corporate, rather than personal, outlook for General Motors, Raskob resigned his GM finance committee chairmanship. Pierre S. du Pont then relinquished his chairmanship of the GM board of directors to protest his friend's ouster. While Raskob and du Pont remained GM board members, their resignations marked the end of their active involvement in the corporation that they had done much to create. While Sloan's corporate outlook for General Motors did not preclude his later personal financial contributions to the Liberty League, the manager-owners of the DuPont Company made little, if any, distinction between their personal and corporate affairs.[54] Partisan and unapologetic, the Liberty League's transparent connections to the fortunes of the du Ponts, the DuPont Company, and General Motors never ceased to amaze. Charles Michelson, the Democratic National Committee publicist hired in 1929 during Raskob's tenure as Democratic Party chairman, chuckled at his one-time employer's "dupontifical" publicity.[55] The American Liberty League, cracked Postmaster General James A. Farley, "ought to be called the American Cellophane League," because "first, it's a DuPont product, and second, you can see right through it."[56]

Though DuPont's use of radio before 1935 had been "spasmodic and light," traditional techniques of publicity and promotion were not unknown to the company's advertising and public relations staff.[57] Company specialists engaged the firm of Ivy Lee and T. J. Ross to handle public and legislative relations during the Senate munitions hearings. The arrangement was allowed to lapse with the end of the hearings, and expired on December 31, 1934.[58] Of more lasting significance, DuPont had maintained a small exhibit hall on the boardwalk at Atlantic City since 1916. Of company media before and after the pivotal year 1935, the exhibit medium seems to have been best understood and supported by Lammot du Pont, who generally questioned the value of public relations work, and institutional advertising in particular.[59] In 1935 some 2,600,000 people visited DuPont exhibits at Atlantic City and the Texas Centennial at Dallas, the latter marking the outreach of company exhibits to regional centers. In 1937 DuPont opened an exhibit at the Museum of Science and Industry at Rockefeller Center and committed to a freestanding exhibit building at the New York World's Fair 1939/40.[60]

Of DuPont's investments in new media after 1935, radio's *Cavalcade of America* was scrutinized most critically by Lammot du Pont and members of the company executive committee. Not until Bruce Barton and BBDO came into the picture after the departure of Lee and Ross in early 1935 did the executive committee warm to the idea of a continuing campaign of institutional advertising. Writing to Lammot du Pont, Barton forcefully stated the practical value of such a campaign, emphasizing its effect upon employees, dealers, purchasing agents, shareholders, and overlapping constituencies of ultimate consumers and voters. Barton urged the executive committee to immediately authorize an appropriation "of not less than $500,000 or more than $650,000" for an advertising campaign to change the public perception of DuPont from "'the powder people'" to "peace time manufacturer." "We propose," Barton wrote, "to create a vast constituency which *knows* what DuPont knows about style, and about many other important phases of everyday living, and will be willing to accept readily anything that bears the DuPont name."[61]

A positive expression of corporate social leadership supervised by advertising and public relations specialists, the resulting campaign exemplified a higher concept of public relations that was far removed from the necessity of the company's initial response to the Senate munitions investigation and the in-and-out of party politics that had become manifest in a near-daily cycle of reaction and attack by 1935. By the early 1950s, company advertising and public relations specialists proudly pointed to increasingly favorable opinion polling data associating DuPont with "Better Things for Better Living." Reflecting on BBDO's long and successful relationship with DuPont in 1956, Bruce Barton attributed the turnaround in part to two factors: women's nylons and the *Cavalcade of America*.[62]

Competing product divisions limited the company's use of radio prior to the *Cavalcade*. In 1931 NBC's Pacific Coast network broadcast a program entitled the *DuPont Decorators*, devised to merchandise the company's line of Duco paints. From November 1932 to June 1933 the DuPont Cellophane division sponsored a fifteen-minute morning program twice a week, featuring the Harding Sisters at the organ and piano, with singer Edwin Nell and a talk on etiquette by Emily Post. An attempt by NBC to parlay these intermittent sponsorships into a company-wide program entitled *The Court of King Duco* failed to pass audition at the company's Wilmington, Delaware, headquarters. A pilot program transcribed on speculation by NBC featured the Doric Quartette in the role of the "Duco Decorators," John and Ned as "The Color Schemers," Rita Lane or Lucille Kirtley as "Princess Cellophane," Harry Stanton as "King Duco," and a twenty-piece orchestra, the "Rainbow Harmonists," conducted by Meredith Willson.[63]

In a similar but more successful fashion, Barton and Durstine parlayed DuPont's decision for the *Cavalcade* into a long-term campaign to promote the company as a public-spirited institution. The campaign opened with a series of ten advertisements placed in the *Saturday Evening Post*. Written by BBDO's Douglas Kingston with photographs by Victor Keppler, each advertisement placed DuPont in the daily lives of its often unknowing consumers. The first advertisement, appropriately entitled "It started one Saturday night," pictured a well dressed young couple in a darkened movie theater, their faces lit by the screen's reflection (fig. 10). While the couple stares at the screen, lost in the film and, presumably, in each other, the copy coyly explains DuPont's contributions to their first date. "There's no use talking—Saturday was an exciting day for Amos Hunter. . . . That night he had a date with a girl. THE date with THE girl. So he spent part of the afternoon shining up the old bus with 'Duco' Polish . . . . In the meantime Susie Blossom was busy putting the last frills and furbelows on her new, peach-colored DuPont Rayon dress. Susie was pretty sure that Amos was THE boy. And at eight o'clock sharp, Amos and Susie were on their way in the bright, shiny car . . . bound for the movies to see a hand-holding romance that was made on DuPont film. Neither Amos nor Susie," the ad concludes, "realized how chemical research had touched their lives that day."[64] The copy's fine print reminded readers to tune in the *Cavalcade of America*, and carried the "Better Things for Better Living . . . through Chemistry" tag created for the campaign. Thereafter, DuPont's succinct expression of the personal meaning of corporate enterprise accompanied every advertisement and followed each mention of the company on the *Cavalcade of America*.

BBDO specialists approached the DuPont executive committee with a radio audition presented as a "trial" of two programs. Committee members first listened to a program written and performed by playwright Channing Pollock. The program consisted of a half-hour monologue that a company history later described as "a

Figure 10. Advertisement, "It started one Saturday night," *Saturday Evening Post* 208 (October 5, 1935): 5. Courtesy of Hagley Museum and Library.

sentimental diary . . . full of homely common sense and quiet humor" designed to "appeal to a wide audience and also be a fitting vehicle for DuPont's down-to-earth description of its many products and how they contributed to the comfort and well-being of people everywhere." While DuPont's directors judged Pollock's monologue to be too sentimental and fragile, they found the second program, the "stalwart 'Cavalcade of America' . . . dramatic, vigorous . . . truly representative of DuPont. A fitting frame for DuPont's story of perseverance and achievement." The executive committee instructed BBDO to proceed with "a series of shows dealing with historical subjects—subjects which would implement 'the widespread belief among thinking people that America should be brought back to first principles and given a new realization of the sturdy qualities and stamina and character which built this country.'"[65] A window display set up at company headquarters to merchandise the *Cavalcade* among employees promised "a radio program of unusual technique, which reaches new heights of vivid interest and artistic excellence—linking together little known but thrilling episodes of American life—emphasizing the fine, sturdy fundamentals of American character. The kind of program millions of radio listeners have wanted for many years"[66] (fig. 11).

The debut of the *Cavalcade of America* on the evening of October 9, 1935, starred Walter Hampden in the aptly entitled "No Turning Back." The half-hour program presented two dramas; Hampden took the lead in both. The program concluded with a brief commercial "story of chemistry." Part I featured Hampden as "Edward Winslow," a Pilgrim who chooses to remain in America rather than return to England with the *Mayflower*. Part II featured Hampden as a farmer—a descendant of the first character—whose South Dakota farm is ruined by a plague of grasshoppers. The farmer, too, decides to remain on the land, and in this case, reclaim his family farm from natural disaster. The program's announcer exclaimed the connection. "No turning back—the will to carry on—the refusal to give in. This quality has helped shape the course of American history from the days of the Pilgrims to the present day. People whose names find no important place in history's pages. Who quietly did their job and ask no credit or glory! We salute them: Heroes of the American Cavalcade."[67]

Figure 11.

DuPont Company Headquarters window exhibit, *Cavalcade of America* (October 1935). Courtesy of Hagley Museum and Library.

Critics reacted to the first program by speculating on DuPont's political motive. *Variety* declared the *Cavalcade* to be a somber and dubious entertainment. A reviewer noted that "DuPont a leader, through the [NAM], in providing radio stations with free discs to combat communistic propaganda, has seemingly carried this campaign a step further." Although the *Cavalcade* included a "story of chemistry" advertisement mentioning various DuPont products, "the sales copy is primarily institutional so that the impression is given that the sponsor is more concerned with what America is thinking than what America is buying. That in itself marks the program as exceptional." The reviewer credited Hampden with a "smooth job," but wondered at the intent of author and director Kenneth Webb. While Webb made his characters believable, his script's "exhortations to patient, plodding see-it-through Americanism are close enough to familiar homiletics to have a familiar ring to native ears, but it still is a sermon. Program may," continued the reviewer, "if such is the DuPont motive help galvanize the already conservative thinking to stout resistance against the stirrer-uppers of revolt and dissatisfaction. Question remains—will the average person bother to listen? And that's hard to believe."[68]

Reaction to the broadcast among NBC network specialists was understandably bitter. Stanley High complained that the *Cavalcade* was "terrible" and in no way comparable to that summer's *American Adventure*. "The music was poor and I thought the casting was likewise bad," High reported. "Walter Hampden had too cultivated a voice to play the part of a farmer and the rest of the cast sounded like a bunch of Vermonters rather than Kansans." "The plot wasn't substantial enough to be called flimsy. The action was slow and the climax sounded like a page out of Horatio Alger—and a poor page at that."[69]

Other reviewers, however, seemed to warm to the *Cavalcade*'s educational and entertaining attributes. A Women's National Radio Committee endorsement, worked into the introduction of a *Cavalcade* episode entitled "Faith in Education," for example, opined that "The story of America's progress is drama as absorbing as fiction and on this half hour it is particularly entertaining. Don't let the word 'educational' fool you for this program will hold your interest from start to finish. We recommend it especially as family entertainment and suggest that the children be allowed to sit up and hear it."[70]

BBDO's aggressive merchandising of *Cavalcade* involved celebrated authors, dramatists, actors, actresses, educators, and historians. From 1935 to 1938 the *Cavalcade*'s historical advisers included Dixon Ryan Fox, the president of Union College and the New York Historical Association, and Professor Arthur M. Schlesinger of Harvard. The arrangement enabled BBDO to merchandise the program as a contribution to the "new social history" with which Fox and Schlesinger as co-editors of the twelve-volume *A History of American Life* had become identified. The series set aside the usual political framework of historical narratives for a topical treatment of social subjects. Fashioning an American past from the source material of everyday life, *A History of American Life* enlarged the field of historical inquiry to include the totality of human experience. In 1937 Schlesinger explained that the historian "cannot allow his choice of subject matter to be governed by what lies conveniently at hand in newspaper files and other conventional historical sources. He is constantly asking questions, many of which can be answered only by prying into unexpected holes and corners." The authors of *A History of American Life*, for example, had expanded their investigation of primary source material to include "diaries, personal correspondence, travel accounts, advertisements, pictures, artifacts and other museum objects, books of etiquette, popular songs, cookbooks, works of fiction, scientific publications and a wide variety of ephemera."[71] The approach never seemed more timely than in the Depression, when the self-conscious search for a usable past placed renewed emphasis on the discovery of the native qualities, values, and traditions of the common man.

The *Cavalcade* consulting arrangement formalized contact between the historical profession and the amateur historians who populated the program-building departments of the networks and Madison Avenue agencies. So fully did Fox enter into the collaborative spirit of the program that he initially sought no compensation for his labors, considering the work "a good national service."[72] It provided an outlet for the promotion of Fox's interests in state and local history as well. As president of the New York Historical Association from 1929 to 1945, he turned the organization into what one of its later directors described as "less of a society and more of an educational force, seeking to tell the story of Everyman as he labored, built, played, thought and created."[73] Whatever legitimate interests Fox pursued as an apostle of the new social history, he brought to the tasks of program building and merchandising the progressive outlook of the whig theory of history.[74] In a 1931 essay that asked "Are We Better than Our Ancestors?" for example, Fox sought to "detect some trend and, if there has been change, to test it in the terms of progress." Describing a "technique of living" that might have taken even Bruce Barton's breath away, Fox wrote,

> Seated by your fireside you can hear a word as soon as it is whispered on the other side of the Atlantic; men have now flown across that great expanse of ocean almost in a day; we have a well-based expectation that we soon shall see across it. Space is almost obsolete. So habituated are we to all such improvements that what must yet be done to perfect these achievements we know will be done; with such infinitude of premises, prophecy has scarce need of faith. Heating his home with automatic furnaces and cooling it with mechanical refrigeration, man has almost abolished the seasons. To conquer night he needs only press a button. The world's

> work is done not with muscle but with ingenuity, an ingenuity which has made possible a consumption of materials by the humblest that would have aroused the envy of great kings in years gone by.[75]

While chairman of the Columbia University History Department in 1933, Fox acted upon Edward L. Bernays's suggestion to honor the publication of General Motors' company history *The Turning Wheel*. By 1935, the first year of his collaboration with Schlesinger as a *Cavalcade* consultant, Fox's "civilization in transit" had transcended the frontier "man with the axe" for the "pioneers of ideas and special competence" who had followed "in their wake." Fox found native qualities of perseverance, and coupled them to an entrepreneurial flair for risk-taking and adventure. "As the woodsman-farmer with his axe and hoe took a risk, as to whether untamed nature would let him live," Fox argued, "so these men with the book, the scalpel, the compass, to say nothing of the microscope and test-tube, took a risk, as to whether the social soil was deep and rich enough to sustain their specialties."[76]

The DuPont Company's foray into the *Cavalcade of America* proceeded along familiar lines of commercial contact and acquaintance. Fox mistakenly believed the program concept to have originated with BBDO's Roy Durstine and producer Kenneth Webb, "who," he wrote Schlesinger, "has [*sic*] conceived, with some advice from me, an elaborate historical program series entitled 'The American Cavalcade.'" Unaware of the concept's gestation at NBC, Fox added that Durstine and Webb "had a hope that some solid American enterprise might find such a high class program a good thing to which to attach their name. They tried the American Telephone and Telegraph Company, but finally their negotiations failed. They were not disheartened, however, and now have sold their scheme to the DuPont Company." Fox continued, "The latter is anxious, exceedingly anxious, apparently, to build up their business and reputation in the field of the peaceful arts and were much taken with my original suggestion that the whole program eliminate war and violence. Military patriotism is entirely eliminated as a theme; they are more squeamish about this than I was."[77]

In seeking Schlesinger's assistance with the tasks of *Cavalcade* script reading and topic suggestion, Fox expressed a desire to be publicly identified with the program as a historian rather than as a college president. The distribution of program responsibilities among "two or three historians" would lighten the burden and further the interests of the historical profession. "The whole thing," Fox noted without further elaboration, "seems of the kind the American Historical Association had in mind, though, of course, the Association is not being brought into it." An unlikely prospect for DuPont employment given his sympathy for the New Deal, Schlesinger replied that he had "no objections on principle of being associated with

[*Cavalcade*]," though before agreeing to participate he wanted to clearly understand "our responsibilities" regarding services "'creative' or merely critical, to what extent we will be associated in the public mind with the program, etc." "The connection with the DuPont Company bothers me somewhat," Schlesinger wrote, "but I suspect you have safeguarded our interests by the provision for the elimination of military patriotism. Of course there are many other things which might embarrass us, such as the glorification of the employer who maintains the 'American system' of the open shop against the labor unions. I think we should have a pretty clear idea of what the program is going to be before becoming involved in it."[78]

Reassuring Schlesinger, Fox explained that "from time to time" he "made suggestions" to Durstine, "and answered questions out of friendship." Fox added the startling news that Durstine "would be satisfied to deal with me alone and offers me $300 a month as long as this program runs, which will probably be two or three months any way and perhaps much longer." Describing the distance from their prospective sponsor as more apparent than real, Fox concluded, "He pays us and not DuPont."[79] Eventually Schlesinger agreed to join the enterprise, and to accept as compensation $100 of the $300 monthly fee offered by Durstine with the stipulation that Fox, who had already given time to the project, take the lead as the "'central' clearing house" for expediting the work. Despite Fox's assurances, however, Schlesinger remained skeptical of the program's objective. "You seem less concerned than I about the possible danger of becoming involved in an undesirable type of propaganda," he wrote Fox. "Probably you are wise not to be greatly concerned in advance. Of course, we can withdraw from the enterprise at any time if it should appear that the broadcasts are being used for purposes of which we disapprove."[80]

Given the topical framework provided by the BBDO radio department, Schlesinger need not have worried. *Cavalcade* producer Kenneth Webb thanked Schlesinger for agreeing to work with BBDO, enclosing three scripts for review and a list of proposed topics for development. In short order Schlesinger checked the script "Community Self-Reliance" for historical inaccuracies and found none. Turning his attention to the list of topics, Schlesinger suggested that "East Meets West," the story of air mail, dramatize instead the completion of the Union Pacific and the "wedding of the rails." "Heroism in Science" might treat the construction of the Brooklyn Bridge and the discovery of the transmitting cause of yellow fever. Episodes meeting Schlesinger's approval under the topical heading "The Will to Share" featured Clara Barton's struggle to establish the American Red Cross; episodes under "The Humanitarian Urge" featured the story of the Society for the Prevention of Cruelty to Children, and the founding of Hull House by Jane Addams. Only the topic "Freedom of Speech" presented a problem. The producer's inability to come up with a suitable episode spoke volumes about *Cavalcade*'s limitations. Schlesinger wrote, "I appreciate the difficulty of finding a subject during the last half-century which would not involve a good deal of emotional controversy." A good bet, he suggested, might be John Quincy Adams's struggle for the right of petition in the House of Representatives—touching upon the slavery struggle—"I think the subject could be handled without offense to the sensibilities of present-day Southerners."[81]

Schlesinger soon found himself in conference with Durstine and Webb in BBDO's Madison Avenue offices, where he offered further "half-baked suggestions . . . for what they may be worth." These included a program on the contributions of American immigrants ("America: the Melting Pot"), featuring the labors of Jacob Riis to abolish slum conditions in New York, and a second, "The Spirit of Play," showing, for example,"how the frontiersman mixed fun with work in, say, a neighborhood cabin raising." "Thirdly," wrote Schlesinger, "I think we should have a program dealing with the theme of loyalty to family as a phase of the American character. This is somewhat vague in my mind, but I do think that a program which emphasizes love of the home and fireside might work well into the series."[82] As the *Cavalcade of America*'s broadcast sequence played out through early 1936, it became evident that Durstine and BBDO happily concurred.

Suspended between the liberal sensibilities of the new social history represented by the collaboration of Fox, Schlesinger, and BBDO and their conservative sponsor's predilection for attack, the *Cavalcade* offered a counter-subversive drama of "self-reliance," "resourcefulness," and "defiance," animated by the misfortunes of natural phenomena: grasshopper plagues, flash floods, fires, droughts, dust storms, blizzards, ice floes, and log jams. Successful resolution demanded heroic acts of voluntarism, community spirit, and the sterner stuff that defined a heritage. As one flinty character explained, while he helped extinguish a forest fire threatening his town, "What we struggled to get, we fight to keep."[83]

More than Fox, Schlesinger recognized the *Cavalcade*'s limitations as a scholarly product, never more so than when acknowledging Durstine's constant requests for "human interest stories" and "more human incidents."[84] For his part, Fox paid close attention to historical fidelity, not normally the focus of advertising agency life. Fox insisted that the broadcasts be recorded for posterity, a prospect that further stimulated his rigorous examination of scripts for errors of fact and interpretation. "Of course, if the scripts were merely spoken off once it might not matter so much about details," Fox explained, "but I have advised B.B.D.&O. to have each program taken off on a master phonograph record from which other records can be made for schools, clubs, etc. This gives permanent value to the program and, therefore, more *responsibility* for me."[85] Schlesinger, though, quickly realized the impossibility of their position. The best that could be done—in the interest of history—was to alter the announcer's introduction to reflect that liberties had been taken in the interest of entertainment. Schlesinger wrote, "As I have said so many times before, I do not see why our employers insist upon saying that the programs are 'dedicated to telling true stories. . . .' Such statements should be amended to read: 'dedicated to telling stories dealing with true incidents in American History.'"[86] "My own rule of action," Schlesinger later explained to a young assistant who had taken on Fox's duties during a summer break, "is to let dubious statements pass if there is no clear proof to the contrary. I do not think we are obliged to do a real job of historical research on these scripts, but merely to correct factual inaccuracies. As for the literary style employed, that seems to me the business of the well-paid script writers in New York. The most difficult recurrent problem is that of the amount of fictional elbow room which script writers are entitled to. I incline to be liberal in this respect."[87]

An early *Cavalcade* program, "Building and Architecture," for example, followed the historical development of the American iron and steel industry through the love interest of a young Quaker couple. The first of two twelve-and-a-half-minute sketches, a tribute to the carpenters, joiners, masons, plasterers, and glazers of Independence Hall (originally known as the Pennsylvania State House), told the story of the courtship of "Prudence Woolley," daughter of guildsman Edmund Woolley, and "Tyson," a carpenter. Their marriage and family life paralleled the enlargement of the hall, and they glimpsed in Quaker admiration at "uncommon sturdy" door hinges and the peal of the belfry's two-thousand-pound "great bell" (later known as the Liberty Bell), the first cast by an American foundry.

Industrial initiative and incidental love interest packed the program's second half. It continues the story of American iron and steel through "Tommy Coleman," an orphan newsboy on the triangular corner of Fifth Avenue, 23rd Street, and Broadway, the site of the fabled "flat iron" building. An enthusiastic student of steel construction, young Tommy makes the acquaintance of an architect, who helps him land a job in the construction trade. The action picks up twenty-five years later, where atop the steel superstructure of the Empire State Building, a deep-voiced Tom has just led his "rivet gang" past the sixty-fourth floor. A "gangboy," Tom drives his crew of ethnic Irish and Italian steel workers toward a bonus for completing the building before "renting season." Tom confides an additional reason for working so hard: his wife Mary is scheduled for surgery at the New York Medical Center. One of the gang, momentarily missing the point, enthuses, "Oh, the medical center. I work on that job. Good job. Lotsa steel. But it's a heck of a place for a vacation!" After the "might be fatal" operation, the surgeon volunteers a prognosis for Mary's recovery of "full health." The surgeon, it turns out, has used a "new technique." Invited to inspect the tiny instrument that "did the trick," a grateful Tom gushes, "This little gadget—heh, look will ya! Dog-gone it, it's made of steel!"

The "story of chemistry" commercial concluding the broadcast describes the use of acids to "pickle" the exterior steel finish of the Empire State Building (the New York headquarters of the DuPont Company), and offers additional examples of metallurgy's role in improving automobile bodies and making possible the galvanized cable supporting the George Washington Bridge. Following the "story of chemistry," a "special message" recommends upcoming *Cavalcade* broadcasts to school principals and teachers of English, history, and dramatics, a point that Fox had often urged.[88]

The dramatization of the personal significance of enterprise played out in the *Cavalcade*'s striking use of female protagonists. In its first season the *Cavalcade* presented a hierarchical schedule of broadcasts beginning with "Women's Emancipation," the story of Elizabeth Cady Stanton, Lucretia Mott, William Lloyd Garrison, and Susan B. Anthony; "Women in Public Service," the story of Jane Addams and Hull House; "Loyalty to Family," the story of frontier widow Ann Harper; and "Self-Reliance," the story of planter Eliza Lucas's efforts to establish indigo culture in Carolina.

Independent spirit and action anchored in the physical space of the home and related spheres of charitable and civic improvement characterized the *Cavalcade* woman. Huddled around their radio receivers, the *Cavalcade*'s listening audience might know of what "Jane Addams" spoke in partaking the blend of entertainment and information. Describing her "settlement house," Addams explained, "we're like a mission, only not as preachy. We're not a mission—nor a hospital—nor a school. A place to be friendly in for anyone who cares to come. A place where people can drop in. You know, like they might in a small town." The contemporary portion of the program following the Addams sketch featured volunteer "frontier nurses" who tended to the "poverty-stricken mountaineers of Kentucky" from a network of "wayside cabins." The plot involved a sickly child, "Billy," a nurse's horseback ride to his rescue, her intercession between feuding families, and a mountaineer, struck by her kindness, who exclaims in amazement, "treatin' Billy like she was kin!"[89]

Many *Cavalcade* women occupied an idealized domestic space hewn from the wilderness. "Loyalty to Family," for example, dramatized the story of frontier widow Ann Harper and her young family's struggle for existence in Ohio's Western Reserve. Setting the scene, an announcer explained that the family, "the basic unit of our country's social structure, has been a great force for good in America. Since it is largely in the hands of women that the care of our families has been placed, it is to the history of American womanhood that we look this evening."[90] An announcer's introduction to "Self-Reliance," the story of planter Eliza Lucas, noted that "when this continent was settled, womanhood had few traditions of true partnership with men." Yet women such as Lucas "often share an equal burden in a country's progress." Lucas, "beautiful and spirited daughter of the South," made herself "at home" managing her father's struggling Carolina plantation. In a "bold stroke" to fend off his creditors, she undertakes the cultivation of West Indies indigo. Although the crisis ends not with a new export crop, but with her marriage, nevertheless Lucas has laid the basis for a domestic strain of the delicate indigo seed, thereby contributing to the future prosperity of Carolina.[91]

Many *Cavalcade* women turned up as agents of production. "The Search for Iron," broadcast in 1938, for example, dramatized the Merrit family's discovery of the massive iron ore deposit in Minnesota's Mesabi Range. The search, played out over three generations, featured matriarch Hepzabeth Merrit, life in a log-hewn home, and the frontier quest for resources. The story opens in 1857 as Hepzabeth and five of her seven sons arrive on the frontier. The Minnesota frontier, explains a fellow passenger on the ferry steaming across Lake Superior to the rendezvous, is a "grand, wild new land." "A man can think and do as he pleases." "Those woods and rocks," he foreshadows, "hold a lot of secrets. It'll be youngsters like these Merrit kids that'll ferret them out."

On the frontier, familial pride of accomplishment reflects the native qualities and a distinctively American never-give-up determination. As the years pass, Hepzabeth "kept house, cooked, fashioned candles, made clothes for her seven boys and served as nurse for the community." The plot unfolds, significantly enough, during a family meeting in which Father declares that a fortune awaits the discoverers of "a rich lot" of Mesabi iron. Passing the doughnuts, Hepzabeth implores her boys to "figure out a way" to find the elusive ore. Father urges his sons to "look sharp when you're scoutin' around up there. Bring back any rocks that look interesting." Her sons' suggestion that Hepzabeth move to a place where she might "live regular" only strengthens her will to endure. "I brought you boys up here, and I'm going to stay just as long as you do. Your father's right. There is iron up in that range, and the Merrit men are gonna find it! And I'm going to stay right here and fry the whitefish and knit their socks while they do it!" The story comes to its inevitable conclusion years later, as her grandsons mine their lucky find. The discovery of ore so close to the surface affirms Hepzabeth's belief "in the iron and in the Merrit boys. . . . I knew all along it'd be like that." Carried by her grandson to the edge of the pit, she declares the "happiest day in my life . . . to see all this." The concluding "story of chemistry" explained how miners used DuPont dynamite to excavate iron ore from "mother Earth," an example of the modern world's extraordinary engineering feats and of dynamite's use for constructive projects. Not without its lighter moments, "Search for Iron" began, like many early *Cavalcade* broadcasts, with a medley of popular show tunes, in this case "Someday My Prince Will Come" and "Heigh Ho" from Walt Disney's *Snow White and the Seven Dwarfs*.[92]

The front-loaded sentiment of the songs that introduced program segments could carry those segments as subjects worthy of dramatic interpretation. "Songs That Inspire the Nation," for example, paid tribute to Stephen Foster's "Old Folks at Home," Daniel Decatur Emmett's "Dixie," John Philip Sousa's "Stars and Stripes Forever," Irving Berlin's "Alexander's Ragtime Band," and Carrie Jacobs-Bond's "End of a Perfect Day."[93] The popularity of *Cavalcade* stories featuring composers led to "Songs of Home," a program that paid homage to John Howard Payne, composer of "Home, Sweet Home," Stephen Foster, composer of "My Old Kentucky Home," and David Guyan, who transcribed from boyhood memory "Home on the Range, the Home Sweet Home of the West." The Guyan sketch dramatized "Home on the Range" as a folkloric artifact heard by a boy and his mother on the steps of their farm house, close by the "roving cowboys" who played the song. Opening the program for DuPont, an announcer drew the necessary parallels.

> Since this nation is first of all a land of homes, the home songs occupy an important place in our history. And just as music is interpreted in terms of home, so can be the developments of science and industry. The best proof of the service rendered by chemical research lies in the many comforts and conveniences it has brought to every home. These contributions are summed up in the DuPont ideal, "Better Things for Better Living . . . through Chemistry."

Following a brief musical bridge, the narrator folded this thought into the subject at hand.

> Love of home has always been a prominent trademark of the American people. Our country was founded and settled by sturdy pioneers who above all sought permanent homes for themselves and their families. This home loving instinct is reflected by many of our best-known songs . . .[94]

During July and August 1936 the *Cavalcade* presented an episodic history of American band and orchestral music. This "special summer series" featured band leader Arthur Pryor, the father of *Cavalcade* director and BBDO radio department head Arthur Pryor, Jr. The series' program sequence followed the career of the elder Pryor, a popular band leader in his own right who had once played in John Philip Sousa's band. The second in the series, a tribute to the "Gay Nineties," began with an uptempo performance of the ever-popular "Washington Post March." Settling into the history and culture of the Sousa performance as re-created by the Pryors, the program used narration as a bridge to the playing of each composition as a set piece. The first took listeners to the World's Columbian Exposition of 1893, where Sousa had encouraged audiences to sing along with the music. This suggestion was perhaps not lost among *Cavalcade* listeners, who might join in with the cast as the senior Pryor conducted a medley of "Two Little Girls in Blue," "Annie Rooney," "The Band Played On," and "After the Ball."[95]

While the crisply starched martial air and the community sing were no doubt familiar to the *Cavalcade*'s listening audience, they were unfamiliar instruments for men who thought of themselves as chemists and financiers, not entertainers. The *Cavalcade*'s resort to a "special summer series" of musical programs in 1936 suggests that BBDO determined to avoid all dramatic comment during that summer's presidential campaign. Even after the *Cavalcade* returned to the historical anthology formula, stories with a "political angle" remained off limits. Webb told Schlesinger that scripts entitled "Patriotism" and "The Constitution," for example, were "a little too political in content." "Several of our best scripts have been refused because they featured politicians," Webb complained. "Our client feels that any story that might stir up any controversy is dangerous."[96] Not limited to politicians, the ban against controversial subjects extended to Booker T. Washington and Jacob Riis "because of race prejudice." Other topics were forbidden as well. A story about Dorothea Dix, for example, was rejected because "the subject of the insane is too unpleasant for the program."[97] At other times the program's editorial policy limited a full understanding of the chosen subject. The story of Clara Barton, for example, was featured, "and as they wanted it without any war, it was not as complete as it might have been."[98] A similar problem arose when Webb requested "a story about Texas because of the coming Texas Centennial . . . any material we could use which would not depend on war or any controversial subject."[99] In short order, Schlesinger proposed stories treating the "bringing in of American pioneers by Stephen Austin—a story which would center in the conquest of Texas from the wilderness;" another featured the activities of the Texas Rangers, "suppressing the bad men and establishing law and order in the frontier settlement of Texas"; a third dealt with the "self-reliant efforts of the city of Galveston to reestablish their city after the great tidal wave and storm of 1900."[100]

Was the *Cavalcade of America* propaganda? Approving Fox's efforts to supply teachers with broadcast transcriptions, Schlesinger noted that it was indeed, though "not in any objectionable sense."[101] While Schlesinger clearly enjoyed his relationship with the program, his correspondence with Fox reveals a self-deprecating sense of humor, referring to "our masters, the DuPonts," and "my iniquitous connection with the DuPonts," a turn of phrase used to acknowledge receipt of his $100 monthly allotment from Fox.[102] Utterly lacking Schlesinger's sense of irony and detachment, Fox actively promoted the idea that the *Cavalcade* represented a "new twist for history" no less politically significant than the unvarnished diatribes of the National Association of Manufacturers and the American Liberty League that BBDO so desperately sought to replace. Citing the *Cavalcade*'s impact upon the "average undergraduate," Fox confided to Lammot du Pont, "I think it is doing a great deal of good, generally, for the American tradition and particularly for the DuPont Company as an American institution."[103] It was left to Fox to publicly explain the program's dramatization of the past as an exercise in cultural introspection sharpened by the Depression and, by implication, the untested experiments of the New Deal. In the foreword to an anthology of *Cavalcade* stories published in 1937, Fox wrote:

> The program was originally conceived and steadily developed in patriotic faith, informed by understanding and responsible research, to remind us of the purposes and motives on which our fathers and mothers based and built this nation. In it have been heard the inspiring voices of the past, when men and women of public spirit and lofty resolution faced and conquered difficulties which might have wrecked our national undertaking before we could inherit it. We have listened to the authentic life of America, vastly more stirring and persuasive because it is true.

While it would have been easier for the *Cavalcade* to dramatize the "familiar matter of the textbooks, to say again what everybody knows about the great heroes of American history," the program's producers had followed a different plan:

> The dazzling geniuses, the supermen, appear now and then, though in aspects and episodes by no means so well known. For the most part, however, the designers of this program have dipped into the common mass for their instances of heroism, virtue, ingenuity and public service. They have drawn their stories from the great folk of America, the same folk on which we must, and happily can, with full faith now rely. They have tried to analyze the American character and find instances which vividly illustrate American traits and ideals.[104]

If European history seemed more glamorous or closely knit, Fox explained, "That is because our historians have placed too much emphasis on the central government in Washington, and not nearly enough on the different states and sections of the country."[105]

While BBDO projected the *Cavalcade* as the beginning of a long-term institutional campaign, it proved difficult for the du Ponts and their associates in the National Association of Manufacturers, the American Liberty League, and the Republican National Committee to look past the election of 1936. As the election approached, cultivation of corporate public relations was put aside in favor of efforts to unseat Roosevelt and turn out the New Deal. In that summer's heated presidential contest, the *Cavalcade* appeared to be a short-term investment not unlike the du Ponts' many radio investments, ranging from the speech schedule of the Jeffersonian Democrats (the anti-Roosevelt splinter group of the Democratic Party led by John J. Raskob and Al Smith) to plans for a popular dramatic series modeled after radio's *Seth Parker* program. A pilot script prepared at Irénée du Pont's and Raskob's request featured a character named "Goodwin Hollister"("Good" for short), who issued common sense advice in the plain-folks idiom. The series never aired.[106]

NBC's Edgar Kobak was still smarting from the loss of the *Cavalcade of America* to CBS. Kobak reported in December 1935 that Lammot du Pont, Irénée du Pont, and company advertising director William A. Hart "are trying to feel satisfied and pleased with their *American Cavalcade* program, but Mr. Lammot du Pont is hearing from too many of his friends who either tell him they do not think much of the program or that they have not heard it. Of course, this is an institutional job of the highest nature, but I am afraid that it is not doing what they hoped would be done." Noting that DuPont Company president and General Motors board member Lammot du Pont liked the *General Motors Symphony Concerts*, Kobak ordered his specialists to "trail [the DuPont] account closely . . . develop new ideas and find time to bring this business over to NBC."[107]

NBC's pursuit of the DuPont account did not involve Stanley High. In February 1936 High took a leave of absence from his program-building duties at NBC to join President Roosevelt's re-election campaign. High became director of the campaign's editorial and pamphlet publicity and shared responsibility for campaign radio policy with publicist Charles Michelson and the head of the Democratic Party Speakers Bureau. Unofficially, High's new responsibilities included speech writing with FDR, a collaborative process shared with Samuel I. Rosenman and sometimes Thomas Corcoran. Additionally, High carried out an FDR plan to organize businessmen who were favorable to the New Deal. The "Good Neighbor League," a winsome parody of the Liberty League, offered a public platform for pro-business Democrats and disaffected Republicans.[108]

Freed of the obligations of political impartiality as a network executive, High wasted no time airing his differences with the NAM and the Liberty League. "A short time ago," High wrote, "I sat in on a conference of big businessmen—some of the biggest—at which the New Deal was the subject of discussion." Though his fellow conferees warmed to a discussion of relief's "abstract ideals," "It was the effort to put the ideals into practice that hurt." "It was my belief that something could be done about it that was offensive. And it is that which is offensive in the New Deal."[109] Previously engaged at NBC turning speeches into stories, High profitably mined the experience by turning the story into a speech. Appearing on NBC's *Town Hall* to debate the question "Are our liberties in danger?" High declared: "The crisis of the Revolution had its Tories. The present crisis has—or, rather, had its Liberty League. They are of the same blood. Both, in their day, talked the same language, espoused the same objectives and were propelled by the same interests."[110]

High's unsuccessful experience at the hands of the Liberty League and the NAM gave him ample inspiration for writing. The DuPont Company had taken the synopsis for the "American Cavalcade" and inverted its title; High would reclaim the theme on behalf of the New Deal's common man. The theme of democratic reclamation filtered through the campaign speech-writing process, emerging in a recurring Roosevelt attack upon "our resplendent economic autocracy" and "royalists of the economic order."[111] Before officially leaving NBC to join the campaign, High had helped FDR with several speeches in 1935 and early 1936, a period in which the president had used his annual message to the Congress to excoriate "entrenched greed."[112] Leaving little doubt about the objects of his enmity, FDR explained, "They seek—this minority of business and industry—to control and often do control and use for their own purposes legitimate and highly honored business associations; they engage in vast propaganda to spread fear and discord among the people. . . . such fear as they instill today is not a natural fear, a normal fear; it is a synthetic, manufactured, poisonous fear that is being spread subtly, expensively and cleverly by the same people who cried in other days, 'Save us, save us, lest we perish.'"[113]

During the summer and fall of 1936, High and Rosenman contributed to FDR's blistering attack upon business's errant sense of privilege and entitlement. The most dramatic foray came with the "rendezvous with destiny" acceptance speech for the renomination for the presidency at the Democratic National Convention in Philadelphia. Addressing an audience assembled at Franklin Field and a national radio audience as well, FDR recalled that "political tyranny was wiped out at Philadelphia on July 4, 1776."

> Since that struggle, however, man's inventive genius released new forces in our land which reordered the lives of our people. The age of machinery, of railroads; of steam and electricity; the telegraph and the radio; mass production, mass distribution—all of these combined to bring forward a new civilization and with it a new problem for those who sought to remain free.
>
> For out of this modern civilization economic royalists carved new dynasties. New kingdoms were built upon concentration of control over material things. Through new uses of corporations, banks and securities, new machinery of industry and agriculture, of labor and capital—all undreamed of by the fathers—the whole structure of modern life was impressed into this royal service. . . .
>
> It was natural and perhaps human that the privileged princes of these new economic dynasties, thirsting for power, reached out for control of Government itself. They created a new despotism and wrapped it in the robes of legal sanction. In its service new mercenaries sought to regiment the people, their labor, and their property. And as a result the average man once more confronts the problem that faced the Minute Man. . . .
>
> These economic royalists complain that we seek to overthrow the institutions of America. What they really complain of is that we seek to take away their power.[114]

Though High, Rosenman, and Thomas Corcoran contributed to FDR's speech text, the phrase "economic royalists" was High's lasting contribution to New Deal political discourse. The phrase mocking the pretensions of the NAM and the Liberty League dramatized for many the us-versus-them stakes of the presidential contest.[115] In a more private way, the expression was the swan song of High's career as a network program builder. Finding a dramatic presence in the person of the president, High drummed the NAM and the Liberty League from his personal "American Cavalcade" and perhaps that of millions of other Americans as well. The irony did not go unnoticed among High's former employers at NBC, their rivals at CBS, or the *Cavalcade of America*'s producers at Batten, Barton, Durstine & Osborn, whose efforts to dramatize a democratic outlook for their reluctant client labored under the phrase for years.

Chapter Four

The Notoriously Persuasive Voice

Conservative business leaders and their advertising and public relations specialists were never more united in purpose than in the year before the election of 1936. Their political and professional interests converged in a effort to deflate the popularity of the New Deal, applying to this end the tools and techniques of commercial promotion. Willing to invest in any and all means to turn out Roosevelt and upend the New Deal, they flocked to the Republican National Committee (RNC) and to the campaign of the Republicans' presidential candidate, Governor Alfred Mossman Landon of Kansas. The Republicans captured only Maine and Vermont, however, and the crushing electoral defeat in November 1936 called to question the apparatus of advertising and public relations that had been devoted so completely to the effort.

The convergence of political necessity and promotional efficacy began when the Republican campaign attracted what one pundit later described as "a strongly connected group of practical business men and idealists." "In the late weeks of 1935," another confirmed, "it became apparent that a small but determined group of important businessmen were working quietly to take over the direction of the 1936 campaign." From the Republican Party's "inner council" came the announcement that it planned a campaign that disdained traditional "ballyhoo" for modern techniques employed in marketing commodities and "good will" among the public.[1]

Eager to demonstrate the practical value of mass merchandising at the highest level of the campaign, specialists used opinion polling to test campaign themes, pruned network radio schedules to play to regional political strengths, and applied the audience-building techniques of broadcast merchandising. Hill Blackett of Blackett, Sample and Hummert, a Chicago-based advertising agency and radio program builder and one of the top purchasers of network time, led the Republican effort. The public relations division that Blackett headed applied the techniques of commercial promotion to "'unsell' President Roosevelt and his New Deal" and to "sell Governor Landon and his highly advertised 'common sense.'"[2] Bringing an adman's sensibilities to the task, Blackett commissioned opinion survey research of the kind used in his advertising agency's "trade investigations." Blackett asked the A.C. Nielsen Company "to sound out small independent drug store owners in various parts of the country to find out who they are for and why." In September Blackett reported to Landon that Nielsen's investigation indicated "that the Democrats' arguments are based upon ideas that are already popular with many people" and that Landon could anticipate a Democratic "main drive featuring two points: Are you better off now than you were in 1933? (and) Why swap horses now?"[3]

Taking advantage of the flexibility afforded by network radio, Blackett apportioned the campaign's radio budget by region, judiciously cutting the Democratic South from the broadcast schedule, emphasizing instead the agricultural Northwest and Middle West. Blackett also made use of networks in the Northeast and along the Pacific coast. "Men in the bureau," wrote one observer, "declared this was the first time in a political contest 'radio was used intelligently.' Word went out that the medium no longer would be used simply to present the candidate but "to sell the idea of the campaign."[4]

Thomas G. Sabin headed the RNC radio division. A former time salesman at NBC, Sabin's buildup of "broadcast merchandising" invited the Republican high command to think of politics as a commodity. According to his radio division's carefully cultivated press relations, Sabin "brought with him a very pronounced view that politics is a commodity and that while its label and package may differ from that of the commercial package, nevertheless there was a common objective—selling an idea to the public." Early on, Sabin determined that merchandising Republican broadcasts would play "a most important part" in the party's "radio activities." Radio division publicity explained that "the sale of an idea embraces more than simply putting a message over the air. It must follow through with a complete merchandising plan that will not only gain the largest possible listening audience but will make sales in the casting of the voter's ballot in the ballot box." "Giant displays" mounted at the 1936 Republican National Convention described the plan. Merchandising the merchandising idea, the exhibit promoted the use of direct mail and traditional advertising media that "not only vastly expanded the audience listening to programs but paid dividends in making programs more effective." Radio division personnel at the exhibit made a special effort to explain the importance of such tie-ins to Landon campaign "radio captains" and "motor squadron leaders." Enthusiastic exhibit-goers seemed to grasp its connection to the larger scheme of the political-commercial economy's reciprocal effect. As one political worker testified, "I have always thoroughly merchandised my own advertising, but this exhibit has given me pointers not only for the coming political campaign but for more effectively merchandising the advertising of my own business."[5]

The period of openly contested broadcast opposition began in the fall of 1935, as requests escalated for broadcasts of congressional banquet and luncheon talks. Sabin brought to the Republican campaign an insider's understanding of network radio administration, which proved decisive in wresting free air time from his former employer. NBC vice president for programming John F. Royal complained that Sabin's success had brought on a "condition different from any other national campaign situation that we have ever had." "The method of the Republicans, as they have started it," Royal complained, "is to ask for a series of talks by prominent Republican Congressmen and Senators, and after getting this assignment of time, to use every subtle means of getting speakers on the air through noon-day luncheons, banquets and improvised meetings." This situation left Royal "beginning to think that we must handle our politics almost the way we do religion—to the effect that we will assign to a recognized Republican or Democratic organization certain fixed time periods and let them fill these spots with their speakers. In this way all requests for banquets and luncheons and the numerous other methods of chiseling time by Democrats and Republicans would be referred to a central committee."[6]

It was in the context of "chiseling time" that the White House announced that President Roosevelt would for the first time deliver his annual congressional address in the evening at a time certain to attract a large radio audience. Rather than respond in kind with a new round of talk requests, Republican National Committee Chairman Henry P. Fletcher announced an RNC plan to broadcast a series of four half-hour radio dramas entitled *Liberty at the Crossroads*. Approached by party officials seeking a network slot for the series in late 1935, NBC's Royal turned down the drama outright. Accused of protecting the New Deal from the incisive cuts of Republican playlets, Royal deftly parried his visitors' complaint. "If you put it that way," said Royal, "you might stop to think what Clifford Odets and those boys could do with 'Brother, Can You Spare a Dime?'"[7] Later Royal described Labor Stage, Inc., a new play-producing organization backed by the AFL's William Green, as an example of "what we might have expected from Labor if we had accepted the political."[8]

The RNC's *Liberty at the Crossroads* dramatized young couples, cracker barrel personalities, and common sense philosophy made familiar by the National Association of Manufacturers' *American Family Robinson*. Written by playwright Henry Fisk Carlton, the first program presented five skits personalizing the fiscal issues of the New Deal.[9] In one widely publicized skit, a marriage license clerk warns "John" and "Mary" of the burden that high taxes and the national debt impose upon the cost of living.[10] Another skit satirizes a "spending type of American family" who thinks it's "smart to be constantly in debt, who were as they put it, 'spending to prosperity.'"[11] In another, the popular character actors known as the Stebbins Boys satirize New Deal deficits in a world turned upside down. John Stebbins explains: "What's good enough for them that runs our great government is good enough for me! They know what they're doin'—and who am I to stand out agin' 'em! Goin' in debt is fashionable. It's the new way o' doin' things. Spend more than ye get . . . keep the debts jumpin'! Keep 'em exercised and fed so they'll grow fast!"[12]

Long passages of statistics introduced and followed each sketch. Monitoring the first *Liberty at the Crossroads* program broadcast on Chicago's WGN, the radio station owned by *Chicago Tribune* publisher and New Deal opponent Robert R. McCormick, NBC's J. O'Neill noted that though the statistics sounded "convincing," "dramatization most certainly helped no end, making it very listenable."[13] A. R. Williamson, another NBC monitor, believed that the program's producers had "packed it too full, resulting in confusion."[14] Skits broadcast the following week dramatized George Washington's refusal to set himself up "as the dictator of a free people"; another ends with Woodrow Wilson, "the great Democratic president," declaring, "I do not want to live under a philanthropy."[15]

Neither NBC nor CBS allowed the RNC to broadcast *Liberty at the Crossroads*. NBC president Lenox R. Lohr explained that to broadcast the Republican program "would place the discussion of vital political and national issues on the basis of dramatic license, rather than upon a basis of responsibly stated fact or opinion." CBS president William S. Paley agreed. Noting the manipulative effect of drama upon radio audiences inexperienced in making distinctions among similar though politically sponsored programs, Paley warned that "While we realize that no approach to the electorate is ideal, we believe American voters have long been trained to discriminate among the assertions of orators, whereas we do not believe they could discriminate fairly among dramatizations, so that the turn of national issues might well depend on the skill of warring dramatists rather than upon the merits of the issue debated." In reply, RNC chairman Fletcher suggested that the networks' decision to refuse Republican programs had been "affected and perhaps involuntarily controlled by the political party in power which regulates the issuance of your licenses."[16]

Fletcher's complaint reflected the reality of Federal Communications Commission oversight of network affiliates and the potential for congressional anti-trust investigation of the networks themselves—a potential that specialists and network executives sought to circumvent with dramatic radio production. The outright denial of network facilities to the Republicans placed NBC and CBS officials in a duplicitous position, publicly banning the dramatization of political issues while specialists met privately with the NAM and the DuPont Company to model dramatic fare more insidious than any yet rejected by the network. NBC's stage-managing of its defense took the form of a two-pronged attack: first, promoting discussions of "politics" in an oratorical, rather than dramatic, form; second, limiting paid political talks to times between the national nominating conventions of the major parties and election day.[17]

Working behind the scenes, NBC's Alfred H. Morton met with columnist Walter Lippmann to explain the network's denial of facilities for the RNC's *Liberty at the Crossroads*. On the face of it, Morton found Lippmann wholly sympathetic. Lippmann, Morton reported, "thoroughly agreed with our policy of not accepting on our stations politics in dramatized form, and also agreed we could not and should not charge for political broadcast time prior to the conventions." "Incidentally," Morton added, "he does not approve the use of radio for politics at all, claiming that it is not the type of medium which lends itself to free and open debate as readily as does the platform of an auditorium or written statements." Dismissing the propriety of political dramatization out of hand, Lippmann applauded the network's handling of the controversy in the "restrained, simple direct statement being sent to the newspapers." Characteristically, he also suggested that network executives relieve themselves of the controversy by transferring the responsibility for dividing and apportioning time to an outside expert authority.[18] Lippmann might only have guessed at NBC's ongoing efforts to promote a drama of subtlety and indirection among the leadership of the NAM, an undertaking that had gone astray with the DuPont Company's sponsorship of *Cavalcade of America* on CBS. Though Lippmann perhaps may be excused for his limited knowledge of NBC's program-building activities, his misplaced faith in expert authority revealed the limitations of his model for democratic mass culture exemplified by the "restrained, simple direct statement."[19] The statements that NBC's politically active sponsors wished to make through the NAM, the Liberty League, the Crusaders, and the Republican National Committee were simple, direct, and troublesome. No solution was found, save the outright denial of network facilities for dramatized politics, and failing that, further obfuscation with dramatic technique. The immediate controversy ended indecisively. Reporting the outcome of events some months later, NBC president Merlin Aylesworth noted: "It later developed that a majority of the members of the Republican National Campaign Committee were not enthusiastic about the idea nor was the money available for sponsorship."[20]

Refused by the major networks, the Republican National Committee's bid for an election year dramatic series shared the fate of the NAM's *American Family Robinson*. Following the first broadcast of *Liberty at the Crossroads* by transcription on Chicago's WGN, a second program went live over a network similar to that lined up for Fred Clark's *Voice of the Crusaders* talks. The press in turn reported the controversy and published scripts of the suppressed dramas. A re-enactment of the first program's marriage license skit and a dramatization of the network ban—with actors portraying Lohr, Paley, and Fletcher—found its way onto the BBDO-produced broadcast, the *March of Time*. Emanating from CBS's Madison Avenue studios, the broadcast achieved a national network audience equal to any that the RNC might have purchased. At the broadcast's conclusion, no one associated with CBS would admit to having been outwitted. William Paley was said to be "out of town," and his spokesmen intimated that in any event, "he would not care." "This wasn't the whole thing," said one person at the studio, who did not want to be named. "This was just a dramatization of the news."[21]

The issue for the Republican campaign remained what Senator Arthur H. Vandenberg described as "the notoriously persuasive voice of our President on the air." Further efforts to sell the idea of the campaign involved a sensational radio broadcast in which Vandenberg "debated" recorded statements made by FDR and taken from transcriptions of his 1932 Chicago convention appearance and 1933 inaugural address. The illusion of a live debate hinged upon the Republicans' technical proficiency in re-recording the transcription excerpts. Fred Gennett of the Starr Company of Richmond, Indiana, a manufacturer of electrical transcriptions, suggested the idea. Blackett took up the suggestion upon becoming the Republican campaign's director of public relations. Blackett put Benjamin K. Pratt, a former examiner with the Federal Radio Commission who was now with the GOP's Chicago press division, in charge of finding "politically vulnerable excerpts." Henry H. Rahmel, a radio engineer and instructor on leave from the Massachusetts Institute of Technology, selected the most technically viable of the excerpts for broadcast and carefully re-recorded them onto two platters. For the role of the questioner, Blackett sought commentator and GOP announcer William Hard and then Landon himself. When Hard and Landon turned it down, the task fell to Senator Vandenberg. The performance took place in the Tropical Room of the Medinah Athletic Club in Chicago before a studio audience of Republican Party, business, and newspaper officials. "The novelty of the thing came as a complete surprise to everyone in the room," Pratt recalled. "The expressions on their faces when they heard the voice of Roosevelt come from the loudspeaker were amusing. We had the loudspeaker on a little raised platform immediately back of the microphone where Vandenberg and I stood. It was draped and insofar as the audience was concerned, looked merely like a stand. After the first excerpt using Roosevelt's voice we pulled the drapes aside and all could see it was a loudspeaker!"[22]

CBS executives canceled the program shortly before air time—only to reverse their decision minutes before the broadcast. In the ensuing confusion, the network dropped the broadcast from its East Coast chain and deleted the program's recorded portions sent to western affiliates.[23] Senator Vandenberg's questions and comments addressed to the president and the arrangement of recorded excerpts to fashion a dialogue created an illusion of immediacy acclaimed by Republicans. Republican National Chairman John Hamilton demanded that Paley reschedule the broadcast. "The vocal reproduction of the President's own spoken promises in his own familiar voice are so essential to an understanding of the issues in this campaign," Hamilton wrote.[24] Acclaiming the use of the recordings as a "new technique," Vandenberg hastened to add that the program had made scrupulous use of the president's voice. "If it was shocking to anybody, the shock must have resulted from the dramatic emphasis thus put upon the enormous gap between promise and performance." Democrats suggested that the broadcast might have been more interesting if Vandenberg had debated with himself.[25]

The exploitation of FDR's radio style and Vandenberg's defense of the broadcast as a "new technique" alarmed the Democratic campaign, which charged that the Republicans had attempted "to deceive the public into thinking that an actual debate between [Roosevelt and Vandenberg] was in progress."[26] But only part of the broadcast's effect came from the quality of its carefully recorded excerpts, inasmuch as Vandenberg asked the questions and played the answers. Its real effect was dramatic. The day following the broadcast, Roosevelt campaign chairman James A. Farley cabled Vandenberg: "If you broadcast another sham battle tonight, suggest you use some animal noise sound effects with the Roosevelt record. Congratulations, Boy Scout."[27]

The shock of Landon's unexpected defeat reverberated through the nation's board rooms to the offices of the advertising and public relations specialists who had used the campaign to market their skills and specializations. What did Landon's defeat mean for the emerging field of broadcast merchandising and market research? Critics charged that the "chart readers" who had attached themselves to the Republican campaign lacked experience in the management of political symbols and had short-changed Landon's candidacy by pursuing a single-minded attack upon the New Deal. "So detached from the American masses were the Republican politicos," charged one critic, "that many of them were totally unaware of the irresistible Roosevelt undertow perceptible to even the most casual tyro in the street.

They campaigned to the end in a pleasant haze of wishful thinking—blissfully unconscious of the fact that the American public was not even listening to their propaganda." Among the casualties were the *Literary Digest*, mortally embarrassed at its prediction of a Landon landslide based on a straw poll of its subscribers, and the American Liberty League, whose officers quietly suspended operations, retaining only spokesman Jouett Shouse and a token staff.[28]

The rout of the Landon campaign brought with it a professional crisis for advertising and public relations specialists, who found their judgment questioned more closely and their accounts in review. Investments in advertising seemed as tentative as ever, and long-term commitments to institutional promotion an impossibility. Bruce Barton quickly advanced his own ingenious interpretation of the Republicans' November disaster—that FDR's plebiscite confirmed the cumulative power of advertising. "We recently have had a most remarkable national election," Barton wrote to Standard Oil's Walter Teagle, a prospective client, in December 1936. "The President of the United States, seeking re-election, was opposed by two-thirds of the entire press of the country, and by a radio expenditure that must have been somewhere in the neighborhood of 2 or 3 to 1. Yet, with all this opposition of the printed and the spoken word, he is overwhelmingly successful." Did Roosevelt's victory mean that the press and radio had no influence, that the public paid no attention to advertising? Or, did it mean "that the members of our craft are taking money under false pretenses, that some day Business will wake up to discover that we are without influence and throw us all out? Any advertising man with any imagination whatever must have asked himself these questions in the days immediately following November 3rd."[29]

While the Republicans' November disaster led to doubts about the efficacy of advertising, Barton urged that business look to the winning qualities of the administration's continuous projection of the idea that FDR was "trying to do something" for the common man. Unlike his clients, who had yet to accept the election's outcome, Barton had found his answer. He wrote,

> My own answer is clear. I hold that President Roosevelt was the beneficiary of a three-year advertising campaign more powerful and more persuasive than any the country had ever seen. The effect of that advertising campaign was to plant deep in the mind of the average man and woman this simple but all-powerful thought: "*He is trying to do something for me.*" Having that thought firmly fixed in mind, and being convinced of its truth, the common man and woman did not bother to read speeches or listen to them, or even to return his Literary Digest ballot. He did not proclaim his intentions aloud; he just quietly went to the polls and did what he had long ago made up his mind to do. He voted for the leader who, he believed, was trying to something for him.

> What is the lesson of that for Big Business? We live in a democracy where, as Lincoln said: "Public sentiment is everything. With public sentiment nothing can fail; without public sentiment nothing can succeed." The public sentiment of this country is going to be favorable to those businesses which somehow manage to get into the people's minds the thought: *They are trying to do something for us.*[30]

Roosevelt's re-election affirmed the power of sincerity, a point that Barton had urged for years. Its projection called for the sedulous maintenance of an image of selflessness like that of FDR and the programs of the New Deal. "In the years that lie ahead of American business," Barton forecast, "advertising is going to be a more important rather than a less important factor."[31]

Increasingly, specialists resorted to survey and market research to enforce action consistent with their professional goals and corporate interests. The dramatization of corporate social leadership became the focus of program building and broadcast merchandising directed to the client. A client's likes and dislikes could be overridden, if not reduced to irrelevancy, with market and survey research that quantified the tastes and habits of the listening audience. The sale of ideas, having decamped from the dais and dinner plan, vacated the ballot box for the technique of dramatic radio production, where the comprehensive claim of "better living" had established the beachhead of a new vocabulary of business leadership.

The Return of the *Cavalcade*

The foremost popular expression of business leadership to survive the election of 1936, the *Cavalcade of America*, by the early 1940s, had become the commitment to well-merchandised public relations entertainment that its specialists had long sought. Specialists attributed the *Cavalcade*'s longevity to its capacity to assimilate the functions of education and entertainment, each adjusted to fit the circumstances allowed by the changing leadership of the DuPont Company, the inroads of middle management using positivist social research, and the onset of the Second World War, which made possible, and even desirable, the expression of democratic sensibilities. With success came further opportunities to draw upon the work of amateur and academic historians. Acquiring fresh talent after DuPont officials canceled the program, then reversed their decision, BBDO replaced historical consultants Fox and Schlesinger with author and historian James Truslow Adams in November 1938.[1] The program was canceled a second time in June 1939, but after a six-month hiatus, it returned to the air on NBC in January 1940. A new mixture of amateurs and academics now assumed greater responsibilities. *Cavalcade* featured on-air story introductions by Professor Frank Monaghan of Yale and a memorable broadcast performance by poet and Lincoln biographer Carl Sandburg, which signaled the relaxation of the program's editorial outlook. The resulting program, its formulaic drama of the American past culminating in "better living," distanced itself from the Depression-era crisis of business leadership that had called it to being. Increasingly removed from the necessity of its creation, the *Cavalcade* accumulated significant power and appeal. By the 1940s specialists described its entertainment value with the enthusiasm once reserved for its educational function. Ever so slowly, the *Cavalcade* decamped from the usable past for the intimate terrain of "more," "new," and "better living" merchandised with a build-up of stars and stories.

The *Cavalcade* did not change its sponsors as much as outlast them. The promotion of the *Cavalcade*'s educational function relaxed after Lammot du Pont retired from active management of the DuPont Company in 1940. Through the late 1930s, du Pont justified outlays for the company's institutional promotion as education for a public deficient in values conducive to free and unfettered enterprise. In addition to his company's commitment to the *Cavalcade*, du Pont himself oversaw expenditures for exhibits at the Texas Centennial in 1936 and at the Museum of Science and Industry (MSI) at Rockefeller Center in 1937. While traditional exhibit media used the readily understood method of educational display, an appreciation of dramatic radio production eluded du Pont, who, as a condition of investment in it, required constant assurance of its remedial effect. Significantly, Lammot du Pont made his only *Cavalcade* appearance in conjunction with the opening of the company's MSI exhibit, appearing in a "story of chemistry" spot that followed a dramatization of the enterprising career of William Holmes McGuffey of *McGuffey Readers* fame. Du Pont joined MSI and AT&T president Frank A. Jowett and DuPont Company research director Charles M. A. Stein in describing their aspirations for contemporary educational endeavors in the McGuffey tradition. Du Pont's broadcast appearance could not have been more skillfully framed. "The sketch about McGuffey's famous *Readers*," du Pont told listeners, "stirred memories of school days and brought back the times when our teachers took it to task for the way we studied or failed to study our textbooks." Segueing to his company's MSI exhibit, du Pont suggested that its impact rivaled that of the printed page. "As a medium for visual education," du Pont explained, "it shows in a stirring way the progress made since McGuffey's time." In much the same way, du Pont broached the subject of *Cavalcade* specialists' reluctance to allow him to appear on the program, which to his way of thinking pointed up the paradox of his company's investment in radio. "Though the *Cavalcade of America* program is sponsored by the DuPont Company," du Pont explained, "this is the first time our people have permitted me to appear on it. Their judgment has been good. But I will let you decide whether that applies to keeping me off the air in the past, or letting me on now."[2]

Selling the *Cavalcade* idea had proved particularly trying for BBDO's Bruce Barton. He prevailed over Lammot du Pont's "vigorous opposition" to establish the program in 1935, and presumably to re-establish it on an annual basis when the

DuPont Company executive committee canceled it in 1938 and 1939, a period in which a majority of the committee also voted to banish the slogan "Better Things for Better Living . . . through Chemistry" from their executive letterhead. Having reconsidered the May 1938 cancellation of *Cavalcade* (it returned to the air on CBS the following January), at program renewal time in May 1939, the committee, led by Lammot du Pont, again voted to discontinue the company's radio activities. Perhaps feeling pinched by their expenditures for an exhibit at that year's New York World's Fair, the executive committee voted neither to renew nor to replace the *Cavalcade*. The committee, explained Henry B. du Pont to an inquiring family member, felt that any program sponsored by the company in the future "should be somewhat different."[3]

Exhibiting its producers' penchant for staging subjects calculated to attract the loyalty of its sponsor, the final episode of the *Cavalcade* series, broadcast by CBS on May 29, 1939, reprised the previous season's final broadcast dramatizing the life of company founder Eleuthère Irénée du Pont. Played against the backdrop of revolutionary France and the early American republic, the program adopted young Irénée's investiture pledge (the motto of his father, Pierre Samuel) as a leitmotif: "No privilege exists that is not inseparably bound to a duty." The story followed the young du Pont's study of chemistry under the great Lavoisier, and finally Thomas Jefferson's encouragement of the family's commercial ventures in the New World that led to the establishment of a powder yard on the Brandywine River near Wilmington, Delaware. Instead of the usual "story of chemistry" at the broadcast's conclusion, announcer Basil Ruysdael alerted listeners that the *Cavalcade* had indeed come to an end. On behalf of the program's production staff and sponsor, Ruysdael thanked listeners for their many comments received over the course of the 167 broadcasts since October 1935. The reading of listener mail had been a component of early broadcasts; it typically began with the acknowledgment of a laudatory letter or awards conferred by civic and patriotic organizations. "We have a simple request to make of our radio listeners," said Ruysdael. "We will welcome any comment you care to send us." "In the early days of the *Cavalcade*," Ruysdael recalled, "we wondered if we successfully could carry on this rather unique idea: a program high in information content, and so entertaining as to command the attention of a fair share of the great radio audience. However, the sincerity and enthusiasm of the letters that came to us from people in all walks of life quickly dispelled our fears." In a final bid for supportive and useful mail, Ruysdael invited listeners to write to Wilmington for a free copy of the June issue of *DuPont Magazine* and an eight-page picture booklet featuring DuPont's "Wonder World of Chemistry" exhibit at the New York World's Fair.[4]

Letters were not the only means of gauging the program's effect. Accompanying the introduction of DuPont's "Better Living" campaign in 1935, in which the *Cavalcade* played a leading role, company public relations and advertising specialists commissioned surveys designed to measure public opinion about the company. Coming into its own by the late 1930s, the technique of opinion sampling that was closely identified with the commercial surveys of Archibald M. Crossley, George H. Gallup, Elmo B. Roper, and Claude E. Robinson had helped make positivist social research a tool by which management could predict public reactions to the choices of the corporation and state.[5] At the DuPont Company, as perhaps no other, the intransigence of its owner-operators made survey research a burgeoning cottage industry central to specialists' implementation of a corporate outlook. The possession of information provided by survey research became a source of intra-organizational power and authority.[6]

Intent on modifying company president Lammot du Pont's opposition to the *Cavalcade*, DuPont advertising director William A. Hart invited du Pont to attend a presentation of opinion survey work. Hart had commissioned it from the Psychological Corporation (PSC), "in our efforts to apply more research methods to our promotional problems." Such PSC reports typically explored the methodology used to probe individual attitudes toward DuPont, and the sources of those attitudes. The officers of the Psychological Corporation packaged their surveys as scientific investigations of the first order. A report undertaken by ten psychologists in 91 interviews entitled "The Clinical Interview in Public Relations Work," for example, concluded that people would speak freely to survey takers about the labor practices of General Motors, the concentration of wealth among DuPont's owner-operators, and persistent concerns about munitions manufacturing. Causes or sources that respondents gave to explain their attitudes included newspapers, magazines, books (*America's 60 Families*), "'friends living near their plant,'" and "'their radio program.'" The report highlighted the suggestions of individuals "by which companies can improve people's attitudes," including "Stop or change political activity 'By not contributing to movements such as the American Liberty League,'" "'Be more cooperative with the present administration,'" and "'concentrate on their laboratories and get out of the political field.'"[7]

In an attempt to persuade the DuPont executive committee to revisit radio as a source of positive information about the DuPont Company, Hart commissioned a PSC "Test Tube Study" of the *Cavalcade of America's* influence upon public opinion. Since 1937 the PSC had made it its business to track and tabulate public attitudes toward industrial corporations, including DuPont. Returning to a panel of 807 interviewees in Cleveland, Indianapolis, and Buffalo surveyed in November 1938, the PSC reported an encouraging 13 percent increase in favorable opinion toward DuPont among the sample's *Cavalcade of America* listeners. Segregating listeners into two groups—those who could identify the program's sponsor, and those who could not—the PSC noted that among the latter group, 60 percent held a positive opinion of the company. This figure compared favorably to the rating of nonlisteners, of whom only 48 percent indicated a favorable attitude toward DuPont. Acknowledging listeners' predisposition toward the company, nevertheless the PSC concluded that "it would seem difficult to account for the greater percentage . . . on any basis other than the efficacy of the *Cavalcade*."[8]

No matter how crude, survey research provided special data that altered relationships between specialists and their governing executives. What effect the survey may have had on the DuPont executive committee's decision to renew the *Cavalcade*, however, remains unclear. Despite Lammot du Pont's continuing opposition to the program, shortly after voting to cancel the *Cavalcade* for the second time in May 1939, the executive committee again reversed its decision. By a vote of five to four the committee decided to continue the company's radio activities, and to retain the *Cavalcade* in its present form. One vote the other way, and the company would have dropped its radio activities entirely. Having played out the spring 1939 season on CBS without renewal, the *Cavalcade* returned to the air January 2, 1940, on NBC.[9]

The new *Cavalcade*'s merchandising plan reflected NBC's development of institutional programs dating from the mid-1930s, when the network had first attempted to channel escalating demands for speech time into dramatic, yet politically oblique, entertainment. In the interim, NBC had become more cognizant of its relations with outside "pressure groups." An institutional program like the *Cavalcade*, explained NBC's W. G. Preston, Jr., would not only bring revenue to the network. It would also satisfy the "demands of the listening public for a new program pattern—a pattern of programs that will appeal to important pressure groups, and will do much to answer the demands of consumer movements for a revision of some of our current commercial program patterns." Alluding to the *Cavalcade*'s developmental track begun by NBC in the mid-1930s, Preston explained: "Inasmuch as almost all trends in programs start on a sustaining basis, we hope to build a quality of program and to merchandise that type of program so successfully that commercial clients will follow our lead even if they do not buy our shows." Yet in all likelihood they would, for even program-producing advertising agencies had become interested in NBC's merchandising of programs to select "pressure groups."[10]

Pursuing this policy through the late 1930s, NBC enjoyed the distinct advantage of its employment of James Rowland Angell, president emeritus of Yale University, as network "education counselor." Angell stepped into the position vacated by Stanley High, who by joining President Roosevelt's 1936 re-election campaign had unwittingly disqualified himself from future network employment.[11] With characteristic aplomb NBC president Lenox Lohr noted that the energetic Dr. Angell, facing mandatory retirement from Yale at age 68, had merely "chang[ed] his base of educational endeavor from New Haven to New York, from a university to the air." Angell's acceptance of the network post pointed up "a still greater pioneering opportunity" in "educational programs."[12] Awarded a three-year contract at $25,000 per year (said to equal his salary at Yale), Angell was given free rein "to devise and suggest methods" to enliven network sustaining programs, estimated at 4,360 hours annually—44 percent of total network time.[13] Angell promptly proved his worth by adopting the expression "public service" to distinguish sustaining programs from their revenue-producing counterparts, a strategy that further insulated the network from attack by the advocates of nonprofit broadcast education. At the height of Angell's tenure in the early 1940s, NBC public service programs included Walter Damrosch's *Music Appreciation Hour*, current events discussions *America's Town Meeting of the Air* and the *University of Chicago Round Table*, and discussions of art, civilization, and work, respectively entitled the *Pageant of Art* and *On Your Job*.[14]

Whereas Stanley High had ended his career at NBC by ghosting FDR's attack upon "economic royalists," Angell's denunciation of the New Deal in his last year at Yale proved no impediment to network employment. However cloaked in the language of "trends," "dispositions," and "tendencies," Angell's politics were hardly in doubt. For example, he gave a 1936 commencement address entitled "The Moral Crisis of Democracy: Must We Accept Complete Socialization?" that warned that "any actual approach to a general control by government over our economic interests would quickly extend to education and then to religion and the whole range of higher human activities," the inevitable outcome of the expanding role of the state in unemployment relief, public works and taxation.[15] In a speech on the subject of moral "drift" entitled "Second Thoughts after the Election," Angell proved to be unchanged from the first. Questioning the premise of public relief, Angell warned: "Again the disposition of the citizen to look to the state, or the city, or the federal government to take over these philanthropic tasks is apt to be demoralizing to a sense of personal responsibility." Repeating portions of his earlier commencement talk, Angell noted the "shattering effects" of taxation upon philanthropy, not to mention the "far completer socialization of our resources and methods than heretofore, a larger surrender of that individual privilege which we have been accustomed to regard as our intrinsic right as citizens." Angell concluded that "unless public opinion be clearly registered as opposed to further similar encroachment—and the recent election certainly disclosed no dominant opposition—it may confidently be expected to spread until in effect, whatever the name, we shall have something beginning to represent a collectivist state."[16] The week that NBC publicly announced his new position as network education counselor, Angell delivered what would be his last commencement address, a discourse on the subject of "a bastard democracy deriving from communistic sentiment and ideology." His examples included President Roosevelt's unsuccessful attempt to pack the Supreme Court, and the nettlesome influence of "small pressure groups" upon the Congress exemplified by the sit-down strike, a tactic developed by "small pressure groups to terrify and coerce majorities on behalf of their purely selfish interests."[17]

The New Deal's friends volunteered that Angell's appointment as NBC's education counselor exemplified a disturbing trend in itself. Reviewing Angell's "unforgivable address against the President," Rabbi Stephen Wise complained to RCA's David Sarnoff that "you and your associates would not dream of inviting anyone of equal capacity, let us say John Dewey, the greatest living American educator, who is as deeply committed to the liberal viewpoint as Dr. Angell is to the reactionary." Perceptively, Wise reasoned that the appointment of a "virulent partisan" meant that NBC "deliberately ranges itself with the foes of liberalism and American progress and is prepared to help those foes to become more articulate and to ensure a lesser opportunity for the hearing of the liberal side of the issues that are at stake today."[18] "Some of us," Wise added in a note to presidential secretary Missy LeHand, "are not fooled about the appointment of Dr. Angell as Director of Radio Education, another one of those nice, smooth things which operate altogether in favor of the supporters of privilege and the enemies of the FDR program."[19] The president instructed secretary Marvin H. McIntyre to "Tell Sarnoff that this was a very, very dumb thing to do—appoint Angell of Yale as Director of Radio Education."[20]

Angell's appointment cast a new light upon the relationship between the White House and network officials, who according to the New Deal's conservative critics, were said to fear for the licenses of their affiliates should they broadcast programs critical of the administration.[21] Liberal reaction to Angell's appointment was the price that NBC officials willingly paid to win the confidence of politically active sponsors. Putting the best face on the situation, publicity about Angell's network position noted that Yale's president emeritus had spent an enjoyable summer abroad contemplating "the relationship of education to radio."[22]

Whatever Angell's reputation as an academician, his reputation as an outspoken critic of the New Deal helped network officials consummate their new relationship with the DuPont Company. Neither Wise nor Roosevelt could have known the difficult task that network officials faced in promoting institutional entertainment. "As you of course know," Angell wrote to Lammot du Pont in early 1940, "the National Broadcasting Company is very greatly interested in the new 'Cavalcade' program and not least because it is employing a type of material which heretofore we have been able to utilize as a rule only on sustaining programs." Moreover, the merchandising of the *Cavalcade* to network pressure groups would capitalize upon its inherent civic appeal. The historical dramas of the *Cavalcade*, Angell explained, "will speedily establish themselves in the minds of school teachers, their pupils, women's clubs and innumerable organizations devoted to the development of social and cultural interests, to say nothing of the general public." "The DuPont Company is in this manner setting an example which is sure to be followed by other great industrial organizations which employ radio for institutional advertising."[23] Amplifying this line of argument in publicity promoting the program, Angell expected *Cavalcade* to "open a new chapter in the evolution of commercial radio by showing how fine entertainment may be combined with the enlargement of knowledge and the enrichment of understanding."[24]

NBC specialists wasted no time preparing an object lesson in broadcast merchandising for the benefit of the DuPont Company executive committee. The first of several promotional events conducted by NBC in early 1940 brought to Radio City the superintendents of education from six states in and about New York and school superintendents from the large cities in the area. As the guests of NBC, the educators listened to presentations on the network's public service goals, dined with NBC and DuPont executives, and attended that evening's *Cavalcade* broadcast, entitled "Tisquantum, Strange Friend of the Pilgrims." In concert with program producer Batten, Barton, Durstine & Osborn, NBC also took the *Cavalcade* on the road for broadcasts modeled on the pressure group concept. The first of three remote broadcasts originated from the Chicago Civic Opera House and starred Raymond Massey in Robert Sherwood's adaptation of Carl Sandburg's *Abraham Lincoln: The War Years*. The second, starring Helen Hayes in "Jane Addams of Hull House," was broadcast from the Milwaukee convention of the General Federation of Women's Clubs. A third program, attended by DuPont's Richmond, Virginia, employees, featured Philip Merivale in "Robert E. Lee" and was based on historian Douglas Southall Freeman's biography *R. E. Lee*. Company and sectional harmony reigned on the Lee program, "portray[ing] the southern leader during the cataclysmic days of the War between the States ending with Lee's optimism as to the future dignity and united power of the American nation"[25] (fig. 12).

A polished publicity barrage prepared under Angell's capable hand linked the need for a usable past with the possibilities of improved and elevated radio technique. The nominally "high level" of production maintained by the *Cavalcade*, a playbill suggested, "even increased, as radio technique has improved, and the listening public's taste has increased in perception and sensitivity." For its part, DuPont had "tried, with the aid of able historians, to base its radio dramas on sincere and honest research into American history." Dramatization of the past came quite naturally to a company whose own development was intertwined with the

FIGURE 12.

Cavalcade broadcast, "Robert E. Lee," Richmond, VA (April 23, 1940).

Courtesy of Hagley Museum and Library.

growth of the United States. The parallels were many. "With many strange and bewildering doctrines being advanced for experiment throughout the world, it was the opinion of the sponsors that they could be of public service in recalling to [the] American people the origins of our unique freedom through dramatic stories of the men and women who won it, and those who fought to hold it." Repeating his private assurance to Lammot du Pont, Angell explained that the *Cavalcade of America* would set a "brilliant new pattern for sponsored radio productions . . . in a period when world-shattering events are following one another with unprecedented rapidity, and the importance of a knowledge of history and of the prodigious forces which are at work in it was never greater." The *Cavalcade*, Angell concluded, "presents on the air the most significant personalities and the most dramatic events in the centuries-old history of the western world, culminating in the creation and development of the United States."[26]

With the program's renewal came a new and more aggressively merchandised roster of historians, authors, and educators. The lineup for 1940 included biographer Marquis James, twice winner of the Pulitzer Prize and author of *Alfred I. du Pont: The Family Rebel*; Carl Carmer, author and folklorist; and Frank Monaghan, an assistant professor of history at Yale (fig. 13). The former assistant editor of the *Dictionary of American Biography*, Monaghan brought to the *Cavalcade* extensive professional public relations experience gained during his four-year tenure as research director and historian of the New York World's Fair. After joining the fair corporation in its planning stage in 1936, Monaghan supervised the opening day re-enactment of George Washington's triumphant inaugural tour from Mt. Vernon to New York City. The fair's ostensibly commemorative purpose, the celebration of the 150th anniversary of Washington's inauguration and the establishment of the federal government under the Constitution, was accomplished by horseback, stagecoach, and bus—and then forgotten in the progress talk of the "World of Tomorrow."[27]

The historical consultant for all *Cavalcade* programs, Professor Monaghan performed comparable promotional tasks for BBDO, rattling on about the "colorful and sturdy traditions of America's past" in a booklet mailed to 50,000 educators. Monaghan prepared program introductions, which he himself delivered on the air: "Amerigo Vespucci, 'How a New World Was Named'"; "Mehitabel Wing, 'A Ride Earlier, More Dramatic than Paul Revere's'"; "Thomas Jefferson Goes Shopping (And Writes an Immortal Document)"; and "Benedict Arnold, 'The Tragedy of a Man Who Twice Saved and Once Betrayed a Nation.'"[28] For the fall 1940 broadcast season, Monaghan prepared a second booklet entitled "History in This Hour" that featured Angell's earlier endorsement of the *Cavalcade*'s "'recognized place in our national life'" and a Walter Lippmann essay that "poignantly lamented the fact that some 'debunking' historians have emptied history 'of all the elements of greatness—that

FIGURE 13.

***Left to right:* Frank Monaghan, Carl Carmer, and Marquis James, *Cavalcade of America*'s history board, in the office of program producer Arthur Pryor, Jr. *(far right)* (December 13, 1939). Courtesy of Hagley Museum and Library.**

is to say, of the conviction that history is not the meaningless tale of a race of mercenary idiots but the record of great men and great peoples struggling indomitably to rise out of the sloth and squalor of their barbaric origins.'"[29] Like the *Cavalcade* of 1935–1939, the *Cavalcade* of the early 1940s championed a notion of the historical past of the common man. "History may seem to be *written* in terms of the great characters," Monaghan explained, "but the common folk—the unwritten, unsung and inarticulate little people—*made* it to an equal degree."[30] DuPont's dramatization of history assimilated documentary expression with a vengeance. Yet rather than use the drama of social fact to illuminate human problems, the *Cavalcade* brought the technique to bear upon the institutional problems of the corporation. As a gloss upon the program's merchandising plan, the documentary idea held understandable appeal. The promotion of the program as an actuality added the value of special proof to the subjects selected for broadcast, each of which by Monaghan's count underwent over 200 hours of preparation to ensure "dramatic interest, historical significance and historical authenticity."[31]

With Monaghan, Carmer, and James on board, the program production and merchandising arrangement that was allowed to lapse with James Truslow Adams in 1939 was revived. Once again, the *Cavalcade* spun human interest stories from what Schlesinger had once described as "oddments" and anecdotes drawn from a lifetime of research.[32] Monaghan, for example, contributed the story of Enoch Crosby, a Revolutionary era cobbler and American double agent, who was revealed to listeners as the inspiration for James Fenimore Cooper's *The Spy*.[33] However estimable a gambit, stories of the historically obscure did not become the *Cavalcade*'s sole concern, for specialists recognized the advantage of featuring characters familiar to listeners, many of whom regarded historical figures as voices of authority. Other specialists recommended that the *Cavalcade* emphasize well-known figures and events, believing that isolated and relatively unknown incidents were simply unpopular.[34]

The ideal protagonist was heroic yet humble. Of the 781 *Cavalcade* radio broadcasts from 1935 to 1953, biographical treatments of George Washington and Abraham Lincoln led the list (fifteen programs each), followed by Benjamin Franklin (nine) and Thomas Jefferson (eight). Washington personified a recurring metaphor, linking America's revolutionary struggle for freedom to business's modern-day struggle to escape the regulatory tyranny of the New Deal. In "George Washington Refuses a Crown," a drama coinciding with the opening of the New York World's Fair, the future president dismisses the monarchical intentions of the Continental Army officers who would make him king. Taking stock of the "grave uneasiness afoot" sown by discontent, discouragement, and distrust, Washington warns the officers that their clamor will end in popular revolt and the collapse of freedom. "No man, king or otherwise," Washington tells them, "has the right to set himself up over the destinies of a free people." The program's commercial announcement then leads listeners through DuPont's "Wonder World of Chemistry" fair exhibit, conceived as a "play" in four "acts": research, laboratory control, manufacturing, and a marionette show that dramatized the meaning of chemistry in daily life.[35]

With the outbreak of the Second World War, denunciations of despots increased. In a dramatization of the first inauguration, entitled "Plain Mr. President," the *Cavalcade*'s Washington warns away enemies of freedom everywhere. Invoking the "sacred fire of liberty and the destiny of the republican form of government . . . staked on the experiment entrusted to the American people," Washington prays that "the invisible hand of the almighty being guide the people of the United States to wise measures, for our free government must win the affection of its citizens and command the respect of the world." The weekly "story of chemistry," retitled "news of chemistry's work in our world," cheerily notes that "Washington, the practical economist, would no doubt have been pleased with modern house paints that actually clean themselves."[36]

Until U.S. entry into the war, the *Cavalcade* and its "news of chemistry" commercials adopted a distinctly isolationist stance. A commercial preceding Carl Sandburg's "Abraham Lincoln—The War Years," for example, recalls the sudden stoppage of raw materials exported to the United States during the First World War. Announcer Thomas Chalmers then describes the DuPont Company's exemplary production of synthetic materials since that time—man-made rubber, dyestuffs, fertilizers, yarn made from wood pulp, coal, air, and water, "to name a few of chemistry's unending stream of developments" that might now isolate America from war-torn Europe. "Our liberation from dependence on an undependable world is even now a saga of American enterprise that we might well thrill with pride to hear," Chalmers told listeners. "But perhaps of more importance is the fact that these advances of chemistry and industry are a guarantee that we may look confidently ahead. For once again, as she has in the past, America has found a road wide and straight, along which its cavalcade may roll."[37]

By the fall of 1940 the program's merchandising plan had made unanimous supporters of not only Lammot du Pont but the DuPont executive committee. One company vice president, for example, who had been characterized as "rabid against radio" the previous season, had become "the most ardent booster for radio and for the present show." It was said that Lammot du Pont, who retired as company president that year, had become so interested in the *Cavalcade* that he asked to sit in on the company's radio committee. Having achieved the unanimous endorsement of the DuPont executive committee, NBC specialists recommended that the program be promoted as entertainment, not education, in publicity directed to the general public. A revised program merchandising plan put into effect that fall limited Monaghan's role thereafter to the promotion of the program among NBC's "pressure groups" of the educated and influential. Shorn of Monaghan's on-air introductions associated with the "educational" value of public relations "utilization," program merchandising directed to the general public now emphasized the *Cavalcade*'s "entertainment" values.[38]

Gaining the confidence of their sponsors, who at last warmed to the idea of entertainment, the *Cavalcade*'s producers found themselves able to take advantage of a wider range of story material. This new range of material extended from the program's original basis in the historical past and the world of letters to adaptations of Hollywood screenplays and original works for radio that dramatized democratic sensibilities. In the fall of 1940, the *Cavalcade* presented the story "Wild Bill Hickok," woven around a ballad composed and performed by Woodie Guthrie; "Town Crier" Alexander Woollcott, on loan from CBS, performed his "word picture" of "The Battle Hymn of the Republic"; and a special Christmas night broadcast of Marc Connelly's "The Green Pastures" featured the Hall Johnson Choir.[39]

The adaptation of popular screenplays the following season enlarged upon the plan. In November 1941 the *Cavalcade* presented Henry Fonda in "Drums along the Mohawk"; Errol Flynn in "They Died with Their Boots On"; and, in the weeks following Pearl Harbor, Orson Welles in "The Great Man Votes" and James Cagney in "Captains of the Clouds."[40] The adaptation of *All That Money Can Buy*, a Robert Sherwood screenplay based upon Stephen Vincent Benét's short story "The Devil and Daniel Webster," exemplified the trend toward "stars" and "stories." Like the RKO motion picture, the *Cavalcade* adaptation of this tale of materialism and redemption featured Walter Huston as the Devil and Edward Arnold as Mr. Webster. At the conclusion of the program the cast returns to the microphone to engage in some appreciative word play on behalf of the DuPont Company. "We in Hollywood," Arnold began, "are very happy to have, have the DuPont *Cavalcade* with us. We have a very high regard for *Cavalcade* and a real appreciation of the way things that DuPont, ah, Company gives us for better living."[41] The appearance of stars who volunteered personal feelings about the company spoke volumes for its growing confidence in a corporate public relations strategy inconceivable in the early years of the program. Moreover, the appearance of celebrities known for their upper-case Democratic sensibilities suggested that the *Cavalcade* had lost the opprobrium that had attended its debut in 1935. The showcasing of Carl Sandburg, who played an active role in one memorable broadcast, and the broadcast of Stephen Vincent Benét's *The People, Yes*, also exemplified the change.

The *Cavalcade*'s embrace of Carl Sandburg was all the more striking for his public enthusiasm for the New Deal. In 1926 Sandburg secured his reputation as a biographer with the publication of *Abraham Lincoln: The Prairie Years*. The popular two-volume study of Lincoln's formative experience climaxes with his election in 1860. Laboring into the 1930s, Sandburg published the four-volume *Abraham Lincoln: The War Years* in 1939. One of the New Deal's earliest public champions, Sandburg found parallels in the political crises of the 1860s and the 1930s. Shortly after President Roosevelt's first inauguration, Sandburg published the article "Lincoln-Roosevelt" in Raymond Moley's new magazine, *Today*. In it, Sandburg described section 7(a) of the National Industrial Recovery Act as a second Emancipation Proclamation. The article led to an exchange of letters between Sandburg and Roosevelt and a series of four speeches by Sandburg, a political independent, on behalf of Roosevelt's 1936 re-election campaign. In them, Sandburg enlarged upon the similarities of presidential leadership in 1864 and 1936. No stranger to radio, in 1940 Sandburg delivered a five-minute talk concluding the Democratic Party's election eve broadcast.[42] Always available to read poems and "Lincoln words," Sandburg had by this time become a fixture of the network tributes marking Lincoln's birthday. In January 1941, for example, Sandburg appeared on a CBS broadcast from the Metropolitan Opera, where he read excerpts from *The People, Yes*. Later that year Sandburg collaborated with CBS writer and producer Norman Corwin, who dramatized the poem with an operatic score.[43]

Despite Sandburg's political baggage—which by 1941 included a call for American intervention in the war—the *Cavalcade* made Sandburg himself the subject of a special biographical broadcast entitled "Native Land." The program featured Burgess Meredith as young Sandburg, and Sandburg himself, "prophet and biographer of your Native Land," read poem excerpts culled from *Cornhuskers*, *Slabs of the Sunburnt West*, and *The People, Yes* (fig. 14). Meredith and the *Cavalcade* cast performed the work, dramatizing the poet's method as a colloquial, indigenous, and democratic force. The broadcast opens as Sandburg recites, "Hey you sun, moon, stars and you winds, clouds, rain mist, / Listen to me, listen." In turn, Meredith explains,

> The voice you hear is the voice of a poet. No dead poet, no half-alive poet, trying to sell you a world of his own, but the kind of poet who will happen only once in your native land, in your lifetime. Carl Sandburg. Whether you know him or not, it is certain you have seen him because he's always among you. And whether you like poetry or not, you listen to his poetry because you wrote it yourselves . . .
>
> People of America are trying to say something, and someone is listening. A poet, Carl Sandburg. Who is Carl Sandburg? How did he get that way? It is time we found out. He explains himself and he explains you too. He tells his story, and he tells your story. This man is speaking to you now, so listen, it might be important.[44]

Sandburg then reads the opening verses of "Prairie" from *Cornhuskers*.

> I was born on the prairie and the milk of its wheat, the red of its clover,
>   the eyes of its women, gave me a song and a slogan.
> I speak of new cities and new people.
>
> I tell you the past is a bucket of ashes.
>
> I tell you yesterday is a wind gone down,
>   a sun dropped in the west.
> I tell you there is nothing in the world
>   only an ocean of tomorrows,
>   a sky of tomorrows.[45]

The body of the play commences, as Meredith assumes the role of young Sandburg. As a reporter for the *Chicago Daily News*, he discovers his line of work in "people, yes," plain-spoken contacts, acquaintances, and passers-by. The first interview, "a professor who specializes in what words mean," explains the Indian derivation of "Chicago": "'the place of the skunk, / the river of the wild onion smell, / Shee-caw- go.'" Next, a housewife describes the meaning of her "occupation": "'I am the woman, the home, the family, / I get the breakfast and pay the rent; / I telephone the doctor, the milkman, the undertaker.'" The voice of the housewife segues

Figure 14.

Carl Sandburg and Burgess Meredith performing "Native Land—Part I," *Cavalcade of America* (September 22, 1941). Courtesy of Hagley Museum and Library.

to the street talk of polyglot others: "'You can fix anything / If you get the right fixers.'/ 'Hush baby—hush baby—/ I don't know a thing.' / 'Let it ride / Shoot it all.'"[46] The broadcast concludes with characters comfortably removed from "necessity" and "subsistence." Excerpting the closing verses of *The People, Yes*, Sandburg returns to the microphone to read.

> Once having marched
> Over the margins of animal necessity,
> Over the grim line of sheer subsistence
> Then man came
> To the deeper rituals of his bones,
> To the lights lighter than any bones,
> To the time for thinking things over,
> To the dance, the song, the story,
> Or the hours given over to dreaming,
> Once having so marched.
> . . . .
> In the darkness with a great bundle of grief the people march.
> In the night, and overhead a shovel of stars for keeps, the people march:
> "Where to? What next?"[47]

After an instrumental bridge, Sandburg returns to the microphone. Lending contemporary urgency to the reading of "Lincoln words for now, for this hour," Sandburg reads the conclusion of Lincoln's 1862 annual message to Congress. "*We* cannot escape history. . . . No personal significance, or insignificance, can spare one or another of us. The fiery trial through which we pass, will light us down, in honor or dishonor, to the latest generation. . . . We shall nobly save, or meanly lose, the last best, hope of earth. . . . The way is plain . . . a way which, if followed, the world will forever applaud, and God must forever bless."[48] A concluding "news of chemistry" commercial urges the conservation of automobiles and the protection of engine cooling systems with DuPont Xerone antifreeze during the defense emergency.[49] Such untoward commercial associations were by now commonplace and not unanticipated. Sandburg's selection of poems for broadcast seemed to challenge the market's omnipresence and skewed consciousness. An excerpt from *The People, Yes* wonders: "That baby in Cleveland, Ohio, / in Cuyahoga County, Ohio— / why did she ask: / 'Papa, papa, / what is the moon / supposed to advertise?'"[50] In the context of the broadcast, Sandburg telegraphs his unease with the merchandising of his poetic celebrity by excerpting the peroration of *The People, Yes*. "The people," Sandburg reads, "is a tragic and comic two-face: / Hero and hoodlum: phantom and gorilla twist- / ing to moan with a gargoyle mouth: / "'They buy me and sell me . . . it's a game . . . / sometime I'll break loose . . .'"[51]

Although the possibility of high-profile *Cavalcade* participation was not available to Stephen Vincent Benét in his lifetime, nevertheless the poet's original work for radio shared the celebrity packaging accorded Sandburg in a posthumous

Cavalcade broadcast of "Listen to the People." In the early 1940s Benét assumed public responsibilities in politics and the looming war emergency. An outspoken opponent of isolationism and friend of Roosevelt, Benét publicly called for FDR's re-election with the poem "Tuesday-November-1940." Benét's play "Listen to the People" was first broadcast on NBC July 4, 1941, in a time period immediately preceding a Roosevelt presidential address. The play featured soliloquies by a succession of characters who challenge—and in the end, affirm—American resolve in the face of totalitarianism. In 1943 the *Cavalcade* broadcast the play, casting Ethel Barrymore in the role of narrator. In keeping with *Cavalcade* editorial policy, the script did not include Benét's troubled pictures of the Depression era ("the apple-sellers in the streets . . . the empty shops, the hungry men"). The program's producers also tinkered with the soliloquy of "A totalitarian voice," who urges Nazi-American collaboration. The Goebbels-like character explains, "We can give you your own Hess, your own Himmler, your own Goering—all home grown and wrapped in *tissue*," a conscious substitution for the DuPont Company trademark "cellophane" that appeared in Benét's original text.[52]

Elsewhere editors pared the soliloquy of "An older voice, conservative," who in Benét's text describes her unfortunate "Aunt Emmeline," who "had to shoot her third footman. / (He broke his leg passing cocktails and it was really a kindness.)" Though shorn of this aside, Benét's round parody of the conservatism of the *Cavalcade*'s sponsors was allowed to stand. "An older voice, conservative" relates:

> My dear fellow, I myself am a son of a son of a son of the
> American Revolution,
> But I can only view the present situation with the gravest
> alarm,
> Because we are rapidly drifting into a dictatorship
> And it isn't my kind of dictatorship, what's more.
> The Constitution is dead and labor doesn't know its place,
> And then there's all that gold buried at Fort Knox
> And the taxes—oh, oh, oh!
> Why, what's the use of a defense-contract if you can't make
> money out of your country?
> Things are bad—things are very bad . . .
> And, if you let the working-classes buy coal, they'll only
> fill it with bathtubs.
> Don't you realize the gravity of the situation, don't you?
> Won't you hide your head in a bucket and telegraph your
> congressman, opposing everything possible, including peace and war?[53]

Narrator Ethel Barrymore reads a tribute to Benét, especially written for the broadcast by Carl Sandburg. "How well did he know that men of ideas vanish first when freedom vanishes," Barrymore reads. "Stephen Benét was a whimsical man. It would have pleased him to know that a radio play he wrote goes marching on, like John Brown's body."[54]

Though the carefully altered subtext of Benét's work went "marching on," the *Cavalcade*'s Benét program, the participation of Sandburg, and presence of a stable of scriptwriters of known democratic sensibilities underscore the formula's malleability, and thus its true meaning. According to scriptwriter Arthur Miller, the *Cavalcade* consciously traded in ambiguity, a condition that Miller attributed in part to the "doubleness" that allowed writers to work on the program as long as they hid their copies of the *Nation*, *New Masses*, and the *Partisan Review* when visiting the offices of BBDO. Miller recalled the *Cavalcade* as "more like a form of yelling than writing." An aspiring playwright then dividing his time between Brooklyn Navy Yard war work and *Cavalcade* rehearsals at NBC's studio 8H, Miller won the attention of Orson Welles and the lasting gratitude of producer Homer Fickett with a script-in verse dramatizing the life of Mexican president Benito Juarez. Others followed. Given biographies and monographs to turn into scripts, Miller revisited the story of the Merrit brothers' discovery of iron ore in the Mesabi Range. The Mesabi story, Miller recalled, was "the most brutally rapacious corporate tale I had ever heard." The monographs given Miller documented John D. Rockefeller's wresting away of the massive ore deposit from the hard-scrabble Merrits. At first failing to purchase the rights to the ore, Rockefeller later obtained them as the undercapitalized Merrits floundered in debt. Miller queried Fickett why DuPont desired to dramatize such a story. "They don't see it the way we do," Fickett explained. "The Merrit boys were just unable to manage this kind of wealth, and it was in the country's interest, and humanity's interest, that the one who could manage it should." "In other words," Miller wondered, "God's in his heaven." "He sure as hell is," replied Fickett.[55]

Author and editor John Driscoll began his career with BBDO as a writer for the *March of Time* radio program and found success in Hollywood when one of his *Cavalcade* scripts became the basis for the motion picture *Knute Rockne—All American*, starring Pat O'Brien and Ronald Reagan. In 1947 Driscoll received screen credit for *The Hucksters*, an adaptation of novelist Frederic Wakeman's satire of the crudities of commercial radio, starring Clark Gable and Sidney Greenstreet.[56] Greenstreet's portrayal of an insensitive soap manufacturer, widely appreciated as a caricature of tobacco magnate George Washington Hill, drew fire from the DuPont Company magazine, *Better Living*. "Movies," complained a caption above a portrait of a scowling Greenstreet, "often portray business men as grasping and greedy individual in luxurious office or suite."[57]

Like Driscoll, writer Peter Lyon came to the *Cavalcade of America* from BBDO's *March of Time*. The grandson of publisher S. S. McClure and son of a DuPont Company plant manager, Lyon divided his energies between the *Cavalcade* and the wartime radio dramas sponsored by the Congress of Industrial Organization. The CIO's dramas alternated on a weekly basis on NBC with the talks and interviews of the American Federation of Labor's *Labor for Victory*. Lyon also contributed scripts to ABC's sustaining *Labor—USA*. Lyon's sketches, which dramatized CIO activities and concerns, employed actors with whom he worked on the *Cavalcade* and the *March of Time*. *Cavalcade* program ideas and suggestions, Lyon later recalled, followed no pattern, except to establish a framework for DuPont's discussions of "better things for better living."[58]

Other *Cavalcade* production staff came to BBDO after careers with the Federal Theater Project. George Kondolf, the chief story editor of BBDO's Radio Department and *Cavalcade* producer from 1943 to 1945, joined BBDO after producing seven Broadway shows and serving as the director of the Federal Theater Project in Chicago and in New York. While in the FTP Kondolf produced E. P. Conkle's Lincoln drama "Prologue to Glory" and Arthur Arent's "One Third of a Nation," a "Living Newspaper" plea for adequate housing. Coming under the scrutiny of congressional opponents convinced of its subversive design, the FTP ended in 1939. The FTP's original production of "Prologue to Glory," however, lived again on the *Cavalcade*. Adapted for radio by Arthur Arent and Robert Tallman, the play aired in 1944. Though "Prologue to Glory" appeared on the *Cavalcade*, "One Third of a Nation" did not, despite Arent's and Kondolf's frequent collaborations.[59]

The reprise of stories exploited a bankable past of *Cavalcade* scripts owned outright by the DuPont Company. Previously broadcast scripts underwent continual revision for use through the 1940s, and they proved an eventual boon when the program moved to television in 1952. The *Cavalcade* especially valued the wit and inventiveness of Benjamin Franklin, for example, presenting the elder statesman and inventor as the series' most ingratiating propagandist for "better living." "Dr. Franklin Takes It Easy," by Erik Barnouw, the seventh of nine *Cavalcade* broadcasts to feature a Franklin character, told the "story of how Benjamin Franklin's amazing inventive genius was coupled with a new concept of the freedom to be won for the human spirit—freedom from drudgery, discomfort and want—through intelligence." While acknowledging Franklin's inventive genius, the *Cavalcade* presented its Franklin less as an inventor than as a consumer of inventions. Reprised starring Charles Laughton in 1941, Barnouw's script, originally entitled "Dr. Franklin Takes It Easy," became "The Laziest Man in the World." Program host Walter Huston introduced Laughton, who, Huston explained, had played "heroes, rogues, great men and simple men of all faces and temperaments." "If you were to visit as I do the motion picture studios here in Hollywood," Huston told listeners, "you would find there is no actor who has portrayed the widest possible range of characters." In "real life" Franklin had played as many roles: diplomat, prophet, scientist, revolutionary statesman, wit, moralist, sage, writer, publisher, and inventor. From Franklin's earth-drawn mind had come the folding step stool, a mechanical arm to retrieve things from high places, bifocal lenses, and the celebrated Franklin stove. Through the narrative device of a young and inquisitive character, Franklin's granddaughter Debby, listeners learn of these and more. Setting the tone of the broadcast, Laughton's Franklin tells Debby of the inspiration of his many discoveries and inventions: he hates work. When he demonstrates a Leyden jar at an "electric Christmas party," a spark knocks him to the floor; during a thunderstorm, he confirms the electrical properties of lightning and that it might be arrested with rods, sparing people's homes, churches, and public buildings from fire. Having taken in a program full, Debby realizes that Grandpa has been building better things for better living. The conclusion of the broadcast and the beginning of yet another "lesson" leave Franklin and little Debby practicing her spelling. The first word: "T-O-M-O-R-R-O-W."[60]

The *Cavalcade* proved most pernicious in adapting literary reputations to the corporate end. Literary figures whose lives were dramatized in the early 1940s included Emily Dickinson, Herman Melville, Edgar Allan Poe, O. Henry, and Walt Whitman. The *Cavalcade* allowed more than usual dramatic license in a program on Walt Whitman, presenting a "radio fantasy" in which Whitman materializes at Coney Island and encounters a Depression-era young couple. The couple mistakes the silver-tressed Whitman for a refugee from an island sideshow. Engaging the couple in conversation, Whitman learns of their reluctance to marry, and indeed, their uncertain future. Launching an aside on shareholder democracy, Whitman explains that they share a people's capitalism of factories, railroads, farms, department stores, schools, colleges, symphony orchestras, and art collections. "Your country," he allows, "is what you make it. . . . I have what I have." Next, Whitman ascends a skyscraper and engages a riveter in a similar conversation. Later Whitman meets a waitress in a combination hash house and filling station.[61]

Young couples, riveters, waitresses, poets—the *Cavalcade*'s sponsors had come far from bankrolling the speeches and addresses of the NAM and the Liberty League. A dramatization of the life of the late Will Rogers indicates how facile a venue the *Cavalcade* had become. Brought to life on the *Cavalcade*, Rogers becomes the mouthpiece that his industrialist friends and acquaintances had encouraged him to be.[62] The victim of an airplane crash in 1935, in the year before his death Rogers had turned his rapier-like wit upon Liberty League organizers Edward F. Hutton, Irénée du Pont, and John J. Raskob. A private banquet at Los Angeles attended by 250 businessmen honoring the barnstorming industrialists attracted Rogers' attention. "They got a plan . . . called Liberty League," Rogers cracked in his syndicated newspaper column "Daily Telegrams." "They feel that under the New Deal that the United States Constitution is the forgotten man." Imagining Hutton, du Pont, and Raskob "doing a modern Paul Revere and going down the valleys in three private railway cars arousing the people," Rogers recommended the millionaires' "barnstorming tour" to his readers. "If they happen to play your town, get all the big wigs out. They are darn nice fellows and got the best show on the road this season." "Three hundred million dollars worth of talent."[63]

Reading a *Cavalcade* script shorn of such wisecracks, Rogers's friend Cal Tinney struggles through the Depression with a counter-subversive simulation of Rogers's wit.

> *Announcer:* The Twenties were tumbling to a chaotic close. Prosperity. Bull markets. America riding the crest. The talkies, Cellophane and streamlining. And then 1929. Black Thursday and the bubble burst. Headlines, bread lines, bonus marchers, and Will Rogers, continuing to voice the common sense of the American people.
>
> *Rogers:* Seems funny to hear the people carryin' on about this country bein' broke. How can it be broke. This is the first time the nation ever went to the poor house in an automobile.
>
> *(laughter)*
>
> *Rogers:* Just one thing worries me right now. That's all this talk about me runnin' for President. Now as long as it was a joke, is [*sic*] O.K. Now once and for all this country's got enough problems to face without puttin' a professional comedian in the White House.

In the final scene Rogers flies into an Alaskan fog, his fate sealed "as a spokesman of a fabulous era in American life. Will Rogers—whose memory belongs to the great tradition that is the *Cavalcade of America!*"[64]

The *Cavalcade*'s return to the air in 1940 represented a victory for network, public relations, and advertising specialists who sought an end to the troublesome talks beloved of their largest clients and sponsors. In the six years from 1934 to 1940, speeches gave way to the persona of "just folks," the serials of the National Association of Manufacturers and the Republican National Committee, and the *Cavalcade of America*'s drama of "first principles" in a new land with a new way of thinking. The *Cavalcade* signaled an appreciation among specialists and business leaders alike that popular mass media could, in the long run, re-establish a political climate conducive to the expansion of corporate enterprise. Continuous institutional promotion and a relaxed on-air presence were well on their way to wider acceptance as America entered the Second World War. Business's contest with the administration for social and political leadership would continue, specialists hoped, divorced from rhetorical reaction and counter-productive short-term effects.

After the war, the dramatic anthology became the preferred vehicle of corporate public relations among the clients of Batten, Barton, Durstine & Osborn, with tremendous significance for television in the 1950s. BBDO-produced programs included the *Cavalcade of America*, the *General Electric Theater, U.S. Steel Hour (Theatre Guild on the Air)*, and the *Armstrong Circle Theater*. The prototype of well-merchandised institutional entertainment, *Cavalcade* set the precedent for them all, including the merchandising of programs undertaken by *General Electric Theater* host and program supervisor Ronald Reagan.

The dramatic anthology became the central expression of corporate public relations, the product of an ambitious, consciousness-shaping operation that by the early 1950s had learned to appreciate the value of public relations education less, and that of outright entertainment more. By dramatizing the personal meaning of enterprise, specialists wondered, entertainment like this might save the system itself.

Talkers versus Doers: The Sponsored Motion Picture

A memorandum on commercial movies prepared for discussion at the J. Walter Thompson advertising agency in 1938 addressed the current and potential applications of film to business's sales and institutional problems. The conclusion reached by the memo's authors, Thompson executives Wallace Boren and Fred H. Fidler, was that the screen's influence on "the American standard of living—on style, recreation, decoration, etc. . . . seems destined for a much broader use for both intra-organization and public propaganda." "One commercial picture produced for an automobile manufacturer," for example, "was recognized by Stalin as an excellent technique for his own campaign to combat the Soviet workman's fear of technocracy." Closer to home, they added, "A major studio has under consideration an entertainment picture the subtheme of which is freedom of the press." Closer still, they acknowledged the "need for an interpretive 'humanization' of business to labor" and recommended film to the nation's industrialists "for whom 'Fireside Chats' over the radio are not a practical medium."[1]

A shift from the rhetorical to the dramatic occurred as America's largest industrial corporations entered the entertainment business—and entered to stay, as the most expeditious way of asserting their social and political leadership. The dramatization of the personal meaning of corporate enterprise, like commercial radio, propelled to new heights a popular culture of sponsored films, exhibits, and fairs. It held sway until specialists made television their promotional medium of choice in the early 1950s. Representative entertainments in this period include sponsored motion pictures, traveling shows, and the seminal exhibitry of the New York World's Fair 1939/40, which largely abandoned the promotion of manufacturing processes of earlier fairs and expositions for the dramatization of the personal meaning of enterprise in the "World of Tomorrow."[2] Specialists made clear business's stake in entertainment. Public relations counselor Bernard Lichtenberg, for example, welcomed the New York World's Fair 1939 as an opportunity to counter "the New Deal propaganda." Just as the Roosevelt administration made use of documentary films such as Pare Lorentz's *The River* and the *Living Newspaper* on the New York stage "to get across a message in an entertaining way," noted Lichtenberg, "so exhibitors at the New York World's Fair may be counted upon to stress the entertainment angle in presenting their story."[3]

One indicator of business's willingness to invest in the sponsored picture medium was the increasing use of sponsored pictures in fair exhibits. Some six years earlier at Chicago's Century of Progress, 43 companies employed films. The Northwestern Railroad, Union Carbide & Carbon, Elgin Watch, Sears Roebuck, and Western Union screened films in "semi-open" spaces with liberal seating. Ford, General Motors, Chrysler, and Studebaker presented "closed shows" to capacity crowds in air-conditioned theaters.[4] At the New York World's Fair, films became integral components of exhibits. At the Trylon and Perisphere, the fair's thematic centerpiece, 70-mm transparencies of murals and clouds, projected above the city diorama inside the Perisphere, provided atmospheric effects. In the Transportation Zone, the focal exhibit taken over by the Chrysler Corporation featured a compilation film on the improvement and advance of transportation. The film came to a climax with the off-screen launch of a miniature suborbital rocket ship to London, cued by the firing of engines on the screen[5] (fig. 15).

Motion pictures occupied a special place in the hearts of advertising and public relations specialists, who believed that entertainment that carried business's story could re-establish the proper climate for the autonomous expansion of corporate enterprise. But even so, many ambitious and expensive films betrayed their sponsors' leaden and unremitting urge to command from the top. Pictures packed with compelling special effects ground out messages in mechanical and wooden ways. Making an engine of the screen itself, Ford, Chrysler, and General Motors demonstrated a special fascination with the stop-action animation of automobiles that assembled themselves in the absence of workers. Though specialists continually warned of the dangers of dullness, pomposity, and boredom, a literal manner of expression pervaded the short subject field through the 1940s.

Sponsored motion pictures did dramatize the inadequacy of radio talk and the static demonstrations of manufacturing processes that had once defined the in-

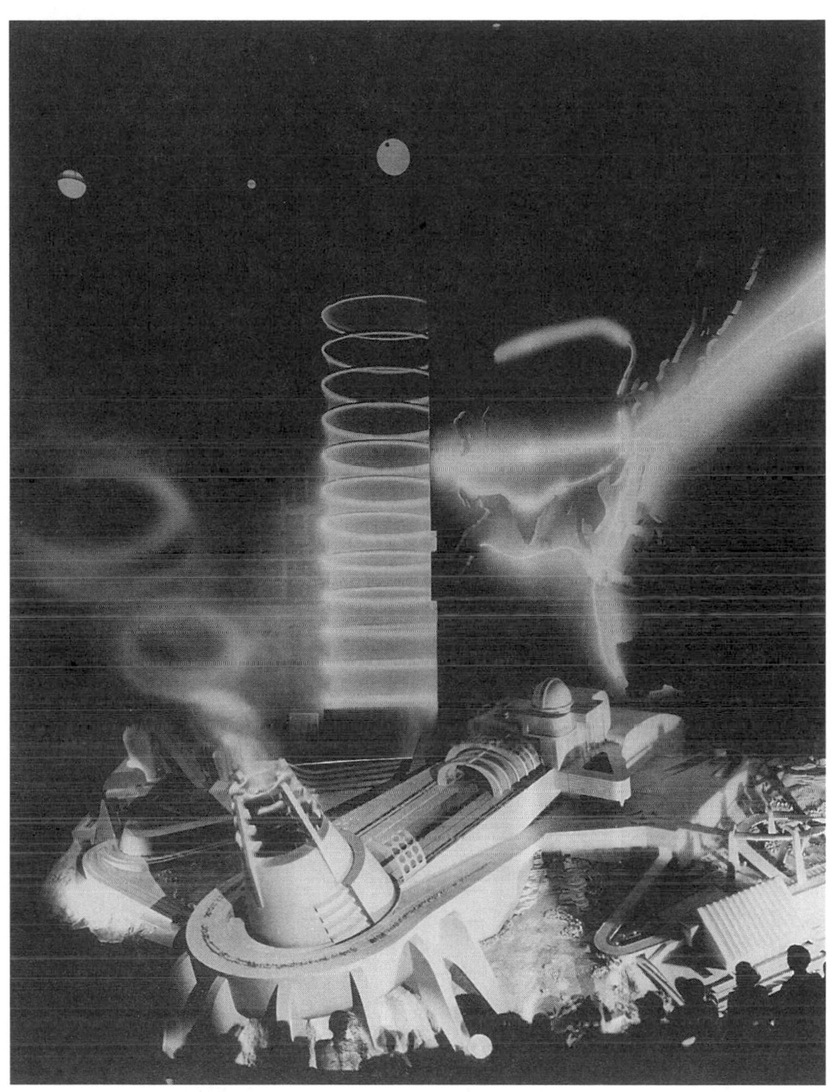

Figure 15.

Rocketport exhibit, Chrysler Corporation, New York World's Fair (1939).

Edward J. Orth Collection, Smithsonian Institution.

dustrial film. As if attempting to raise the cinematic consciousness of the business community, the opening scene of Westinghouse's *The Middleton Family at the World's Fair* (1939), for example, depicts a father and his dispirited son listening to a radio talk. The film presents radio talk as ineffectual discourse perpetuated by business's critics, the "talkers." Father and son argue about future opportunities for young people, allowing the father to establish the reason for the family's visit to the fair. "You've heard all the talkers," he tells his son. "Now you're going to see the doers." Begun by radio, the argument will be decided by the fair-in-a-film.[6]

The *Middleton Family* suggests the enormous confluence of media and ideology that was marshaled for the popular promotion of corporate enterprise on the eve of the war. Part public relations strategy, part answer to the aspirations of the Depression decade, the drama of "more," "new," and "better" became inseparably bound with broadcast and screen entertainment. Moreover, we can see in sponsored pictures intended for popular audiences from the late 1930s through the late 1940s the specialists' attempts to transcend the limits of rhetoric and the printed word of traditional publicity for the subtleties of dramatic expression that personalized the meaning of corporate enterprise.

After the turn of the century, motion pictures assumed various sales, training, and educational functions. In some of the earliest sponsored motion picture films, produced between 1909 and 1912, Ford demonstrated the manufacture of the Model T; General Electric, the work-saving possibilities of home and farm electrification; and the National Association of Manufacturers, the responsibility for workplace safety shared by factory owners and employees.[7] Joining the media of visual instruction, the film became an active agent of the modern corporation. John C. Patterson, the president of the National Cash Register Company, for example, produced participatory spectacles for sales conventions and noontime screenings. They were comparable to the "high class" entertainments produced by traveling picture exhibitors Lyman Howe and E. Burton Holmes, who interspersed lantern slides and sound recordings with complex sequences of short films.[8] Shadowing the growth of the theatrical film industry, specialized industrial picture producers built studios in New York, Chicago, and Detroit, where they established relationships with corporate clients not unlike those of Madison Avenue agencies. Allying with General Motors, for example, filmmaker Jamison Handy, a Patterson protégé, parlayed a contract to supply sales training filmstrips to every Chevrolet dealer in the country into a motion picture, exhibit, and convention production company that by the 1950s had become the country's largest employer of theatrical talent (fig. 16). With headquarters in a former church on Detroit's Grand Avenue, Handy employed by 1935 a staff of over 400, including 12 cameramen, 8 directors, 28 writers, 6 sales representatives, 36 advance men, 80 projectionists, and a musical director. His staff in-

Figure 16.

Chevrolet sales convention musical, 1954. Courtesy of Rick Prelinger.

cluded artists, still photographers, accountants, letterers, animators, and a convention department that produced executive talks, playlets, and traveling shows. Servicing clients Oakland-Pontiac, Chevrolet, Coca-Cola, and General Electric, Handy produced in a typical year from 750,000 to 800,000 filmstrips and 70 motion pictures, staged from 18 to 20 conventions and six to eight road shows.[9]

If the filmstrip represented the low end technologically of industrial film development, the talking sales picture represented the potential of its high end. Audiences for sponsored films increased with the improvement of portable projection equipment and the organization of projection services, such as Western Electric's Modern Talking Picture, whose advertisements featured uniformed projectionists, panel trucks, and the motto "Any place, any time." Introducing sound-on-disc and sound-on-film systems in the late 1920s, Western Electric's subsidiary Electrical Research Products, Inc., aggressively promoted the immediacy and intimacy of screen talk while suggesting film's applicability to the extension of managerial authority and the routinization of work. "Makes personal appearances in 10 cities at once," exclaimed one Western Electric advertisement, which shows a tuxedo- clad executive delivering an after-dinner talk to, presumably, his guests[10] (fig. 17).

Coinciding with the onset of the Depression, the advent of the talking sales film ushered in a state of cinematic arrest, ironically, at the very moment that business most needed to explain itself. Though little evidence remains to suggest the effect of screen talks on theatrical audiences during the Depression, the little that does remain suggests that, like business's radio talks, the sponsored screen was

FIGURE 17. Advertisement, "Makes personal appearance in ten cities at once," Electrical Research Products, Inc. (1930). Courtesy of Robert Finehout.

hampered by business's transparent and self-interested defense of its own interests and activities. A 1934 Ford newsreel attacking the Roosevelt administration's proposal for an inheritance tax, for example, presented a talk read over a compilation of factory scenes punctuated with animated charts and graphs. According to Upton Sinclair, who saw the film one evening in a Pasadena, California, neighborhood theater,

> Some little diagrams were shown, illustrating how much of great fortunes it was proposed to take by an inheritance tax. . . . Then came the question on the screen: "What would such an inheritance tax law do to the Ford fortune? How would such a great factory be divided up?" And then we saw some pictures of some Ford workers, and the dread question was asked: "What would this tax program do about their jobs?"
>
> Of course, we can understand that was the crux of the whole thing; that was what the makers of the movie were really concerned about—the welfare of the workers at the Ford factory! Oh, yeah![11]

Ford's disingenuous analogue perhaps left even critics who were sympathetic to business wondering: Was business talking to itself?

FIGURE 18.

The audience of Chrysler's three-dimensional film *In Tune with Tomorrow,* New York World's Fair 1939. Courtesy of Herbert Rolfes.

The shortcomings of such films were not necessarily matters of talk per se. A film might stumble upon stop-action animation at the scene of production. The orchestration of assembly operations in Chevrolet's *Precisely So* (1937), a Taylor-like time-motion fantasy, for example, featured finished automobiles that flew from a factory paced by the superimposed sweep hand of a stopwatch.[12] Upping the ante, Chrysler Corporation invested in two Loucks & Norling films entitled *In Tune with Tomorrow* (1939) and *New Dimensions* (1940) to show at the New York World's Fair. They simulated the manufacture of a Plymouth sedan employing three-dimensional cinematography, the latter in Technicolor[13] (fig. 18). Of the three leading automakers Ford first introduced stop-action animated sequences in *Rhapsody in Steel* (1934), a film that drew 5,000 persons daily to the company's Century of Progress exhibit. A Technicolor sequel entitled *Symphony in "F"* (1939) shown at the New York World's Fair reprised the stop-action animation of assembly operations at Ford's River Rouge plant.[14] In each, the interrelated processes of making an automobile were presented, set to a symphonic score. The "specially composed music," a press

FIGURE 19.

Scenes from *Rhapsody in Steel*, Ford Motor Company's 1934 Century of Progress film. Ford Collection, National Archives at College Park.

release explained, "depicts the roar of the machines, the hum of the lathes, and the music of the motors."[15]

Rhapsody in Steel, the earlier and arguably more cinematic of the two, opens with a montage of research and development activities, overlaid with the half-dissolved image of Henry Ford (fig. 19). A series of rapid, geometrical wipes cuts to draftsmen working their slide rules, to workers testing belts and leaf springs, to designers conferring over drawings, to men making steel, and at last, to a Model A blueprint. From the blueprint, a diagonal wipe begins a second montage of manufacturing processes, represented by a dramatically lit overhead crane, ladles, ingot molds, and steel slabs—all intercut with flames flaring across the screen. The camera alights on the faces of workmen who, when pictured in closeups as individuals, perform autonomously some distance from the assembly line: an engineer with calipers, a crane operator, a die maker, a machinist at his lathe. Workers, pictured at a distance, from the side, or from the back, labor anonymously tending the routine of the assembly line. A whistle blows and production halts. Hands return tools across the counter of the tool crib, where other hands put them away. As the plant comes to a complete stop, the shift punches a time clock and their feet head for the door.

Once the assembly line has closed for the evening, a "tiny imp" materializes from the V8 insignia on the radiator grille of the last Model A assembled that day. Promptly checking the assembly line's posted production schedule, the animated imp notes that the factory's quota of 4,999 has fallen one car short of the schedule of 5,000. With great anthropomorphic fanfare the imp sets out to build the car. Pan-like, the imp animates a dizzying array of engine blocks, camshafts, transmissions, springs, and chassis and body parts. Assembling from all corners of the Rouge, the parts begin a parade and, in one sequence, perform a square dance. As the "rhapsody" becomes more urgent and martial, the car's final assembly takes place. Proud of the handiwork reflected in the beautifully turned-out Model A, the imp moves the production counter to 5,000 and resumes the form of a V8 logo, this time on the automobile that has met the posted production quota.

Ford publicists promoted composer Edwin Ludig's *Rhapsody in Steel* score as an original contribution to the art of industrial film. Ludig, whose previous work included incidental music for the Broadway productions of David Belasco, composed the score after having spent several weeks at the River Rouge "studying the sounds of the machinery."[16] Five years later Ludig reprised the concept for Ford's New York World's Fair exhibit, where *Symphony in "F"* introduced a live-action "ballet" of transportation progress entitled "A Thousand Times Neigh." Alternately described as a musical comedy, the ballet incorporated fashion models, "Dobbin" the horse, and, inevitably, new Fords (fig. 20).

In the years between the Century of Progress and the New York World's Fair, profound changes in American labor relations made new interpretive demands on Ford's production processes. Where *Rhapsody in Steel*'s symphonic soundtrack idealized a factory of robot-like efficiency and control, the *Symphony in "F"* soundtrack spoke to the morality of work. Its animated factory figures labor to a chorus that urges

> Work work work
> We'd rather be busy than shirk
> It's fun to be giving
> New standards of living so
> Work work work.
>
> Work work work
> No one of us ever will shirk
> We'll make people wealthy
> And happy and healthy so
> Work work work.[17]

Animated columns of purchase orders march through the countryside, emphasizing the latent consequences of "Work work work." The Ford exhibit's George F. Putnam, however, dismissed the film with the observation that "It makes no unmistakable point," and complained that it "fails completely to give the idea that the motor in-

FIGURE 20.

Ballet, "A Thousand Times Neigh," Ford exhibit, New York World's Fair 1939. Courtesy of Herbert Rolfes.

dustry spreads employment, though it seems to try to express that. In places, the music alone seems to be the main idea. I refer to those over-long sequences showing the marching order blanks." Believing "that actual scenes from the Rouge are more interesting, Putnam declared the integration of stop-action figures with documentary sequences of the factory to be "a puzzling combination of 'Snow White' and an educational, industrial reel." "I think," he concluded, "we ought to pick one or the other."[18]

Jamison Handy used animation and documentary techniques for client General Motors, though never in the same film. For example, *'Round & 'Round* (1939), a film made for General Motors' Department of Public Relations, used the technique of stop-action "dolls in motion" to explain the trickle-down economy of "Widget-land" (fig. 21). *From Dawn to Sunset* (1937), a Handy film made for GM's Department of Public Relations after the Flint sit-down strike, used documentary techniques to picture the prosperity spread by the corporation's longstanding policy of administrative decentralization (fig. 22). Closely associated with the managements of DuPont and General Motors, the concept of administrative decentralization acquired added value as an operating logic in overcoming the production bottlenecks ably exploited by the UAW during the strike. Just as the post-strike logic of redundant supply and assembly operations lent new meaning to the concept, its latent consequences acquired the aura of a community-based share-the-wealth scheme on the screen. Bustling plants and plant communities constituted its core argument. *From Dawn to Sunset* pictures an army of interdependent workers and salaried personnel awakening to a montage of alarm clocks, well-dressed children, and pleasant suburban streets that lead through the gates of Chevrolet plants throughout the country. During the day the purchasing power of paychecks fuels the local economies of twelve plant cities.[19] As an indication of the urgency with which GM desired to put its message before the public, that same year the corporation established a circulating film library to complement the distribution of pictures arranged by Handy, in order to the blanket the theater, club, and school circuits.[20]

Under increasing pressure to justify the consequences of their operations as strikes rocked the coal, steel, and auto industries, other managements took on the burden of direct film distribution as well. In 1937 the National Association of Manufacturers opted for the "intensive and expensive" distribution of films as a matter of urgency in placing industry's message before the public. By 1938 the NAM had placed a total of four short theatrical films in circulation: *Men and Machines; America—Yesterday, Today and Tomorrow; Frontiers of the Future;* and *America Marching On*. A tally of attendance that year reported showings in 4,809 theaters averaging 1,725 persons per theater, totaling some 8,307,766 persons. The program's total cost, including production, prints, promotion, and distribution, came to

FIGURE 21.

Scenes from General Motors'

'Round & 'Round (1939).

Courtesy of Rick Prelinger.

FIGURE 22.

Scenes from General Motors'

From Dawn to Sunset (1937).

Courtesy of Rick Prelinger.

$83,000 for a per capita distribution figure of $.0098—about one cent. The films' subsequent nontheatrical distribution reduced the per-capita figure to $.0026. Specialists reported showings in 259 schools, colleges, and universities and in one hundred Civilian Conservation Corps camps, in addition to screenings at 65 companies and to permanent deposits in school systems in Cleveland, Buffalo, Elgin (Illinois), Los Angeles, Baltimore, and Philadelphia.[21]

The NAM's *Men and Machines* (1937), one of two short subjects packaged as a series entitled "Let's Go America,"set out "to explode the old Frankenstein fiction of the machine ruining man." The picture's plot pitted the time-tested truths of "Dad" against the unproven economic theories of "Ted." A NAM publicity kit explained: "In a sidewalk discussion with a friend, Lowell Thomas narrates the story of an old retired machine shop foreman, Dad. Dad's son, Carl, has a young friend, Ted, who believes that machines are 'ruining' the country. When Ted tells Dad his theory, Dad goes into the facts." In the NAM's plans for merchandising *Men and Machines* to the patrons of neighborhood theaters, however, could be seen the glimmer of an arresting array of consumer goods, which stood apart from the picture's fact-laden argument. NAM publicists suggested that theater owners "contact stores selling automobiles and modern mechanical implements like vacuum cleaners, refrigerators, kitchen equipment, etc. Ask them to display window cards tying-up the movie with the articles they're selling." The window cards read, "If you work . . . or want to work, see this dramatic talking picture." A suggestion for decorating theater lobbies was more provocative. "One suggestion which can be reproduced with wide variations is to exhibit a dummy of a tired, untidy woman, with a lined face, bent over an old fashioned washboard, with the dummy of a modern woman, neat and fresh-looking, operating modern washing machine by merely pressing a button with her finger."[22] In the theater lobby, if not upon the screen, the NAM had created the personal setting in which to dramatize its enterprise ideology, in a way that the mere representation of manufacturing processes could not. The display of push-button progress recalled the early advertisements of General Electric, General Motors, and others that had promoted the electric lamp and the automobile self-starter as symbols of business's social service in the 1920s. What redefined this strategy for the 1930s was the ratcheting up of its personal focus into a comprehensive political claim. What was new was less this claim's dramatization at the point of consumption than the fact that the claim had become widely understood as the point of entertainment.

The planners of the television system exhibited at the New York World's Fair were well aware of exhibitors' investment in a showmanship of domestic settings and situations, which were destined to become staples of television entertainment. In 1939 Lenox Lohr, NBC president and the nominal marketer of RCA's television system, outlined for RCA President David Sarnoff a company plan to study fair exhibits. "More knowledge," Lohr explained, "can be gained of an industrial company in an hour's study of its exhibit than in months of questions with agencies and clients, since every product, aim and purpose of the company is visually presented." In appreciation of the fair's lessons for television, Lohr noted that "[the fair] offers an excellent opportunity for the television programming staff to view exhibits which are presented with subtle merchandising and strong entertainment value; . . . since the present exhibits are the best known methods in motivated visual presentations to the ultimate consumer conceived by industry." Lohr particularly liked the short theater show at the Westinghouse exhibit entitled "The Battle of the Centuries," which pitted the dishwashing talents of "Mrs. Drudge" against those of "Mrs. Modern," a dishwasher operator[23] (fig. 23).

Illuminating the shadowy recesses of the World's Fair's stage shows, the drama of "more," "new," and "better" represented an important change in the way that business impressed its entrepreneurial outlook upon the public. The theatrical expression of better living included the "dramatic spectacle" staged by DuPont in the refurbished center hall of its 1940 exhibit, where visitors attended the "birth of a crystal." Accomplished by means of Polarized light, a musical score, and "poetic

Figure 23.

"Mrs. Modern" *(left)* and "Mrs. Drudge" stage "The Battle of the Centuries" dishwashing competition, Westinghouse exhibit (1939), New York Worlds' Fair 1939–40. Records, Manuscripts and Archives Division, The New York Public Library, Astor, Lenox and Tilden Foundations.

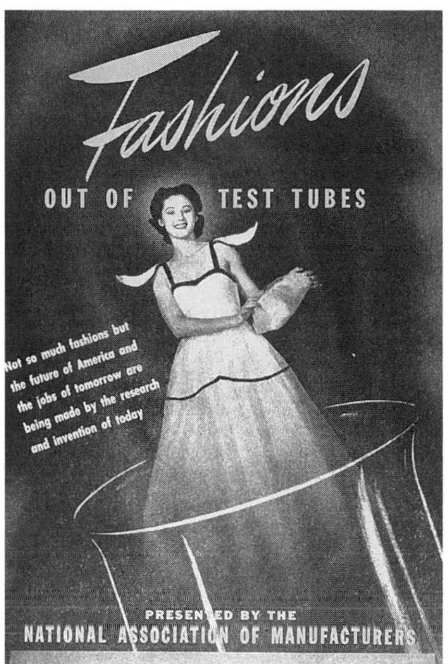

FIGURE 24.
Playbill cover, "Fashions out of Test Tubes," NAM (1940). Courtesy of NBC Collection, State Historical Society of Wisconsin.

narrative," the crystal dramatized "the universal beauty which scientists comprehend in the orderly workings of natural laws" and the "ultimate nature of matter, which until now has been reserved for scientists working in the seclusion of their laboratories." The orderly workings of natural laws carried through "into the beauty added to familiar things by scientific research," symbolized by "Miss Chemistry," a model "garbed in the products of chemistry" who emerged from a giant Lucite test tube.[24] "Though no one can foretell the future," Miss Chemistry cautioned, "man's hopes and aspirations point to what might be."[25] Expanded to include the products of American Viscose, Eastman Kodak, U.S. Rubber, Monsanto Chemical, Celanese, B. F. Goodrich, and Owens-Corning, the show played the National Association of Manufacturers' Congress of American Industry convention and "Modern Pioneer" dinners celebrating the 150th anniversary of the American patent system. Like DuPont's World's Fair exhibit, its road show equivalent, entitled "Fashions out of Test Tubes," was neither a fashion show nor an attempt to compare man-made fibers with those of nature. A playbill explained, "This presentation, a dramatization of industry forging ahead through research and science, is a dramatic challenge to those who claim there are no longer any frontiers for Americans"[26] (fig. 24).

Perhaps nowhere was the change from demonstration to dramatization more evident than at General Motors' "Highways and Horizons" exhibit. Five years earlier, at the Century of Progress, General Motors had exhibited the final stages of

FIGURE 25.

Left to right: **Norman Bel Geddes, Alfred P. Sloan, Jr., Richard H. Grant, Wiliam S. Knudsen, and Charles F. Kettering, inspecting the street of tomorrow, General Motors exhibit model (July 20, 1938). New York World's Fair 1939–40. Records, Manuscripts and Archives Division, The New York Public Library, Astor, Lenox and Tilden Foundations.**

the manufacture of Chevrolets on a facsimile assembly line. In the course of planning the corporation's 1939/40 fair exhibit, officials abandoned plans to re-exhibit the assembly line and chose instead designer Norman Bel Geddes's "Futurama," a diorama of future progress based upon present science and invention projected for 1960 (fig. 25). The most popular exhibit at the fair, "Futurama" transported visitors in sound chairs two abreast over the vast diorama as if making a transcontinental flight over the United States. The narrative piped into visitors' ears featured the progress talk that was fast becoming General Motors' institutional hallmark. Like DuPont's "Miss Chemistry," GM's Alfred P. Sloan, Jr., carefully explained that the Futurama offered not a prediction, but an inspiration of "a greater realization that the future can be made a better place in which to live."[27]

Exiting the Futurama, visitors could wander freely about a full-scale street intersection, bounded by an apartment building, an automobile salon, an appliance showroom, and a 600-seat auditorium. The auditorium presented GM's "Previews of Progress" stage show, "as colorful as anything to be found on the carnival midway." The show's host broadcast to the audience with a "personalized radio station," and demonstrated the "television telephone," the "frig-o-therm" (freezes and cooks), the "talking flashlight" (photoelectric cell), and "a breath-taking array of new inventions and discoveries" that included unbreakable lenses and yarn made from milk. "Previews of Progress," gushed a press release, "is regarded as a visual demonstration of what science has done, is doing, and more important, must yet do in the days to come. It is being called a prologue to the Fair itself, for no visitor can spend 40 minutes in the GM Auditorium without feeling that he or she has had a mental tuning-up for the world to come."[28]

Noting the range of attention-getting devices available to fair exhibitors in the late 1930s, specialists reported the increasing number of films that were used to "put on a show" and create the holiday atmosphere believed conducive to sales and institutional public relations. *Business Screen* reported that there were over 600 films screened at the fair in 1939 (404 in standard 35 mm, 191 in 16 mm, the majority projected with sound). The total included projections of transparencies and film loops integrated with exhibits, changing programs of educational films and documentaries, and sponsored films that complemented stage shows or stood alone as special attractions.[29]

Reporting on the experience of leading film exhibitors at the 1939 fair, the editors of *Film News* noted that exhibitors "now rate moving pictures well ahead of most static exhibits," a claim borne out by the enlargement and construction of new theaters for the 1940 fair season. Chrysler added a larger screen (40 by 60 feet) for showings of a new three-dimensional Technicolor picture entitled *New Dimensions*. Lines of visitors waiting to see Chrysler's 1939 3-D film *In Tune with Tomorrow*, *Business Screen* reported, had been as long as those at General Motors' Futurama. Across the street at Ford, a new 420-seat theater offered *Symphony in "F"*. At the United States Steel Subsidiaries exhibit, improvements included dioramas that forecast how steel might serve in the future. The exhibit showed prefabricated steel housing, a radio-controlled hydroponic tomato farm, a working model of traffic control in the City of the Future, and a futuristic 250-seat theater for showing U.S. Steel's Technicolor documentary, *Men Make Steel* (1937).[30]

Challenged to interpret the latent consequences of industrial enterprise, film makers made use of home and community life to prop up the demonstrations of production processes that had once defined the industrial film. Noticeably, work was displaced as an industrial subject in the films exhibited at the fair in 1940. Consider, for example, the modification of U.S. Steel's *Men Make Steel*. Made by Roland Reed Productions, the industrial picture branch of Hollywood's Selznick International, *Men Make Steel* documented the production of steel from iron ore. Its Technicolor cinematography and symphonic score won critical acclaim and theatrical success. Pare Lorentz, reviewing the film in *McCall's*, declared it the most beautiful color film ever made. "The dull blues of the gigantic furnaces; the red and gold fountains of molten steel, the squat Bessemers pouring their great ladles against a dark sky—these are thrilling and awe-inspiring photographs," Lorentz wrote. Lorentz praised the film's use of real-life steel workers, the kind of dignified, tough working men "that [lent] a conviction to the picture no routine cast of film players could achieve." He believed that only the intrusion of a "banal" shot of a worker stuffing a paycheck into his pocket compromised the picture's overall effect, by suggesting that the manufacturing processes pictured on the screen might have political significance.[31] But by 1939, Richard Griffith, in a review of films at the fair, dismissed *Men Make Steel* with the comment that "a blast furnace in Technicolor is still a blast furnace."[32]

Brought up to date for showing in the new theater of the revamped U.S. Steel Subsidiaries exhibit in 1940, a new Technicolor prologue introduced the original film's demonstration of steel-making, using the drama of steel consumption. According to a copyright synopsis filed by the Jam Handy Organization, the prologue's producer:

> A newly married couple ponder over the furnishings and equipment of their new home while the Narrator relates steel's contributions to present day living, and what the U.S. Steel labels mean on products made of steel. In the completed home the young newlyweds see for themselves the big part quality steel plays in the comfort, pleasure and service of daily life.[33]

As aspirations of newlywed couples displaced work and demonstrations of production processes, industrial films took on the domestic stage craft of theatrically released feature films.

None of the sponsored films conceived to dramatize the personal meaning of industrial enterprise in the 1930s approached the level of production of Westinghouse's *The Middleton Family at the World's Fair* (1939) (fig. 26). The *Middleton Family* incorporated fair exhibitry and radio in its plot, and the film itself played a role in a larger institutional public relations campaign incorporating those media. To merchandise the Westinghouse exhibit, company specialists built a year-long ad campaign around the visit of a "mythical 'typical' family to the Fair." The campaign began in April 1939 with four-color advertisements in the *Saturday Evening Post, Collier's*, *Life*, *Liberty,* and the *Country Gentleman*. In serial strip story format, the ads introduced the Middletons, "a 'family of folks you know' who have just come to the Fair." The first ad of the series finds the Middletons inspecting the Westinghouse exhibit's "Singing Tower of Light." "With a possible 20,000,000 people visiting the Fair," explained Westinghouse advertising manager Syd Mahan, "the probable audience the Westinghouse exhibit could hope to attract without advertising would be at most 5,000,000. By taking the story to the readers of five magazines, we reach a possible 12 million people seven times, actually taking them through the high

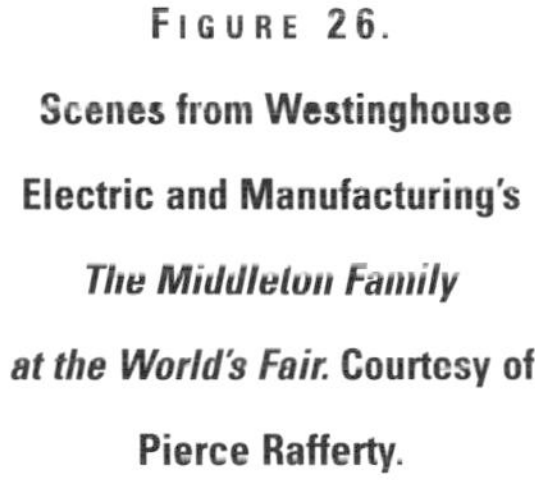

Figure 26.
Scenes from Westinghouse Electric and Manufacturing's *The Middleton Family at the World's Fair.* Courtesy of Pierce Rafferty.

points of our exhibit."[34] The idea carried into the exhibit's "Letters Home" radio contest. Broadcast from a studio in the Westinghouse exhibit building, the contest awarded prizes to letter writers and their addressees. To merchandise the letter-writing idea, the exhibit included a writing room where visitors could compose letters on stationery and post them free of charge. For fair goers who were perhaps too occupied to compose a letter, special stationery provided a "Dear ———" narrative of the exhibit experience. Sprinkled with first-person colloquialisms ("my wanderings, if placed end to end would resemble a plate of spaghetti"), the cursive text toured the main attractions: the "Elektro the Moto-Man stage show," and the "Student Science Laboratory of the American Institute Science and Engineering Clubs," where "young physicists literally made electrons jump through hoops."[35] The *Middleton Family* film, in turn, featured each exhibit element, promotional device, and medium in the campaign.

Prized by today's documentary film makers for its Technicolor cinematography and location shots of the fair, the *Middleton Family* cast the New Vocabulary in a domestic comedy-drama that one observer characterized as "a Westinghouse equivalent of the Hollywood Jones Family."[36] Ostensibly about a family's visit to the fair, the *Middleton Family* never ventures beyond the Westinghouse exhibit, a fact that amused critics and befuddled viewers expecting a tour of the fair rather than a distillation of its message. Nevertheless, audiences might identify with the Middletons, who travel from their home in Indiana to visit Grandmother in suburban New York, and of course, the fair.

As character types populating the fair's exhibits and stage shows the Middletons are familiar enough. Tom Middleton, the amiable father, is a self-reliant, successful small-town businessman. Wife Jane marvels at the Westinghouse electrical living exhibits and the dishwasher, about which she will needle him later. Daughter Babs, a stylish college art student, lives in New York with her capable grandmother. Son Bud, a mischievous and insufferable wisecracker, is, like many of his older friends, resigned to the inevitability of unemployment and government relief after high school.

At the outset the *Middleton Family* makes telling use of radio as a device to establish the subtext of scarcity and dwindling opportunity, later dispelled by the fair-in-a-film. Significantly, the first words spoken in the film come from a radio. A commentator, noting the 600,000 young Americans "stepping hopefully out into the world this year, looking for their first jobs," wonders "What can this young generation look forward to? What hope is there for youth in the world of tomorrow?" The film uses the commentator as a device to suggestively equate radio talk with business's idle social critics. The commentator's talk engages Tom Middleton and Bud in a father-son discussion, which allows Dad to establish the reason for the family's vacation at the fair—but only after Bud tunes out the commentator in mid-sentence. Flipping the dial to the swing band that plays through the background of the rest of the scene, Bud holds his finger in the air and begins to jitterbug in a shuffling and dispirited way. Tom Middleton registers his disappointment not so much with Bud's rudeness as with his lack of ambition and interest in the future.

> *Bud:* [*changing station*] Sorry Dad, he's breakin' my heart.
>
> *Tom:* I should think you'd be interested in hearing about opportunities for young people.
>
> *Bud:* What opportunities. Say, do you know the motto of the last graduating class?
>
> *Tom:* Something lofty, no doubt.
>
> *Bud:* Yeah—W.P.A. here we come. That's super lofty.
>
> *Tom:* Well I guess times change. When I was your age, I—
>
> *Bud:* I know, you were working for a hardware jobber, and you kept right on 'til you saved enough to open your own store.
>
> *Tom:* Yes. And I don't see—
>
> *Bud:* 'Cause times change like you said. We got all the hardware stores we need. All the grocery stores, all the doctors, all the lawyers, all the everything.
>
> *Tom:* But it don't stand to reason that a country with our record could all at once lack—
>
> *Bud:* No? You just try and get a job.
>
> *Tom:* Maybe it is difficult but it's worse to be a quitter. Now you've got years of school ahead of you. Yet you let your friends talk you into believing you're licked already.
>
> *Bud:* Oh they know what they're talkin' about.
>
> *Tom:* Now listen son, I wasn't going to tell you this, but you're the reason we came here all the way from Indiana. You've heard all the talkers. Now I'm going to show you the doers. That's why I brought you and your mother to the Fair.
>
> *Bud:* Holy smoke, the Fair! I forgot where we were!

Dad's juxtaposition of "talkers" and "doers" positions the radio talk as an intrusive device that is capable of starting arguments, yet incapable of sustaining interest in them. The entertainments of the fair soon convert Bud into an attentive and enthusiastic student of tomorrow.

The plot of the *Middleton Family* turns on the affection of Babs for her two suitors, Nicholas Makaroff and Jim Treadway. Nick Makaroff, she tells her family, has "been in America since he was a little boy. But he knows the world like we know Main Street." Her art teacher and current boyfriend, Makaroff favors bow ties and abstract painting. His rival, Jim Treadway, dated Babs in high school, but Babs has broken off their "understanding." While Treadway confides in Bud an urge to "plow into a line now and then," he has given up football for bigger kicks: electrical research. For the present, he is superintending the Westinghouse exhibit as "backstop for the guys" (guides), chasing down answers to visitors' questions. In contrast to the affable and self-effacing Treadway, the sullen Makaroff sneers at the exhibit he is about to tour as the Westinghouse "temple of Capitalism." He vows to not enjoy himself.

In the Westinghouse exhibit's Hall of Power, Treadway and Makaroff tangle. The meaning of the fair emerges from the conflict in ways that the exhibit itself only begins to suggest. For example, in one scene played in front of a model traction railway, Treadway handily deflects Makaroff's pointed questions about automation and unemployment. The clash of personalities is hardly complex, but even as stock types the characters are nevertheless remarkable for challenging and confirming the exhibit's rhetorical subtext. The most striking aspect of Makaroff as a character type is his complete alienation from the fair and its conception of the average visitor. Inveighing against machines as "Frankenstein's monsters" and against displays of consumer appliances as "capitalist sucker traps," Makaroff lies beyond the regenerative power of better living. A synopsis put it bluntly: "Makaroff is not a bad character; he just hasn't any. He's good-looking, dark, attentive, well-dressed, smooth. He has the shallow mind and glib tongue of the parlor pink—the type which finds it easier to belittle and tear-down than to be constructive. He has never been successful, so he salves his failure by pooh-poohing the achievements of a system from which his own deficiencies bar him."[37]

While Makaroff finds an opponent in Treadway, Makaroff finds an effective foil in Grandmother Harrison. An afternoon at home finds Bud writing a prize-winning essay to Westinghouse's "Letters Home" radio contest, Babs and Makaroff going over some of his abstract paintings, and Treadway bemoaning Babs's new interest in art. Taking Treadway aside, Grandmother encourages him to believe that he and Babs have more in common than he suspects. "Most women you'll find, pick husbands who see the world as they do," she explains. "Who think as they do about religion, war, politics, yes, even communism. They do it unconsciously. It's bred into them from childhood." "Yes," counters Treadway, "but they can make mistakes, too."

As Grandmother and Treadway affirm the homogeneity of their world, meanwhile on the veranda out back, Babs questions Makaroff about the abstract forms pervading his paintings. Tom Middleton, holding a pair of scissors and a bouquet of cut flowers, stops to ask what the couple are looking at. "A good piece of abstract painting, don't you think?" asks Makaroff, passing a canvas to Middleton. Struggling to orient the picture, Middleton becomes ensnared in the discussion. "It's just that I'm sort of used to looking at pictures of people and objects,—uh, you know." "Why?" replies Makaroff. "If you want a house or a flower, you can go and look at them, or if you want them represented you can have them photographed. So why allow them to intrude into pictures?" Returning the painting to Makaroff, Middleton heads inside. The flowers, he mutters, need a drink.

Though the *Middleton Family* expends considerable energy embellishing Makaroff's party credentials, in the film's denouement Babs's estrangement from him is presented not as an ideological matter but as romance gone bad. Babs's story remains that of romance betrayed by insincerity and deceit, because she is incapable of making the connection between ideology and personal meaning. Her perceptive grandmother, on the other hand, whose attractive suburban home attests to the counter-subversive comforts of more, new, and better, makes it for her. Grandmother suggests that Babs show Makaroff the decorated room displays of the Hall of Electrical Living to soften him up a bit and suggest what a young lady might like in the way of a home life. "Oh Nick doesn't care about that. He wouldn't care if . . . ," Babs replies. The romance unravels with Grandmother's discovery that the ring that Makaroff has given Babs—"a polychromatic study in harmony" passed through his family for over a dozen generations as its "official seal of betrothal"—is nothing but a piece of costume jewelry. It is, in fact, a replica of a ring in a Moscow museum. This climactic though not unanticipated turn of events leaves Babs clinging to Jim Treadway, the Westinghouse man from back home.

The *Middleton Family* begs to be considered as an entertainment whose every moment refutes visually the Keynesian thesis of the "mature economy" of scarcity and dwindling opportunity. The material circumstances and props of the Middleton's home life exude a cheery optimism and constitute the stage upon which ideological issues play as matters of personal convenience and well-being. The home, in short, measures the meaning of the system. This is dramatized in a variety of ways: Grandmother's groaning sideboard is replenished by her cook, Elvira (who declares "If appetites is houses, I'd own half of Harlem by now"); and clothing and furnishings are rendered in appealing Technicolor.

High production values paid dividends in audience acceptance. Modern Talking Picture successfully exhibited the *Middleton Family* for 1,366 Parent Teacher Associations in the early 1940s. A survey of the PTA audience conducted by the public relations firm of Fuller & Smith & Ross, Inc., found an average attendance per show of 182.8 individuals, comprised of 30.2 men, 75.4 women, 37.5 boys, and 39.7 girls. The report promoted the "discovery" of the value and effect of professional film production and national distribution.[38]

Though the fair was a passing phenomenon, the success of domestic drama in the sponsored motion picture was not, and here the *Middleton Family* must be considered as a prototype of wartime and postwar entertainment. With the coming of the Second World War, dreams of modernity such as the happy home life of the *Middleton Family* were put on hold for the duration, later to flower as the common currency of television.

Chapter Seven

Creative Discontent

By 1940 the sponsored motion picture had arrived as a medium of business leadership. On the eve of America's entry into the Second World War, business could hardly regard the medium with indifference. During the war, films routinized training and work, papered over dissident labor-management relations, and linked the home and fighting fronts with the drama of common sacrifice and struggle. Though the war had cut short the aesthetic expectations of industrial picture producers, the sponsored picture medium emerged from it with an enhanced reputation for "idea communication." Within and without the workplace, the postwar problems of economic reconversion and the removal of legal barriers to top-down anti-union discourse with the passage of the Taft-Hartley Act heightened business's communicative challenge. Leaving the factory for home and family life, the quest for a personally meaningful New Vocabulary of business leadership proceeded. First-person narrative material was offered by company personnel departments, whose specialists charted the nuances of human behavior, believed to be the last variable in the production equation. Applying the lessons of "human relations," the specialists studied the phenomena of leadership and communication in small groups to gain insight into the attractions of unionism. Specialists busied themselves surveying employee wants and desires, the better to come up with effective employee and public relations media for their restless audiences.[1]

The war had renewed interest in publicity devices and techniques ranging from single-sheet posters to the officially packaged information campaigns of the Office of War Information.[2] Production incentive imagery for war workers ignored the difficult past of labor-management relations, the war emergency providing an ostensible truce in the conflict. Wartime conditions included the official imposition of wage and price controls, a "no strike" pledge from labor, and spotty implementation of labor-management coordinating committees in war production plants.[3] Company posters, employee magazines, and films invited workers to think of themselves not as union members—or, for that matter, as employees—but rather as Uncle Sam's production soldiers.[4]

Driven to enlarge Americans' productive and imaginative capacities for Total War, the nontheatrical picture industry converted to the crash production of training films that reflected the noncoercive values of democratic social engineering.[5] The major producers included Burton Holmes Films, Inc., Detroit's Jam Handy Organization, Inc., Audio Productions, Inc., Bray Studios, Inc., and Pathescope Company of America, Inc.[6] The Jam Handy Organization, for example, already had in production 24 instructional films for pre-flight training at the time of U.S. entry into the war. Eventually Handy produced some 2,000 training filmstrips and films for the Army and 5,000 subjects for the Navy. In total the government spent $20 million for Handy films, filmstrips, and training devices for radar, airplane maintenance, guided missiles, and aerial gunner instruction (the latter a mockup cockpit with projected planes and simulated battle noises) (fig. 27). Some 1,100 officers and gunnery instructors participated in Handy's "train the trainer" program. The most enjoyable project, producer Jamison Handy later recalled, was "getting women marines to teach marines how to fight."[7] Building upon the success of the public relations films that its clients had exhibited at the New York World's Fair, Handy consolidated its reputation as the film maker of record for the nation's largest industrial corporations.[8] By virtue of its position with General Motors and U.S. Steel, Handy found itself at the core of the nation's conversion problems.[9]

Motion pictures promoted business's reputation for over-the-top production of war materiel. GM-Handy films, for example, dispelled questions of managerial competence that had been raised during the defense emergency, when UAW Vice President Walter Reuther had embarrassed the auto industry with a "500 planes a day" proposal to streamline aircraft production.[10] In early 1942 General Motors' advertising agency Campbell-Ewald learned that the UAW had readied an advertisement for national distribution that attributed the auto industry's production gains "to the magnificent efforts of labor and the operations of what they claimed was essentially the Reuther Plan, adopted for want of adequate leadership by employer management." Acting quickly, Campbell-Ewald prepared a GM ad headlined "Good

FIGURE 27.

Aerial tail gunner seated at an audiovisual training device faces projected images of enemy airplanes, Jim Handy Organization, about 1944. Courtesy of Image Bank.

News from the Production Front." An agency specialist later claimed that "the effect was electric and set in motion the entire series of General Motors wartime advertisements, not to mention campaigns by other companies which more or less followed the General Motors lead. But it was a close call. The union might easily have gained the same start and carried it through to the same conclusions." Corporate claims to the contrary set the tone for GM public and employee relations media keyed to the slogan "Victory is Our Business."[11]

Though lavish film entertainments on the order of the *Middleton Family* were out for the duration, dramas with friendly characters and familiar settings drawn from everyday life promoted management's full-throttle identification with the government's war effort. General Motors' *Close Harmony* (1942), for example, featured a barber shop setting, in which "one of the customers successfully answers the questions of the other customers and the employees of the shop in regard to the conversion of American factories from peacetime to war production."[12] Collapsing the distance between the home and the fighting fronts, U.S. Steel's film *To Each Other* (1943) (figs. 28 and 29) recounted the corporation's stupendous production achievements. Taking its title from the Declaration of Independence ("we pledge to each other our lives, our fortunes, our sacred honor"), the picture casts Walter Brennan as an elderly "steel man" who reads a letter from his son "somewhere overseas." As

Figure 28.

Scene from *To Each Other*. Courtesy of Rick Prelinger.

Figure 29.

Trans-Lux newsreel theater marquee featuring U.S. Steel's *To Each Other*, Rockefeller Center, 1943. Courtesy of Rick Prelinger.

ladles, ingots, and sheets roll across the screen, the steel man tallies the contributions of women workers, and talks about shipyard prefabricated subassembly sections and other production innovations in mills across the country. From a hillside overlooking U.S. Steel's Homestead works—on the very spot where before the war his son too had decided to become a steel man—the elderly worker fights back a tear to confide proudly a "kick in being in it together . . . fighting for the day of victory—'the day when you'll be coming home.'"[13]

The war interrupted the progress of indigenous labor films, which had seemed poised to take off in 1940. The UAW-CIO's *United Action Means Victory* (1940), for example, contrasted the union's working class Americanism with that of management during the General Motors tool and die strike of 1939. Produced and directed by Michael Martini with the assistance of Frontier Films, *United Action* chronicles the history of the strike and the community support won by the strikers. The action features flag-carrying pickets ringing GM plants and scenes of home and family life acted out by the strikers themselves. The film's voice-over continuity concludes with a query—"Want to know who's next?"—to Henry Ford, whose Ford Motor had yet to recognize the union.[14]

Though the timely production of labor films ground to a halt after Pearl Harbor, full employment created new audiences for labor film programs. Under President R. J. Thomas, the UAW-CIO film department built the largest film library of any union in the country. With some 450 prints, the library included short subjects from the U.S. Army and Navy, the U.S. Office of War Information, the British Information Service, and the U.S. Coordinator of Inter-American Affairs. By 1944 the UAW-CIO claimed a circulation of 5.5 million for films presented under its auspices. Films circulated among community organizations and 375 UAW locals, 175 of which owned 16 mm projectors. Not until 1944 did the UAW resume film production, making an animated cartoon short in support of President Franklin D. Roosevelt's re-election. Borrowing a title and a railroad metaphor from financier James P. Warburg's campaign book (which opposed Roosevelt's re-election in 1936), the UAW-CIO's *Hell Bent for Election* deployed the momentous image of a New Deal campaign train, whose spirited locomotive personified FDR. The animated short played to an estimated audience of 4 million CIO members and community groups. The high point of the picture's distribution came in Detroit, where the UAW film department's Tony Marinovich projected it one evening against the General Motors Building. With the possible exception of *Hell Bent for Election*, the film audiences of GM management and the UAW rank and file seldom intersected.[15]

Open labor-management conflict near the war's end taxed the return of all but the most bombastic modes of discourse. To manage the postwar economic shocks and the dislocations of reconversion, business turned to many of the same promotional tools and techniques that had proven successful on the production front during war. Many in business believed that such techniques could dispel the atmosphere of disunity and distrust stemming from the lifting of price and wage controls and the subsequent strikes that swept the auto, steel, and electrical industries.[16] Seeking a totality of effect commensurate with their wartime efforts, advertising and public relations specialists responded with a comprehensive campaign to sell the preeminence of free enterprise ideology. Easily convinced of the need for such a campaign, the National Association of Manufacturers and allied industry groups had already launched a legislative attack in Washington seeking "equalizing amendments" to the Wagner Act, and redoubled commitments to the remedial economic education of their employees and the public alike.[17]

The passage of the Taft-Hartley Act in 1947 cut short an emergent film aesthetic of industrial human relations. The employer "free speech" provision of the new law opened the workplace and workers' homes to the kind of aggressive antiunion proselytization previously outlawed as an unfair labor practice under the Wagner Act. Taft-Hartley section 8(c) expanded the scope of permissible employer speech to include language containing "no threat of reprisal or force or promise of benefit." Moreover, the new law removed barriers to the presentation of management messages on company time.[18] Almost immediately, the sanction of unbridled business discourse resulted in a proliferation of factory pamphlet racks and letters sent to the homes of employees by upper management.[19] Correspondingly, letter writing became a predominant feature of the tightfisted theatrical shorts of the National Association of Manufacturers and allied industry groups, whose protagonists, like their eager sponsors, demonstrated an uncinematic propensity for writing things down.

There were notable exceptions to this approach, however. General Motors used films for intra-organizational communication, a practice limited by the Wagner Act to audiences of salaried personnel assembled for division service manager meetings and plant advisory groups.[20] Films for distribution to the club and school circuit recalled the corporation's first push into sponsored pictures following the Flint sit-down strike in 1937. By 1948 General Motors had placed in circulation fifty institutional and educational film subjects totaling 4,400 prints. Made available to any group on request, in 1947 GM films were shown 152,000 times to audiences totaling 15.6 million people, of which 70 percent comprised school groups. Titles included *We Drivers* (1937), a perennial favorite used for driver education; *On to Jupiter* (1939), the inspiration of GM vice president for research Charles F. Kettering, in which a doubting business executive learns that the world was not "finished"; and *To New Horizons* (1940), which featured an armchair tour of GM's popular New York World's Fair exhibit, "Futurama." Between the 1937 inception of film library activities and 1948, General Motors estimated that 117.5 million people had seen its films. The total cost of production and distribution came to $3,134,000, or 2.6 cents per head.[21]

Spurred to develop more and better motivational tools for the postwar era, the newly organized General Motors Employe Cooperation Staff contracted with the Jam Handy Organization, desirous of dramatic shorts broaching the discussion of difficult subjects with difficult audiences. *Experiment* (1946), described by a Handy synopsis as "an interesting picture," dramatized "the general subject of getting people to agree with you—especially in supervisor-worker relationships." "The acting is good, the direction excellent, the pace fast, the idea put across with a minimum of obviousness." A second picture, entitled *The Easier Way* (1946), "presents a case for motion study in particular and shows how skeptics can be convinced that motion study is a good thing." The picture "demonstrates how teaching can be done by indirection. This is a particularly invaluable technique where there may be resistance to an idea or where there are mature people to be dealt with who might resist 'teaching.'"[22]

The dramatization of appropriate supervisory behavior included *The Open Door* (1945), a five-reel all-dialog picture treating the thorny issue of foreman unionism (fig. 30). After the war, foremen frequently found themselves on the wrong side of the "collar line." Regarded by management as the linchpins of the communications-in-industry movement, foremen themselves often allied with the production line workers from whose ranks they had won promotion and looked to unionism for protection from managerial authority. Industry-wide, the rapid expansion of war production had resulted in an absolute increase in the number and percentage of foremen. General Motors, for example, employed between 18,000 to 20,000 foremen in fifteen plants. Reconversion posed uncertainties for those recently promoted to the position. Many looked to unionism as a mechanism with which to confirm seniority and arbitrate grievances.[23]

Subtitled "The Story of Jim Baxter, His Family and His Job," *The Open Door* addresses the ambiguities of supervision that trouble a machinist who finds himself promoted to the position of foreman. The film poses a question: Is a foreman a member of management, or one of the boys? The answer unfolds as Baxter contemplates foreman unionism with his co-workers, his supervisors, and, significantly, his wife. The film opens as Baxter thinks aloud in a flashback to another day at the plant where his foreman "gets the devil from both sides." Now promoted to foreman, Baxter wonders where he stands. Ruth, his wife, a character given the improbable dimensionality of a company stooge, argues against Baxter's taking orders from "some outside union official—who doesn't even work in the plant." Perhaps, she suggests, her husband should avail himself of the plant manager's Open Door.

Figure 30. Scenes from *The Open Door*. Courtesy of Rick Prelinger.

Returning to work only to find himself summarily transferred to another job—supervising women—Baxter takes up the question of foreman unionism with his immediate supervisor and the plant manager, who iterate the foreman's responsibilities as a member of management. As the film cuts from the plant office to the Baxter living room and, later, to the kitchen, Ruth Baxter reiterates the point as if completing a sentence. "A foreman is in business . . . must stand on his own feet," she tells her husband. "A man is promoted on an individual basis, not because of membership in a group." Taking the argument to the kitchen, she vows "free enterprise for the individual." The representation of foremen by a "third party," she warns, will nullify their usefulness. Stiffened by the comforts of a home life that preclude escape from his responsibilities to management, Baxter decides that foremen owe allegiance to the corporation after all.[24]

The following year Handy deployed the cast and production crew of *The Open Door* in General Motors' *Doctor in Industry* (1946), "The Story of Kenneth Randall, M.D." (fig. 31). The film focuses upon occupational health and safety issues, such as the remediation of hazardous working conditions and the company control of employee medical records, matters long contested by the UAW. Designed for "premiere" showings of film library subjects to General Motors Club audiences and guests, *Doctor in Industry* dramatizes a young physician's struggle against the wishes of his father as well as factory owners' failure to make industrial hygiene a function of modern management. In flashbacks the film visits the career of "Kenneth Randall," "the personification of those who saw the need for industrial medicine." Moved to action by a succession of accidents at a local mill, young Randall's success in rehabilitating injured workers earns him a reputation as a "factory doctor." Unimpressed by his son's altruism, Father cautions Randall that factory medicine erodes the prestige of private practice. Moreover, as a salary man, how will a physician represent the interests of both his patients and his employer? For a time, local doctors shun Randall, until they realize that they benefit from the patients that he refers to them. Gradually winning acceptance for his practice on the eve of the First World War, Randall now helps to rehabilitate wounded soldiers. Resuming his industrial career after the armistice, Randall develops an interest in environmental conditions, dust samples, and oils and writes a history of occupational diseases. Offered a job with a "large auto manufacturer," Randall realizes his lifelong ambition: to be part of a large organization. Becoming director of medical activities, in a final flashback Randall reflects upon the corporation's preparations for World War II: the hiring of full-time staffs of nurses and technical assistants; the importance of a filing system for employee medical histories; treatment rooms; control of dust and fumes; a medical department that works with safety staff; a philosophy of preventative medicine; an induction program for employees, especially women—and on and on.[25]

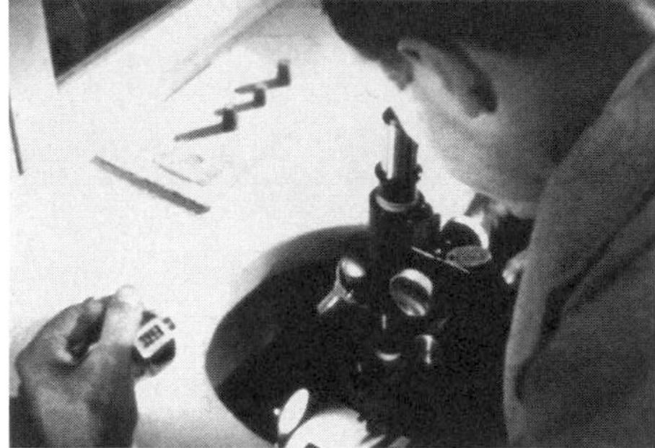

Figure 31. Scenes from *Doctor in Industry*. Courtesy of Rick Prelinger.

In both *The Open Door* and *Doctor in Industry*, the individual focus of industrial human relations finds dramatic meaning beyond the plant gate. The remediation of supervisors' unrest, like the remediation of factory environmental conditions, turns home and community life into settings for fact-finding, discussion, self-analysis, and accommodation, which determine the course of production.[26] The denouement of *The Open Door*, after all, unfolds in the Baxter kitchen, not in the plant manager's office. *Doctor in Industry* concludes with oratory and awards and takes place at the dais of a banquet hall filled with applauding professional colleagues and peers.

What is striking about Handy's postwar film work for General Motors is the way in which the concepts of corporate personnel management neatly converge with the cinematic aspirations of the industrial picture producer. During the war, Handy might have tackled the issues of foreman unionism or industrial hygiene in a filmstrip or film staged at the scene of production and punctuated with voice-over narration. By 1947, however, the abandonment of facile narrative economies had become a matter of cinematic pride. In a bid to further shake its reputation as a producer of "nuts-and-bolts" industrials, Handy began production of *Strange Interview* (1947), a six-reel salesmanship fantasy dramatizing Benjamin Franklin's "principles and philosophy of man-to-man relationships." Handy officials ranked *Strange Interview* with *The Open Door* and *Doctor in Industry* as examples of its finest work, and they directed sales and contract men to use the film to promote sales of "all dialogue" pictures dramatizing "intangible ideas" and "human relationships."[27]

For industrial clients who still insisted upon seeing tangible production processes depicted on the screen, Handy prepared pictures in two lengths: one was for clients who thrilled to a factory viewpoint, and a second, shorter version was for general audiences, for whom the scene of production was less attractive than all-dialogue drama. U.S. Steel's *Unfinished Business* (1948), for example, told of the company's "record-breaking peacetime production accomplishments, made possible by thousands of men like Jim Robbins." The picture appeared in twenty-three- and nine-minute lengths, in order to "bracket the target with two pictures to get maximum effectiveness per dollar." The former was directed toward stockholders and employees, the latter to the theater-going public.[28] The longer version committed to film a simplified statement of the corporation's 1947 annual report. Its lengthy statistics could be removed by a scissor cut, "in the interest of getting long usage." Handy's George B. Finch explained that U.S. Steel had commissioned *Unfinished Business* to counter criticism of its handling of the postwar steel shortage, by picturing "what they are doing to meet the unprecedented demand for steel—to show record peacetime production alongside of expansion operations . . . where their income is going . . . that they are taking care of their own folks in re-employing veterans." Because "they do not wish to appear defensive," Finch added, "the shortages we all know of are identified with the life of one particular returned veteran."[29] Not unlike Handy's wartime production *To Each Other*, the postwar era's *Unfinished Business* aspired to "Human Steel," intercutting the usual scenes of "unsurpassed productive capacity" with the promise of a loved one's return from overseas — in this case, the veteran Jim Robbins, whose poignant homecoming bore a striking resemblance to those in William Wyler's *The Best Years of Our Lives* (1946).

Making similar bids for audience participation, in 1940 the leaders of the National Association of Manufacturers turned to Hollywood in search of dramatic values that would lead to theatrical success. Consistent with the popular goal of its ambitious consciousness-shaping operations, the NAM Public Relations Advisory Committee concluded: "Generally speaking, the motion picture producers can do a better job for us, if they can be persuaded to do it, than we can do for ourselves." The committee proposed to undertake "a frank approach to John Hancock at Lehman Brothers, Mr. [Winthrop W.] Aldrich and others who finance the movie industry. . . . with this entree, NAM would be in a position not only to discuss with major producers the possibility of producing feature pictures reflecting favorably on industry (in contrast to "Grapes of Wrath," "Boy Slaves," etc.) but, more specifically, would be able to suggest industrial subjects to the producers of 'shorts.'"[30]

Thereafter, the NAM dealt exclusively in playlets dramatizing recognizable human situations.[31] In *Your Town—The Story of America* (1940), "Gramps" treats "Jerry" to a front porch recollection of "the industrial vision of one man [that] changed the sleepy rural village into a thriving manufacturing community, as scores of other American communities have been changed." Directed by Robert R. Snody of *Middleton Family* fame, the ten-minute short "embodie[s] in its swift narrative . . . the whole story of American history, civics and economics."[32] *American Anniversary* (1943) tells the story of "Joe Karnack," an immigrant who celebrates citizenship while eagerly eating an "anniversary cake" and explaining that in America there is "more cake than I ever see."[33] On the homefront of *Postmark—U.S.A.!* (1943), produced for the NAM by the Educational Film Division of Paramount Pictures, a father writes to his aviator son, "Bill Smith," "'somewhere out there'" (fig. 32). Promotional literature supplied to theatrical exhibitors explained:

> With all the vividness of the life, comedy, drama, and homely philosophy of "regular folks," Bill Smith learns in his letter all the news from back home, as written by his loving dad. It unfolds in his mind, as it does on the screen, all the warmth and tender feeling of those pleasant memories of familiar scenes in the comfy old living room at home . . . with mother, dad, and sis around a cozy fire.
>
> There also are the factory and all the gang at work giving him the stuff with which to fight . . . Main Street with its familiar church, its busy shops, its old town hall . . . the girl he left behind him . . . the local movie—all those things which go to make up the American way of life our boys are fighting and dying to preserve.

FIGURE 32. Poster, *Postmark—USA!* (1943), NAM Collection. Courtesy of Hagley Museum and Library.

> Out on the firing line, Bill Smith knows what that means . . . because he can feel what the "other side" has missed through years of regimentation and strangulation of liberty, thought, and individual endeavor, by dictator beasts who call themselves men.[34]

Three to Be Served (1943), another NAM-Paramount collaboration, "packed the whole story of American business—the theory on which it is based" into the "simple story" of three teenagers who "go into business to earn money for summer camp." Undertaking the manufacture and sale of chemical "garden sprays," "they find they must overcome all the traditional difficulties of older businessmen."[35]

By the early 1950s, executives whose companies had used institutional advertising during the war to maintain public awareness of their products and services looked back upon the experience as a successful period in the development of their public and employee relations. Those who had used institutional advertising to keep their company's names and products before the public during the war reported increased market shares with the return of full-scale consumer production; but more important, business leaders asserted that their well-advertised sacrifice and struggle had improved postwar government relations as well. General Motors chairman Alfred P. Sloan, Jr., for example, claimed that GM had come out of the war with "the best position in public relations that it had ever enjoyed." Sloan's remark was cited in a report compiled by "Po" Field, the Campbell-Ewald executive who had directed the auto maker's war advertising. Field buttressed the agency's claim that its client had achieved such a favorable position by the performance of its war duties "to the fullest" and the equally important use of institutional advertising to *"let the public know about it."*[36] The close association of General Motors with the government's war effort created an image of corporate responsibility not without political advantage or irony. The exercise of government relations in wartime helped business blunt government regulation in peacetime, Field explained. He added:

> The paradox created is this: That by generous cooperation and skillful attunement to the popularized sentiments, business helps government in the long run to defeat itself in the continuing effort to control business.
>
> The better a business acquits itself in popular opinion during a war, the more difficult it becomes for politicians to stigmatize that business later as a wholly selfish institution, blind to public interests and the peoples' welfare . . .
>
> So, in using the term "government relations," we have in mind the dual factors of *friendly* relations in wartime, *strong* relations in the area of postwar politics.

The development of a postwar political climate favorable to big business led Field to assert that there was a direct connection between the practice of wartime institutional advertising and the prevalence of postwar political conservativism.

> In our opinion, it is doubtful whether the friends of business represented by the so-called "conservative" elements in both parties of our present government could have won such strong public support, as recent *popular* voting has shown, had not business in World War II provided—and advertised—such unquestionable cooperation and unimpeachable patriotism.[37]

The wartime experience of selling ideas in the absence of products suggested that the peacetime continuation of institutional advertising might win for business an unassailable position of social and political leadership. The tracts of the Association of National Advertisers, the American Association of Advertising Agencies, and the Chamber of Commerce of the United States stressed that "the exclusive product-selling usages to which advertising was successfully put in the pre-atomic era are insufficient to modern times," and predicted that "public service advertising will be as effective in the competitive era as it was in the war."[38] The consensual veneer laid by wartime institutional advertising compared favorably with the corporate liberalism that emerged from the experience of industrial mobilization and further demonstrations of the shared responsibilities of business and government for economic planning and growth. A similar managerial thesis characterized the organization of the Committee for Economic Development and the Advertising

Council, whose public service campaigns promoted a conception of corporatist rapprochement with the state that was slightly more liberal than that of the NAM.[39]

Survey research brought to bear new kinds of private information that lent credence to strategies of meaning and drama. At a meeting of corporate advertisers, advertising account executives, pollsters, and publicists, sponsored by the Association of National Advertisers in April 1946, specialists told each other of the harmonious polity that awaited the development of new mechanisms to explain the business system to employees and the public. "You and I may disagree with many of their ideas and attitudes," explained Everett Smith of the Macfadden Wage Earner's Forum, "but the starting point in influencing them is to know the attitudes which must be met." Delivering a rousing pronouncement reminiscent of the call to arms issued in 1941 by War Advertising Council co-founder James Webb Young, BBDO's Henry H. Haupt exclaimed: "We have before us the opportunity to knock out the *only* dangerous weakness of the greatest economic system the world has ever known—the system's inability to explain itself." Haupt urged the assembled specialists to "get Gallup, Roper, Robinson, Nielsen and other researchers to go to work on new kinds of information—new techniques to interpret our way."[40] Claude E. Robinson of the Opinion Research Corporation opined that "management is for the good things in life; . . . but you wouldn't think so from gossip in the marketplace." Management's messages, he warned, "must be made to penetrate or management's leadership will go the way all products go that are not properly merchandised." "In manufacturing and distributing social leadership the same competitive rules apply" as in product selling: make a better social product, and merchandise the social product better than the competitor. If business insisted upon boring the public with talk of its "prerogatives," Robinson argued, let them "then be sold to the buying public in terms of the public's interest. . . . *It is an easy sale provided we talk simply about the buyers' interest rather than our own.*"[41]

Specialists seeking values beyond ownership concluded that the words "private" and "free" had been repeated so often and used so widely that they had lost their meaning. Decrying the overuse of "free enterprise," public relations counselor John Orr Young suggested that the expression's repetition as a slogan "has not added to its popularity or value, because the public hasn't known its meaning. It has grown to be a dull pair of words to the reader because he keeps seeing them in print without concrete specifications."[42] Henry Obermeyer, a correspondent of Bruce Barton's, wrote: "I have often heard you say that in advertising the client often tires of an idea before the public is even aware of it. In this case, however, it's the reverse: The public has tired of 'free enterprise' before the enterprising industrialist has even decided on what it means."[43] *Fortune*'s William Allen Whyte wondered that the public listened at all. A parody of advertising activism entitled "Bull Session" treated readers to a compilation of public-spirited clichés culminating with "Everything is everybody's job"[44] (fig. 33), a tag reminiscent of "Freedom is everybody's business," the slogan of the recently concluded Freedom Train and its industry-led campaign of "National Rededication." The situation had hardly improved by 1956, despite the attention of allied opinion pollsters brought together for an Advertising Council campaign on behalf of "People's Capitalism." Claude Robinson, who conducted a "pilot test" of the title, conceded, "There is no doubt but what the word 'capitalism' has limitations, but we have searched the dictionaries for a better word and do not seem to be able to find one."[45]

The admission was significant, for Robinson had spent the better part of a decade modeling the NAM's public attack upon New Deal–Fair Deal liberalism. With neither success nor exception, the NAM had opposed major New Deal legislation dating to section 7(a) of the National Industrial Recovery Act.[46] Anticipating the association's shifting political fortune with Republican majorities expected in the House and Senate in 1946, the NAM's leaders proposed to "project industrial management into a hard-hitting, constructive force—transforming management from its traditional defensive position of continuously answering the allegations of the collectivists." "Henceforward, NAM's representation of management will be at its proper station—on the offense—with a direct, positive, constructive approach to every problem that arises." The campaign began shortly after the hiring of Earl Bunting, the NAM's former president, as full-time managing director, and Holcombe Parkes, the former publicist of the Southern Railway System and the Association of American Railroads, as NAM vice president for public relations.[47]

Robinson's exhortations to "merchandise the social product better than the competitor" figured as the mainstay of the NAM's "pro-public" campaign to roll back the "Three Roadblocks": the Office of Price Administration, the "inequalities" of the Wagner Act, and government spending.[48] Though the NAM's public relations policy committee acknowledged that contention and reaction had contributed to the association's marginalization in the recent past, its members rationalized their perennial defeat in the Congress with Robinson's interpretive survey data, noting that "collectivist ideology has penetrated into the thinking of many segments of our population that are as American as apple pie."[49] Framing their communicative problem in this way required little modification of the NAM's political position, only the public perception of change, inasmuch as "views were presented constructively, not argumentatively, and 'in the *public* interest.'"[50] An article placed by Parkes in *Railway Age* magazine explained the operating premise "that the strength of anti-capitalist political leaders with the public lay in their promises of specific benefits to the electorate—whether they could actually deliver these benefits or not—while business leaders were weak in popular support because they promised nothing but only 'viewed with alarm.'"[51]

BULL SESSION

. . . Sometimes it doesn't take much to get a guy to wondering.

You probably never heard of me. I'm just a plain guy. Name of Joe Smith. But in a way I'm a pretty important fella. At least that's the way Doc Hibbard put it.

Guess I must have been really spouting off. But Doc just looked at me with those twinkling eyes of his. "Business profits too big?" he said, with a chuckle. "Why, son, they're as American as apple pie."

He pointed to little Tim Taylor—he's Ed Taylor's boy—selling newspapers on the corner.

"Tim there, for instance. When you talk about monopolies and more taxes on big business, that's the fellow you're attacking. 'Cause if you wrap up every big question about our free-enterprise economy, what he does answers it.

"Tim knows what the American Way is, all right. Lot of folks seem to think you can get something for nothing. Not Tim. No siree, you don't catch him running to the government for handouts. Don't hear him hollerin' about security, either."

Doc tapped his pipe and went on. "There was a fellow once put it pretty well—'Let not him who is houseless pull down the house of another.' "

Doc paused a moment and then, very softly, continued. "The codger who said that, son, was a fellow called Abe Lincoln."

I guess that's when I began to see things differently. And brother, take it from me, maybe it's time all of us did.

Maybe it's time we stopped biting the hand that feeds us. Maybe it's time we got behind the Tim Taylors.

Let's let the snake-oil peddlers yell all they want about their isms and their "security." Me . . . I'll take vanilla.

Yessiree, it doesn't take much to get a guy to wondering these days.

Everything is everybody's job

Figure 33.

"Bull Session,"

***Fortune* 42 (September 1950): 80. © 1950 Time, Inc.**

The NAM's most impressive feat of "pro-public" transmogrification was the suppression of its more belligerent members' intractable opposition to the Wagner Act. Acknowledging the political impossibility of overturning the act's guarantees to labor and the practical advantages of its revision by a sympathetic Congress, in early 1947 the NAM joined in supporting the legislation that would become the Taft-Hartley Act.[52] Heralding the NAM's "new look," in January 1947 a single-sheet newspaper advertisement headlined "For the good of all" called for "impartial administration of improved laws primarily designed to advance the interests of the whole public while still safeguarding the rights of all employees." Advertisements in April and May continued the campaign with the headlines, "How about Some Pro-Public Legislation?" "Industry-wide Bargaining Is No Bargain for You," "The Road to Freedom for the American Worker," and "Who Wants the 'Closed Shop'?" The "new look" targeted "The great, unorganized, inarticulate, so-called 'middle-class'; The younger generation . . . and The opinion-makers of the nation." The traditional run of printed disbursements included clipsheets and monthly periodicals, which were mailed to teachers, women's club leaders, farm leaders, and clergymen.[53] The pursuit of editorial effects extended to the modeling of an experimental "grassroots" technique, the "teen-age press conference," in which high school and college newspaper editors met industry spokesmen to learn and presumably report on the NAM's views.[54]

The campaign's "pro-public" appeal consigned labor to extra-public status. The campaign outraged rank-and-file contributors to the UAW-CIO's *The Searchlight*, a widely read paper published by Flint, Michigan, Chevrolet Local 659. Decrying the "Nasty Atrocious Mischief Makers in Other Words N.A.M.," *Searchlight* contributor Don Chapman took issue with the association's newfound concern for the enactment of "Pro-Public Legislation." Chapman asked: "Who is the public? The greatest portion of it is just plain everyday workers and the NAM doesn't give a tinkers damn about the worker, so what they want is legislation."[55] Industry observers wondered just whose views the NAM did represent, noting that the so-called "spokesman for industry" had consistently predicted the onset of a state-run society from 1900 right up to 1948.[56] Others, reporting the NAM's latest public relations "renovation," wondered how the oppositional tactics that had sustained its membership during the Depression could inform a positive program capable of meeting the challenge and complexity of postwar prosperity.[57]

With the return of open labor-management conflict exacerbated by the lifting of price and wage controls, strikes, and "pro-public" publicity, many advertising and public relations specialists concluded that what was needed was a campaign to banish disunity and distrust. Such thinking animated the corporate sponsors of the Freedom Train, a traveling exhibit of documents and manuscript materials organized with the financial assistance of Paramount Pictures and the Advertising Council and with the tacit support and encouragement of the Office of the U.S. Attorney General and the National Archives, whose Education Staff arranged for loans of the crucial exhibit documents. During the Freedom Train's transcontinental tour from September 1947 to January 1949, an estimated 3.5 million visitors viewed its 131 documents, which were mounted in three specially converted passenger rail cars. The "precious cargo" included Jefferson's manuscript draft of the Declaration of Independence, Thomas Paine's *Common Sense*, the Bill of Rights, Lincoln's reading copy of the Gettysburg Address, the Petition of the National Woman Suffrage Association, Nazi and Japanese surrender documents, and a selection of Treasury Bonds.[58] The preparation of an exhibit catalog fell to former *Cavalcade of America* historical consultant Frank Monaghan, who called exhibit organizers' attention to a letter written by John Jay, purported to use the word "Americanize" for the first time.[59]

In the hands of Advertising Council specialists, the Freedom Train became the symbolically charged hook for a year-long campaign of "National Rededication." The train's local appearances climaxed with a community-based ceremony in which individuals took the "Freedom Pledge," signed the "Freedom Scroll," and pledged to abandon partisan political baggage for "Americanism."[60] An experience most intensely merchandised to school and labor groups, the campaign's appeal to "common heritage" and "active citizenship" appeared at times to be little more than an outgrowth of the communications-in-industry movement. Leading Advertising Council specialists, however, stopped short of folding economic education into Freedom Train merchandising. They went to great lengths to distinguish the train's umbrella campaign of "National Rededication" from the "American Opportunity"/ "Miracle of America" economic education campaign that had been simultaneously undertaken by the council for the Joint Committee of the Association of National Advertisers, American Association of Advertising Agencies, and the Chamber of Commerce of the United States[61] (fig. 34).

While Advertising Council leaders quietly refused their members' requests to turn the Freedom Train into a vehicle for economic education, sympathetic specialists noted that economic education had only scratched the surface in using proven commercial techniques to frame an appeal. In a rambling article published in *Business Screen* magazine, the Psychological Corporation's Henry C. Link noted that surveys revealing the public's indifference toward capitalism reflected the inadequacies of the traditional techniques and means used to communicate its significance. "To be sure," Link reassured readers, "many are sold on America's comforts, but they are *not* sold on the principles, the taproots, which have made those comforts possible. The real America lies not in her present wealth, her present luxuries, but rather in the system which produced them." Dismissing factual presentations of abundance as ineffective, Link suggested that employers instead learn to emulate the language of emotional appeal. Link recommended that employers study, for example, the series

Figure 34.

Advertisement, "Comes the Revolution!"

Records of the American Heritage Foundation, folder: economic campaign, box 210, RG 200.

Courtesy of National Archives at College Park.

of articles then appearing in the *Ladies' Home Journal* that described the tastes and spending habits of American families. Each month the *Journal* focused upon a "typical" family, describing "how they live, what they earn, how they spend it." The series used "all kinds of families" "from wage workers to company executives." "People have hearts as well as minds, passions as well as brains," Link explained, "and when they *do* read one of the many ads or pamphlets thrust upon them, they interpret the facts in terms of their own emotional attitudes and moral standards. Therefore, we say, emotional appeals should be used to sell free enterprise even if this means a decrease in the number of facts presented." The way to greater meaning lay in the use of emotional appeals to model effective incentives. To this end, Link proposed that corporate communicators hammer home the personal meaning of free enterprise using first-person narrative material gleaned from 25-word description employee contests.[62]

The publication of Link's suggestion happened five months after General Motors' announcement of just such a contest. Sponsored by the GM Employe Relations Department, the "My Job and Why I Like It" contest (MJC) invited all hourly rate workers and some salaried personnel to "look at the doughnut instead of the hole." As incentives, contest organizers offered 5,145 prizes including refrigerators, home freezers, radios, automatic washers, and electric ranges and irons. Forty contestants received first place prizes of new automobiles and publication of their winning essays in a booklet entitled *The Worker Speaks*.

The contest idea came up in early 1947 at a GM Employe Relations staff conference. As discussion ensued, the Research Section staff seized upon the contest idea as an "opportunity to obtain *documentary and narrative material* of the type we were seeking—material which might subtly reflect certain basic employee attitudes."[63] Contest objectives included the encouragement of "constructive attitudes" among workers, and as an occasion "to place certain educational bulletins in the hands of employees that would indicate some of the benefits derived from employment with General Motors."[64] Collated data satisfied multiple needs, not the least of which, according to GM vice president for Employe Relations Harry B. Coen, was the documentation of the modern corporation as a progressive and stabilizing social force. A former Ford automobile dealer and production plant superintendent, Coen joined the Chevrolet Division of General Motors at Flint in 1933. Promoted to manager of Chevrolet operations in the wake of the UAW-CIO sit-down strike, in 1939 Coen transferred to the GM central office in Detroit as a member of the personnel staff specializing in labor relations, later becoming director of labor relations. In the preface to *The Worker Speaks*, Coen explained, "The inspiration behind this unusual experiment—an inquiry into the attitudes of General Motors men and women—was generated by the popular fiction that people employed in such large enterprises as ours were 'slaves of the conveyor belt'—'were just numbers'—'were without incentives to progress'—'were plodding in a mass to their hopeless destiny' and finally were ripe for revolution against the American form of government and the whole Free Enterprise System."[65]

From 174,854 employees (58 percent of the work force) came a flood of contest submissions. They ranged from one to twenty pages in length, and, if placed on top of one another, the corporation claimed, they would have made a stack six stories tall. Forty coding clerks trained by academic consultants in content analysis read, classified, and tabulated entries. From the initial coding and sorting of entries emerged ten themes most discussed by respondents, listed in order of predominance: "supervision," "associates," "wages," "attitude toward work," "pride in company," "management," "insurance plans," "pride in product," "benefits from wages," and "pride in stability of company." By cross-checking contestant entry cards and employment records, research staff compared "contest participants with non-participants as to age, length of service, sex, marital status, kind of work, etc." The result: "The majority of General Motors workers find many things interesting and satisfying about their jobs."[66]

The United Auto Workers greeted the MJC with incredulity. The UAW's Walter Reuther dismissed the contest as "a one-sided opinion poll of the workers" bought with "valuable prizes" for the purpose of gathering "employee statements to the effect that General Motors is a kindly, fatherly and understanding employer, sympathetic to the workers' problems and needs, which will later be used in so-called goodwill advertising." Stripping away the sociological pretense of "a frank cross section of opinion from its employees," Reuther charged that the corporation "wants material for a high pressure publicity and advertising campaign that will try to convince prospective car-buyers that General Motors employees are just as contented as Carnation's cows."[67] Flint Local 659's *The Searchlight* published letters unlikely to appear among the corporation's prize-winning sample. Under the banner headline, "My Job Why! Do I Like It?" the UAW's Rosco N. Hodges wrote,"I like my job because we have a union in our shop that has made it a very good place to work." A letter addressed to "Mr. Dupont [*sic*], Owner of General Motors," concluded, "So long as you have the CIO to make the Company do good things, I like my job. Signed, your servant, Joe." Another, addressed to "Mr. Chevrolet," contrasted union solidarity during the Flint sit-down strike with the working-together spirit fostered by the corporation's employee relations and institutional advertising.[68] Flint's Jimmy Kiger offered contest odds. "If you're a good writer and a Grade-A liar, GM will take a few crumbs from that mountain of profits you've made for them—and award you with an exquisite prize. You gotta be good at it though because your chance is 1 in 10,000." Kiger concluded, "These contest letters will be used against you and everything you've worked and fought for to build better job conditions through your union movement . . . in the circulars and pamphlets GM mailed to you they are dirty enough to ask you to get your whole family to help cut your throat!"[69]

Letters of first-place prize-winning contestants used attention-getting devices that even a trained advertising or employee relations specialist might envy. William Joseph Kelly of GM's Overseas Operations Division, for example, submitted an organization chart with his letter "to eliminate superfluous words and definite confusion in trying to describe my job to you." "I am an employee of one of the largest corporations in the United States, an Institution which in itself is a symbol of Americanism." Thomasene Lewis, a stenographer on the legal staff of the corporation's central office in Detroit, fashioned her prize-winning entry as a wartime reminiscence to her sister. "Each day . . . I learned about the operation of the many

General Motors Divisions through my work and through GM fact-filled publications, lobby exhibits, and 'Previews of Progress.' Through this growing knowledge of General Motors, I became aware of the part business plays in an individual's life, of the cooperation of business with the government, and the actual working of democracy." Lawrence E. Hunt, a test engineer with the Delco-Remy Division, submitted a one-act play "from real life," inspired by a MJC poster headline, "Get Your Family to THINK—WRITE—WIN."[70]

Contestants who demonstrated familiarity with employee relations media provided gratifying examples of their effect. While one prize-winning contestant reported that her co-workers dismissed the MJC as a ploy ("Do they expect us to tell a lie and win a prize, or tell the truth and get fired?"), other winning contestants described the employee magazine *GM Folks*, company exhibits, and even safety posters as benefits of General Motors employment. Completing the communicative circle of effect, one prize-winning contestant described her recent visit to the Freedom Train, while others mentioned Chevrolet's Soap Box Derby and GM's traveling exhibit of diesel-powered passenger comfort, the "Train of Tomorrow." Though none of the top forty prize-winning contestants mentioned the corporation's motion pictures, one contestant thought to enclose a homemade 16 mm film with his MJC entry. The six-minute silent Kodacolor film pictured "the contestant talking about the contest with his family, writing his letter and then dropping it into the corner mailbox."[71]

Though an employee-made film about the writing of a letter appeared as a novelty in the marginalia of *The Worker Speaks*, the letter-film was on its way to becoming the sine qua non of postwar economic education, which, like the MJC, capitalized upon Taft-Hartley's relaxation of top-down access to workers. As a narrative economy, the letter-film applied management's mass-mail idea to the screen. The result, a near-bottomless capacity for fact-laden argument, overwhelmed the emotional subtleties of dramatic indirection. Like a pink slip in a pay envelope, the letter-film could be nasty, brutish, and short. RKO Pathé's *Letter to a Rebel* (1948), for example, the sole motion picture product of the advertising industry's "American Opportunity" economic education campaign, features an irritable editor who exchanges epithets with his son's campus newspaper. Goodyear Tire & Rubber's *A Letter from America* (1950) features a Russian emigrant who writes of the freedom he enjoys as an American rubber worker. In Chrysler Corporation's *The Birthright* (1954), the strangest and most wonderfully inept example of the genre, an expectant father contemplates the uniquely productive values of capitalism's "creative discontent" in a letter to his newborn son. Each picture shared the narrative continuity of postwar corporate economic education: the comparison and contrast of ideological systems, the linkage of democratic freedom and free enterprise, and, most tellingly, a penchant for writing.

Taking up the pen, *Letter to a Rebel* (issued under the imprimatur of the Motion Picture Association's Eric Johnston) proclaims that "the American story of freedom, abundance and opportunity is the great drama in the world today." The picture begins as "R. M. Gregory," editor of the "*Monroe Gazette*," types a response to an anti-capitalist editorial published by his son in the "*University Daily News*." "That my son, Andy, was the proud author of this deathless prose startled me a bit." "I looked at Andy's editorial again, and I realized that someday *he'd* be running the Gazette. I couldn't tell him what to think. But I wanted to be sure that *he* was *thinking*." As the footage flashes by, the senior Gregory reads a bitter denunciation of his son's handiwork. Ruling out the possibility of reconciliation, the film visits the ancestral past of family liberals who were capitalists too—cued by great-grandfather's flintlock rifle, grandfather's abolitionism, and the many modern acts of consumption that make up daily life in Monroe: the miracle of canned pineapple at the local grocer and inexpensive gasoline at the corner filling station, the enlightened discussion of local issues by a free press in an atmosphere of "free labor" made possible by "free enterprise" in which "even the little guy" can triumph over "big business."[72] The script won the approval of the American Heritage Foundation's Thomas D'Arcy Brophy, who encouraged "exhibitors to show this film the week after the Freedom Train is in town."[73]

Goodyear Tire & Rubber's *A Letter from America* (fig. 35) adopted a more congenial tone in line with the corporation's longstanding inculcation of working-class citizenship.[74] The picture features "Karl," an immigrant rubber worker who describes the productive capacity of American enterprise in a letter to his sister "Freida" and her family behind the Iron Curtain. His purpose in writing, he explains to a colleague, is to expose the misstatements and untruths spread by propagandists "back in the old country." His immediate inspiration comes from a radio commentator who has suggested that listeners "who have friends and relatives over there write and tell them the truth about America." On the evening after his fiftieth birthday, in the fiftieth anniversary year of Goodyear's founding as "a typical free American enterprise," he begins to tap out a letter on his office typewriter.

The letter unfolds in a series of flashbacks. Arriving in America, eighteen-year-old Karl finds "none of the rags, none of the sharp pinched faces of hunger I had left behind." "I thought it was Sunday. Everyone seemed on a holiday." In a flashback set in the old country, little Freida asks Karl what he thinks heaven is like. "Oh, I don't know," he says. "What do you think?" Freida thinks "it is a big cool woods filled with wild strawberries. And you can pick as many as you want to. What do you think it is like?" Karl can only smile and shake his head. "I don't know," he says. But now he knows. "It's living in America."

Arriving at Akron, Ohio, he lands a job alongside "Cousin Rudy" at "the rub-

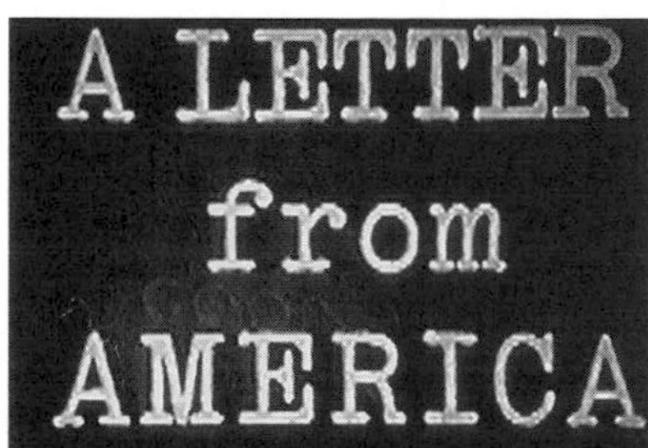

FIGURE 35.

Scenes from *A Letter from America*.

Courtesy of American Archives of the Factual Film.

ber company," where the two perform "hard, dirty work" in the compounding room. As Karl's guide to things American, Rudy explains the peculiarities of democracy. The first lesson occurs when "Kronsky," a co-worker, complains "If our government wasn't so rotten, they'd step in and tell these guys how to run this business. Heh, what do they care about the workin' man?" Karl quietly wonders that perhaps Kronsky has "too much free speech." Not so, says Rudy. "That's where you and Kronsky both make your mistakes." Taking Karl aside, Rudy patiently explains. "You could say to a fellow like Kronsky right now, 'Do you believe in American freedom?' And he'd say, 'You bet your life.' He'd be ready to fight for it. But—he hears someone say, 'The government ought to step in and do so and so'—he starts repeating it like a parrot. Never stopping to think that what he's yelling for would be knocking one of the props right out from under us." "So you come along, and you say 'He hadn't ought to be allowed to say such things . . . that's too much free speech.' And when you do that, Karl, you are taking a sock at another one of our freedoms." Taken aback, Karl protests that he did not mean it that way. "Of course you didn't," says Rudy. "But you understand don't you, that anytime you start to fool around with any one of our freedoms, you're liable to mess up the whole works."

A second lesson follows an exchange in which Kronsky warns that the installation of a mixing machine in the compounding room will put them all out of a job. Soon Karl is the wiser. Mechanical mixers, he learns, improve working conditions, reduce costs, and multiply employment throughout the land. In most cases, he writes, expanding economies of production brought by mechanization absorb willing workers—in his case, a less physically demanding job in the tire building department. His new foreman, recognizing that Karl "has stuff in him," suggests that he apply for the "squadron" of roving workers trained in all aspects of production. Exercising "individual initiative" and "freedom of choice," Karl takes up the suggestion. He joins the squadron and in the process takes a pay cut from the piece-rate wage paid to tire builders, in exchange for the opportunity to gain a working knowledge of the plant's operations. "Can you imagine," he asks, "that happening in one of those countries where the government tells you just what work you can do, and tells your employer what he can pay you?"

The final lesson plays out in a kitchen conversation with Rudy and his wife, Millie. Owing to Rudy's promotion to foreman, the couple have a comfortable middle-class home in Goodyear Heights. Karl's inquisitive "Rudy, there was a funny one today," introduces a discussion of shareholder democracy. A new hire, Karl tells Rudy, wanted to see the owner of the company. "I knew there was more than one," Karl wonders. "But who are they?" Who indeed. "There're three of them right here in this kitchen," replies Rudy. A quick trip around the plant and the surrounding community completes the picture, with the camera alighting upon the tire inspector, the stock boy, the scientist, the stenographer, the receptionist, and residents of the town including the small businessman, the banker, the professor, the farmer, the dress maker, and the piano teacher. "Rudy, that makes us sound like capitalists," Karl gasps. "We are," Rudy continues, drying a teacup. "Capitalists American style. In this country anybody who puts up the money to run any business is a capitalist . . . of course some put up more, some put up less. It's a matter of degree." "But you and me," Karl stammers, "a lot of people that put up their money are—are workers." Rudy nods. "Most of them." Karl asks, "Then what is the difference between capital and labor?" "Oh there isn't any, really," Rudy replies. More perplexed than confused, Karl wonders, "Well then what is all the fuss about?"

Segments intercutting sister Freida's spartan home in the old country provide the backdrop for the questions of her incredulous children. Hearing of Uncle Karl's "free enterprise," her daughter Ilsa asks, "Momma, what's a free surprise?" And well she might, for Karl's work on the squadron and part-time study at Goodyear Industrial University and special night classes at the University of Akron have led him to a professional career in applied scientific research.

A Letter from America concludes as it began, in the afterhours solitude of Karl's laboratory office. Interrupted by a telephone call from his wife (hinting of a family life removed from the scene of production), Karl promises to come home soon. Returning to his typewriter, he concludes: "Some of the newer crowd think it is smart to be cynical—to make light of the great principles that brought us where we are today—not realizing that when they do they are playing right into the hands of those who would destroy our way of life."[75]

Not unlike the immigrant Karl, the protagonist of Chrysler Corporation's *The Birthright* entertains an "inspired and creative discontent" (fig. 36). The film opens in a hospital waiting room, where "Jonathan Jones," a young Chrysler engineer, learns of the unspecified complications of his wife's delivery. Upset that nothing can be done to alter the course of nature despite modern medicine's progress to date, Jones becomes increasingly agitated. A physician, having delivered the news, offers "Here, take these . . . something to calm those jitters. Read a book. Look out the window. Smoke your head off. Write a letter to somebody. It's the best therapy in the world." Jones, now visibly relaxed, lights a cigarette and gathers himself at a desk and begins to write. "My dear son, today is your birthday. Congratulations . . . what should a father write to his son in these circumstances? When you read this, you'll already have a pretty good idea about what living is all about. Honor, truth, integrity—so what can I give you now that will help you most? A key to unlock the best doors of life. I know a word that says exactly what I want to say. Discontent—not the vicious destructive kind that robs a man of character, but the positive sort that has been behind every important accomplishment since time began."

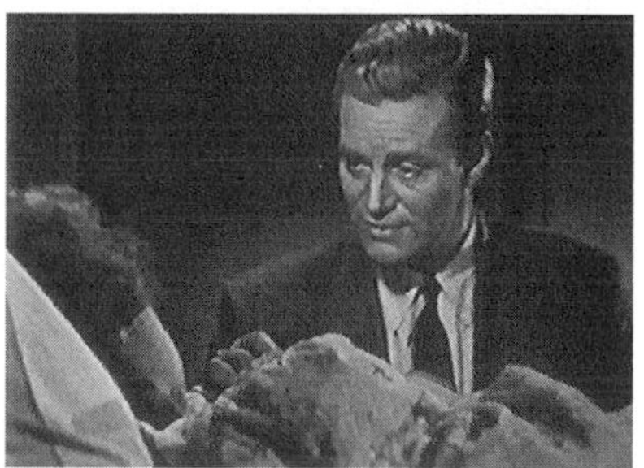

Figure 36.

Scenes from *The Birthright*. Courtesy of American Archives of the Factual Film.

Historical examples and Chrysler products punctuate the action as Jones writes into the wee hours of the morning. The first of several elaborately staged costume dramas opens in Plymouth, England, in 1620, with ancestor "Christopher Jones . . . an inspired and discontented man." A master without a ship, Jones becomes captain of the *Mayflower*. "Determined, uncompromising," "not content to stay in a land where it is a capital crime to think free," Captain Jones embarks upon a new way of life. "You might call it," his letter-writing descendant concludes, "a kind of American birthright." The same spirit, Jonathan Jones writes, animated the early republic. "Washington and the men at Valley Forge," for example, "had it. Theirs was an unwillingness to accept domination, the tyranny of wrong thinking by somebody else." A similar spirit inspired the heroes of American invention represented by "Sam Morse," who was "discontent with the slowness of communication between men's minds."

A soliloquy about "unsung heroes" segues to the story of "Sam Slater." Alternately described as "discontent with the selfishness and domination of greedy men" and "a fugitive from stupidity and greed," Slater treats fellow "guildsmen" who are violently opposed to the power loom to an extemporaneous speech. He promises "Better wages for less work. Easier weaving for less toil." Turning to the Chrysler Corporation for contemporary examples, Jones finds "the same drive toward perfection—the same lack of content with second-rate things—the same inspired restlessness" among its work force. He touches upon a draftsman here, a foundry man there, and even an assembly line worker, all of whose "determined, creative, restlessness" leads to production efficiencies, often despite the received knowledge of "experts." The corporation's engineering staff, who are "actually paid to be discontent," overcome obstacles and resistance to change as they develop four-wheel hydraulic brakes and streamlined passenger car design, the latter represented by the ill-fated "Airflow." Adding his personal experience, Jones recounts the development of the rubber motor mount and the 235 horsepower "hemi" engine. "'But what of it?'" he imagines his son saying, "'Research is our job.'" "Yet without the spark of creative discontent that makes a man seek truths above and beyond the call of duty, nothing of great consequence is ever accomplished." Looking to the future, Jones notes the corporation's metallurgical research, work with irradiated substances, and electron microscopy—all "magic tools" for exploring "worlds never before seen and to glimpse possibilities there that stagger the imagination. Because to anyone with the drive of inspired discontent, nothing is wholly impossible." "Well, son," Jones writes in conclusion, "that's the key, if you want it. Discontent. Inspired and creative. Never satisfied with anything short of perfection. No matter what the obstacles might be. This key is yours, as your honest American birthright."

Despite such bids for audience participation, *The Birthright* has surprisingly little to say to a work force otherwise unsympathetic to the impatient outlook and philosophy of its "discontented" protagonist, whose overbearing approach to labor relations appears drawn from the worst features of the communications-in-industry movement. *The Birthright* comes to a climax when a passing thunderstorm interrupts the hospital's electrical service, and thus the letter. Rushing to the hospital basement in search of the emergency generator, Jones finds only a hapless maintenance man in a grease-stained undershirt who is desperately trying to start the generator's balky engine. In a tension-filled exchange, so overplayed that it is painful to watch even today, the hero takes command as only an unsung hero can. "Lay off, you idiot, you're just running the battery down." "Give me your tools." "GIVE ME YOUR TOOLS!" The startled maintenance man wonders, "Hey, you a mechanic?" "I'd better be," Jones mutters, stripping off his jacket. Setting to work, Jones quickly discovers that the generator's "float hinge pin" has "crystallized completely." Installing a replacement fashioned from the belt buckle of the maintenance man, Jones cranks the wheezing machine to life, restoring the hospital's electrical service. Dumbstruck, the maintenance man exclaims, "By golly, I'da bet money it couldn't have been done." Jones replies, "There's always somebody that'll say that." The scene dissolves to mother Jones and her newborn baby, "Christopher," whose cries reveal that he too is "not too contented."[76]

The sponsored picture had finally arrived, a poignant symbol of postwar economic and political education. This could be seen in films-within-films, which altered attitudes and beliefs as their characters watched. As a narrative economy, the film-within-a-film constituted a slight improvement upon the letter-film. Instead of employing a character who composed and read a letter over a compilation of stock footage, it was populated by characters much like its working-class audiences, who admired the projector and dimmed the lights. The United Electrical, Radio and Machine Workers' *The Great Swindle* (1948), for example, features "Tom Gray," a working-class consumer invited to see the "The Big Squeeze," the film-within-a-film (fig. 37). Billed as the UE's "answer" to NAM pro-public "propaganda," *The Great Swindle* attributed postwar inflation to monopoly control in the coal, steel, and auto industries and to the NAM's successful attack upon price controls. *The Great Swindle*'s opening sequence introduces Tom Gray. While shopping for the weekend, Tom has found most of the things he wants, but not all of them. What Tom needs most, *The Great Swindle* suggests, is an understanding of inflation. While shopping, Tom encounters several plausible yet conflicting explanations for shortages and high prices. Standing on line at the local grocer's, he overhears a fellow customer complain that there is no butter, only margarine; no steak, only hamburger. "Newspapers," a narrator interjects, "blamed the OPA [Office of Price Administration]. Not only one paper, or two, but practically all of them. The radio blamed OPA . . . the

Figure 37. Scenes from *The Great Swindle*. Courtesy of Rick Prelinger.

people were confused." Next, Tom passes two men on a street corner arguing the logic of "the more you produce, the more you buy. Production goes up, prices go down." Seeking refuge from the mounting din of claims and counter-claims, Tom ducks into a barber shop for a haircut. But to no avail. Two customers are debating the contents of a full-page NAM newspaper ad.

> *Customer One:* Yes sir, our business leaders are not afraid to call a spade a spade. Listen: "If OPA is permanently discontinued, the production of goods will mount rapidly and through free competition prices will quickly adjust themselves to levels consumers are willing to pay."
>
> *Customer Two:* Bull, just plain bull.
>
> *Customer One:* My dear boy, they know what they are talking about. They are the men who run industry.
>
> *Customer Two:* Aw, they're just a bunch of sharks.
>
> *Customer One:* Listen. Just listen to this: "The members of the National Association of Manufacturers have no intention of rocking the inflation boat. Now or at any other time."
>
> *Customer Two:* Oh no, not at all. Just take off controls. That's all. Why brother, they'll skin us alive.
>
> *Customer One:* Young man, you sound just like a Red. These are the men that know what they are talking about.

As Customer One drops the newspaper to the floor, Tom bolts from his waiting chair, retrieves the ad, and quickly exits the shop as the barber exclaims, "Hey! You're next, sir!"

Digesting the NAM's free market logic, Tom dreams of buying a new car. This dream sequence features a salesman whose exaggerated presentation of the car and a succession of falling prices—"Special today (courtesy NAM)"—carry the argument. Awakening from his dream in the cinematic aftermath of a Republican Congress, "scrapped promises," and an "orgy of profiteering," Tom nevertheless rationalizes the inevitability of inflation. Tom's brother-in-law "Pete," however, will have none of it. Maybe, Pete suggests, Tom should join him for a free movie at the union hall "on this wages and prices thing. It's supposed to be good." In the union hall sequence before the screening of "The Big Squeeze," *The Great Swindle*'s film-within-a-film, Tom and Pete admire the local's new 16 mm projector. They agree that films build attendance, and in Tom's case, a dawning realization of the true causes of inflation. Having viewed "The Big Squeeze," "Tom begins to realize the necessity of joining [Pete] and the Union in their struggle for better wages and better representation in Congress in order to halt the hurtful effects of monopoly upon the common man."[77]

At the opposite end of the political spectrum, a film-within-a-film changes the thinking of the working-class protagonist of *Albert in Blunderland* (1950), a cartoon send-up of New Deal–Fair Deal liberalism. The animated "Albert" falls victim to the foibles of a "planned economy," which is parodied in a dream sequence in which he becomes "boss" and is made to witness a state-sponsored "free movie." Beset by the regulatory intrusions of the state "planning board," Albert awakens from the dream more satisfied with his "way of life" and disabused of the notion "that a government-controlled society would prove a better lot."[78] Produced and directed by animator John Sutherland of "Chiquita Banana" fame, *Albert in Blunderland* was one of a series of approximately ten MGM feature cartoons underwritten by the Alfred P. Sloan Foundation and distributed by the "National Education Program" of Harding College of Searcy, Arkansas. Between 1947 and 1950 the Sloan Foundation contributed grants totaling some $597,870 to the Harding program, a sum apparently dedicated to the production and distribution of animated features. Other titles in the series included *Make Mine Freedom* (1948), in which "Dr. Utopia" peddles a tonic "ism" in exchange for "freedom"; *Inside Cackle Corners* (1951), a widget-land of small appliance production and consumption; and *Meet King Joe—The American Working Man* (1950) whose denim-clad Joe reigns over a surfeit of consumer goods from a throne astride a conveyor belt.[79]

A comic book distributed by the CIO, in an unsuccessful bid to unseat Senator Robert A. Taft in 1950, offered additional evidence of the sponsored screen's centrality as tool and symbol of the postwar era's fractious labor-management relations. Entitled *The Robert Alphonso Taft Story*, the comic pictures the film-making exploits of a Taft senatorial campaign committee led by "J. Phineas Moneybags," or "JPM" for short (fig. 38). "My plan," he announces on the first page, "is to put out a moving picture of the life of our GR-R-REAT candidate, ROBERT ALPHONSO TAFT! We'll make 'em show it in schools, factories, union league clubs—oops—excuse that dirty word 'union,' boys!" In the following frame, a cigar-chomping accomplice chimes in, "Under the Taft-Hartley law, we can make the working people look at it too—in the plants." Taft campaign adviser Lou Gulay traced the comic book to New York publisher Eliot Kaplan, concluding that Kaplan's brother, the cartoonist Al Capp, had done the art work.[80]

Corporate public and employee relations specialists appeared to be as actively engaged in tit-for-tat film making with their union opponents as the capitalists of the CIO's comic *Taft Story*. If the United Electrical Workers made a film attacking General Electric, then General Electric would make a bigger picture, and in color. *By Their Works* (1949), for example, a "reply" to the UE's *Deadline for Action* (1946), opens with GE president Charles E. Wilson seated at his desk explaining, in the words of *Business Screen*, "what General Electric is and what it hopes to become." Wilson's opening remarks depict the General Electric research staff "not

FIGURE 38.

Comic book panel, *The Robert Alphonso Taft Story*. Ralph E. Becker Collection, Smithsonian Institution.

only as the possessors of great minds, but as ordinary human beings like you and me." Setting the tone for the film's presentation of the rest of "the people of General Electric," *By Their Works* toured "around the country to the many plants which make G.E. products." Though "General Electric is one of the largest corporations in the world," *Business Screen* concluded, "the film points out that size depends on the public choice, for the company truly operates at the pleasure of the people."[81]

Among the cinematic exceptions in the field of corporate communications was Standard Oil of New Jersey's *Louisiana Story* (1949). Filmed on location in Louisiana's Petit Anse Bayou country by documentarian Robert Flaherty, the picture takes as its theme the harmonious coexistence of floating oil rigs and Cajun culture, as experienced through the eyes of a curious young boy. Flaherty undertook the project in 1946 with assurances from Jersey's public relations department that it would not exploit the picture directly, a policy consistent with the corporation's other ventures in photography and painting.[82] Jersey specialists specifically rejected the dominant discourse of "economic education" that sold the "Free Enterprise system per se." Specialists instead recommended "an indirect approach . . . based on a well-conceived communications effort built around the Company rather than dealing with 'understanding the business system.'"[83]

In contrast, the NAM's resumption of dramatic film production after Taft-Hartley signaled a renewed bid for public attention. In *The Price of Freedom* (1949), the association's most ambitious postwar film, the son of a newspaper editor visits Germany and learns how freedom had eroded in an atmosphere of mistrust, disunity, and apathy. He recognizes these very conditions in his hometown upon returning to America[84] (fig. 39). The picture featured a Hollywood cast, high production values, and a "philosophy of idea communication." The NAM's Holcombe Parkes explained that the "philosophy of idea communication through the motion picture medium . . . , while not new, has not heretofore been a feature of sponsored films." "This philosophy," Parkes continued, "discards the fiction of the '12 year old mentality' of the average movie audience and substitutes for that limiting fiction the concept of the audience as a group of thinking Americans thoroughly capable both

Figure 39.

Pamphlet, *The Price of Freedom* (1949), NAM Collection.

Courtesy of Hagley Museum and Library.

of grasping ideas without being clubbed over the head and of voluntarily contributing a translation of the ideas presented to their own lives and interests."[85]

Produced and directed by Jack Chertok, the Academy Award–winning producer of *The Corn Is Green* (1945), *The Price of Freedom* offers a comment upon complacency in postwar political life. Set in the familiar terrain of the village editor, the film opens with a flashback, as "Fred Vollmer" recalls the early days of his career at his family's newspaper, the *Franklin Leader*—"the smell of printers ink and paste . . . the clatter of typewriters and the rumble of the presses downstairs." Fred's success as a popular "Town Talk" columnist measures the depth of his aloofness. "Mac," the paper's elderly editorial assistant, tells Fred that "Town Talk" is a gratuitous feature that his grandfather and founding editor Peter Vollmer never would have published. "Slick writing of cheap gossip," Mac complains, "doesn't make a good newspaper. A newspaper has an obligation to make people think, and take a stand on things that count. That's the kind of newspaper your grandfather ran. . . . There was a man who ran a newspaper . . . not a sheet filled with a lot of prattle."

Challenged to write "something serious," Fred announces to his father and editor Tom Vollmer, "It's about time we took a stand on some things that count." Without inquiring of his son just what those things might be, the elder Vollmer demurs. He informs Fred that as the *Leader*'s publisher, he has "found it best to compromise on these things." The confrontation establishes the father as a trimmer whose reluctance to publish suggests that the time-tested truths of American conservativism require more forceful and youthful leadership.

His father's rejection begins Fred Vollmer's odyssey from "key-hole columnist" to crusading editorialist. Traveling to war-torn Europe, Fred visits his editor-grandfather's brother, Uncle Johann. A schoolmaster jailed by the Nazis, repatriated by the Allies, and recently returned to teaching, Uncle Johann imparts a "lesson"—a startling confession of complicity in prewar Germany's descent to totalitarianism. "Step by step the government took over control of everything for us—our work—our music—our theater, press, and radio—finally our *thinking*." Startlingly close to the NAM's longstanding analysis of the New Deal, Uncle Johann's lesson foreshadows the column that Fred will write upon his return to Franklin. Back at home, he discovers the tell-tale conditions of "apathy, ignorance and confusion. An atmosphere in which disunity and fear could be cultivated. I had to do something about it. I had to write it down . . . And this time I really had something to say—and I said it. I didn't pull any punches—I called it 'The Price of Freedom.'"

Again, his father is unimpressed. "Things," Tom Vollmer explains, "aren't that bad." Fred counters, "people don't have to be conquered by an army to lose their freedom. It can *slip* away . . . painlessly. . . . It can be traded for pretty-sounding guarantees of a better life without working for it." After consulting with the sympathetic Mac and rereading the piece (as the film cuts from the manuscript to the office portrait of founding editor Peter Vollmer), Tom tells Fred that his piece will appear on page one, effecting their reconciliation and heralding a new leading voice for the *Franklin Leader*.[86]

Industrial publicists and public relations executives judged *The Price of Freedom* to be obscure and of limited popular appeal. The editors of the usually sympathetic *Business Screen* magazine, for example, wondered what the disagreement between father and son was all about. "The son's articles . . . from the examples quoted, seem as innocuous and typical of most newspaper attitudes as the philosophy of Little Orphan Annie." The character of Uncle Johann—played "to the hilt" by Michael Chechov—was more credible. There the motivation lay closer to the NAM's "philosophy of idea communication."[87] Hill & Knowlton's Merrick Jackson confided to John W. Hill that *The Price of Freedom* "probably will appeal to a good many persons who take a somewhat intellectual view of the passing scene. It is less likely to persuade anyone that we are all in a war for survival." "It lacks, it seems to me, any tangible bid for audience participation. Few in the audience will be able to do what the main character did; namely, get his job back with his newspaper, change his father's conservatism overnight and publish a series of articles on the laziness, stupidity and confusion of his neighbors." Jackson concluded that "we are beyond the point of knowing just what to do and we need vigorous, articulate leadership. I am not certain we have it here." The problem, Jackson suggested, was not what, but how.[88]

The further development of the NAM's film dramas collided with the realities of the dawning television age. Soon after the premiere of *The Price of Freedom*, NAM vice president for public relations Holcombe Parkes joined Jack Chertok's Apex Productions, presumably to advance the concept of idea communication among the politically active businessmen with whom he had come in contact through the NAM. After *The Price of Freedom*, the NAM completed two additional dramatic short subjects with Chertok entitled *The Quarterback* (1950) and *Joe Turner, American* (1950). The NAM then invested in a film project that proposed something different: a telefilm series featuring regional manufacturing centers, plants, and facilities. The series became known as *Industry on Parade*. NAM director of radio and television George W. (Johnny) Johnstone conceived the series in the summer of 1950. Categorizing the existing supply of industrial and public relations pictures as "unacceptable . . . technically or story-wise" for television, Johnstone contracted with the film unit of NBC News. They produced a 13 1/2-minute pilot program with "footage behind the plant gate" that conformed to the public service standards of television "program acceptance," i.e., "non-commercial, educational and entertaining." The pilot and subsequent series won wide acceptance, and by 1955 weekly installments of *Industry on Parade* appeared in the nation's 285 television markets. Johnstone and his successor, Arthur Rank, described the series' voice-over narration format as an editorial virtue rather than a liability. As program publicity directed to the attention of NAM members carefully explained, "No live sound—actual voices, sound effects, etc.—is ever used. For this reason, no ceremonies, speeches, meetings, celebrations or the like are ever covered for this newsreel." After television syndication, NAM regional offices placed the films in school and library depositories. "As the inventory of back prints builds up," a press release explained, "and the program is integrated into the curricula of more and more schools, the saturation of the potential audience should become as complete as that of the television audiences."[89]

While *Industry on Parade* returned to voice-over narration close to the scene of production, the dramatic construction known as idea communication played on among the independent producers who found themselves on the ground floor of the telefilm market in the early 1950s. Jack Chertok, the producer of a filmed annual report for General Mills entitled *Operation '46*, went on to introduce a generation of television viewers to General Mills' *Lone Ranger*. From DuPont's *This Is Nylon* (1948) and *The DuPont Story* (1951), in which the company's present day officers played themselves, Chertok's Apex Productions proceeded apace, to telefilm episodes of the *Cavalcade of America* and the *General Electric Theater*.

Chapter Eight

Showmanship Triumphant

In the years following the Second World War, the leaders of the National Association of Manufacturers, Chamber of Commerce of the United States, and allied advertising industry groups redoubled their efforts to establish the preeminence of free enterprise ideology. The titles of their campaigns echoed the rhetorical inadequacies of business's concerted opposition to the anti-corporate features of New Deal–Fair Deal liberalism: "American Opportunity," "Our American Heritage," and the curious "How Our Business System Operates" employee education campaign organized at DuPont and General Electric.[1] Noting the proliferation of "economic education" in the late 1940s, observers began cataloging and criticizing the American business creed.[2] More recently, historians struck by the success of wartime industrial mobilization have heralded the corporate liberalism of business leaders who acknowledged the shared responsibilities of business and government for postwar planning and growth.[3] Other historians, more impressed with the veneer of consensus laid by wartime employee and public relations advertising, have argued that industrial mobilization taught lessons less about liberalism than about the sheer totality of effort and effect required to affect the apathy and indifference of Americans toward their business system.[4]

If that totality of effort and effect led to the rhetorical excesses of the American Way and the remedial economic education of bar graphs and pie charts, its dramatization demanded the props and settings of an idealized private life, and of entertainment unimaginable twenty years before. By the early 1950s, for example, General Electric vice president for public relations Chester H. Lang marveled at the success of Bing Crosby's radio show in "pioneering in economic education." "Crosby's easy-going style," explained Lang, "sells free enterprise and good human relations in a manner that is enjoyed by the public and has won the plaudits of industrial and financial leaders."[5] DuPont's magazine *Better Living*, comparing "the Marx named Karl" with "the Marx named Groucho," asked: "Which Marx Gets the Biggest Laugh?" "Funny thing is, that only under capitalism is there ever enough money for comedians"[6] (fig. 40). The nation's public relations and advertising specialists had made the giddy discovery of culture recaptured or, at least, in sight. By 1954 corporate public relations specialists anticipated a generation coming to maturity with no first-hand knowledge of the Depression—or as General Electric's Lang put it, "no adult exposure to the violent anti-business propaganda of the 'depression' years." In the meantime, said Lang, there was work to be done combating the "Four Roadblocks":

- Centralized government, chipping steadily away at our traditional freedoms;
- Confiscatory taxes, threatening our ability and our customers' ability to grow;
- Politically powerful labor;
- And the outmoded, but still potent, fear of big business.

"The opinions the young people form now, as they grow up," Lang explained, "will determine the climate in which we will operate in the decades of their maturity." "Television offers us the most effective medium ever created by man for the communication of ideas and attitudes."[7] As DuPont's F. Lyman Dewey suggested, the depth of the company's investment in television, and in particular in dramatic programs, affirmed its executive committee's appreciation of the fact that there was no longer a question of "*shall we as DuPont representatives use these powerful tools of communication* but shall we use them well."[8]

General Electric had long technical and practical experience with the television medium. The public introduction of the electronic television system, including the establishment of scientific and technical standards, the manufacture of transmitters and receivers, and the inauguration of a program service all coincided with the New York World's Fair 1939. Though the fledgling system's economic future was far from certain, by 1939 television had become an institutional symbol of jobs, research, and preparations for the future (fig. 41). In February of that year a General Electric magazine advertisement asked:

> What Is Television? Just another gadget—another form of entertainment? No. It represents another step forward in man's mastery of time and space. It will enable us, for the first time, to see beyond the horizon. And, in addition, it will create new jobs for today and tomorrow.

FIGURE 40.
Advertisement, "Which Marx Gets the Biggest Laugh?" *Better Living* 6, no. 2 (March–April 1952): 34. Courtesy of Hagley Museum and Library.

KARL

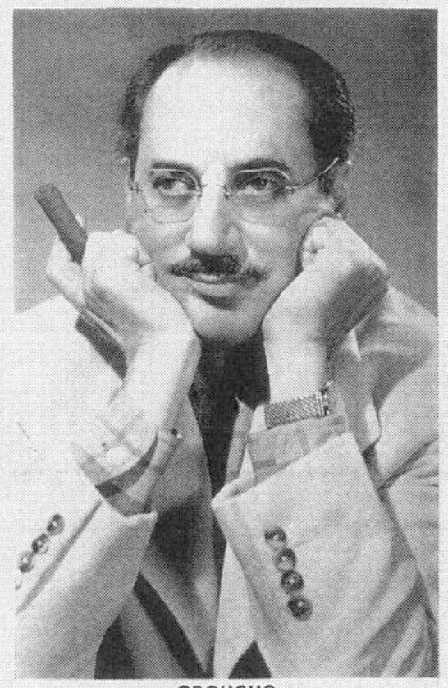

GROUCHO

Which Marx Gets The Biggest Laugh?

The Marx named Karl, founder of communism, was a dour character who lived in the Nineteenth Century. A deadpan kind of comic of the Buster Keaton-Ned Sparks type, his act was to say funny things as though they weren't funny at all.

The Marx named Groucho, on the other hand, is an out-and-out yak man. He's funny all the way.

You get Groucho's lines right away. Karl's become funny only over the long pull—a few decades or so. Trouble is, sometimes, that a lot of mischief goes on before people get the humor of it. Subtle, Karl's stuff is.

Like where he says capitalism leads to the concentration of wealth in the hands of the few and the impoverishment of the people as a whole. You don't get that one until you try to find a place to park down-town amid all the impoverished people shopping like mad in the department stores. When you do, it kills you. Nobody is *that* funny.

Or like where Karl says the only answer is for workers to seize the tools of production and hand them over to the government to run. You don't get that until you see newsreels of the new Russian automobiles, and see that they'd be sneered off any used-car lot in America. Then you're doubled up in the aisle, especially when you see that only Generals and Commissars are riding at all. Even Groucho isn't so funny, after all.

Or Karl's line about the miserable hovels in which workers must live, stiff with cold as they huddle about the charcoal brazier. You don't get that until Saturday night when you hear the furnace click on and you notice that the only thing huddled around the charcoal brazier are the hamburgers. That stretches you out holding your sides.

Funny thing is, that only under capitalism is there ever enough money for comedians. So when it comes to comics, we've made our choice. Groucho can stick to romantic roles, where both he and his countless admirers will have more fun. We'll stick to Karl. He's the biggest laugh of all times.

150th Anniversary

BETTER THINGS FOR BETTER LIVING . . . THROUGH CHEMISTRY

FIGURE 41.
Advertisement, "What Is Television?" General Electric, 1940.

What Is TELEVISION?

JUST another gadget another form of entertainment? No. It represents another step forward in man's mastery of time and space. It will enable us, for the first time, to see beyond the horizon. And, in addition, it will create new jobs for today and tomorrow.

New products make new jobs. That's been the history of radio, of the automobile, of electric refrigerators and movie cameras and air conditioning. It's been the history of hundreds of other devices and services that have come from the research laboratories of industry. That's why, in the last 50 years, the number of factory jobs in this country has doubled. And why, in addition, millions of other jobs have been created—selling, servicing, and obtaining raw materials for the new products.

It often takes years of costly, painstaking research to develop a laboratory experiment into a useful product ready for the public to enjoy. This has been the case with television. As long ago as 1930, Dr. E. F. W. Alexanderson and other General Electric engineers demonstrated television to a theatre audience in Schenectady, N. Y. When, after years of labor, television is ready for the public, it will bring to the people of America a new product that will add to their comfort and enjoyment, raise their living standards, and create new employment for today and tomorrow.

G-E research and engineering have saved the public from ten to one hundred dollars for every dollar they have earned for General Electric

NEW YORK—VISIT THE "HOUSE OF MAGIC" AT THE FAIRS—SAN FRANCISCO

> New products make new jobs. That's been the history of radio, of the automobile, of electric refrigerators and movie cameras and air conditioning. It's been the history of hundreds of other devices and services that have come from the research laboratories of industry . . . When, after years of labor, television is ready for the public, it will bring to the people of America a new product that will add to their comfort and enjoyment, raise their living standards, and create new employment for today and tomorrow.[9]

Looming above the copy on the page, a cathode ray tube beams an image of workmen approaching a factory. The upper right corner of the page pictures a worker assembling a power chassis. Subsequent advertisements featuring television abandoned the point of production for home-based settings, sporting events, and the occasional abstract representation of progress, each encased in a finely finished cabinet.

In public demonstrations of the new medium at the fair, the small screen achieved a personal focus that transcended advertisement. At the General Electric, Westinghouse, and RCA exhibits, fairgoers could see themselves on closed-circuit television. Some visitors recorded their friends' television appearance in snap shots, and exhibitors issued souvenir cards to their guests, certifying that "——— has been TELEVISED." Stylized radio-television living rooms invited fairgoers to consider the home as the location for television reception. For example, the "Radio Living Room of Tomorrow" created by John Vassos, the designer of RCA's streamlined television cabinetry, featured a "combination radio, television, record-player and record-recording set, facsimile receiver, and sound motion picture projector . . . built into the furnishings."[10] The 1940 fair carried out this vision in television home displays. Enlarged to nearly twice its original size, the RCA television exhibit featured a "Television Suite" of ten separate air-conditioned viewing rooms "furnished as typical American living rooms where television may be seen under circumstances approximating those in the home." Elsewhere at the 1940 fair, "America at Home," "an exhibit of living in America—around the clock and around the map," featured Vassos's "Musicorner," a room incorporating bleached mahogany modular furniture, indirect lighting, soundproofing, 16 mm sound film projector, radio, phonograph, television receiver with pop-up screen, and a small library of books and records[11] (fig. 42).

Among the fair's sympathetic critics, Gardner Harding wondered if the "vigorous conception of the future . . . may set new bounds to the resources of our daily living." Walter Dorwin Teague, the designer of the U.S. Steel, Westinghouse, and DuPont exhibit buildings, submitted "that better household equipment and better mechanical devices are of no real value unless they are easy first essays in the fundamental redesign of our world: harbingers of a wholesale reorganization of our chaotic scene."[12]

By 1940 that world had taken on a decidedly modern appearance, with the home presented as a metaphoric link between industrial civilization and "better liv-

FIGURE 42.

Designer John Vassos's "Musicorner," in "America at Home," "an exhibit of living in America—around the clock and around the map," New York World's Fair, 1940.

ing" in tantalizing proximity to television. Between its television studio and its viewing area, General Electric entertained exhibit goers with the "Phantom House," a "fast-moving and amusing demonstration" of "the story of Mr. and Mrs. Tom Morrow, newlyweds, and what happens when Mr. Morrow's mother-in-law comes to visit them" (fig. 43). The drama occurred "within a glass house, giving visitors the opportunity to see and listen in on this domestic triangle, and learn how the newlyweds solve the problem raised by the mother-in-law's insistence that she stay with them." The solution involved electric living, which dramatized "the story of electric appliances for the home with a light touch."[13] In this instance television appears not to have entered the picture to speed the solution, but it is hard to recall when, since then, it has not.

A symbol of the "world of tomorrow," television had become by the early 1950s the predominant medium for the dramatization of that world. Reintroduced to the public after the war, television eclipsed radio as the focus of family attention in the home, and from this unique position it assumed the promotional functions of the fair itself. It was a propitious time for television, whose technological form neatly fit the emergent stage craft of business leadership, which embraced the

FIGURE 43.

"Phantom House," General Electric exhibit, New York World's Fair 1939.

Edward J. Orth Collection, Smithsonian Institution.

objects, advantages, and pleasures of home life. Inviting prospective consumers to an open chair, the merchandising of receivers talked of expanding "horizons" and "vistas," while home "theatricalization" raised questions of orientation and behavior in television's space.[14] More than the static subject of a magazine page or an exhibit, the television home became an active setting and the actual location where the New Vocabulary of business leadership would play in entertaining ways.

Television was the beneficiary of radio's institutional sponsorships, and its leading program type was the dramatic anthology. By the late 1940s, corporate advertising and public relations specialists had made the anthology program their broadcast formula of choice. The dramatic anthology formula had been most closely identified with the institutional clients of Batten, Barton, Durstine & Osborn—United States Steel, sponsor of the *Theatre Guild on the Air* (renamed the *United States Steel Hour* in 1949); DuPont, sponsor of the *Cavalcade of America;* and General Electric, sponsor of television's *General Electric Theater.*[15] In varying degrees, each show was designed around an educational premise. U.S. Steel's *Theatre Guild on the Air* featured distinct entertainment and educational "components." By arrangement with New York's Theatre Guild, the program presented adaptations of plays with little bearing upon corporate "messages" (i.e., intermission talks), and vice versa. The separation of the program's dramatic and editorial control extended to U.S. Steel executives' admirable defense of their program in an era of rampant blacklisting; it simultaneously provided one of radio's last examples of corporate voice advertising read by corporation officers themselves. DuPont's *Cavalcade of America* continued to be, as it had been since 1935, a catalog of selective historical properties that had proved their value in easing the show's reluctant sponsors toward a more corporatist outlook succinctly expressed as "better living." General Electric, a latecomer to the sponsorship of anthology drama, was, of the three, the most conceptually advanced. Consistent with the goals articulated by chief executive officer Chester Lang, the *General Electric Theater* sought maximum entertainment value for the corporation's television investment.

The transfer of the dramatic anthology formula from radio to television in the early 1950s signaled anew specialists' determination to reconstruct a cultural climate conducive to the autonomous expansion of enterprise.[16] After the war, the executive officers and board members of U.S. Steel became willing converts to anthology drama showcasing company voice advertising. Their radio program, *Theatre Guild on the Air*, helped to promote the corporation's course of action during postwar reconversion, a period that saw the lifting of price and wage controls intertwined with negotiation of agreements with the Truman administration and the United Steel Workers of America.[17] Among BBDO radio clients using the anthology formula for institutional promotion, U.S. Steel was unique in contracting for program production and, effectively, dramatic control outside of its advertising agency. That responsibility fell to the Theatre Guild. Founded in 1918, the guild aspired to produce plays not then found in the commercial theater repertory. Co-founder and managing director Lawrence Langner championed the work of George Bernard Shaw and Eugene O'Neill. Through the 1920s and 1930s the guild staged their work and that of others including Maxwell Anderson, Elmer Rice, Sidney Howard, William Saroyan, George Gershwin, Richard Rodgers, and Lorenz Hart. Performing in them was a distinguished company of actors and actresses whose leading lights included Lynn Fontanne and Alfred Lunt. By 1945 a back catalog of some 200 guild productions provided a ready source of adaptable material for *Theatre Guild on the Air*. Under contract to U.S. Steel, the guild supplied plays and casts. Artistic control was retained by Langner, whose long career as a patent attorney representing such clients as inventor Charles F. Kettering allowed him easy access to the world of corporate affairs. The actual broadcast was produced by BBDO's George Kondolf, the former director of New York's Federal Theater Project. It was directed by Homer Fickett, the former director of radio's *March of Time* and the *Cavalcade of America*.[18]

The autonomy enjoyed by the Theater Guild in the selection and casting of plays, and the confinement of U.S. Steel's corporate messages to two intermissions, conformed to the broad goals of public relations education and entertainment desired by the corporation. In addition to the program's "commercial aspects," explained U.S. Steel public relations director J. Carlisle MacDonald, its "two main objectives were (1) To create a better general understanding of the affairs of United States Steel through a series of weekly, informative messages explaining the Corporation's policies and describing its wide-spread activities (2) To provide the nation's vast listening audience with the finest in dramatic entertainment by bringing into millions of homes every Sunday evening the greatest plays in the legitimate theatre." A cartoon in an early playbill, entitled "2 Ways to Keep Folks' Ears Glued to Their Radios," reinforced this statement of purpose. The first frame pictured a man pasting another man's head to a radio: "Get some glue, go into folks' homes, and literally glue their ears to their radios. Then whatever program comes along, they're stuck with it. Trouble is, they resent this method." The second frame pictured a man posting a playbill: "Put on an all-star dramatic hour like *The Theatre Guild on the Air* and millions of folks will gladly (and of their own accord) glue their ears to their radios. Week after week, too!" Exemplifying the rewards of such thinking, the first season's plays ("building bigger and bigger audiences for U.S. Steel") included *I Remember Mama*, *On Borrowed Time*, and *The Front Page*, and featured the Lunts, Walter Huston, Katherine Hepburn, Ray Milland, Helen Hayes, Frederick March, Pat O'Brien, and Walter Pidgeon.[19]

The hour-long *Theatre Guild on the Air* featured two intermission talks, prepared by BBDO and read by announcer George Hicks, the "Voice of United States Steel." A former ABC radio newsman who had broadcast the Normandy invasion, Hicks brought his dispassionate reportorial style to the delivery of each week's talks.[20] The first talk described the policies and objectives of the umbrella corporation, and the second described the activities of a subsidiary of "United States Steel—the industrial family that serves the nation." At intermission time, announcer Hicks served up chestnuts of institutional promotion: paeans to the widespread ownership of USS corporation stock among all classes of individuals and institutional stockholders, such as banks, insurance companies, schools, colleges, and hospitals; and to the re-employment of veterans, the upgrading and training of personnel, and so forth. An anthology of plays including two intermission talks published in 1947 suggests the program's aspiration to low-pressure salesmanship. A talk between the acts of Sidney Howard's *They Knew What They Wanted*, for example, described the latent consequences of U.S. Steel's vast scale of production, namely, the employment of men and the movement of raw materials. Striving to convey the personal meaning of it all, the text concluded, "So, next time you use any product of steel from a can opener to an automobile, remember—you are benefitting from the skills and energies of literally millions of men who have helped to transfer the raw materials from the earth into the steel out of which come many things to make our lives more comfortable."[21]

Over and again, the U.S. Steel board of directors expressed satisfaction with their radio program, renewing it on an annual basis from 1946 through 1949. Chairman of the board Irving S. Olds and president Benjamin F. Fairless remained sold on the bifurcated production arrangement, due in part to the corporation's prestigious association with the Theatre Guild, and in part to the public platform that the program provided for Fairless, who personally took to the air to explain the corporation's position during the steel strike of 1949. BBDO's U.S. Steel account executive Carroll P. Newton, however, chafed under the Theatre Guild's extraordinary degree of control of the program. Newton regarded the guild as a disinterested third party that was complicating what should have been a program-producing arrangement between client and agency. Relegated to advisory status, Newton nevertheless worked to inject Fairless's talks with a human touch, meanwhile attempting to enlarge the pool of dramatic material considered by Langner for the guild's part of the program. Believing that "we are seriously scraping the bottom of the barrel on plays," Newton failed to sell Langner the idea of using material from sources other than the legitimate stage.[22] Anticipating U.S. Steel's move to television, and with it the improved prospect of an agency-produced show, with MacDonald's blessing Newton changed the program's title to the *United States Steel Hour*. MacDonald cautioned Newton, however, to not sell anything but a Theatre Guild program when discussing the corporation's move to television. As discussions proceeded, Newton advised his fellow BBDO specialists not to sell any other than a dramatic program over which its sponsor could "maintain complete editorial control."[23]

The divisive issue of program control could not be as easily suppressed when the corporation responded to BBDO's blacklisting of television performers. While advertising and public relations specialists cited the subtle impact of their dramatic anthology programs in combating "roadblocks" from without, the greatest testament to the anthology formula's malleability lay in the lengths to which agency specialists went in checking the appearance of its misdirection from within. Perversely, the practice of blacklisting acknowledged the manipulative possibilities of dramatic production that program builders had promoted since the mid-1930s. Aspiring to more active client service in February 1949, Newton discussed with U.S. Steel chairman Irving S. Olds the steps taken by BBDO "through a special department in our research set-up to give our clients an immediate check on the activities of any person or persons connected with 'subversive organizations.'"[24] That same year, the editors of *Counterattack*, an anti-Communist newsletter busily compiling dossiers on allegedly "subversive" artists in radio and television, encouraged subscribers to write to U.S. Steel complaining of writers and actors appearing on the *Theatre Guild on the Air*. Rising to the guild's defense (presumably without checking with Newton), Olds replied, "Such individuals are considered on the basis of their ability in their respective fields, and in no way on account of ideological, social, or religious beliefs they may hold." Unbowed, *Counterattack* concluded: "U.S. Steel . . . seemingly doesn't care whether its money goes to Communist Party members or fellow travelers."[25]

As the practice of blacklisting enveloped commercial broadcasting, BBDO president Ben Duffy warned U.S. Steel away from the Theatre Guild's continuing to employ actors and actresses who were rightly—or wrongly—accused of Communist sympathies. Suggesting that even well-planned advertising sometimes achieves "'opposite results,'" Duffy wrote,

> During this past season, certain individuals have appeared on the Theatre Guild program—and at least one other is scheduled to appear—who may contribute to creating the "opposite results" we mentioned. While nothing may develop publicly, we want to go on record that your agency did and does recommend against the use of such talent.
>
> Again, let us repeat, it is not a question as to whether or not these people are guilty or innocent. It is simply a question of the public reaction to the corporation which sponsors them. We believe in protecting the advertiser's interest, especially in view of the fact that there is sufficient talent for radio and television without the use of people who could be questioned.

Duffy reminded MacDonald that contractually, neither U.S. Steel nor BBDO had the right to approve casts, and he recommended that no future contract with the Theatre Guild "be approved without this right spelled out unequivocally."[26]

A letter received from the Syracuse, New York, headquarters of American Legion anti-Communist activist and grocery store owner Laurence A. Johnson brought the matter to a head. In early November of 1952, Newton reported that Lawrence Langner had "offered to furnish to us a list of names from which the Guild would agree to cast." BBDO, in turn, would "study these names and make recommendations on them." Furthermore, "any *new* people not on that list would be checked in advance of engagement." Despite the fact that BBDO's "experience has convinced us that we *cannot get proof* of the validity of charges that have been made against certain performers," Newton nevertheless concluded, "we should be in as strong and safe a position as it is possible to be on such a controversial subject."[27]

While Newton and Langner wrangled over *Theatre Guild on the Air*'s dramatic control, Newton found himself at odds with a minority of U.S. Steel's board of directors who wished to conduct the corporation's affairs without the expense of a radio program or, for that matter, advertising of any kind. While Olds, Fairless, and a majority of the board consistently voted to renew their *Theatre Guild on the Air* program, a minority led by U.S. Steel finance committee chairman Enders M. Voorhees criticized the program's million-dollar-plus annual appropriation, an amount certain to increase if and when the corporation moved to television. Newton believed

Voorhees to be the leader of "powerful influences" within the corporation who were "working to get many more officials of U.S. Steel actually on the program to read their messages." The same board members, Newton noted, had "always wanted to stand up and counterattack all the various elements of the Administration who are hostile to big business and to U.S. Steel."[28]

Fearing that the board might indeed vote to abandon the program, Newton argued that U.S. Steel could not afford to abandon its advertising in "the confused and critical atmosphere of public opinion which is going to prevail in the country up to and perhaps beyond, the election of 1952." Awaiting the board's decision in January 1950, Newton proposed a bridge of institutional advertisements. Though proposed for "national magazines," the campaign's platform-building objective would become increasingly familiar as a rationale for cumulative investments in television. On behalf of BBDO (with apologies to Alexander Pope), Newton explained,

> "Little drops of water, little grains of sand, make the mighty ocean and the pleasant land."
>
> We are trying to build a better landscape for the Corporation. We advise you not to attempt to do it in advertisements full of arguments and the statement of principles. Instead we suggest a continuing series of advertisements built on human interest, in which cumulative effect would gradually, week by week, build this subconscious impression in the public mind: "That's a pretty good company! A company like that is a good thing for the United States." What we envision for the corporation in the current atmosphere of public opinion is something more human, more interesting.[29]

Renewing their radio program for 1951, the board made available limited funds for television, approving plans for a series of occasional telecasts.

U.S. Steel's first telecast came on Christmas night of 1951, with a special presentation of Charles Dickens' *A Christmas Carol.* The hour-long production starred Sir Ralph Richardson as Ebenezer Scrooge. The opening credits are superimposed upon a snowy night in Dickens's London, and then the scene shifts to the warmth of a contemporary urban apartment. Outside, visible through a picture window decorated with a large wreath, snow falls on the city below. Seated on a couch in front of the window, announcer George Hicks introduces corporation chairman Irving S. Olds, "to speak for U.S. Steel and to tell you a little bit about why tonight's play was selected." Olds begins,

> Good evening. I should like to tell you how pleased I am to be permitted to say a few words of welcome on behalf of United States Steel. You are participating in our first venture in television. I trust you may find this program to be a fitting end to what I hope has been for you a most happy Christmas Day—one spent pleasantly at home with those who are close and dear to you.

> Tonight, United States Steel sponsors a television presentation of one of the best known, and I believe the most touching of all Christmas stories, Charles Dickens' *A Christmas Carol*. A distinguished cast has been assembled to bring you this beloved, century-old tale, which so vividly illustrates the power of human love and sympathy. Its spiritual character gives a deep and sacred meaning to Christmas. It is my fervent prayer that this presentation again tonight may in some way aid in establishing peace on earth and bringing good will to men everywhere.[30]

The opening scene establishes Richardson's Scrooge as a social malcontent with neither sympathy nor time for the less fortunate. So too is the ghost of Jacob Marley, "doomed to wander here, because in life I never looked upon the goodness of my fellow men. My spirit never went beyond our counting house!"

Though many latter-day adaptations of the *Carol* have emphasized the Christmas feast at the home of the Cratchits, the denouement of U.S. Steel's *Carol* occurs in the spartan office of Scrooge and Marley on the next business day.[31] Awakened from his dark dream, Scrooge exhibits the manner of social reclamation and purpose not unlike that which Newton, Duffy, and Barton urged upon their institutional clients. Encouraging Cratchit to stoke up the office coal stove, Scrooge declares, "It's you Bob Cratchit, to whom I am indebted," and he announces an increase in Cratchit's wages, proclaiming, "Prosperity reigns where harmony dwells."[32]

Entering television on a regular basis in October 1953, the new *United States Steel Hour* debuted with "P.O.W.," a dramatization of "brainwashed" Korean War veterans struggling to adjust to life at home. Announcements of Steel's upcoming television schedule noted that the *Steel Hour* would emphasize "upbeat" drama taking "Americana" for its theme, featuring adaptations of theatrical plays and original works for television. Programs telecast in the following weeks included *Hope for a Harvest, Tin Wedding, Man in Possession,* an adaptation of William Dean Howell's *The Laphams of Boston,* and, direct from Broadway, Henrik Ibsen's *Hedda Gabler,* starring Tallulah Bankhead.[33]

With the formula's successful transfer to television in 1953 appeared new and dramatically experienced critics, too much involved in the program. BBDO's Bruce Barton and Carroll Newton found themselves spending more, rather than less, time with U.S. Steel officials and, on occasion, their wives, fending off complaints of programs' psychological dimensions and "defeatist" attitude. Among them, Barton reported, Mrs. Clifford F. Hood wondered, "'Why can't we have some plays built on the Horatio Alger theme that America is a great place for a young man to make his future, as great as it ever was,' etc."[34] Newton had in fact tried to inject such material into the show. "The fact of the matter is, Bruce," Newton explained, "that it is very hard to find good stories of this kind and even more difficult to get good writers to write originals on this theme."[35]

The production of commercials posed no such difficulty. Instead of the talks and progress reports from Fairless and other officials, viewers met "Mary Kay and Johnny, United States Steel's television family team." Typical presentations featured all-steel Cyclone fence ("the all-day babysitter") and U.S. Steel kitchens ("so many cabinets—you'll want them all"). One memorable series of commercials aired during *The Laphams of Boston* and featured U.S. Steel Homes' "The Westerner," a prefabricated steel house erected on a television sound stage. "The star," a press release explained, "is on the large side . . . the biggest product ever sold on the air." "Her roof and front were cut away, so that Mary Kay and Johnny . . . could stroll with the camera and an estimated 15 million viewers through the six-room, completely-furnished house."[36]

The DuPont Company's leap to television in 1952 offered further evidence of the company's satisfaction with its dramatic anthology the *Cavalcade of America*. On radio, the *Cavalcade* had established the dramatic anthology as the broadcast formula of choice among a generation of public relations and advertising specialists, and with its reluctant sponsor, in a period when continuous institutional promotion was not generally practiced and the value of radio in prosecuting even short-term campaigns was not fully appreciated. Because its sponsor's previous use of radio had been limited to underwriting the anti-administration talks of the American Liberty League, the National Association of Manufacturers, and other business groups, *Cavalcade* represented a signal event in the conservative seedtime of modern broadcast entertainment. Though the *Cavalcade*'s sponsors never relinquished their editorial prerogative, after 1939 they quietly acceded to their specialists' attempts to bury its more troublesome aspects in the subtext of "Better Things for Better Living . . . through Chemistry."

The postwar *Cavalcade of America* exorcised whatever doubts its sponsors may have harbored about the value of dramatic radio production. The *Cavalcade* provided a refuge of sanity and reason in an otherwise treacherous popular culture, in which, as one listener complained, "the villain is always a manufacturer, a business man, or anyone who has accumulated a little wealth." "What a relief it is to hear a program which tells the truth about the American scene, and does it in an interesting story fashion."[37] The *Cavalcade*'s grounding in the past certainly appealed to the company's executive committee, who deemed the formula appropriate given the DuPont Company's history. From time to time the program revisited the story of company founder Eleuthère Irénée du Pont, a script that company officials and family members conscientiously combed for interpretive errors and omissions. Invited to comment on a script entitled "An American from France" that aired in 1950, for example, former company president and chairman Lammot du Pont questioned the use of the word "democracy." "It is my understanding," du Pont explained, "that in the early days of this country, democracy was not regarded as a desirable form of government—in fact, the authors of the Constitution guarded against it, the word is not mentioned in the Constitution, and, in certain respects, a republican form of government is guaranteed. The attraction of democracy could not have brought men to our shores. 'Liberty' would be a better word to use, although 'freedom' would do."[38]

The DuPont Company executive committee's growing acceptance of entertainment could be seen in the *Cavalcade*'s introduction of contemporary story subjects and a willingness to mix the actual and the fantastic. While all *Cavalcade* episodes traded in the suspension of disbelief to revisit the historical past, after the war specialists increasingly used devices such as dreams to move the story along. In one "radio fantasy," for example, a Freedom Train visitor beset by "these uncertain times" and "strikes, inflation, another war?" experiences exhibit documents in a series of encounters with their authors.[39] The commemoration of the one hundredth anniversary of the birth of Thomas Alva Edison, for another, garnered an endorsement of radio entertainment as a rational strategy of business discourse, which, in Edison's case, could be dramatized as the culmination of his life's work in science and invention. "In a way, a broadcast like this is the climax of things I worked at," the *Cavalcade*'s Edison explains. "In a way I can't help being here. This microphone and the tubes in your radio. I had a hand in them. So when those tubes light up and bring you a voice from far off, in a way it's me talking." The broadcast opens as Edison, making ready for yet another evening of honorific banquet talk, demonstrates his latest "amazing invention," the "talk-harnessing machine." "All those speeches, all that talk, all that hot air. If only it could be harnessed for useful work," he wonders. Connecting a diaphragm to a ratchet, then to a doll, and then to a saw resting upon a block of wood, Edison speaks, the diaphragm fills, the doll saws. "After dinner oratory converted into labor benefiting man!"[40]

Freed of "all that hot air," the *Cavalcade*'s free enterprise subtext continued unabated through the late 1940s. DuPont's William H. Hamilton described the program's editorial objective as "Positive Americanism." Hamilton explained, "It is just another way of expressing the American way of life. We have endeavored to acquaint our listening audience with a keener, broader understanding and appreciation of the freedoms that have secured for America the highest standard of living of any country in the world—the belief in the individual which strengthens our democracy politically and affords us tremendous economic strength."[41] At times, company public relations and advertising specialists seemed incapable of any other than dramaturgical expression. When the DuPont Company became entangled in an antitrust suit in 1949, for example, the *Cavalcade* dramatized the benefits of large-scale monopoly in programs like "Wire to the West," the story of the Western Union's consolidation of rival telegraph companies; "Beyond Cheyenne," "a story about how the packing industry started as small business and became big business and in so doing made better and cheaper meat available to the American people"; and "The Immortal Blacksmith," about the origin of the electric motor. Invented by Tom Davenport, it "never amounted to anything until big companies took hold of it and converted its power into conveniences for the millions."[42] Its sponsor's reluctance to broadcast a more explicit defense spoke for a certain dramatic success.

Yet by 1949 the *Cavalcade*'s producers had begun to chafe under their client's constraints on "action and attitude of the performers," which BBDO radio department head Arthur Pryor believed were "modifying and emasculating our shows." The *Cavalcade*, Pryor concluded, was "too precious" and "not gutsy enough."[43] *Cavalcade* musical director John Zoller acknowledged the demographic disparity among listeners in the 20- to 35-year-old age category. "I think all of us know what the elements are that help bring in the high ratings. But we all know, too, that many of these elements are not generally wanted by the client." "We can continue to strive for that good clean show, with PA [Positive Americanism], with gentle words and gentle music and gentle sounds, kind to all, hurting no one, and keeping our regular listeners happy; or, we can take a tip from the Mr. D.A.s and the F.B.I.s." Seeking a solution, Pryor proposed that the group "consider the material for its dramatic value first, and justify it from the PA and historical standpoint second."[44] Along this line, other BBDO specialists questioned history's relevance to postwar audiences. BBDO's Bill Millard, for example, sought to relax the program's exclusive emphasis upon the American past by interjecting contemporary events and personalities. He wanted "Names in the news like Eisenhower or Lucius Clay or Ralph Bunche . . . action which has had direct effects on the lives of *Cavalcade* listeners. . . . The story of the Berlin airlift is much more interesting today than Washington's crossing of the Delaware."[45] For producer Kenyon Nicholson, the *Cavalcade* had plateaued with a self-selecting audience for whom "[n]either contemporary [n]or historical subjects make much difference. . . . *Cavalcade* seems to have created its own followers—an audience conditioned to Better History through DuPont."[46]

DuPont's decision to adapt its *Cavalcade* radio properties for television allowed little consideration for what has since become known as the golden age of television drama. Like many sponsors, DuPont executives calmly justified their decision for television with projected declining costs per thousand viewers, which by 1955 would be comparable to the peak year achieved by radio in 1948.[47] Commenting upon the program's transfer to television in 1952, DuPont Company publicist Lyman Dewey confidently asserted that the typical *Cavalcade* viewer "abstracts [*sic*] the meaning for himself" without need of an explicit statement from the company identifying DuPont with the "rugged scene of America's struggle."[48] A brochure promoting the *Cavalcade*'s second television season suggested: "It's America's own thrilling story . . . replete with drama, romance, humor! Each performance brings you a true story of the achievements of the men and women who have given us our heritage. Here's an exciting, inspirational TV show you'll want your whole family to enjoy—regularly."[49] It appears that the DuPont Company never considered any other than a *Cavalcade* television program. DuPont's first television experience was an experimental *Cavalcade* telecast of "Children of Old Man River" on NBC's WNBT in February 1946. Not until 1950 did the company's executive committee authorize an active investigation of television, approving a budget for the production of four *Cavalcade* films to be used as a "television test."[50] A complete reliance on telefilms ensured the prescribed interpretation of scripts, expanded the scope of production limited by the television studio, and lent the program a finished look that specialists felt reflected the company's stature. The use of telefilms allowed for additional economies in the rebroadcast and syndication of programs.[51] Shorn of their four-minute "Story of Chemistry" commercials, *Cavalcade* telefilms later found their way into circulation in schools, where they were "put to good use."[52]

By early 1952, BBDO's Arthur Pryor, Harold Blackburn, "Hi" Brown, and John Driscoll had evaluated eighteen "approved" *Cavalcade* radio subjects for their television "picture values." Not surprisingly, six Benjamin Franklin scripts led the list. Specialists especially valued Franklin as a character of wit and inventiveness. The first regularly scheduled *Cavalcade* telecast entitled "Poor Richard" continued the tradition. In the drama the "old and obstinate" Franklin is sent to delay surrender talks with the British, allowing General Washington to escape capture and fight another day. The program's conclusion finds Franklin "on his knees praying for Liberty and Peace and the ability to deserve them."[53] Later telecasts reprised other *Cavalcade* favorites, including Eli Whitney's implementation of serial musket production in "The Man Who Took a Chance." The tale begins with the roll of a printed crawl upon the screen: "The story of our country is told best in the lives of its people . . . those men and women whose courage and vision have led us forward!" From President Thomas Jefferson, young Whitney learns the importance of thinking "big." "We're a young country," Jefferson explains. "We must prosper and grow. But today we are in grave danger. If we are to survive we must call on men with initiative and daring. Men who think in big terms. You Whitney, are such a man." Closing the telecast, a four-minute commercial "Story of Chemistry" contrasts the spinning wheel with modern textile and dye making.[54]

The new *Cavalcade* did find an audience in the competitive environment of 1950s television. The easing of the program's radio audience into the new setup was accomplished with the continuation of radio broadcasts through the first six months of the *Cavalcade*'s television season. Sadly, some radio listeners could not come along. For example, Elma H. Franklin, the wife of a blind listener, wrote of her husband's disappointment. A small stockholder and longtime listener, he had considered *Cavalcade* "his *special dividend* from DuPont."[55] From the fringe of television reception in rural Indiana came a letter from Edward L. Johnson, a listener whose poignant reminiscence of growing up with the *Cavalcade* best summed up what the program had done for the DuPont Company. Johnson wrote:

> I am now twenty-eight years old and can remember some of the "milestones" of "Cavalcade's" radio lifetime.
>
> When I was a boy I used to listen faithfully to your program, and was encouraged to do so by my parents.
>
> I remember the fine "Lincoln Day" broadcasts starring Raymond Massey and many other things. I remember with pride the time in the fourth or fifth grade when we started studying about rubber.
>
> Just prior to this I had sent in my name in answer to an offer you had made at the conclusion of one of your broadcasts concerning the thrilling new discovery of "man made" rubber. In reply I received a small, green, smelly eraser in a cardboard "Story folder" relating the discovery of DuPont's new product—Duprene. Was I proud to take that to school; in fact I think in my own small way I was proud of DuPont.
>
> I feel that your broadcasts have always been an education in themselves, certainly they gave me the first real conception of how chemistry affected me in daily living.
>
> Now I am married, have left my native city of Philadelphia and have moved to a tiny farming community in southern Indiana, where I am raising two small boys of my own. The one, being just now six years old, is just now becoming curious of the world around him, and because I know how I felt about your program when I was smaller, though not quite that young, we had taken to listening to your program together, with me trying to fill in a little in the way of explanation where it was over his head. Needless to say we enjoyed your program very much, maybe partly because we were enjoying it together, but nevertheless we did.
>
> Now, however, comes the part where we are left, and feel almost that an injustice has been done us. We are near no big cities and hence have no television station within normal range, and the cost of a set, an antenna, and booster, etc., to bring in the nearest station some 150 miles away makes it beyond the realm of what the ordinary family could afford to spend for such things, even as desirable as they might be. To keep one's family well fed and clothed and sheltered, seems sometimes to be quite a problem itself these days. And so we who have known your program much of our life, who received our first lessons in applied chemistry from it, as well as little fellows who have just begun to know you, feel sort of cheated now that we are just "left."
>
> I realize that your step in changing over to television is just proof of the fact that your company has always stayed abreast of the times; still it hurts a little to know that myself and probably many others like me can't help but feel a little left [*sic*] down.[56]

Company advertising and public relations specialists, too, might wax nostalgic for their radio program as the *Cavalcade* entered the competitive market for television entertainment.

As ever, merchandising directed to the general viewing public leavened the programs' educational purpose with entertainment value. Promotional material accompanying the *Cavalcade*'s second telecast, entitled "All's Well with Lydia," for example, presented "the Revolutionary War story of Lydia Darragh, American patriot and Philadelphia widow, who by her cleverness gained information instrumental in an American victory." Spot announcement texts were supplied to local television stations, to be read "while you are showing the Cavalcade action." They asked: "Was she minx or patriot?" A second exclaimed, "Lydia Darragh's receptive ear ready smile and pink cheek are more dangerous to British hopes than a thousand muskets!"[57]

In a bid to freshen up the series' historical venue with the trend toward "actuals" then in favor on BBDO's *General Electric Theater* and *Armstrong Circle Theater*, during the 1954–1955 television season the *Cavalcade* introduced contemporary story subjects such as "Second Story," the story of Illinois high school football coach Mark Wilson, with the Cleveland Browns' Otto Graham, who played himself; "Man on the Beat," a police drama; "The Gift of Dr. Minot," the story of the 1934 Nobel Laureate in Medicine and his treatment of anemia; and "Sunrise on a Dirty Face," a drama about juvenile delinquency. The favorable reception of these stories led to a change of title in the 1955–1956 television season. Retaining an option on the American past, the *DuPont Cavalcade Theater* debuted with "A Time for Courage," a dramatization of the story of "Nancy Merki and the swimming coach who led her to victory over polio and to Olympic stardom." Subsequent weeks featured a historical–contemporary story mix including "Toward Tomorrow," a biography of Dr. Ralphe Bunche; "Disaster Patrol," an adventure story about the Civil Air Patrol; "The Swamp Fox," featuring Hans Conreid in the role of General Francis Marion; and "Postmark: Danger," a police drama drawn from the files of U.S. postal investigators.[58] DuPont's new interest in contemporary relevance, however, was misread by Batten, Barton, Durstine & Osborn, its longtime advertising agency and program producer. Rejecting a script entitled "I Lost My Job," a DuPont Company official testily explained to BBDO's Jock Elliott that "on 'Cavalcade' or in any other DuPont advertising, we do not want to picture business in a bad light, or in any way that can be interpreted as negative by even a single viewer. It just seems axiomatic that we'd be silly to spend advertising money to tear down the very concept we're trying to sell."[59] Though this incident suggests the sponsor's reluctance to assimilate a reality different from its own, nevertheless by the 1956–1957 television season that sale had moved to new settings and locations far from the *Cavalcade*'s capsule demonstrations of free enterprise at work. Spurred by an editorial confidence in the value of entertainment, the newly renamed *DuPont Theater* all but abandoned the historical past as an educational prerequisite for an evening's entertainment.

The decision to emphasize contemporary story subjects came after a thorough examination of other companies' institutional television programs. In the summer of 1955, DuPont advertising director W. E. Gordon met with representatives of General Electric, U.S. Steel, and the Aluminum Company of America (sponsor of the recently canceled Edward R. Murrow program *See It Now*), "all of which have had television programs with objectives similar to 'Cavalcade.'" At Alcoa, public relations director John Fleming surprised Gordon by offering to share sponsorship of the *Cavalcade* with DuPont. Fleming, however, declined to participate in Gordon's proposal to pool company resources for investigative audience research if the package included U.S. Steel. Steel's J. Carlisle MacDonald and GE's J. Stanford Smith expressed interest in collaborating on a research project, Gordon reported, "which might measure the effectiveness of our respective company programs to a greater degree." Of the three, Gordon found GE specialists the most willing to venture into outright entertainment for "company voice" television. "General Electric," Gordon noted, "is after maximum audience per dollar invested, and therefore they have not been concerned with the educational aspects of their program. They use a popular drama format and spend as high as $15,000 per program for 'star' talent."[60]

In contrast to the DuPont Company, General Electric's integration of television with its institutional activities was not as smoothly accomplished, despite the company's history of technical and practical experience with the medium. During the Second World War, for example, General Electric's experimental station WRGB Schenectady had produced over 950 live talent shows in order to evolve "the basic techniques of good television." Telecasts included musical variety shows, short-form dramas, tests of commercial formats, and movies, which were relayed upstate from NBC's transmitter in New York City.[61] In the fall of 1948, General Electric first entered commercial television with a show entitled the *Dennis James Carnival*, which the company dropped after one performance. A quiz program entitled *Riddle Me This* substituted for twelve weeks and was also dropped. In April 1949 GE returned to the air with *The Fred Waring Show*, produced by Young & Rubicam for the company's Appliance, Electronics, and Lamp Divisions. In November 1951 GE transferred production to Batten, Barton, Durstine & Osborn, introducing the *General Electric Theater* in February 1953 as an all-company project sponsored by GE's department of public relations services.[62]

The decision for a "theater" format was made after careful study and consideration of alternative formats and interviews with the executives of "leading companies" sponsoring television programs devoted primarily to institutional messages. These included U.S. Steel, DuPont, the Aluminum Company of America, Ford, the Electric Light and Power Companies of America, Reynolds Metals, and the Aluminum Company of Canada. General Electric specialists specifically rejected the press conference format of *Meet the Press* and *Youth Wants to Know*, "in which people of all shades of opinion express ideas regarding business and our economic climate." "Because these programs thrive on dramatic conflict," GE specialists concluded, "the issues discussed are usually very controversial and frequently inimical to business. The colorful and controversial figures featured are often persons who are either uninformed or deliberately hostile to business enterprise."[63]

The *General Electric Theater* debuted in the fall of 1953 with a mixed schedule of live and telefilm half-hour programs conceived to attract the largest audience available to television for institutional and product messages. The addition of Ronald Reagan to the program in October 1954 reflected the company's decision to pursue a continuous, consistent, corporate voice (fig. 44). The short-form television drama would serve as the keystone of an ambitious and far-reaching program of employee and public relations. Reagan's role as program host would bring needed continuity to the series' disparate program offerings. The casting of Don Herbert of TV's *Watch Mr. Wizard* fame in the role of "General Electric Progress reporter" established a clear-cut company identity for institutional advertisements. As part of its overall public relations plan, General Electric aggressively merchandised the program among its employees, their families, and their communities. In the first of many promotional tours, Reagan traveled to twelve General Electric plant cities in November 1954 to promote the program idea, to further his identity as spokesman, and to become familiar with company people and products. By the time *General Electric Theater* concluded its eight-year run in 1962, Reagan claimed to have visited 135 of GE's research and manufacturing facilities and to have met some 250,000 individuals. In later years, Reagan's biographers would look back upon the tour as the platform upon which the future president of the United States honed his already-considerable skill as a communicator.[64]

Conceived as tightly controlled entertainment, not education, the new *General Electric Theater* attracted top Hollywood stars to dramatic roles calculated to appeal to the largest possible audience. By December 1954, after only four months on the air with Reagan as program host, *General Electric Theater* achieved Nielsen top-ten status as television's most popular weekly dramatic program. The formula accommodated live telecasts that originated from both coasts and, increasingly, made use of telefilms and Hollywood talent available to Revue Productions, the motion picture production company of the Music Corporation of America (MCA). An unprecedented Screen Actors' Guild (SAG) talent waiver that was granted to MCA-Revue during Reagan's tenure as SAG president in 1952 and again in 1954 enabled MCA-Revue to dominate the telefilm industry. The talent waiver allowed MCA-Revue

FIGURE 44.

General Electric Theater host Ronald Reagan, about 1954.

Courtesy of the Ronald Reagan Library.

to simultaneously represent artists and employ them in the telefilms that it produced.[65] MCA's stars appeared on Revue's *General Electric Theater*, and ratings soared. Many made their television debuts in dramatic roles. Joseph Cotten starred in "The High Green Wall," an adaptation of Evelyn Waugh's *A Handful of Dust*; Jack Benny starred in "The Face Is Familiar," a comedy about a man whose face no one could remember; Alan Ladd starred in "Committed," a mystery about "an author who advertises for trouble and finds it." Joan Crawford made her only 1954 television appearance in "The Road to Edinburgh," a story of "terror on a lonely road." "The Long Way Around" featured Ronald and Nancy Davis Reagan, who solved "a unique marital problem to reunite a family." In a direct dramatic tie-in with a company-voice theme, Burgess Meredith portrayed "Edison the Man," a telecast coinciding with GE's commemoration of "Light's Diamond Jubilee."

General Electric Theater saturated its audience with genial progress-talk in Reagan's introductions, segues, and closing comments, and in Herbert's commercials. From the viewpoint of its sponsors, the program's entertainment component seemed beside the point, which was audience "recall scores," "impact studies," and the "penetration" of company messages culminating with the motto, "Progress is our most important product."[66] Commercials from the 1954 fall season included "Kitchen of the Future," "Lamp Progress," "Jet Engine Advancement," "Turbosupercharger Progress," "Sonar Development," "Atomic Safety Devices," and so on. "Kitchen of the Future" achieved the highest impact score ever recorded by Gallup-Robinson (90 percent audience recall), which reported that the program's commercials were "the leading institutional campaign on television for selling ideas to the public."[67] Closing out a November 1956 Herbert progress report on GE's steam turbine generators and their contributions to "progress toward a fuller and more satisfying life," Reagan reiterated, "In the meantime, remember: From electricity comes progress; progress in our daily living; progress in our daily work; progress in the defense of our nation; and at General Electric, progress is . . ."[68]

By 1957 *General Electric Theater* had hit stride with a top-rated program package, the equal of the company's early technical proficiency in television. While GE's product divisions developed individual sponsorships that reached appliance, lamp, and electronics consumers via *The Jane Froman Show*, *The Ray Milland Show*, *I Married Joan*, *Ozzie and Harriet*, and *Today*, the *General Electric Theater* aspired to the overarching sale of "Total Electric" living. The positioning of kitchen appliances as agents of social progress, for example, fused the promotional interests of company-wide corporate management and its product divisions. A February 1957 *General Electric Theater* telecast featuring Jimmy Stewart celebrated the first anniversary of the electric utilities' "Live Better Electrically" program and "National Electric Week." The closing commercial featured Nancy and Ronald Reagan in the kitchen of a Total Electric home. "When you live better electrically," Reagan told viewers, "you lead a richer, fuller, more satisfying life. And it's something all of us in this modern age can have." In his 1965 autobiography *Where's the Rest of Me?* Reagan recalled that GE installed so many appliances in his Pacific Palisades home that the electrical service soon outgrew the usual cupboard-sized panel and required a three-thousand-pound steel cabinet out back. The *General Electric Theater* was no less loaded with the progress idea, offering a materialism soaked in personal and social improvement, and expressed over and again by Reagan: "Progress in products goes hand in hand with providing progress in the human values that enrich the lives of us all."[69]

Epilogue

The early 1950s found Bruce Barton contemplating his retirement and, to his displeasure, spending more and more time with television. He complained of the stentorian tone of the announcers on the *U.S. Steel Hour* and *General Electric Theater* and wondered, "Why do these big corporations have to introduce their programs with a voice that sounds like the voice of an auctioneer or a train announcer—THE UNITED STATES STEEL SHOW?"[1] Seeking a commensurate totality of effort and effect, two years earlier Barton had launched a campaign within BBDO to get "U.S. Steel to spend 25 million dollars on television." He explained to BBDO president Ben Duffy, "The Steel Corporation, which is the cornerstone of the whole capitalistic structure, ought to be thinking not in terms of ordinary advertising expenditures or campaigns, but thinking 'What can we do that would be so dramatic and so public spirited that millions of people would say, "Wasn't that a wonderful thing for the Steel Corporation to do?"'" "The cost, under the tax laws," Barton noted, "would be trivial compared with the benefit." It would be a model for "almost all our larger accounts."[2] Ruminating upon the cumulative power of advertising and big event programming, Barton prodded DuPont advertising director William A. Hart: "About your idea of having industry join in a great television show on research, how can we get five or six companies interested to join—an oil company, a chemical company, an automobile company, an electric company?" "A really bang-up science program," Barton confided to DuPont account executive Maurice Collette, financed by "a half-dozen top industries would rank next to the Kefauver show." "I'd be willing," wrote Barton, "to have it be the closing chapter of my advertising career."[3] Forever thinking in terms of personal meaning and triumphant showmanship, Barton inquired in February 1951 of his old friend Henry Luce, "Are you old enough to remember the crowd of apple sellers that suddenly blossomed on the street corners of American cities in the last days of Mr. Hoover's term? Things like that just don't happen. Somebody organized that show, and it was a terrifically effective job. Who did it?"[4] The following year, Luce's *Life* magazine published a DuPont Company photograph that had appeared in the pages of DuPont's employee magazine *Better Living*. "Why we eat better" pictured a family of four posed in a refrigerated locker piled with foodstuffs[5] (fig. 45).

With little to look back upon in the Depression decade, advertising and public relations specialists made their best case for business leadership with a paste-up history of people and products, and a highly selective but compelling vision of future progress based upon current science and invention. With the return of commercial television following the Second World War, the New Vocabulary appeared as tightly controlled entertainment rather than education. Much as the apple sellers on the street corners of memory summed up the 1930s, specialists worked to ensure that "better living" would become the visual shorthand of the 1950s. Linking the politics of "better living" to the Cold War, consumerism invited Americans to think of consumption as a political act. Total Electric living, automobile tailfins, and television became freighted with heightened personal and political meaning.[6] Equating consumption with power, the New Vocabulary addressed the individual at home, not at the ballot box. In startling continuity oddly reminiscent of the encounter between Jim Treadway and Nick Makaroff in the *Middleton Family at the World's Fair*, Vice President Richard M. Nixon and Soviet Premier Nikita Khrushchev traded barbs as they toured an American-made "People's Capitalism" exhibit in Moscow. The most memorable of views exchanged that day occurred as the two leaders inspected the appliances of a model kitchen.[7]

As "better living" became better understood as a political claim, businessmen tempered their propensity for reaction and attack with entertaining expressions of social leadership. Coupling the qualities of play and fun with the world of purchasable goods, the New Vocabulary moderated the ham-handed conservatism of business leaders drawn to television production. As television entertainment became entrenched as a function of middle management, so did the anthology program formula. A publicity still picturing the program team of DuPont's *Show of the Month* in 1961, for example, featured charts of upcoming program subjects, and in the shadows, the elements of the formula: "suitability," "appeal," "risk," and "cost" (fig. 46).

The New Vocabulary might displace but would never quite replace the old. While center firms such as General Electric anticipated communicating business's

FIGURE 45.

Photograph, "Why We Eat Better" (1951). Courtesy of Hagley Museum and Library.

FIGURE 46.

Left to right: **Lyman Dewey, DuPont advertising department; Charles M. Hackett, public relations; Edward Pechin, Hugh Horning, and Charles Crowley, advertising department (1961). Courtesy of Hagley Museum and Library.**

social goals to a generation of Americans with no first-hand memory of the Depression, by the early 1960s business found that that generation had social goals of its own, particularly in the areas of civil rights, consumer protection, and environmentalism. In 1966 public opinion pollster Louis Harris described the public image of U.S. business as "bright, but flawed."[8] Specialists set out to narrow the distance between corporate claim and performance said to be as great as the so-called generation gap. Not only had society become more impersonal and complex, they argued, but increasingly polarized and problematic.[9]

The bifurcated campaign strategy of Socony Vacuum's corporate successor Mobil Oil begun in 1971 suggested that business remained of two minds in its approach to the public. The first, insistent and impetuous, adopted a confrontational approach using op-ed advertising in the *New York Times*, the *Washington Post*, and other papers. The second, entertaining and ingratiating, capitalized upon the dramatic anthology program formula that would become the cornerstone of the making-possible program environment of the Public Broadcasting Service.[10] Yet by the late 1970s, the same specialists perhaps wondered just what effect their long-term advertising campaigns had bought. Increasingly business found itself the subject of critical television news stories treating the environment, the OPEC oil shock, inflation, and recession.[11] Moreover, critics charged that public television, a leading outlet for "company voice" advertising, had become a prime example of "logo America," in which "the only price a company will charge for its public service activities is the right to display its logo."[12] Near the opposite end of the political spectrum, conservatives dismissed PBS's broadcast schedule as a "monotonous diet of left-wing politics," though it would have been difficult to find such programs equaling the possibilities, much less access, available to the corporate advertiser.[13] Mobil, for example, financed an hour-long PBS documentary program criticizing the anti-business thrust of prime-time network television drama. Hosted by writer Benjamin Stein, *Hollywood's Favorite Heavy: Businessmen on Prime Time TV* used clips from *Dallas*, *Dynasty*, and *Falcon Crest* to contend that television had destroyed youth's outlook on business and business ethics. A peculiar assumption, wrote one reviewer, since television itself was a business, and advertising had made consumption "the nearest thing to religion for most Americans."[14] Mobil, however, had decided that it could not countenance the likes of Blake Carrington, J. R. Ewing, and other stereotypes of rapacious businessmen in prime time.

The lessons of the New Vocabulary are forgotten and rediscovered by a new generation of specialists. Evidence of this rediscovery may be seen in the personally meaningful language of the Republican Party's "Contract with America" and in a recent proposal for a more effective "Language of the 21st Century."[15] While such efforts look toward the future, specialists are perhaps too caught up with the inner workings of their predictive models of effect to be aware of the fact that the models themselves are old enough to have a past—much like the persistent corporate rhetoric of jobs, consumer benefits, and further elaborations of the latent consequences of the profit motive that have left audiences exclaiming "Oh, yeah!" since the days of Upton Sinclair.[16]

The 1987 suspension of the equal time provision of the Federal Communications Commission's Fairness Doctrine, followed in the 1990s by the erosion of the "no offense" premise of commercial radio, are the respective cause and symptom of the breakup of the broadcast spectrum into a freewheeling market for partisan talk—an eventuality unacceptable to the specialists who imagined and built a national audience for network radio in the 1930s. Now, as then, the New Vocabulary affords far more insidious potential as a method for sustaining a corporatist political outlook extending to the realm of common sense and the everyday, where political talks, democratic ideals of fairness and equal time, and even the prerequisite of an in-and-out party system are treated as irrelevancies.[17]

Although anthology drama has lost its historical relationship with the dislocations of the 1930s that called it to being, the anthology formula, like its sponsors' assumptions about the place of "big event" programming in viewers' lives, has remained unchanged since the days of Bruce Barton and Alfred P. Sloan, Jr. In 1989, for example, "Mark of Excellence Presentations" carried on GM's continuing campaign of association with national life and culture. A magazine advertisement promoting GM's making-possible sponsorships of *Bill Moyers's In Search of the Constitution*, *George Washington: The Forging of a Nation,* and Ken Burns's *The Civil War* pictured a family of four positioned in front of their television receiver. The ad's copy explains, "General Motors has found a way to keep people in their seats without using seat belts. We do it with quality television programming"[18] (fig. 47). Focused through the lens of corporate necessity, the historical past as seen on TV is as selectively authentic as it was in the heyday of radio's *Cavalcade of America*. Filled with the drama of human interest and emotion, the historical past has achieved a noncoercive stasis among corporate sponsors and program producers. The parameters of interpretive possibility are sufficiently understood by program producers who seldom, if ever, require prompting. Commenting on his ongoing 15-million-dollar sponsorship package with General Motors for the PBS films *The Civil War*, *Baseball*, and *Lewis and Clark*, Ken Burns noted that General Motors had neither discussed his films' content with him nor did they need to. "They don't tell me how to make films," Burns explained, "and I don't tell them how to make cars."[19]

By the mid-1990s the noncoercive values of family entertainment had helped underwrite the corporate consolidation of the broadcasting and cable industries, resulting in an unprecedented industrial and media concentration that critics charged had become a "national entertainment state" and a "culture trust."[20] General Electric got over its aversion to current events panel discussions featuring colorful and controversial personalities, and sponsored the *McLaughlin Group* and *This Week with David Brinkley* to showcase the latest incarnation of its New Vocabulary slogan, "We Bring Good Things to Life." The DuPont Company opted out of television drama, but its institutional magazine advertisements continued the tradition of conveying messages from specialist to client within the body of the client's paid space. A DuPont "better living" advertisement tells, for example, the human story of new plastics applied to the prostheses of Bill Demby, a Vietnam veteran who lost his legs to a Viet Cong rocket[21] (fig. 48). The ad pictures Demby playing in a pickup basketball game, in a blur of movement and sudden action. The representation of the game and its players is literally beside the point of the copy carefully inserted in large letters on a graffiti-covered playground wall: DRAMA.

FIGURE 47. **Advertisement, "General Motors has found a way . . ."** ***New York Times Magazine*** **(January 7, 1990): 21.**

FIGURE 48. **Advertisement, "If Bill Demby . . ."** ***New York Times Business World Magazine*** **(June 11, 1989): 5.**

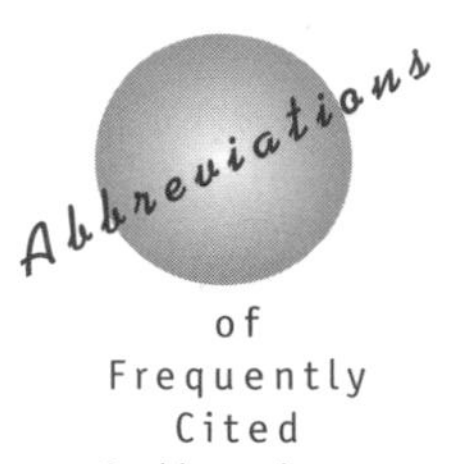

Abbreviations of Frequently Cited Collections

AAFF	American Archives of the Factual Film, Iowa State University, Ames.
AHF/NACP	Records of the American Heritage Foundation, National Archives at College Park, MD.
AMS/HUA	Arthur M. Schlesinger Collection, Harvard University Archives, Cambridge, MA.
BBDO	Batten, Barton, Durstine & Osborn, Inc., Library, New York.
BB/SHSW	Bruce Barton collection, State Historical Society of Wisconsin, Madison.
BPHL	Broadcast Pioneers Historical Library collection, University of Maryland at College Park.
DuP/HL	E. I. du Pont de Nemours and Company, Inc., collection, Hagley Library, Wilmington, DE.
ELB/LC	Edward L. Bernays collection, Manuscript Division, Library of Congress, Washington, DC.
FC/NACP	Ford Collection, National Archives at College Park, MD.
FDRL	Franklin D. Roosevelt Library, Hyde Park, NY.
FT/NA	Records of the Freedom Train, National Archives Building, Washington, DC.
GM	General Motors Corporation, Detroit, MI.
HL	Hagley Library, Wilmington, DE.
KN/SHSW	Kenyon Nicholson collection, State Historical Society of Wisconsin, Madison.
LC	Library of Congress, Washington, DC.
MoMA	Museum of Modern Art, New York.
NACP	National Archives at College Park, MD.
NAM/HL	National Association of Manufacturers collection, Hagley Library, Wilmington, DE.
NBC/LC	National Broadcasting Company collection, Motion Picture, Broadcasting and Recorded Sound Division, Library of Congress, Washington, DC.
NBC/SHSW	National Broadcasting Company collection, State Historical Society of Wisconsin, Madison.
NMAH/SI	National Museum of American History, Smithsonian Institution, Washington, DC.
NYWF/NYPL	New York World's Fair Corporation collection, New York Public Library, New York.
PA	Prelinger Associates collection, New York.
RL	Walter P. Reuther Library, Archives of Labor and Urban Affairs, Wayne State University, Detroit, MI.
SHSW	State Historical Society of Wisconsin.

Introduction

1. Dan Schiller, *Theorizing Communication: A History* (New York: Oxford University Press, 1996), pp. 45, 67, passim; Jackson Lears, "A Matter of Taste: Corporate Cultural Hegemony in a Mass-Consumption Society," in *Recasting America: Culture and Politics in the Age of Cold War,* ed. Larry May (Chicago: University of Chicago Press, 1989), pp. 38–57; Roland Marchand, "Where Lie the Boundaries of the Corporation? Explorations in 'Corporate Responsibility.'" *Business and Economic History* 26 (fall 1997): 80–100.

2. William Graebner, *The Engineering of Consent: Democracy and Authority in Twentieth-Century America* (Madison: University of Wisconsin Press, 1987), pp. 26, 64–65; Eugene E. Leach, "Mastering the Crowd: Collective Behavior and Mass Society in American Social Thought, 1917–1939,"*American Studies* 27 (spring 1986): 99–114; Robert B. Westbrook, "Politics as Consumption: Managing the Modern Election," in *The Culture of Consumption: Critical Essays in American History, 1880–1980,* ed. Richard Wightman Fox and T. J. Jackson Lears (New York: Pantheon, 1983), pp. 143–173; for first-person accounts of encounters with Bernays, who kept visitors au courant until his death in 1995 at the age of 103, see Sidney Blumenthal, *The Permanent Campaign* (New York: Simon & Schuster, 1982), pp. 27–43; Stuart Ewen, *PR! A Social History of Spin* (New York: Basic Books/Harper Collins, 1996), pp. 3–18.

3. Bruce Barton, "The Public," a speech delivered before the Congress of American Industry, in conjunction with the annual convention of the National Association of Manufacturers, December 4, 1935, *Vital Speeches of the Day* 2 (December 16, 1935): 174–177.

4. Loren Baritz, *The Servants of Power: A History of the Use of Social Science in American Industry* (Middletown, CT: Wesleyan University Press, 1960), pp. 118, 134; Elizabeth A. Fones-Wolf, *Selling Free Enterprise: The Business Assault on Labor and Liberalism, 1945–1960* (Urbana and Chicago: University of Illinois Press, 1994), p. 78, passim; Howell John Harris, *The Right to Manage: Industrial Relations Policies of American Business in the 1940s* (Madison: University of Wisconsin Press, 1982), pp. 171 173.

5. For literary variations on this theme see William Leach, *Land of Desire: Merchants, Power, and the Rise of a New American Culture* (New York: Pantheon Books, 1993), pp. 4–5, 9.

6. Roland Marchand, "The Fitful Career of Advocacy Advertising: Political Protection, Client Cultivation, and Corporate Morale," *California Management Review* 29 (winter 1987): 128–156; Marchand, "The Inward Thrust of Institutional Advertising: General Electric and General Motors in the 1920s,"*Business and Economic History* 18 (1989): 188–196.

7. As media theorist and critic Todd Gitlin notes, "hegemonic ideology is extremely complex and absorptive; it is only by absorbing and domesticating conflicting definitions of reality and demands on it, in fact, that it remains hegemonic. . . .What permits it to absorb and domesticate critique is not something accidental to capitalist ideology, but rather its core." Todd Gitlin, "Prime Time Ideology: The Hegemonic Process in Television Entertainment," in *Television: The Critical View,* ed. Horace Newcomb (New York: Oxford University Press, 1994), pp. 516–536.

8. Antonio Gramsci, "The Study of Philosophy," in *Selections from the Prison Notebooks,* ed. and trans. Quintin Hoare and Geoffrey Nowell Smith (New York: International Publishers, 1971), cited in Stuart Hall, "The Toad in the Garden: Thatcherism among the Theorists," in *Marxism and the Interpretation of Culture,* ed. Cary Nelson and Lawrence Grossberg (Urbana and Chicago: University of Illinois Press, 1988), p. 55.

9. David Paul Nord, "An Economic Perspective on Formula in Popular Culture," *Journal of American Culture* 3 (spring 1980): 17–31; T. J. Jackson Lears, "Making Fun of Popular Culture,"*American Historical Review* 97 (December 1992): 1417–1426.

10. The first night's guests included financier E. F. Hutton and editor William Allen White. Barton to Harrison McCann, 29 September 1932, and script, "Address by Bruce Barton, Monday October 3, 1932 on behalf of the Republican Party," folder: Republican Party-1932, box 57 Bruce Barton papers, State Historical Society of Wisconsin-Madison (hereafter BB/SHSW).

11. Roy S. Durstine, "Curtain Going Up on Act II of Advertising," talk at *Advertising & Selling* Annual Awards Dinner, 24 February 1937, BBDO library, New York (hereafter BBDO).

12. Batten, Barton, Durstine & Osborn, *The Wedge* (n.d.), cited in Kenneth Goode and Zenn Kaufman, *Profitable Showmanship* (New York: Prentice-Hall, 1939), pp. 84–86.

13. Michael M. Sokal, "The Origins of the Psychological Corporation," *Journal of the History of Behavioral Sciences* 7 (1981): 54-67; Leonard W. Doob, "An 'Experimental' Study of the Psychological Corporation," *Psychological Bulletin* 35 (April 1938): 220–222; Paul S. Achilles, "A Reply to Dr. Doob's Comments Concerning the Psychological Corporation,"*Psychological Bulletin* 35 (October 1938): 548–551.

14. Psychological Corporation, *The Perils of Peace: A Study of Public Opinion and Morale* (New York: Psychological Corporation, 1941). *The Perils of Peace* drew inspiration (and its title) from the comments of General Electric president Charles E. Wilson, whose "Can We Save Free Enterprise?" appeared the following month in the *American Magazine*. See Charles E. Wilson as told to Beverly Smith, "Can We Save Free Enterprise?" *American Magazine* 132 (November 1941): 36–37, 64–65.

15. Psychological Corporation, *A Study of Radio Listening Habits and Preferences* (New York: Psychological Corporation, October 11, 1934), vertical pamphlet files, Broadcast Pioneers Historical Library, Washington, D.C. (hereafter BPHL), that has since moved to the Hornbake Library, University of Maryland–College Park; *Annual Report of the Psychological Corporation Marketing and Social Research Division* (New York: Psychological Corporation, 1950), folder: Psychological Corporation (NYC) correspondence, brochures and annual reports, box 59: public relations department, acc. 1410 series III, Records of E. I. du Pont de Nemours and Company, Inc., Hagley Library, Wilmington, DE (hereafter DuP/HL). For an identification of the PSC's corporate clients see Psychological Corporation, "Test-Tube Study of the Influence of 'Cavalcade of America' on attitudes toward the DuPont Company," 16 August 1939, and memo, William A. Hart to Lammot du Pont, 18 August 1939, folder: Advertising Department 1939–1940, box 4: Advertising Department: 1937–1952, acc. 1662 Administrative Papers, DuP/HL.

16. Psychological Corporation, *The Perils of Peace*.

17. The omission is puzzling not for lack of notice by contemporary critics of entertainments with which business challenged the New Deal and its work. See for example, Strother Holland Walker and Paul Sklar, *Business Finds Its Voice: Management's Effort to Sell the Business Idea to the Public* (New York: Harper & Brothers, 1938).

Chapter 1

1. T. J. Jackson Lears locates advertising's personal voice in the turn-of-the-century shift from the Protestant ethos of "salvation through self-denial" to "therapeutic self-realization." See Lears, "From Salvation to Self-Realization: Advertising and the Therapeutic Roots of the Consumer Culture, 1880–1930," in Fox and Lears, eds., *The Culture of Consumption*, pp. 1–38. Roland Marchand, in his study of modern advertising, notes that modernity is but a condition of the personal, the lubricant of a distended consumer society; see Marchand, *Advertising the American Dream: Making Way for Modernity, 1920–1940* (Berkeley: University of California Press, 1985), pp. 9, 11–12. Beyond the historiography of getting and spending, the *personal* looms large in the cultural landscape of the 1930s. Warren Susman finds it in the concept of the "average American" central to the decade's thinking and planning, whose monuments include public opinion polling and exposition architecture incorporating crowds; see Susman, "The People's Fair: Cultural Contradictions of a Consumer Society," in Susman, *Culture as History: The Transformation of American Society in the Twentieth Century* (New York: Pantheon, 1984), pp. 211–229. Lary May finds the Depression era's aspirations for private life poignantly reflected in the notions of celebrity of the cinema audience; see May, *Screening Out the Past: The Birth of Mass Culture and the Motion Picture Industry* (Chicago: University of Chicago Press, 1983), pp. 240–241. Documentary expression, taking as its subject the personal and specific, has profoundly influenced the way in which we think about the 1930s; see William Stott, *Documentary Expression and Thirties America* (Chicago: University of Chicago Press, 1986); Roy Emerson Stryker, *In This Proud Land* (New York: Galahad Books, 1973); Carl Fleischhauer and Beverly W. Brannan, eds., *Documenting America, 1935–1943* (Berkeley: University of California Press, 1988); Pete Daniel, Merry A. Foresta, Maren Stange, and Sally Stein, *Official Images: New Deal Photography* (Washington, DC: Smithsonian Institution Press, 1987). For comment on contemporary photojournalism and "working in corporate public relations," see Maren Stange, *Symbols of Ideal Life: Social Documentary Photography in America, 1890–1950* (New York: Cambridge University Press, 1989), p. 108.

2. Cited in Arthur P. Molella, *FDR, The Intimate Presidency: Franklin Delano Roosevelt, Communication, and the Mass Media in the 1930s* (Washington, DC: National Museum of American History, Smithsonian Institution, 1982), p. 50.

3. Ira R. T. Smith, with Joe Alex Morris, *"Dear Mr. President . . .": The Story of Fifty Years in the White House Mail Room* (New York: Julian Messner, 1949), p. 156. Smith reported that Roosevelt received from 5,000 to 8,000 letters a day, and "on some occasions, thousands more" (p. 150).

4. Leila A. Sussmann, *Dear FDR: A Study of Political Letter-Writing* (Totowa, NJ: Bedminster Press, 1963), p. 113.

5. Francis Perkins, *The Roosevelt I Knew* (New York: Viking Press, 1946), p. 72; Harold L. Ickes, *The Secret Diary of Harold L. Ickes*, vol. 1 (New York: Simon & Schuster, 1954), p. 695, cited in William E. Leuchtenburg, *Franklin D. Roosevelt and the New Deal 1932–1940* (New York: Harper & Row, 1963), pp. 193, 330–331; on "air showmanship," see "Will Roosevelt Rule by Radio?" *Radio Fan-Fare* (combining *Radio Digest*) 30 (June 1933): 8–9, 50; typescript, "The Republican Party," p. 2 and attached letter, C. M. Chester to Barton, 23 July 1942, folder: Republican Party 1933, 1942, box 57, and Barton, memorandum to

Mr. Teagle (Standard Oil New Jersey), 7 December 1936, and attached memorandum, Tax Cummings to Barton, 11 November 1952, folder: Cummings, Thayer (Tax) 1940–1955, box 14 BB/SHSW; on "New Deal," see Russell D. Buhite and David W. Levy, eds., *FDR's Fireside Chats* (New York: Penguin, 1993), p. xv; Samuel I. Rosenman, *Working with Roosevelt* (New York: Harper & Brothers, 1952), pp. 71–72, 78–79; T. V. Smith, "The New Deal as a Cultural Phenomenon," in *Ideological Differences and World Order,* ed. F. S. C. Northrop (New Haven: Yale University Press, 1949), pp. 208–228.

6. Frederick Lewis Allen, *Since Yesterday: The Nineteen-Thirties in America* (New York: Harper & Brothers, 1940), p. 233; George Wolfskill and John A. Hudson, *All but the People: Franklin D. Roosevelt and His Critics* (New York: Macmillan, 1969), pp. 5–11, 120; George Wolfskill, *The Revolt of the Conservatives: A History of the American Liberty League, 1934–1940* (Boston: Houghton Mifflin Co., 1962; Westport, CT: Greenwood Press, 1974), pp. 106–110.

7. "The Case against Roosevelt," *Fortune* 12 (December 1935): 102–107, 140.

8. Robert Bendiner, *Just around the Corner: A Highly Selective History of the Thirties* (New York: E. P. Dutton & Co., 1968), pp. 69–70.

9. David Vogel, "Why Businessmen Distrust Their State: The Political Consciousness of American Corporate Executives," *British Journal of Political Science* 8 (January 1978): 45–78; Alan Brinkley, "The Idea of the State," in *The Rise and Fall of the New Deal Order, 1930–1980,* ed. Gary Gerstle and Steve Fraser (Princeton, NJ: Princeton University Press, 1989), pp. 85–121; James Holt, "The New Deal and the American Anti-Statist Tradition," and Ellis W. Hawley, "The New Deal and Business," both in *The New Deal: The National Level,* vol. 1, ed. John Braeman et al. (Columbus: Ohio State University Press, 1975), pp. 27–82; Mark H. Leff, *The Limits of Symbolic Reform: The New Deal and Taxation, 1933–1939* (New York: Cambridge University Press, 1984), pp. 133–134, 156–164; Robert F. Burk, *The Corporate State and the Broker State: The Du Ponts and American National Politics, 1935–1940* (Cambridge, MA: Harvard University Press, 1990), pp. 21, 250, passim; Douglas B. Craig, *After Wilson: The Struggle for the Democratic Party, 1920–1934* (Chapel Hill: University of North Carolina Press, 1992), pp. 274–295, passim; Charles W. Cheape, *Strictly Business: Walter Carpenter at DuPont and General Motors* (Baltimore, MD: Johns Hopkins University Press, 1995), pp. 128–130; Wolfskill, *The Revolt of the Conservatives,* passim; Richard S. Tedlow, "The National Association of Manufacturers and Public Relations during the New Deal," *Business History Review* 50 (spring 1976): 25–45.

10. Wolfskill, *The Revolt of the Conservatives,* passim; Tedlow, "The National Association of Manufacturers."

11. "The N.A.M. Aids F.D.R.," *New Republic* (n.d.): 161, folder: speech material, business vs. New Deal, box 9, PPF 1820, Franklin D. Roosevelt Library, Hyde Park, NY (hereafter FDRL); *New York Times,* 6 December 1935, p. 18.

12. The NAM used the expression "unit thinking and action" to describe the organization's objectives and techniques. See R. W. Gable, "N.A.M.: Influential Lobby or Kiss of Death?" *Journal of Politics* 15 (May 1953): 253–273.

13. "Personal and Otherwise," *Harper's* 176 (January 1938): endpaper.

14. "He Was There" (ca. 3 September 1935), folder: speech material, business vs. New Deal, box 9, PPF 1820, FDRL.

15. George S. Brady, "Employment Conditions under the Hoover Administration," in pamphlet "Then and Now," folder: speech material, business vs. New Deal, box 9, PPF 1820, FDRL.

16. Editorial, "Big Business Declares War," *St. Louis Star and Times,* n.d., folder: speech material, business vs. New Deal, box 9, PPF 1820, FDRL.

17. Colby M. Chester, "Business Team Play," *Today Magazine* (January 18, 1936), folder: Ce-Ch (Colby Chester) ca. 1926, 1940s–1961, box 11, BB/SHSW.

18. Edgar M. Queeny, *The Spirit of Enterprise* (New York: Charles Scribner's Sons, 1943), pp. 20, 38.

19. Paul W. Garrett, "Public Relations—Industry's No. 1 Job." Delivered at the twenty-first annual convention of the American Association of Advertising Agencies on Friday, April 22, 1938, at the Greenbrier, White Sulphur Springs, West Virginia (New York: General Motors, 1938), p. 6, pamphlet collection, Hagley Library.

20. Jon. A. Senneff, Jr., to Lammot du Pont, 25 March 1938, folder: Advertising Department (#C-24) Jan. 1938–Nov. 1938, box 4, Advertising Department, 1937–1952, acc. 1662, DuP/HL.

21. Hall suggests that today's specialist, content to manage the "dominant circle of ideas," assumes that it is neither necessary nor desirable to "directly prescribe the mental content of the illusions that supposedly fill the heads of the dominated classes." Stuart Hall, "The Toad in the Garden: Thatcherism among the Theorists," in *Marxism and the Interpretation of Culture,* ed. Nelson and Grossberg, pp. 35–73, esp. p. 44.

22. Burton Bigelow, "Should Business Decentralize Its Counter-Propaganda?" *Public Opinion Quarterly* 1 (April 1938): 321–324.

23. On The Crusaders, Inc., see United States Congress, Senate, *Investigation of Lobbying Activities: Hearings before a Special Committee to Investigate Lobbying Activities*, 74th, 75th Congress (1935–1938), 8 vols., pp. 1731–1834, cited in Erik Barnouw, *The Golden Web: A History of Broadcasting in the United States*, vol. 2, *1933 to 1953* (New York: Oxford University Press, 1968), pp. 14–15; on the American Liberty League, see Frederick Rudolph, "The American Liberty League, 1934–1940," *American Historical Review* 56 (October 1950): 19–33.

24. Eugene E. Leach, *Tuning Out Education: The Cooperation Doctrine in Radio, 1922–38* (Washington, DC: Current, 1983).

25. Robert W. McChesney, *Telecommunications, Mass Media, and Democracy: The Battle for the Control of U.S. Broadcasting, 1928–1935* (New York: Oxford University Press, 1993), pp. 115, 164–165.

26. L. A. Van Patten to Philips Carlin, 7 May 1934, and John F. Royal to Richard C. Patterson, 4 August 1934, folder 29, Crusaders–1934, box 4, central files correspondence, National Broadcasting Company papers, State Historical Society of Wisconsin (hereafter NBC/SHSW).

27. Frank M. Russell to R. C. Patterson, 14 February 1935, folder: 372 Political Broadcasting 1924–35, National Broadcasting Company papers, Motion Picture, Broadcasting and Recorded Sound Division (hereafter NBC/LC).

28. John F. Royal to Richard C. Patterson, Jr., 16 February 1935, folder: 372 Political Broadcasting 1924–35, NBC/LC.

29. Royal to Patterson, 12 November 1935, folder 37 political broadcasts-policies 1935, box 40, NBC/SHSW.

30. Alva Johnson, "Profiles: Vaudeville to Television—III," *New Yorker* 22 (October 12, 1946): 36–46, cited in Louis E. Carlat, "Sound Values: Radio Broadcasts of Classical Music and American Culture, 1922–1939" (Ph.D. diss., Johns Hopkins University, 1995), p. 95.

31. M. H. Aylesworth to Members of the Board of Directors, 25 October 1935, folder: 372 Political Broadcasting 1924–35, NBC/LC.

32. Barton, "The Public," pp. 174–177.

33. "Word Man," *Newsweek* 70 (July 17, 1967): 78–79; Leo P. Ribuffo, "Jesus Christ as Business Statesman: Bruce Barton and the Selling of Corporate Capitalism," *American Quarterly* 33 (summer 1981): 206–231.

34. Typescript, "1st rough," folder: Hansen, Leon ca. 1955–1961, box 24, BB/SHSW; "Word Man," *Newsweek* (July 17, 1967): 78–79; Harford Powell, "Tiger Man," *Advertising and Selling* (January 19, 1933): 22–23, 54.

35. Barton to Henry G. Weaver, 9 November 1940, folder: General Motors Corp, 1940–1956, box 77, BB/SHSW; Terry Hynes, "Media Manipulation and Political Campaigns: Bruce Barton and the Presidential Elections of the Jazz Age," *Journalism History* 4 (Autumn 1977): 93–98; John E. Hollitz, "Eisenhower and the Admen: The Television 'Spot' Campaign of 1952," *Wisconsin Magazine of History* 66 (Autumn 1982): 25–39; George Seldes, "Barton, Barton, Barton and Barton," *New Republic* 96 (October 26, 1938): 327–329.

36. Susman, "Culture Heroes: Ford, Barton, Ruth," in *Culture as History*, pp. 122–131; see also Ribuffo, "Jesus Christ and Business Statesman"; Richard M. Huber, *The American Idea of Success* (New York: McGraw-Hill Book Company, 1976), pp. 196–209; Stephen Fox, *The Mirror Makers: A History of American Advertising and Its Creators* (New York: William Morrow & Company, Inc., 1984), pp. 101–112.

37. Press release, 5 July 1967, Barton: Photos, BBDO.

38. Barton, "The Public."

39. For examples of GM's advertisements, see Neil H. Borden, *Advertising Text and Cases* (Chicago: Richard D. Irwin, 1950), pp. 503–504, 509–510; GE's early institutional ads pictured a homemaker tending a washing machine accompanied by the headline, "Any woman who does anything which a little electric motor can do is working for three cents an hour!" Advertisement, "The initials of a friend," folder: GE 1937–1946, BBDO; Marchand, "The Inward Thrust of Institutional Advertising"; Marchand, "The Corporation Nobody Knew: Bruce Barton, Alfred Sloan, and the Founding of the General Motors 'Family,'" *Business History Review* 65 (winter 1991): 825–875.

40. Barton to J. D. Danforth et al., 29 June 1951, folder: General Electric, box 76, client correspondence, BB/SHSW.

41. John Matthew Jordan, "Technic and Ideology: The Engineering Ideal and American Political Culture, 1892–1934" (Ph.D. diss., University of Michigan, 1989).

42. Bruce Barton, "This Magic Called Radio," *American Magazine* 93 (June 1922): 11–13, 70, 72.

43. Ibid.

44. Herbert Butterfield, *The Whig Interpretation of History* (1931: reprinted New York: W. W. Norton & Company, 1965), pp. v, 11, 24, cited in Peter Novick, *That Noble Dream: The "Objectivity Question" and the American Historical Profession* (New York: Cambridge University Press, 1988), pp. 13, 273–274; John M. Staudemaier, "Perils of Progress Talk: Some Historical Considerations," in *Science, Technology, and Social*

Progress, ed. Steven L. Goldman (Bethlehem, PA: Lehigh University Press, 1989), pp. 268–293.

45. Barton, "The Public."

46. George Sumner Albee, mss. for *Sponsor* magazine article, "The DuPont 'Cavalcade of America,'" and attached letter, Maurice Collette to Albee, 3 March 1947, folder 23, box 11, acc. 1803, DuP/HL.

47. General Electric Co., *More Goods for More People at Less Cost: A Tribute to American Industry* (New York: General Electric Co., 1940), trade catalog collection, Hagley Library.

48. Paul Garrett to Barton, 24 January 1944, and Barton to Garrett, 25 January 1944, folder, General Motors Corp., 1940–1956, box 77, client correspondence, BB/SHSW; for examples, see Borden, *Advertising Text and Cases,* p. 541.

Chapter 2

1. Walker and Sklar, *Business Finds Its Voice,* pp. 28–30, 45, 47–48, 51–53.

2. *The 1936 All-American Soap Box Derby,* Jam Handy Picture Service for Chevrolet Motor Company, Prelinger Associates Collection, New York (hereafter PA).

3. Walker and Sklar, *Business Finds Its Voice,* pp. 51–52.

4. Typescript, Roy S. Durstine, "Curtain Going Up on Act II of Advertising," 24 February 1937, BBDO: Personnel: Durstine, BBDO.

5. Simon Frith, "The Pleasures of the Hearth: The Making of BBC Light Entertainment," in *Formations of Pleasure,* ed. Tony Bennett et al. (Boston: Routledge & Kegan Paul, 1983), pp. 101–123. On the acculturation of the "middlebrow" in America, see Joan Shelley Rubin, *The Making of Middlebrow Culture* (Chapel Hill: University of North Carolina Press, 1992), pp. 266–329.

6. Durstine, "We're on the Air," pp. 623–631; on his parody of clients, see Durstine, "Curtain Going Up on Act II of Advertising."

7. Joseph K. Hart, "Radiating Culture," *Survey* 47 (March 18, 1922): 948–949, cited in Susan J. Douglas, *Inventing American Broadcasting, 1899–1922* (Baltimore: Johns Hopkins University Press, 1987), p. 309; Michele Hilmes, *Radio Voices: American Broadcasting, 1922–1952* (Minneapolis: University of Minnesota Press, 1997), pp. 1–33, passim.

8. Douglas, *Inventing American Broadcasting,* p. 317, passim; Philip T. Rosen, *The Modern Stentors: Radio Broadcasters and the Federal Government, 1920–1934* (Westport, CT: Greenwood Press, 1980), p. 11, passim; Hugh G. J. Aitken, *The Continuous Wave: Technology and American Radio, 1900–1932* (Princeton, NJ: Princeton University Press, 1985), pp. 22–23, passim; Susan Smulyan, *Selling Radio: The Commercialization of American Broadcasting, 1920–1934* (Washington, DC: Smithsonian Institution Press, 1994), pp. 37–64, passim; John W. Spalding, "1928: Radio Becomes a Mass Advertising Medium," *Journal of Broadcasting* 8 (winter 1963–1964): 31–44.

9. For glimpses of programming staff at NBC and CBS, see Carlat, "Sound Values" (Ph.D. diss.), passim; Thomas Williams, "NBC Cuts a Five Candle Cake," *Radio Digest* 28 (December 1931): 30, 89–90; Erik Barnouw, *A Tower in Babel: A History of Broadcasting in the United States,* vol. 1, *To 1933* (New York: Oxford University Press, 1983), p. 250; and Barnouw, *The Golden Web,* pp. 70–71; on agencies, see J. Fred MacDonald, *Don't Touch That Dial! Radio Programming in American Life from 1920 to 1960* (Chicago: Nelson-Hall, 1970), pp. 31–33; on network promoters and critics, see Smulyan, *Selling Radio,* pp. 73–75.

10. Powell, "Tiger Man," pp. 22–23, 54.

11. "Roy S. Durstine Dies; Leader in Advertising," New York *Herald Tribune,* 12 November 1962, p. 22; typescript, "Data about Roy Sarles Durstine for 'Broadcasting'" (1936), BBDO: Personnel: D, BBDO.

12. Durstine, "Curtain Going Up on Act II of Advertising."

13. Typescript, "Data about Roy Sarles Durstine for 'Broadcasting'" (1936), BBDO.

14. Typescript obituary, "Arthur Pryor, Jr.," 25 May 1954, BBDO: Personnel: Former: Pryor, Arthur, BBDO; Sloan's appearance is noted in the daily radio program listing, *New York Times,* 25 December 1928, p. 10.

15. Durstine, "We're on the Air." As media historian Douglas Kahn notes, "despite the cultural pervasiveness of sound, there was no artistic practice outside music identified primarily with aurality." Kahn, "Introduction: Histories of Sound Once Removed," in *Wireless Imagination: Sound, Radio, and the Avant-Garde,* ed. Douglas Kahn and Gregory Whitehead (Cambridge, MA: MIT Press, 1992), p. 2.

16. Neil Harris, "John Philip Sousa and the Culture of Reassurance," in *Perspectives on John Philip Sousa,* ed. Jon Newsom (Washington, DC: Library of Congress, 1983), pp. 11–40.

17. Harriet Menken, the theater critic for the Theatre Guild and host of WOR's *Town Talk,* followed network dramatists engaged in the process. Menken, "The Play's the Thing," *Radio Digest* 28 (May 1931): 23, 106; and Menken, "Front Row Centre for Radio Drama," *Radio Digest* 26 (February 1931): 29, 96; Peter Dixon, "Supplying Drama to Radio Audiences," *The Drama Magazine* 21 (October 1930): 7–8, 20.

18. Novick, *That Noble Dream,* p. 193.

19. "Colonial revival" describes the antiquarian and anti-immigrant impulses of the 1920s, reflected in the display of a world "untainted" by industrial processes. Wendy Kaplan, "R. T. H. Halsey: An Ideology of Collecting American Decorative Arts," *Winterthur Portfolio* 17 (spring 1982): 43–53; Elizabeth Stillinger, *The Antiquers* (New York: Alfred A. Knopf, 1980), pp. 188–189, 233, passim; Karal Ann Marling, *George Washington Slept Here: Colonial Revivals and American Culture, 1876–1986* (Cambridge, MA: Harvard University Press, 1988); Michael Kammen, *Mystic Chords of Memory: The Transformation of Tradition in American Culture* (New York: Alfred A. Knopf, 1991), p. 340; William Rhodes, "Roadside Colonial: Early American Design for the Automobile Age, 1900–1940," *Winterthur Portfolio* 21 (summer/autumn 1986): 133–152. On the organization of the American Association for State and Local History, see Charles B. Hosmer, Jr., "The Roots of AASLH," and Cary Carson, "Front and Center: Local History Comes of Age," both in Frederick L. Rath, Jr., et al., *Local History, National Heritage: Reflections on the History of the AASLH* (Nashville, TN: American Association for State and Local History, 1991), pp. 7–22, 67–108.

20. Rockefeller and Henry Ford each undertook the re-creation of model colonial communities. See Charles B. Hosmer, *Preservation Comes of Age: From Williamsburg to the National Trust, 1926–1949* (Charlottesville: University Press of Virginia, 1981), pp. 11–73; John M. Staudemaier, "Clean Exhibits, Messy Exhibits: Henry Ford's Technological Aesthetic," in *Industrial Society and Its Museums, 1890–1990: Social Aspirations and Cultural Politics,* ed. Brigitte Schroeder-Gudehus (Langhorne, PA: Harwood Academic Publishers, 1993), pp. 55–65; Geoffrey C. Upward, *A Home for Our Heritage: The Building and Growth of Greenfield Village and Henry Ford Museum, 1929–1979* (Dearborn, MI: Henry Ford Museum Press, 1979), pp. 3–4, 15.

21. Typescript, Arthur Pryor, Jr., "Building a Radio Program," September 23, 1931, BBDO: Depts: Radio, BBDO.

22. Advertisement, "Come to New England! See Where History Was Made," *Saturday Evening Post* 200 (April 21, 1928): 120–121.

23. Advertisement, "Come to New England This Summer and See the Workshop of the Nation," *Saturday Evening Post* 200 (June 2, 1928): 106–107. The apportionment of the campaign's advertising budget among media appears to have favored what Warren Susman and others have described as a "people of the book." See Susman, *Culture as History,* pp. 160–161; Myron Lounsbury, "'Flashes of Lightning': The Moving Picture in the Progressive Era," *Journal of Popular Culture* 3 (spring 1970): 772–787. The disproportionate weighting of print to drama bears striking similarity to the ongoing political relations campaign of Socony's corporate successor, the Mobil Corporation. Laurence Jarvik, "PBS and the Politics of Quality: Mobil Oil's 'Masterpiece Theatre,'" *Historical Journal of Film, Radio and Television* 12, no. 3 (1992): 253–274; Jarvik, *PBS: Behind the Screen* (Rocklin, CA: Prima Publishing, 1996), pp. 237–258; Irwin Ross, "Public Relations Isn't Kid-Glove Stuff at Mobil," *Fortune* 94 (September 1976): 106–111, 196–202; on Mobil's op-ed advertising, with examples, see Herb Schmertz with William Novak, *Good-bye to the Low Profile: The Art of Creative Confrontation* (Boston: Little, Brown and Company, 1986), pp. 133–175.

24. Typescript, "BBDO Short History (proposed 75th anniversary publication), 9/2/66," BBDO.

25. *Westinghouse Magazine* (November 1929): 2–3.

26. "Radio Salute," *Westinghouse Magazine* (February 1930): 11.

27. "Salute to Cities Continue," *Radio Digest* 25 (August 1930): 62.

28. Advertisement, Westinghouse Electric and Manufacturing, "Putting the Romance of Industry on the Air," *Radio Digest* 27 (June 1931): 3.

29. Ibid.

30. "Salute to Cities Continue," *Radio Digest* 25 (August 1930): 62.

31. Bruce Barton, *A Parade of the States* (New York: Doubleday, Doran & Co., and Garden City Publishing, 1932), pp. v, 197–198.

32. Duke Parry, "Hear America First! 'Parade of States' a Musical Pageant and Salutation to All Sections," *Radio Digest* 27 (November 1931): 20–21, 89–90.

33. Sloan later wrote, "When I first attended a world's fair I began to realize that science applied to industry portended the abolition of poverty." Alfred P. Sloan, Jr., *Adventures of a White-Collar Man* (New York: Doubleday, Doran & Company, 1941), pp. 3–6, quote p. 194; Sloan, *My Years with General Motors* (Garden City, NY: Doubleday & Company, 1963), p. 17; "Alfred P. Sloan Jr.: Chairman," *Fortune* 17 (April 1938): 72–77, 110–114.

34. Sloan, *My Years with General Motors,* pp. 19, 22–24.

35. Alfred D. Chandler, Jr., and Stephen Salsbury, *Pierre S. du Pont and the Making of the Modern Corporation* (New York: Harper & Row, 1971), pp. 435–437, 450–456; Alfred D. Chandler, Jr., *Strategy and Structure: Chapters in the History of the Industrial Enterprise* (Cambridge, MA: MIT Press, 1962), pp. 89–91; Stuart W. Leslie, *Boss Kettering* (New York: Columbia University Press, 1983), pp. 149–180, 191–194; Sloan, *My Years with General Motors,* pp. 221–226, 235–237.

36. Sloan, *My Years with General Motors,* pp. 45–56; Chandler and Salsbury, *Pierre S. du Pont and the Making of the Modern Corporation,* pp. 473–474, 493–496; Chandler, *Strategy and Structure,* pp.

130–142, 145–153; Donaldson Brown, *Some Reminiscences of an Industrialist* (Easton, PA: Hive Publishing Co., 1977), pp. 59, 63–68; Arthur J. Kuhn, *GM Passes Ford, 1918–1938: Designing the General Motors Performance-Control System* (University Park: Pennsylvania State University Press, 1986), pp. 56–57, 63–64, 111–117, passim.

37. Sloan, *My Years with General Motors*, pp. 58–70, 238–247, 276; Chandler and Salsbury, *Pierre S. du Pont and the Making of the Modern Corporation*, pp. 512–518; Chandler, *Strategy and Structure*, pp. 142–144; James J. Flink, "Sloanism," in *Encyclopedia of American Business History and Biography: The Automobile Industry, 1920–1980*, ed. George S. May (New York: Bruccoli Clark Layman, Inc., and Facts on File, Inc., 1989), pp. 414–417; Richard S. Tedlow, *New and Improved: The Story of Mass Marketing in America* (New York: Basic Books, 1990), pp. 166–175; Daniel Raff, "Making Cars and Money in the Interwar Period," *Business History Review* 65 (winter 1991): 721–753; Kuhn, *GM Passes Ford*, pp. 82–95.

38. For program classifications, see Harrison B. Summers, *A Thirty-Year History of Programs Carried on National Radio Networks in the United States, 1926–1956* (New York: Arno Press, 1971). Gerald Perschbacher notes that by 1937 General Motors topped the NBC list of advertisers with expenditures of nearly $550,000, part of a trend among automobile advertisers who in the first six months of 1936 spent over $20 million for 22.8 percent of that year's total advertising dollars. See Perschbacher, "Auto Makers in Radio," *Old Car News & Marketplace* (November 12, 1992): 9.

39. Borden, *Advertising Text and Cases*, pp. 503–504; Sloan, *My Years with General Motors*, pp. 104–105; Marchand, "The Corporation Nobody Knew," pp. 825–875.

40. An interpreter of "Anglo-Saxon folk culture," Powell had helped organize the White Top Folk Festival in his native Virginia earlier that year. David E. Whisnant, *All That Is Native and Fine: The Politics of Culture in an American Region* (Chapel Hill: University of North Carolina Press, 1983), pp. 218–246.

41. Barton, *A Parade of the States*.

42. Parry, "Hear America First!"

43. M. H. Aylesworth to Lawrence Richey, 20 August 1932, folder 1, General Motors Co.–1932, box 10, NBC/SHSW.

44. Barton, *A Parade of the States*; advertisement, "The New General Motors Radio Program 'The Parade of the States,'" *Radio Digest* 28 (December 1931): 9.

45. Paul Garrett to M. H. Aylesworth, 7 July 1932, folder 1, General Motors–1932, box 10, NBC/SHSW.

46. Synopsis, "The Problems of the States," folder 1, General Motors–1932, box 10, NBC/SHSW.

47. Burke Boyce to Bertha Brainard for Mr. Royal, 20 July 1932, folder 1, General Motors–1932, box 10, NBC/SHSW. The last novel by Emerson Hough, *The Covered Wagon*, became a theatrical feature film in 1923. See "'The Covered Wagon,' Epic of the Oregon Trail," *Review of Reviews* 67 (June 1923): 643–647.

48. A. P. Sloan, Jr., to Charles T. Fisher, 7 February 1933, folder: correspondence, GMC February 1933, box 176, Edward L. Bernays Collection, Manuscript Division, Library of Congress (hereafter ELB/LC).

49. Typescript, "General Motors" (n.d.) and Samuel Crowther to Bernays, 29 December 1932, folder: notes GMC, box 177, ELB/LC; William E. Akin, *Technocracy and the American Dream: The Technocrat Movement, 1900–1941* (Berkeley: University of California Press, 1977), pp. 61–62, 80–89, 111–112; for general discussion and background of "technological unemployment," see Peter J. Kuznick, *Beyond the Laboratory: Scientists as Political Activists in 1930s America* (Chicago: University of Chicago Press, 1987), pp. 18–25.

50. Paul Garrett to Bernays, 16 March 1933; Bernays to Garrett, 17 March 1933 and 28 March 1933; folder: General Motors Corporation March 1933, box 177, ELB/LC.

51. Paul Willard Garrett, "A Bigger and Better General Motors" (October 3, 1931), folder: General Motors Corp. June–July 1933, box 177, ELB/LC.

52. "Leaders Put Faith in the Machine Age to End Depression," *New York Times*, 9 January 1933, pp. 1, 3; "The Machine's Friends Reply to the Technocrats," *Literary Digest* (January 21, 1933): 6. A year later Bernays called Garrett's attention to the caroming of "another of our ideas, you may recall, come to life on the front page of the *Times*" in physicist Robert Millikan's attack upon Technocracy. Bernays to Garrett, 23 February 1934, and attachment, "Leaders Deny Science Cuts Jobs; Warn against 'Research Holiday,'" *New York Times*, 23 February 1934, pp. 1, 10, folder: General Motors Corporation February 1934, box 177, ELB/LC.

53. Sloan to Fisher, 7 February 1933, folder: correspondence, General Motors Corporation February 1933, box 176, ELB/LC.

54. "Corporation History Stressed at Dinner," *New York Times*, 16 November 1933, p. 29; and note, folder: Columbia Broadcasting System 1929–1930, box 135, ELB/LC.

55. The "top men" included Charles F. Kettering, vice president in charge of research, General Motors Corporation; Glenn Frank, president of the University of Wisconsin; Harvey Wiley Corbett, of Corbett, Harrison and MacMurray, architects; Carl R. Gray, president, Union Pacific Railroad; Robert E. Wilson, vice president and director of research, Standard Oil Company of Indiana; Aylesworth, president of NBC; Morris

Fishbein, editor, American Medical Association *Journal;* and Walter B. Pitikin, professor of journalism, Columbia University. R. C. Witmer to Edgar Kobak, 4 May 1934, folder 29, General Motors Jan.–Aug. 1934, box 27, NBC/SHSW.

56. M. H. Aylesworth to C. M. Chester, 23 July 1934, folder 26, General Foods Company–1934, box 27, NBC/SHSW.

57. Telegram, Alfred P. Sloan, Jr., to Aylesworth, 16 May 1934, folder 29, General Motors Jan.–Aug. 1934, box 27, NBC/SHSW.

58. Sloan to Aylesworth, 5 June 1934, folder 29, General Motors Jan.–Aug. 1934, box 27, NBC/SHSW.

59. Paul Willard Garrett to Aylesworth, 3 August 1934, folder 29, General Motors Jan.–Aug. 1934, box 27, NBC/SHSW.

60. Garrett to Roy C. Witmer, 21 August 1934, folder 29, General Motors Jan.–Aug. 1934, box 27, NBC/SHSW; "Luxury Motors Pay to Keep Harmony on the Air," *Newsweek* 4 (October 20, 1934): 29–30.

61. R. H. White to Witmer, 13 February 1935, folder 7, General Motors–1935, box 37, NBC/SHSW.

62. Press release, "General Motors to Sponsor Concert Series over NBC, for release October 2, 1934," folder 28, General Motors Sept.–Dec. 1934, box 27, NBC/SHSW.

63. David L. Lewis, *The Public Image of Henry Ford: An American Folk Hero and His Company* (Detroit: Wayne State University Press, 1976), pp. 315–329; "Toscanini on the Air," *Fortune* 17 (January 1938): 62–68, 112, 120; Harvey Pinney, "The Radio Pastor of Dearborn," *Nation* 145 (October 9, 1937): 374–375; for examples of talks, see William J. Cameron, *The Ford Sunday Evening Hour Talks* (Dearborn, MI: Ford Motor Company, 1936).

64. White to Witmer, 13 February 1935, folder 7, General Motors–1935, box 37, NBC/SHSW.

65. Sloan to Aylesworth, 19 November 1934, folder 28, General Motors Sept.–Dec. 1934, box 27, NBC/SHSW.

66. Sloan to Aylesworth, 2 January 1935, folder 7, General Motors–1935, box 37, NBC/SHSW.

67. Artists expected to appear in following programs included violinist Yehudi Menuhin, Arturo Toscanini (returning to the program in a concert prepared especially for radio), Paul Whiteman, and George Gershwin. Aylesworth to Sloan, 5 January 1935, folder 7, General Motors–1935, box 37; press release, 11 December 1934, folder 28, General Motors Sept.–Dec. 1934, box 27, NBC/SHSW.

68. Sloan to Aylesworth, 10 January 1935, folder 7, General Motors–1935, box 37, NBC/SHSW.

69. "When Our Young Folks Learn to Drive," General Motors Concerts, 6 October 1935, folder 7, General Motors–1935, box 37, NBC/SHSW.

70. "Sloan Sees Doom of Regimentation," *New York Times,* 12 December 1934, p. 6; Edward Angly, "Both Sides Gird for New Battle in Auto Strike," *New York Herald Tribune*, 25 January 1937, p. 8.

71. Continuity for "The Right to Work," broadcast 24 January 1937, folder 45, General Motors–1937, box 53, NBC/SHSW.

72. Royal to David Sarnoff, 23 January 1937, folder 45, General Motors–1937, box 53, NBC/SHSW.

73. "Paragraph in question in General Motors program, Sunday January 31," folder 45, General Motors Corp., 1937, box 53, NBC/SHSW.

74. Sidney Fine, *Sit-Down: The General Motors Strike of 1936–1937* (Ann Arbor: University of Michigan Press, 1969), pp. 192, 303–312.

75. "Human Rights and Property Rights—Inseparably Bound," broadcast 14 February 1937; Garrett to Robert Wohlforth, 23 February 1937, folder 45, General Motors–1937, box 53, NBC/SHSW.

76. Borden, *Advertising Text and Cases,* p. 503.

77. Roy C. Witmer to Lenox R. Lohr, 8 June 1939, folder 55, General Motors–1939, box 68, NBC/SHSW; on NBC, Royal, and Toscanini, see "Toscanini on the Air," *Fortune* 17 (January 1938): 62–68, 112–120; and Joseph Horowitz, *Understanding Toscanini: A Social History of American Concert Life* (Berkeley, CA: University of California Press, 1994), pp. 152–153.

78. Paul W. Garrett, "Public Relations—Industry's No. 1 Job," delivered at the twenty-first annual convention of the American Association of Advertising Agencies on Friday, April 22, 1938, at the Greenbrier, White Sulfur Springs, West Virginia, pamphlet collection, Hagley Library.

79. Robert R. R. Brooks, *When Labor Organizes* (New Haven: Yale University Press, 1937), p. 76.

80. The latter series of messages appeared on 15,000 billboards in 2,827 cities and towns in 48 states; the daily circulation was conservatively estimated at 65 million. "Industry Speaks to Millions," folder: outdoor posters 1937, box 113; "Telling Industry's Story Outdoors to All Americans," folder: 1937 Telling Industry's Story Outdoors, box 113, acc. 1411, series I, National Association of Manufacturers Collection, Hapley Library, Wilmington, DE (hereafter NAM/HL). On Campbell-Ewald's creation of the NAM bill-

boards, see United States Congress, Senate, Committee on Education and Labor, *Violations of Free Speech and Rights of Labor. Report . . . Pursuant to S. Resolution 266 (74th Congress), Labor Policies of Employers' Associations. Part III, National Association of Manufacturers* (Washington, DC: Government Printing Office, 1939), pp. 168–170 (hereafter *LaFollette Committee Reports*).

81. Brooks, *When Labor Organizes*, p. 76.

Chapter 3

1. Wolfskill, *The Revolt of the Conservatives*, pp. 228–231; Tedlow, "The National Association of Manufacturers," pp. 25–45.

2. Pamphlet, "Which Way America? Facts about the Crusaders," folder 29, Crusaders–1934, box 25, NBC/SHSW.

3. Barnouw, *The Golden Web*, pp. 14–15; for NBC speakers, speech titles, and broadcast dates, see Royal to Patterson, 4 August 1934, folder 29, Crusaders–1934, box 25, NBC/SHSW; card for Mutual and Yankee networks beginning 9 October 1935, folder: Crusaders 1932–1939, box 14, BB/SHSW.

4. NBC broadcast eight talks in this manner from June 18 to August 20, 1934. The first speaker and the Crusaders' "radio director," U.S. Navy (ret.) Rear Admiral Robert H. Harris, delivered a talk entitled "The American Civilization." Subsequent broadcasts featured the NAM's Robert L. Lund on "The Rare Ability of the American Businessman"; F. M. Law, president of the American Bankers Association, on "What the Banks Are Doing to Aid in Business"; Dr. Virgil Jordan, president of the National Industrial Conference Board, on "Our National Wealth and Income"; Colonel Robert McCormick, publisher of the *Chicago Tribune*, on "The Rising Red Tide in America"; Nobel laureate physicist Robert A. Millikan, on "Excess Government May Spoil the American Dream"; New York congressman Fred A. Britten, on "Americanism on Trial"; and Colonel Frank Knox, the publisher of the *Chicago Daily News* and future Republican Party vice presidential candidate, on "Business Free or in Chains." L. A. Van Patten to Philips Carlin, 7 May 1934; Royal to Frank Mason, 7 June 1934; Royal to Patterson, 4 August 1934; Royal to Aylesworth, 29 October 1934, folder 29, Crusaders–1934, box 25, NBC/SHSW.

5. U.S. Senate, *Investigation of Lobbying Activities: Hearings before a Special Committee to Investigate Lobbying Activities*, 74th, 75th Congress (1935–1938), 8 vols., pp. 1748–1750 (hereafter *Black Committee Reports*), cited in Wolfskill, *The Revolt of the Conservatives*, pp. 230–231, and Barnouw, *The Golden Web*, pp. 14–15; for contributors and organizations, see "List of Contributors," *Black Committee Reports, Digest of Data*, p. 1, and Burk, *The Corporate State and the Broker State*, pp. 220–226.

6. Business leaders who agreed to support the Crusader campaign publicly by serving on the National Advisory Council were Edwin M. Allen, president of Mathieson Alkali Works; George G. Allen, president of Duke Power Co.; Thomas H. Blodgett, chairman of American Chicle Co.; Colby M. Chester, president of General Foods Corp.; Donald K. David, president of American Maize Products Co.; Francis B. Davis, Jr., president of U.S. Rubber Co.; William M. Greve; Elon H. Hooker, president of Hooker Electrochemical Co.; Fred I. Kent; Lee W. Maxwell, president of Crowell Publishing Co.; Thomas H. McInnerney, president of National Dairy Products Corp.; George Monroe Moffett, president of Corn Products Refining Co.; Jos. A. Moore, chairman of The Butterick Co.; Ridley Watts; S. Clay Williams, president of R. J. Reynolds Tobacco Co.; Joseph Wilshire, president of Standard Brands, Inc. "Report of Meeting Held in the Directors Room, General Foods Company, 250 Park Avenue on July 9th, 1934"; on Hutton, see Aylesworth to Patterson, 23 July 1934, folder 29, Crusaders–1934, box 25, NBC/SHSW.

7. The Crusaders requested to sponsor fifteen-minute programs "for the exclusive purpose of speeches opposing radicalism, NRA, socialism, etc." R. C. Witmer to R. C. Patterson, 24 October 1934, folder: 372 Political Broadcasting 1924–35, NBC/LC; Royal to Patterson, 4 August 1934, folder 29, Crusaders–1934, box 25; Niles Trammell to Lohr, 11 January 1936, folder 33, General Mills–1936, box 46, NBC/SHSW; on Lasker, see also Barnouw, *The Golden Web*, pp. 9–18.

8. Wolfskill, *The Revolt of the Conservatives*, p. 230.

9. Trammell to Lohr, 11 January 1936, folder 33, General Mills–1936, box 46, NBC/SHSW; Charles F. Sarjeant, ed., *The First Forty: The Story of WCCO Radio* (Minneapolis: T. S. Denison & Co., 1964), pp. 69–77.

10. George B. McClelland, memorandum for file, 7 July 1933, folder 52, General Mills–1933, box 17; on Davis's attempts to sponsor news, see Trammell to Lohr, 11 January 1936, folder 33, General Mills–1936, box 46, NBC/SHSW.

11. James Gray, *Business without Boundary: The Story of General Mills* (Minneapolis: University of Minnesota Press, 1954), pp. 172–178, 182, cited in Marchand, *Advertising the American Dream*, pp. 353–354, n. 63; Summers, *A Thirty-Year History*, pp. 43, 45, 48; John Dunning, *Tune in Yesterday: The Ultimate Encyclopedia of Old-Time Radio, 1925–1976* (Englewood Cliffs, NJ: Prentice-Hall, 1976), pp. 61 *(Betty and Bob)*, 311–314 *(Jack Armstrong)*.

12. John F. Royal to Janet MacRorie, 31 October 1935; Royal to Edgar Kobak, 11 November 1935; MacRorie to D. S. Shaw, 10 January 1936; Dorothy Kemble to Bertha Brainard, 27 April 1938, folder: 358 Policy–Program Policy 1929–50, NBC/LC. Concerned with maintaining the appearance of political im-

partiality, one NBC official sought to rename the Red network, "particularly obnoxious to many people who associate the word 'red' with political implications." Frank E. Mason to Lenox R. Lohr, 29 November 1938, folder: 326 Owned & Operated Stations–Changes in Call Letters & Sign Offs, NBC/LC.

13. Royal to Aylesworth, 29 October 1934, folder 29, Crusaders–1934, box 25, NBC/SHSW; review, "Horse Sense Philosophy," *Variety* 118 (May 1, 1935): 38.

14. *LaFollette Committee Reports*, pp. 208–220; Harry H. Millis and Emily Clark Brown, *From the Wagner Act to Taft-Hartley: A Study of National Labor Policy and Labor Relations* (Chicago: University of Chicago Press, 1950), pp. 281–291; V. O. Key, *Politics, Parties, and Pressure Groups* (New York: Thomas Y. Crowell Company, 1958), pp. 99–100.

15. Tedlow, "The National Association of Manufacturers"; *LaFollette Committee Reports*, pp. 44–47.

16. During the period January 1, 1933, to November 1, 1937, contributions received from DuPont and General Motors led the list ($118,600 and $66,520, respectively), which when combined comprised less than 5 percent of the association's total income received from 3,008 member contributors in the same period (*LaFollette Committee Reports*, pp. 50–51, 211–213); see also Philip H. Burch, Jr., "The NAM as an Interest Group," *Politics and Society* 4 (fall 1973): 97–130.

17. *LaFollette Committee Reports*, pp. 215–218.

18. The story typically emphasized what pro-labor legislation did not define in the way of rights and remedies. *LaFollette Committee Reports*, p. 127; Tedlow, "The National Association of Manufacturers"; Rexford G. Tugwell, *The Democratic Roosevelt: A Biography of Franklin D. Roosevelt* (Garden City, NY: Doubleday & Company, 1957), p. 336.

19. Outlining the public relations committee's plan of operation in 1933, NAM chairman Robert L. Lund explained, "The job, it will be recognized, is similar to that which has been done for individuals and large corporations by men such as Ivy Lee, Brenys [*sic*], Bruce Barton, and others." Tedlow, "The National Association of Manufacturers"; *LaFollette Committee Reports*, pp. 154–155, 212.

20. "N.A.M. Public Information Program 1940 (for discussion by Public Relations Advisory Group, Tuesday, February 20, 1940)," folder 74, NAM–Public Information Program–1940 (Mr. Mullen's files), box 78, NBC/SHSW. For a comparative listing and description of activities during the period 1937–1938, see *LaFollette Committee Reports*, pp. 159–167.

21. Schiller, *Theorizing Communication*, p. 45.

22. *American Family Robinson* episode 20, cited in MacDonald, *Don't Touch That Dial*, pp. 254–256; Tedlow, "The National Association of Manufacturers."

23. *American Family Robinson* 20, cited in MacDonald, *Don't Touch That Dial*, p. 254.

24. *American Family Robinson* 21, collection of J. Fred MacDonald.

25. *American Family Robinson* 21 and 22, cited in ibid.

26. *American Family Robinson* 26 and 27, cited in ibid.

27. "'American Family Robinson' Program Now in Third Successful Year," *World News* 4, no. 6 (June 1937): 1, 5; *Centerville Herald*, vol. 1, nos. 1 and 2 [n.d.], folder: Radio–American Family Robinson, box 156, acc. 1411, NAM/HL.

28. James P. Selvage to Noel Sargent, 2 July 1935, folder: Radio–American Family Robinson, box 156, acc. 1411, NAM/HL.

29. L. H. Titterton to Royal, 16 October and 20 October 1934; Titterton to Bertha Brainard, 4 December 1934, folder 31, American Family Robinson–1934, box 23, NBC/SHSW.

30. On the matter of the NAM and "unlimited time," Royal wrote: "In my opinion, we cannot do this. While they are our biggest clients, there is a much bigger question facing. That is the very question of our existence for 'public interest, convenience and necessity'. We should give them every possible cooperation except where it interferes with our policies. It is true that our policies have had to change with the times and we must always be prepared to meet new situations." Royal to Patterson, 20 February 1935, folder 40, National Association of Manufacturers–1935, box 39, NBC/SHSW.

31. F. N. Bard to Walter B. Weisenburger (cc: R. C. Patterson), 14 February 1935, folder 40, NAM–1935, box 39, NBC/SHSW.

32. Royal to Patterson, 20 February 1935, folder 40, NAM–1935, box 39, NBC/SHSW.

33. "Democrats' St. Paul," *Time* 27 (June 1, 1936): 27.

34. Stanley High, "Radio's Policy Disarms Its Critics," *Literary Digest* 118 (August 11, 1934): 23.

35. High to Royal, 6 September 1935, folder 63, High, Stanley, 1936, box 46, NBC/SHSW.

36. Press release, "Stanley High Is Named NBC Director of Talks," 28 October 1935, Central Files Correspondence, folder 44, High, Stanley (NBC Director of Talks) Oct.–Dec. 1935, box 37, NBC/SHSW.

37. Horace Newcomb and Paul Hirsch, "Television as a Cultural Form," in *Television: The Critical View*, Newcomb, pp. 503–515.

38. High to Royal [n.d.], received and stamped 19 February 1935, folder 40, NAM–1935, box 39, NBC/SHSW.

39. Memorandum, "Notes on Conference between Messrs. Colgate, Kobak, Morton, High" [n.d.]; Lammot du Pont to James P. Selvage, 25 March 1935, folder 40, NAM–1935, box 39, NBC/SHSW.

40. High, "General Objectives of American Cavalcade" [n.d.], folder 40, NAM–1935, box 39, NBC/SHSW.

41. High to Bell, 20 February 1935, folder 40 Nat'l Assn of Mfgrs, 1935, box 39, NBC/SHSW.

42. Ibid.

43. Lammot du Pont to Selvage, 25 March 1935; Walter B. Weisenburger to Kobak, 3 April 1935; Alfred H. Morton to Royal, 1 May 1935, all in folder 40, NAM–1935, box 39; Kobak to Lammot du Pont, 6 April 1935; Lammot du Pont to Kobak, 9 April 1935, all in folder 13, DuPont de Nemours Co., E. I.–1935, box 36, NBC/SHSW.

44. Contemporary observers attributed the popularity of *Cavalcade* (and of the BBC's similar *Scrapbooks*) to audiences for whom the play and its spinoffs became "a revelation of history." Susan Briggs, *Those Radio Times* (London: Weidenfeld & Nicholson, 1981), pp. 12–14; "'Cavalcade' as a Film Outshines the Play," *Literary Digest* 115 (January 28, 1933): 15.

45. Burke Boyce to Alfred H. Morton, 22 April 1935, folder 40 Nat'l Assn of Mfgrs, 1935, box 39, NBC/SHSW.

46. Review, "Town Hall of the Air," *Variety* 118 (5 June 1935): 34; "Town Meetings on the Air," *Survey* 71 (August 1935): 238; Weldon Melick, "National Heckle Hour," *Reader's Digest* 28 (June 1936): 42–46.

47. Morton to David Rosenblum, re American Adventure and Town Hall programs, 27 July 1935, folder 55, American Adventure–1935, box 33, NBC/SHSW.

48. Durstine to Sarnoff, 28 April 1936, folder 29, BBDO–1936, box 44, NBC/SHSW.

49. Barton to Paul Markman, 12 March 1956, folder DuPont 1950–1957, box 76, BB/SHSW; L. L. L. Golden, *Only by Public Consent: American Corporations Search for Favorable Opinion* (New York: Hawthorn Books, 1968), pp. 235–247.

50. Chandler and Salsbury, *Pierre S. du Pont,* pp. 47–54, 358–360, 381–386, 427–430; Chandler, *Strategy and Structure,* pp. 54, 56–57, 78–91, Joseph Frazier Wall, *Alfred I. du Pont: The Man and His Family* (New York: Oxford University Press, 1990), pp. 36–65, 180–196.

51. John E. Wilitz, *In Search of Peace: The Senate Munitions Inquiry, 1934–36* (Baton Rouge: Louisiana State University Press, 1963), pp. 21–23: 34–35, 74, 122–126; H. C. Engelbrecht and F. C. Hanighen, *Merchants of Death* (Garden City, NY: Garden City Publishing Company, 1934), pp. 22–37, 179–180, 248–249; "Arms and the Men," *Fortune* 9 (March 1934): 52–57, 113–126.

52. The Roosevelt administration's announcement of the reopening of the dormant suit came in 1935, shortly before the Liberty League's Mayflower Hotel banquet featuring Al Smith. Tried in 1936, du Pont was ordered to pay $800,000, Raskob $1,100,000. The Supreme Court refused to hear the case on appeal in 1942 and the penalties stood. Roy Haywood Lopata, "John J. Raskob: A Conservative Businessman in the Age of Roosevelt" (Ph.D. diss., University of Delaware, 1975), pp. 249–251.

53. Roy Norr, "Public Confidence and How to Lose It," folder: Charles Michelson, box 11, Stephen T. Early papers, FDRL.

54. Cheape, *Strictly Business,* pp. 117, 120–122, 127; Chandler and Salsbury, *Pierre S. du Pont,* pp. 584–587.

55. Charles Michelson, *The Ghost Talks* (New York: G. P. Putnam's Sons, 1944), p. 144. As Douglas B. Craig perceptively notes, "If Michelson could make Herbert Hoover a national villain within two years, the league reasoned, it could do the same with FDR." Craig, *After Wilson: The Struggle for the Democratic Party, 1920–1934* (Chapel Hill: University of North Carolina Press, 1992), pp. 182–186, 286.

56. Wolfskill, *The Revolt of the Conservatives,* p. 212, cited in Burk, *The Corporate State and the Broker State,* p. 221.

57. The DuPont Company established an Advertising Division in April 1911, and a Publicity Bureau in February 1916. In October 1935 this bureau became the Publicity Department; it became the Public Relations Department on April 1, 1938. "History of the Public Relations Department," E. I. du Pont de Nemours & Co., 20 October 1954, typescript, pamphlet collection, HL; Chandler, *Strategy and Structure,* pp. 94–95.

58. T. J. Ross to Lammot du Pont, 7 January 1935, folder: Jan.–March, box 20, 1935 general correspondence, acc. 1813 Willis F. Harrington, DuP/HL.

59. Asked to comment by *Nation's Business* editor Merle Thorpe upon the practice of institutional advertising exemplified by U.S. Steel in 1937, Lammot du Pont replied that upon encountering a U.S. Steel magazine ad, "the thought passed through my mind, 'What is U.S. Steel trying now?' The effect was unpleasant—a sort of revulsion against the Steel Corporation. Perhaps this was due to the fact that for many years it has appeared to me as a corporation not run in the interest of its stockholders, and therefore one that does not stick to its business. It seems to me that . . . generally speaking, a corporation which

does not sell to the public, the public individually, is not justified in advertising to that individual public. You will probably observe that the DuPont Company does not follow this principle. Probably 90 percent of our products is not sold to the public, and yet we do advertise to the public. Perhaps DuPont is justified for special reasons, but those special reasons are rare, and I cannot see that the Steel Corporation has them. Pride of the salesman is all right, and so is the pride of the workman in his work, but that pride should be in the accomplishment and not the applause of the public." Lammot du Pont to Merle Thorpe, 2 June 1937, folder: Advertising Department (#C-24) Jan. 1937–Dec. 1937, box 4, acc. 1662, DuP/HL.

60. DuPont's Grasselli Chemicals also exhibited at the Great Lakes Exposition, held at Cleveland in 1936. "At the Dallas and Cleveland Expositions" and Margaret E. Lott, "The Showcase of an Industry," *DuPont Magazine* 30 (midsummer 1936): 5–7; pamphlet, "What You Should Know about the DuPont Company. Prepared by the Publicity Department for the Information of Employees" (May 1937), p. 9, folder: publicity matters, 1930–1937, box 64, acc. 1662, administrative papers, DuP/HL; David J. Rhees, "Corporate Advertising, Public Relations and Popular Exhibits: The Case of DuPont," in *Industrial Society and Its Museums, 1890–1990,* ed. Schroeder-Gudehus, pp. 67–75. With notable compromises, DuPont and Ford held out the longest "for an older vision of the great fairs as places of popular education in new techniques and industrial processes." Roland Marchand, "Corporate Imagery and Popular Education: World's Fairs and Expositions in the United States, 1893–1940," in *Consumption and American Culture,* ed. David E. Nye and Carl Pedersen (Amsterdam: VU University Press, 1991), pp. 18–33.

61. Barton to Lammot du Pont, May 18, 1935, folder: Advertising Dept., July 1932–Dec. 1935, box 3, acc. 1662, DuP/HL, cited in Rhees, "Corporate Advertising, Public Relations and Popular Exhibits."

62. Barton to Paul Markman, 12 March 1956, folder DuPont 1950–1957, box 76, BB/SHSW.

63. Harry F. Anderson to J. Overall, 16 June 1934, and J. R. Overall to John H. Bachem, 27 September 1934, folder 59, DuPont–1934, box 25, NBC/SHSW.

64. George Sumner Albee, mss. for *Sponsor* magazine article, "The DuPont 'Cavalcade of America,'" and attached letter, Maurice Collette to Albee, 3 March 1947, folder 23, box 11, acc. 1803, DuP/HL; advertisement, "It started one Saturday night," *Saturday Evening Post* 208 (October 5, 1935): 51.

65. Albee, "The DuPont 'Cavalcade of America,'" DuP/HL.

66. Photograph, "Wilmington exhibit October 1935 (no. 10135-B), pictorial collections, DuP/HL.

67. Script, "No Turning Back," *DuPont Presents the Cavalcade of America* 1 (October 9, 1935). A relatively complete set of scripts for the period 1935–1939 can be found in the stack collection of the Library of Congress; a complete list of *Cavalcade of America* broadcasts can be found in the Music Reading Room of the Motion Picture, Broadcasting and Recorded Sound Division, Library of Congress; broadcast transcriptions and playbills can be found in the collection of the HL.

68. Review, "Cavalcade of America," *Variety* 120 (October 16, 1935): 44.

69. High to Royal, 10 October 1935, folder 13 DuPont–1935, box 36, NBC/SHSW.

70. "Faith in Education," *Cavalcade of America* 5 (November 6, 1935), DuP/HL.

71. The series' first four volumes published in 1927 included James Truslow Adams's *Provincial Society* and Alan Nevins's *The Emergence of Modern America*. The 1930s saw publication of Schlesinger's *The Rise of the City*, Arthur Charles Cole's *The Irrepressible Conflict,* and Ida Tarbell's *The Nationalizing of Business*. The 1944 publication of John Allen Krout's and Fox's *The Completion of Independence* completed the series as first conceived. A thirteenth and final volume, Dixon Wecter's *The Age of the Great Depression,* appeared in 1948. A. M. Schlesinger, "An Editor's Second Thoughts," in *Approaches to American Social History,* ed. William E. Lingelbach (New York: D. Appleton-Century Co., 1937), pp. 80–101; Schlesinger, *In Retrospect: The History of a Historian* (New York: Harcourt, Brace & World, 1963), pp. 72, 111–113, 199–200; Novick, *That Noble Dream*, pp. 178–179.

72. Dixon Ryan Fox to Arthur M. Schlesinger, August 31, 1935, folder: E-F, 4/1/35–4/1/36, box 11 correspondence, HUG 4769.305, Arthur M. Schlesinger collection, Harvard University Archives (hereafter AMS/HUA).

73. Walter Muir Whitehill, *Independent Historical Studies: An Inquiry into Their Research and Publication Functions and Their Financial Future* (Boston: The Boston Athenaeum, 1962), p. 336, quoting from a 1957 report by Louis C. Jones, cited in Cary Carson, "Front and Center: Local History Comes of Age," in *Local History, National Heritage: Reflections on the History of AASLH*, by Frederick L. Rath, Jr., et al. (Nashville, TN: American Association for State and Local History, 1991), p. 86.

74. Butterfield, *The Whig Interpretation of History*, pp. 5, 11, 24, 26–27.

75. Dixon Ryan Fox, "Are We Better than Our Ancestors?" in Theodore Sizer, et al., *Aspects of the Social History of America* (Chapel Hill: University of North Carolina Press, 1931), pp. 68–69.

76. Dixon Ryan Fox, *Ideas in Motion* (New York: D. Appleton-Century Company, 1935), p. 4.

77. Fox to Schlesinger, August 31, 1935, folder: E-F 4/1/35–4/1/36, box 11 correspondence, AMS/HUA.

78. Fox to Schlesinger, August 31, 1935, and Schlesinger to Fox, September 4, 1935, folder: E-F 4/1/35–4/1/36, box 11 correspondence, AMS/HUA.

79. Fox to Schlesinger, September 19, 1935, folder: E-F 4/1/35–4/1/36, box 11 correspondence, AMS/HUA.

80. Schlesinger to Fox, September 24, 1935, folder: E-F 4/1/35–4/1/36, box 11 correspondence, AMS/HUA.

81. Webb to Schlesinger, September 28, 1935, and Schlesinger to Kenneth Webb, October 2, 1935, folder: B 4/1/35–4/1/36, box 11 correspondence, AMS/HUA.

82. Schlesinger to Webb, October 8, 1935, folder: B 4/1/35–4/1/36, box 11 correspondence, AMS/HUA.

83. "The Will to Rebuild," *Cavalcade of America* 4 (October 30, 1935), DuP/HL.

84. Telegram, Durstine to Schlesinger, October 31, 1935, folder: B 4/1/35–4/1/36, box 11 correspondence, AMS/HUA.

85. Fox to Schlesinger, October 24, 1935, folder: E-F 4/1/35–4/1/36, box 11 correspondence, AMS/HUA.

86. Schlesinger to Fox, December 14, 1935, folder: E-F 4/1/35–4/1/36, box 11 correspondence, AMS/HUA.

87. Schlesinger to Frederick Bronner, July 15, 1937, folder: B 3/1/37–3/1/38, box 12 correspondence, AMS/HUA.

88. Ibid.

89. "Women in Public Service," *Cavalcade of America* 14 (January 8, 1936), DuP/HL.

90. "Loyalty to Family," *Cavalcade of America* 18 (February 5, 1936), DuP/HL.

91. "Self-Reliance," *Cavalcade of America* 30 (April 29, 1936), DuP/HL.

92. "The Search for Iron," *Cavalcade of America* 129 (April 6, 1938), DuP/HL.

93. "Songs That Inspire the Nation," *Cavalcade of America* 22 (March 4, 1936), DuP/HL.

94. "Songs of Home," *Cavalcade of America* 35 (June 3, 1936), DuP/HL.

95. "The Development of Band Music in America," *Cavalcade of America* 41 (July 22, 1936), DuP/HL.

96. Webb to Schlesinger, December 18, 1936, folder: B 4/1/36–4/1/37, box 11 correspondence, and Webb to Schlesinger, July 22, 1937, folder: W 3/1/37–3/1/38, box 12 correspondence, AMS/HUA.

97. Webb to Schlesinger, November 22, 1935, folder: B 4/1/35–4/1/36, box 11 correspondence, AMS/HUA.

98. Webb to Schlesinger, July 22, 1937, folder: W 3/1/37–3/1/38, box 12 correspondence. Schlesinger pointed out that Barton had nursed in the Civil War and the Franco-Prussian War before starting her campaign for American participation in the Red Cross. Schlesinger to Webb, July 21, 1937, folder: W 3/1/37–3/1/38, box 12 correspondence, AMS/HUA.

99. Webb to Schlesinger, April 22, 1936, folder: W 4/1/36–3/1/37, box 12 correspondence, AMS/HUA.

100. Schlesinger to Webb, April 23, 1936, folder: W 4/1/36–3/1/37, box 12 correspondence, AMS/HUA.

101. Schlesinger to Webb, December 27, 1937, folder: W 3/1/37–3/1/38, box 12 correspondence, AMS/HUA.

102. Schlesinger to Fox, February 23, 1937, folder: E-F 4/1/36–3/1/37, box 11 correspondence; and June 21, 1938, folder: E-F 3/1/38–1/1/39, box 13 correspondence, AMS/HUA.

103. Fox to du Pont, 3 April 1937, folder: Advertising Department (#C-24) Jan. 1937–Dec. 1937, box 4, acc. 1662, DuP/HL, cited in Roland Marchand, typescript, "Creating the Corporate Soul," 11 April 1997.

104. Dixon Ryan Fox, foreword to *The Cavalcade of America*, ed. Fox and Arthur M. Schlesinger (Springfield, MA: Milton Bradley, 1937), p. viii. On Fox's role in selecting scripts and preparing the foreword, see Fox to Webb, October 2, 1937, folder: W 3/1/37–3/1/38, box 12 correspondence, AMS/HUA.

105. "New Twist for History," *BBDO Newsletter* (October–November 1936), file: BBDO–Dep'ts: Radio, BBDO.

106. Burk, *The Corporate State and the Broker State*, p. 236.

107. Edgar Kobak, cc: Shaw, Hitz, Overall, 6 December 1935, folder 13, DuPont–1935, box 36, NBC/SHSW.

108. Roosevelt to Lohr, 12 February 1936, folder 63, High, Stanley–1936, box 46, NBC/ SHSW. One of High's last acts as an NBC employee was to suggest that network officials meet to consider "just what precisely we would do if a flash came through that the President had been shot down." "The present political bitterness makes an assassination of the President more possible than normally," High explained. "That is why the Secret Service are taking unprecedented precautions." "It is impossible to cover every exigency in advance but I do think a general policy and a general line of procedure could be worked out."

High to Royal, 1 February 1936, folder 63, High, Stanley–1936, box 46, NBC/SHSW. On High's campaign responsibilities, see memorandum, FDR to the Postmaster General, 26 March 1936, folder: Stanley High 1936, box 46, OF 300, FDRL.

109. Stanley High, "A Republican Takes a Walk," *Forum* 95 (May 1936): 261–267.

110. "Abstract of Debate by Stanley High," 30 April 1936, folder 63, High, Stanley–1936, box 46, NBC/SHSW.

111. Samuel I. Rosenman, *The Public Papers and Addresses of Franklin D. Roosevelt,* vol. 5 (New York: Random House, 1938), pp. 16, 233.

112. Rosenman, *Working with Roosevelt,* p. 99. On "economic autocrats" and "economic royalists," see James Holt, "The New Deal and the American Anti-Statist Tradition," in *The New Deal,* ed. Braeman, Bremner, and Brody, pp. 27–49.

113. Rosenman, *The Public Papers and Addresses of Franklin D. Roosevelt,* vol. 5, pp. 13–14, 16–17; Stanley High, *Roosevelt—and Then?* (New York: Harper & Brothers, 1937), pp. 21–22.

114. Ibid., pp. 232, 235.

115. Rosenman, *Working with Roosevelt,* pp. 106–107; Kenneth S. Davis, *FDR: The New Deal Years, 1933–1937: A History* (New York: Random House, 1986), pp. 634–637.

Chapter 4

1. Harold Lord Varney, "Autopsy on the Republican Party," *American Mercury* 40 (January 1937): 1–12; and Turner Catledge, *New York Times,* 16 August 1936, sec. 4, p. 3E, cited in Ralph D. Casey, "Republican Propaganda in the 1936 Campaign," *Public Opinion Quarterly* 2 (April 1937): 27–44.

2. Catledge, *New York Times,* 16 August 1936. Biographer Donald McCoy describes Landon's image as "unglamorous but sound, homely, and forthright." McCoy, *Landon of Kansas* (Lincoln: University of Nebraska Press, 1966), p. 266.

3. Hill Blackett to Alfred M. Landon, 18 September 1936, Blackett correspondence, Alfred M. Landon papers, Kansas State Historical Society, Topeka, Kansas.

4. Catledge, *New York Times,* 16 August 1936.

5. "We Believe in Broadcast Merchandising," [August 1936] folder 15 political broadcasts; RNC, July–October 1936, box 49, central files correspondence, NBC/SHSW.

6. John F. Royal to Richard C. Patterson, Jr., 12 November 1935, folder 37 political broadcasts-policies 1935, box 40, NBC/SHSW .

7. Alva Johnston, "Profiles: Vaudeville to Television—III," *New Yorker* 22 (October 12, 1946): 36–46.

8. John F. Royal to Richard C. Patterson, Jr., 14 October 1935, and attached clipping "New Stage Group Set Up by Labor," *New York Times,* 14 October 1935, folder 34 political broadcasts Oct.-Dec. 1935, box 40, NBC/SHSW; for an assessment of Labor Stage's work, see Michael Denning, *The Cultural Front: The Laboring of American Culture in the Twentieth Century* (New York: Verso, 1996), pp. 296–297, passim.

9. Ralph M. Jennings, "Dramatic License in Political Broadcasts," *Journal of Broadcasting* 12 (summer 1968): 229–246; Thomas Whiteside, *The Relaxed Sell* (New York: Oxford University Press, 1954), pp. 33–48; Barnouw, *The Golden Web,* pp. 51–52; "Republicans' Skit Put on Air by News Coup," *New York Herald Tribune*, 16 January 1936, p. 16.

10. "Republican Drama," *Time* 27 (January 27, 1936): 20, cited in Jennings, "Dramatic License in Political Broadcasts," 229–246.

11. J. O'Neill to S. Strotz, 14 January 1936, folder 14, Political Broadcasts-RNC Jan.–June 1936, box 49, NBC/SHSW.

12. "Republican Skit Assails Spending," *New York Times,* 15 January 1936, pp. 1, 13.

13. J. O'Neill to S. Strotz, 14 January 1936, folder 14, Political Broadcasts-RNC Jan.–June 1936, box 49, NBC/SHSW.

14. A. R. Williamson to Sidney Strotz, 16 January 1936, folder 14, Political Broadcasts-RNC Jan.–June 1936, box 49, NBC/SHSW.

15. "Republican Skit Assails Spending," *New York Times*, 15 January 1936, pp. 1, 13; "Republicans Give New Air Skits Here," *New York Times*, 22 January 1936, pp. 1, 14.

16. "Radio Chains Bar Republican Skit but Party Gets Chicago Outlet," *New York Times*, 14 January 1936, pp. 1, 17; Merrill Denison, "Editorial Policies of Broadcasting Companies," *Public Opinion Quarterly* 1 (January 1937): 64–82; "Republican Drama," *Time* (January 27, 1936): 9.

17. Frank M. Russell to Lenox Lohr, 8 January 1936, folder 14, box 49, NBC/SHSW.

18. Alfred H. Morton to John F. Royal, 18 January 1936 and attachment, "Luncheon with Walter Lippmann Thursday January 16th," and Walter Lippmann, "The Radio Controversy," *New York Herald Tri-*

bune, 18 January 1936, p. 15, all in folder 72 political broadcasts, general Jan.–June 1936, box 48, NBC/SHSW.

19. Stanley Aronowitz, "Is Democracy Possible? The Decline of the Public in the American Debate," in *The Phantom Public Sphere*, ed. Bruce Robbins (Minneapolis: University of Minnesota Press, 1993), pp. 75–92.

20. M. H. Aylesworth to Members of the Board of Directors, 25 October 1935, folder: 372 Political Broadcasting 1924–35, NBC/LC.

21. "Republicans' Skit Put on Air by News Coup," *New York Herald Tribune*, 16 January 1936; "Republican Drama," *Time* (January 27, 1936): 9; "Radio Chains," *New York Times*, 14 January 1936, pp. 1, 7.

22. "Pratt Explains Origin of Vandenberg Disc Broadcast," *Heinl Radio Business Letter* (November 3, 1936): 2–5, attached to letter, Harry C. Butcher to Marvin McIntyre, 4 November 1936, folder: CBS 1936–1939, OF 256, FDRL.

23. For a running account of the incident, see *New York Times*, 18, 19, 20, 21, and 30 October 1936. WGN, the *Chicago Tribune* station, broadcast the program in its entirety, transcriptions of which can be found in the Arthur H. Vandenberg papers, Bentley Historical Library, University of Michigan, Ann Arbor.

24. "Air Ban on Vandenberg Linked to Deal with James Roosevelt," *New York Sun*, 19 October 1936, pp. 1, 15; "Ask Rebroadcast for Vandenberg," *New York Times*, 19 October 1936, pp. 1, 3.

25. "Will Press Attack, Says Vandenberg," *New York Times*, 21 October 1936, p. 20; "Ask Rebroadcast for Vandenberg," *New York Times*, 19 October 1936, pp. 1, 3; "Byrnes Accuses Vandenberg," *Los Angeles Times*, 23 October 1936, p. 7.

26. "Rebroadcast Demanded on Vandenberg's Radio 'Debate,'" *New York Herald Tribune*, 19 October 1936, pp. 1, 6.

27. Telegram, Farley to Vandenberg [n.d.], scrapbook no. 8, p. 159, Arthur H. Vandenberg papers, Michigan Historical Collections, Bentley Historical Library, University of Michigan, Ann Arbor.

28. Varney, "Autopsy on the Republican Party"; on the suspension of league operations, see Wolfskill, *The Revolt of the Conservatives*, pp. 246–249.

29. Barton, memorandum to Mr. Teagle (Standard Oil New Jersey), 7 December 1936, and attached memorandum, Tax Cummings to Barton, November 11, 1952, folder: Cummings, Thayer (Tax) 1940–1955, box 14, BB/SHSW; the Republicans and their allies reportedly spent $14,198,202.92 during the campaign, while political groups supporting FDR spent $9,228,406.85. *Senate Investigation of Campaign Expenditures in 1936*, Report 151, 75th Cong., 1st sess. (Washington, DC: Government Printing Office, 1937), pp. 27, 29, cited in McCoy, *Landon of Kansas*, pp. 345–346, n. 13; on New Deal executive branch agency public relations activities that critics charged more than made up for the $5 million deficiency, see James L. McCamy, *Government Publicity: Its Practice in Federal Administration* (Chicago: University of Chicago Press, 1939); on the contemporary crisis of the press, see Schiller, *Theorizing Communication*, pp. 43–46, passim.

30. Barton to Teagle, 7 December 1936, and attached memorandum, Cummings to Barton, November 11, 1952, folder: Cummings, Thayer (Tax) 1940–1955, box 14, BB/SHSW.

31. Ibid.

Chapter 5

1. Durstine telephoned Fox to tell him that after some indecision the du Ponts had determined to renew the *Cavalcade* late in the 1938 broadcast season, "but they wanted to follow a little different plan with some ideas of James Truslow Adams." "Consequently," Fox wrote Schlesinger, "our employment will not be continued. He said nice things about us, but that was the gist of it." Fox to Schlesinger, 26 November 1938, folder: E-F 3/1/38–1/1/39, box 13 correspondence, AMS/HUA.

2. "The McGuffey Readers," *Cavalcade of America* 76 (March 31, 1937), DuP/HL.

3. Eight executives voted to drop the motto: J. Thompson Brown, R. R. M. Carpenter, W. F. Harrington, C. M. A. Stine, T. S. Grasselli, J. W. McCoy, W. S. Carpenter, Jr., and M. D. Fisher. Two voted to keep the motto: A. B. Echols and E. E. Lincoln. Lammot du Pont and Henry B. du Pont remained neutral. Wm. A. Hart to Lammot du Pont, 26 July 1938, "Re: The Slogan . . ." August 1938, folder: Advertising Department (#C-24) Jan. 1938–Nov. 1938, and H. B. du Pont to Frank V. du Pont, 26 May 1939, folder: Advertising department (#C-24) Jan. 1939–Dec. 1940, all in box 4, acc. 1662, DuP/HL; Barton to Paul Markman, 12 March 1956, folder Du Pont 1950–1957, box 76, BB/SHSW.

4. "Eleuthère Irénée du Pont," *Cavalcade of America* 167 (May 29, 1939), DuP/HL.

5. Todd Gitlin, "Mass Media Sociology: The Dominant Paradigm," *Theory and Society* 6 (September 1978): 205–253; Claude E. Robinson, "Recent Developments in the Straw-Poll Field," *Public Opinion Quarterly* 1 (July 1937): 45–56 and (October 1937): 42–52; Archibald M. Crossley, "Straw Polls in 1936," *Public Opinion Quarterly* 1 (January 1937): 24–35; Institute for Propaganda Analysis, "Polls, Propaganda, and Democracy," *Propaganda Analysis* 4 (November 11, 1940): 1–6; George H. Gallup, "A Scientific Method

for Determining Reader Interest," *Journalism Quarterly* 7 (March 1930): 1–13; Gallup, oral history interview transcript (New York: Columbia University Oral History Office, 1972); American Institute of Public Opinion, *The New Science of Public Opinion Measurement* (Princeton: AIPO, 1938).

6. Donald Hurwitz, "Broadcast Ratings: The Missing Dimension," *Critical Studies in Mass Communication* 1 (June 1984): 205–215.

7. Psychological Corporation, "The Clinical Interview in Public Relations Work," 27 June 1938, folder: PSC (NYC), correspondence, brochures, annual reports 1947–1950, box 59 Public Relations Department, acc. 1410 series III, DuP/HL; on the PSC and promotional problems, see William A. Hart to Lammot du Pont, 18 August 1939, and Hart to Members Executive Committee: L. du Pont, W. S. Carpenter, Jr., J. Thompson Brown, J. E. Crane, A. B. Echols, W. F. Harrington, J. W. McCoy, C. M. A. Stine, and T. S. Grasselli, 18 April 1938, folder: Advertising Department 1939–1940, box 4 Administrative Papers, acc. 1662, DuP/HL.

8. Psychological Corporation, "Test-Tube Study of the Influence of 'Cavalcade of America' on Attitudes toward the DuPont Company," 16 August 1939, and memo, Hart to Lammot du Pont, 18 August 1939, folder: Advertising Department 1939–40, box 4 Administrative Papers, acc. 1662, DuP/HL.

9. W. G. Preston to Dr. James R. Angell, 28 August 1940, folder 68, DuPont, June–Dec. 1940, box 76, NBC/SHSW.

10. W. G. Preston, Jr., to Royal, 20 May 1940, folder: 395 Program Dept—Education Division 1934–40, NBC/LC.

11. In the matter of High's reemployment following the campaign, NBC vice president for programming John F. Royal wrote: "In my opinion, I think it would be a mistake for us to take him back regardless of any alleged influence he may have with the President." Royal to Lohr, 24 December 1936, folder 63, High, Stanley, box 46, NBC/SHSW.

12. "Dr. Angell as Educational Counselor of the National Broadcasting Company," *School and Society* 46 (July 3, 1937): 12–13; on Angell's network appointment and the collapse of educator opposition to commercial radio reflected in the reorganization of the National Committee on Education by Radio, see McChesney, *Telecommunications, Mass Media, and Democracy,* p. 231.

13. "Angell to NBC," *Time* 30 (July 5, 1937): 52; in December 1937, *Education by Radio* reported Angell's salary to be $37,000. Cited in McChesney, *Telecommunications, Mass Media, and Democracy,* pp. 231, 340, n. 17.

14. "Elder Statesman," *New Yorker* 17 (September 6, 1941): 12.

15. James Rowland Angell, "The Moral Crisis of Democracy," *Vital Speeches* 2 (August 1, 1936): 670–674.

16. James Rowland Angell, "Second Thoughts after the Election," *Vital Speeches* 3 (December 1, 1936): 98–101.

17. Angell, "A Bastard Democracy: The Danger and the Method of Avoidance," New Haven, 22 June 1937, *Vital Speeches* 3 (July 15, 1937): 578–580.

18. Wise to Sarnoff, 28 June 1937, folder: NBC, PF 477, FDRL.

19. Wise to Margaret LeHand, 29 June 1937, folder: NBC, PF 477, FDRL.

20. "Memo for Mac," 3 July 1937, folder: NBC, PF 477, FDRL.

21. See, for example, Steele, *Propaganda in an Open Society,* pp. 17–20, 127–132, passim; Betty Houchin Winfield notes that from 1938 to 1940 the increasing rate of radio station ownership by conservative newspaper publishers "outraged" FDR. Winfield, *FDR and the News Media* (Urbana: University of Illinois Press, 1990), p. 110.

22. While in England Angell visited the BBC, presumably to become better acquainted with the comparable advantages of the American system of broadcasting. "Dr. Angell as Educational Counselor of the National Broadcasting Company," *School and Society* 46 (July 3, 1937): 12–13.

23. Preston to Angell, 28 August 1940, folder 68, Du Pont, June–Dec. 1940, box 76, NBC/SHSW; Angell to Lammot du Pont, 11 January 1940, folder, advertising department 1939–1940, box 4, acc. 1662, DuP/HL.

24. Pamphlet, "New Historical Research and Other New Features in Cavalcade of America" (January 1940), folder 41, Cavalcade of America–1940, box 75, NBC/SHSW.

25. Preston to Angell, 28 August 1940, folder 68, DuPont, June–Dec. 1940, box 76, NBC/SHSW; program title list and synopses, "Cavalcade of America," Music Reading Room, Motion Picture, Broadcasting and Recorded Sound Division, LC.

26. Playbill, "Abraham Lincoln," *Cavalcade of America* (February 13, 1940), CBS library, New York.

27. Alice G. Marquis, *Hopes and Ashes: The Birth of Modern Times, 1929–1939* (New York: Free Press, 1986), pp. 187–188; pamphlet, "New Historical Research and Other New Features in Cavalcade of America" (January 1940), folder 41, Cavalcade of America–1940, box 75, NBC/SHSW.

28. Pamphlet, "New Historical Research and Other New Features in Cavalcade of America," NBC/SHSW.

29. Pamphlet, "History in This Hour," Dr. James Rowland Angell, Walter Lippmann, Dr. Frank Monaghan [Fall 1940], folder 41, Cavalcade of America-1940, box 75, NBC/SHSW.

30. Pamphlet, "New Historical Research and Other New Features in Cavalcade of America," NBC/SHSW.

31. Ibid.

32. Schlesinger to Fox, June 21, 1938, folder: E-F 3/1/38–1/1/39, box 13 correspondence, AMS/HUA.

33. "Tisquantum, Strange Friend of the Pilgrims," *Cavalcade of America* 171 (January 2, 1940); "Enoch Crosby," *Cavalcade of America* 176 (February 22, 1940), DuP/HL.

34. Preston to Angell, 28 August 1940, folder 88, Du Pont, June–Dec. 1940, box 76, NBC/SHSW.

35. "George Washington Refuses a Crown," *Cavalcade of America* 163 (May 1, 1939), DuP/HL.

36. "Plain Mr. President," *Cavalcade of America* 214 (February 19, 1941), DuP/HL.

37. "Abraham Lincoln—The War Years," *Cavalcade of America* 121 (February 13, 1940), DuP/HL.

38. Preston to Angell, 28 August 1940, folder 88, Du Pont, June–Dec. 1940, box 76, NBC/SHSW.

39. "Wild Bill Hickok," *Cavalcade of America* 199 (November 6, 1940); "The Battle Hymn of the Republic," *Cavalcade of America* 203 (December 4, 1940); "The Green Pastures," *Cavalcade of America* 206 (December 25, 1940), DuP/HL.

40. "Drums along the Mohawk," *Cavalcade of America* 252 (November 10, 1941); "They Died with Their Boots On," *Cavalcade of America* 253 (November 17, 1941); "The Great Man Votes," *Cavalcade of America* 257 (December 15, 1941); "Captains of the Clouds," *Cavalcade of America* 264 (February 2, 1942), DuP/HL.

41. "All That Money Can Buy," *Cavalcade of America* 249 (October 20, 1941), DuP/HL.

42. Alfred Haworth Jones, *Roosevelt's Image Brokers: Poets, Playwrights, and the Use of the Lincoln Symbol* (Port Washington, NY: Kennikat Press, 1974), pp. 76–78; North Callahan, *Carl Sandburg: His Life and Works* (University Park: Pennsylvania State University, 1987), p. 150.

43. Penelope Niven, *Carl Sandburg: A Biography* (New York: Charles Scribner's Sons, 1991), pp. 542–543. The poet's study of Lincoln's youth and early career inspired a run of successful stage and screen adaptations as well. *The Prairie Years* became the basis of E. P. Conkle's Federal Theater production, *Prologue to Glory,* and playwright Robert E. Sherwood's *Abe Lincoln in Illinois*. The latter, featuring Raymond Massey, opened a long Broadway run in October 1938. Excerpting Lincoln's rebuttal to Stephen Douglas, Sherwood's and Massey's Lincoln directly addressed the audience, as did Massey, who, out-of-character, explained to the press the play's contemporary parallels. RKO brought the play and Massey to the screen in 1940. With screenplay by Sherwood, *Abe Lincoln in Illinois* opened to a receptive Washington audience including President Roosevelt, who enjoyed a private White House screening. Within months Sherwood joined the Roosevelt re-election campaign, becoming, as had Stanley High four years earlier, a speech-writing collaborator with Samuel I. Rosenman. With Sherwood's arrival FDR's speeches and prepared remarks acquired Lincolnian words. On the way to deliver an address in Philadelphia formally opening the campaign, the president stopped in Wilmington "to read from a speech" in which Lincoln defined "liberty," "the right of each man to do as he pleases with himself, and the product of his labor. . . ." "This year," FDR concluded, "the people, not only of Delaware but of the United States, are all taking a renewed interest in that word 'liberty.'" Jones, *Roosevelt's Image Brokers*, pp. 35–50, 71–74.

44. "Native Land," *Cavalcade of America* 245 (September 22, 1941), DuP/HL.

45. In quoting the Sandburg poems that were excerpted for broadcast, I have taken care to conform to the published form of the verses. *The Complete Poems of Carl Sandburg* (New York: Harcourt Brace Jovanovich, 1976), pp. 79, 85.

46. Ibid., pp. 271–278.

47. Ibid., pp. 616–617.

48. Abraham Lincoln, "Annual Message to Congress," December 1, 1862, in *The Collected Works of Abraham Lincoln,* vol. 5, ed. Roy P. Basler (New Brunswick, NJ: Rutgers University Press, 1953), p. 537.

49. "Native Land," *Cavalcade of America* 245 (September 22, 1941), DuP/HL.

50. *The Complete Poems of Carl Sandburg,* p. 443.

51. "Native Land," *Cavalcade of America* 245 (September 22, 1941), DuP/HL; *The Complete Poems of Carl Sandburg,* p. 616.

52. "Listen to the People," *Cavalcade of America* 338 (April 5, 1943), DuP/HL; Stephen Vincent Benét, "Listen to the People," *Selected Works of Stephen Vincent Benét,* vol. 1: *Poetry* (New York: Farrar & Rinehart, 1942), pp. 474, 483.

53. "Listen to the People," *Calvalcade of America*; Benét, "Listen to the People," *Selected Works,* p. 473.

54. "Listen to the People," *Cavalcade of America.*

55. Arthur Miller, *Timebends: A Life* (New York: Grove Press, 1987), pp. 203–209. Two book-length accounts of the Merrits's discovery, contemporary with Miller's *Cavalcade* work, are Paul De Kruif, *Seven Iron Men* (New York: Harcourt Brace, 1929), and Stewart H. Holbrook, *Iron Brew* (New York: Macmillan, 1939).

56. Resumé and attachments, John Driscoll, folder: 38 biographies, A-M 1948–1952, box 11, series I, acc. 1803, DuP/HL; Alan Havig, "Frederic Wakeman's *The Hucksters* and the Postwar Debate over Commercial Radio," *Journal of Broadcasting* 28 (spring 1984): 187–199; "Industry's Boss," *Better Living* 4 (March–April 1950): 10–11.

57. "Industry's Boss," *Better Living* 4 (March–April 1950): 10–11

58. Erik Barnouw, ed., *Radio Drama in Action: Twenty-Five Plays of a Changing World* (New York: Rinehart & Co., 1945), pp. 80–81; Peter Lyon, telephone interview with the author, 16 January 1987.

59. Resumé, George Kondolf, 12 March 1957, folder: 38 biographies, A-M 1948–1952, box 11, series I, acc. 1803, DuP/HL; John O'Connor and Lorraine Brown, eds., *Free, Adult, Uncensored: The Living History of the Federal Theatre Project* (Washington, DC: New Republic Books, 1978), pp. 15–16, 125–135, 161–173, 220; James Dugan, "Housing Goes to Town," *New Masses* 30 (February 14, 1939): 28–29.

60. "Dr. Franklin Takes It Easy," *Cavalcade of America* 211 (January 29, 1941); "The Laziest Man in the World," *Cavalcade of America* 409 (November 13, 1944), DuP/HL.

61. "I Sing a New World," *Cavalcade of America* 218 (March 19, 1941), DuP/HL.

62. Telegram, Will Rogers to E. F. Hutton [n.d.], attached to letter, Hutton to Irénée du Pont, 15 April 1935, box 205, Irénée du Pont papers, acc. 228 series J (American Liberty League), HL, cited in Burk, *The Corporate State and the Broker State*, pp. 157–158.

63. "Will Rogers Acclaims Paul Reveres De Luxe," *New York Times,* 15 November 1934, cited in James Smallwood, ed., *Will Rogers' Daily Telegrams* (Stillwater: Oklahoma State University Press, 1979), p. 241; "Liberty League Plan Explained at Dinner," *Los Angeles Times,* 14 November 1934, sec. 2, p. 1. Rogers later apologized to Hutton "for just getting too dam [*sic*] fresh." "It was the kind of alleged joke that I am not proud of being the sire of," Rogers cabled. "You boys were no doubt out on a worthy mission, and I had [illegible] just cause to shoot you on your way to get converts." "You must admit," Rogers explained, "that you three boys with your financial standing and background out to save the Constitution, it does lend itself to some little touch of humor. I might not have been capable of just hitting it, but don't you honestly now think that there was a laugh there somewhere. . . . Russia is not running this country, and never will, Tugwell is not running it, and never will, the Constitution is not being trampled on, and never will be, Roosevelt is the one that's doing everything that you are objecting too [*sic*], so change your tactics, change your title, and you will be in the clear, and you will gain strength, and you will have a clear conscience. Anyhow I am not a politician, and I am not taking any what is going on as so dam serious. You say I could do some good if I would do this or that, well I am not out to crusade the country for any cause, this desk is piled with letters two feet high telling me what I ought to do, well I ain't going to do anything, I am paid entertaining wages, not salvation wages, anyhow you are my friend, and your friends are my friends, and I am just a dam fool." Rogers to Hutton [n.d.], attached to letter, Hutton to Irénée du Pont, 15 April 1935, cited in Burk, *The Corporate State and the Broker State*, pp. 157–158.

64. "Will Rogers," *Cavalcade of America* 144 (December 19, 1938); "Will Rogers," *Cavalcade of America* 207 (January 1, 1941), both in DuP/HL.

Chapter 6

1. Memorandum, Wallace Boren and Fred Fidler, 5 February 1938, p. 26, RG 5, U.S. Offices, J. Walter Thompson Company Archive, New York.

2. On the popular products of the 1930s, see Walker and Sklar, *Business Finds Its Voice;* for an introduction to the fair, see the essays by Joseph P. Cusker and Warren I. Susman in The Queens Museum, *Dawn of a New Day: The New York World's Fair, 1939/40* (New York: Queens Museum and New York University Press, 1980); Gardner Harding, "World's Fair, 1939: A Preview," *Harper's* 176 (December 1937): 129–137; Bernard Lichtenberg, "Business Backs New York World Fair to Meet the New Deal Propaganda," *Public Opinion Quarterly* 2 (April 1938): 314–324; and Gardner Ainsworth, "The New York Fair: Adventure in Promotion," *Public Opinion Quarterly* 3 (October 1939): 694–704.

3. Lichtenberg, "Business Backs New York World's Fair."

4. "World's Fair Reveals New Strength of Films as Advertising Media," *Sales Management* 35 (August 15, 1934): 146–148.

5. Richard Griffith, "Films at the Fair," *Films: A Quarterly of Discussion and Analysis* 1 (November 1939): 61–75 (reprinted New York: Arno Press, 1968); "New York Fair Films," *Business Screen* 2, no. 3 (1940): 34; Donald J. Bush, *The Streamlined Decade* (New York: George Braziller, 1975), pp. 155, 166–167.

6. *The Middleton Family at the World's Fair* (1939), Audio Productions for Westinghouse. Director: Robert R. Snody. Cast: Harry Shannon, Marjorie Lord, Douglas Stark, George J. Lewis, Adora Andrews, James Lydon, Ruth Lee, Georgette Harvey. 55 mins, Technicolor, sd. Special thanks to Pierce Rafferty of

Petrified Films, Inc., and Rick Prelinger of Prelinger Associates, Inc., for making this film available to me; script "Westinghouse Presents 'The Middleton Family, Fair Weather' (tentative title)," 31 March 1939, may be found in the collection of the Westinghouse Historical Center, Pittsburgh, PA.

7. On Ford, see Lewis, *The Public Image of Henry Ford,* pp. 114–118; on General Electric, see Joseph Corn, "Selling Technology: Advertising Films and the American Corporation, 1900–1920," *Film and History* 11 (September 1981): 49–58; on the NAM, see Kay Sloan, *The Loud Silents: Origins of the Social Problem Film* (Chicago and Urbana: University of Illinois Press, 1988), pp. 8–9, 31; and Steven J. Ross, "Cinema and Class Conflict: Labor, Capital, the State, and American Silent Film," in *Resisting Images: Essays on Cinema and History,* ed. Robert Sklar and Charles Musser (Philadelphia: Temple University Press, 1990), pp. 68–107; for an overview of the field, see Anthony Slide, *Before Video: A History of the Non-Theatrical Film* (New York: Greenwood Press, 1992); on the dearth of sponsored film scholarship, see Daniel J. Perkins, "The Sponsored Film: A New Dimension in American Film Research?" *Historical Journal of Film, Radio and Television* 2, no. 2 (1982): 133–140.

8. NCR's annual sales conventions and daily noon-hour entertainments were presented in the company's "schoolhouse," a Greek Revival theater with a capacity of 2,300. Stanley C. Allyn, *My Half Century with NCR* (New York: McGraw-Hill, 1967), pp. 17–20; Samuel Crowther, *John H. Patterson: Pioneer in Industrial Welfare* (Garden City, NY: Doubleday, Page & Co., 1923), pp. 251–252; Charles Musser in collaboration with Carol Nelson, *High-Class Moving Pictures: Lyman H. Howe and the Forgotten Era of Traveling Exhibition, 1880–1920* (Princeton, NJ: Princeton University Press, 1991), pp. 5–6.

9. M. R. McKeown, "Detroit: The Commercial Hollywood," *Barron's* 16 (29 June 1936): 11–12; Arthur Edwin Krows, "Motion Pictures—Not for Theatres," *Educational Screen* 19 (February 1940): 58–61.

10. Advertisement, Electrical Research Products, Inc., "Makes personal appearance in 10 cities at once," *Time* 15 (June 16, 1930): 65.

11. Upton Sinclair, "Mobilizing the Movies," *National EPIC News* 2, no. 13 (August 19, 1935): 1.

12. *Precisely So* (1937), Jam Handy Organization for Chevrolet Motor Co., Richard Prelinger, *To New Horizons* (Los Angeles: Voyager Press, 1987) [Laserdisc] .

13. *In Tune with Tomorrow* (1939), see Griffith, "Films at the Fair"; *New Dimensions* (1939), Loucks & Norling Studios for Chrysler Corporation, see "Symphony in Dimension," *Business Screen* 3, no. 1 (1940): 16–19, and 2, no. 6 (1940): 10.

14. Lewis, *The Public Image of Henry Ford,* pp. 307, 330–331; "Camera Eye," *Business Screen* 2, no. 6 (1940): 7, 31. Prints of *Rhapsody in Steel* (200 FC 4339, 4341) and *Symphony in "F"* (200 FC 4355, 4356) may be found in the Ford Collection, National Archives at College Park, MD (hereafter NACP).

15. Press release, 31 August 1934, folder: Motion Pictures, box 4, acc. 545, Henry Ford Museum and Greenfield Village, Dearborn, MI. Ford officials described the "key of F" as "a particularly joyful and melodic one." "Each time the 'Theme in F' is heard, we always find ourselves observing on the screen the Ford idea as the constructive and impelling force towards progress and prosperity." "Camera Eye," *Business Screen* 2, no. 6 (1940): 7, 31.

16. Press release, 31 August 1934, folder: Motion Pictures, box 4, acc. 545, Henry Ford Museum and Greenfield Village, Dearborn, MI.

17. *Symphony in "F"* (200 FC 4355, 4356), Ford Collection, NACP.

18. Compiling suggestions for the improvement of "A Thousand Times Neigh" and the film that introduced it, Putnam noted that "the whole show seems somewhat confused in purpose. It is as though we hadn't decided whether to appeal to the intelligentsia or the proletariat. Consequently, we fall somewhere in between." Memo, GFP to Mr. Black, 28 May 1940, folder: interoffice memos, box 10, acc. 56, Henry Ford Museum and Greenfield Village, Dearborn, MI, cited in Lewis, *The Public Image of Henry Ford,* p. 307, n. 46.

19. *From Dawn to Sunset* (1937), Jam Handy Organization for Chevrolet Motor Division, General Motors Sales Corporation, synopsis, copyright deposit file MU 7768, LC, print, PA. Richard Prelinger notes that *From Dawn to Sunset* "takes up more time showing people getting paid than showing them actually working on the job." Prelinger, *Our Secret Century: Archival Films from the Darker Side of the American Dream,* vol. 2: *Capitalist Realism* (Los Angeles: The Voyager Company, 1996) [CD-ROM].

20. On the GM film library, see Borden, *Advertising Text and Cases,* p. 549.

21. "Report on Motion Pictures Theatrical and Non-Theatrical Showings," folder: Public Relations-Motion Slide Films Rep. of Motion Picture Showings April 27, 1938, box 113, NAM/HL.

22. "Men and Machines," and "America Yesterday Today and Tomorrow," folder: Public relations posters, box 111, NAM/HL.

23. Lenox R. Lohr to David Sarnoff, 1 June 1939, folder 20: New York World's Fair 1939–1940, box 79, NBC/SHSW.

24. Press release, "The 1940 Wonder World of Chemistry," 8 April 1940, folder: DuPont, E. I., box 1005, New York World's Fair Corporation Collection, New York Public Library (hereafter NYWF/NYPL); Roland Marchand, "Part I—The Designers Go to the Fair: Walter Dorwin Teague and the Professionalization of Corporate Industrial Exhibits, 1933–1940," *Design Issues* 8 (fall 1991): 4–17.

25. "Chemistry and the Future," in playbill for "Dr. Franklin Goes to Court," *Cavalcade of America* 200 (November 13, 1940), DuP/HL.

26. Pamphlet, "Fashions out of Test Tubes," presented by the National Association of Manufacturers (1940); "NAM Public Information Program 1940 (for discussion by Public Relations Advisory Group, Tuesday, February 20, 1940)," folder 74 NAM-Public Info Program-1940 (Mr. Mullen's files), box 78, NBC/SHSW.

27. Press release, 22 March 1940; press guide, "General Motors Highways and Horizons Exhibit, World's Fair of 1940 in New York," p. 2, folder: General Motors, box 1005, both in NYWF/NYPL; Roland Marchand, "Part II—The Designers Go to the Fair: Norman Bel Geddes, The General Motors 'Futurama,' and the Visit-to-the-Factory Transformed," *Design Issues* 8 (spring 1992): 22–40.

28. Press guide, "General Motors Highways and Horizons Exhibit," pp. 23–27, folder: General Motors, box 1005, NYWF/NYPL.

29. "New York Fair Films," *Business Screen* 2, no. 3 (1940): 34; Griffith, "Films at the Fair."

30. "World's Fair—1940," *Film News* 1 (May 1940): 1–2; Bob Seymour, "World's Fair Letter," *Business Screen* 2, no. 6 (1940): 10; Lewis, *The Public Image of Henry Ford*, p. 307; "Steel's New York Fair Theatre," *Business Screen* 2, no. 6 (1940): 10. For lists of 1940 World's Fair films, see "World's Fair Supplement," *Film News* 1 (July 1940): 1–8; "Films at the 1940 New York World's Fair," *Business Screen* 2, no. 7 (1940): 14–15.

31. Pare Lorentz, "Men Make Steel," *McCall's* (July 1938), reprinted in Lorentz, *Lorentz on Film: Movies, 1927–1941* (Norman: University of Oklahoma Press, 1975, 1986), pp. 154–156; advertisement, Roland Reed Productions, "Reviewed Like a Hollywood 4 Star Feature," *Business Screen* 1, no. 1 (1938): 57.

32. Griffith, "Films at the Fair."

33. United States Steel Corp., "Technicolor Prologue for Men Make Steel," 20 June 1940, copyright deposit file MU 10685, Motion Picture, Broadcasting and Sound Division, Library of Congress.

34. Press release, "Westinghouse Ad Campaign Based on New York World's Fair," 26 April 1939, Westinghouse Historical Center, Pittsburgh, PA.

35. The letter concluded, "Well, shucks, come and see for yourself." Letter (1940), file: Westinghouse, Orth Collection, National Museum of American History, Smithsonian Institution.

36. Press release, 26 April 1939, Westinghouse Historical Center, Pittsburgh, PA; Thomas M. Pryor, "Tomorrow's Propaganda," *New York Times*, 18 June 1939, sec. 9, p. 4, cited in Warren Susman, "The People's Fair: Cultural Contradictions of a Consumer Society," in Queens Museum, *Dawn of a New Day*, pp. 16–27.

37. Synopsis, "Westinghouse Presents 'The Middleton Family, Fair Weather' (tentative title)," 31 March 1939, Westinghouse Historical Center, Pittsburgh, PA.

38. Advertisement, Modern Talking Picture Service, Inc., "A Report of Showings, Audiences and Total Costs of the Commercial Sound Motion Picture 'The Middleton Family' Prepared for Westinghouse Electric & Mfg. Co. and Fuller & Smith & Ross, Inc.," *Business Screen* 3, no. 4 (1941): 18–19.

Chapter 7

1. Baritz, *The Servants of Power*, pp. 118, 124, 134, 139, 141–143, 154, 168–169, 176–177; Graebner, *The Engineering of Consent*, pp. 70, 73–75, 84–85; Richard Gillespie, *Manufacturing Knowledge: A History of the Hawthorne Experiments* (New York: Cambridge University Press, 1991), pp. 228, 237–238; Howell John Harris, *The Right to Manage: Industrial Relations Policies of American Business in the 1940s* (Madison: University of Wisconsin Press, 1982), pp. 171–173; Fones-Wolf, *Selling Free Enterprise*, pp. 67–107.

2. Mark H. Leff, "The Politics of Sacrifice on the American Home Front in World War II," *Journal of American History* 77 (March 1991): 1296–1318; Frank W. Fox, *Madison Avenue Goes to War: The Strange Military Career of American Advertising, 1941–1945* (Provo, UT: Brigham Young University Press, 1975), pp. 45–67; Robert Griffith, "The Selling of America: The Advertising Council and American Politics, 1942–1960," *Business History Review* 57 (autumn 1983): 388–412; John Morton Blum, *V Was for Victory: Politics and American Culture during World War II* (New York: Harcourt Brace Jovanovich, 1976), pp. 31–39; Allan M. Winkler, *The Politics of Propaganda: The Office of War Information, 1942–1945* (New Haven: Yale University Press, 1978), pp. 62–63; Sydney Weinberg, "What to Tell America: The Writers' Quarrel in the Office of War Information," *Journal of American History* 55 (June 1968): 73–89; William L. Bird, Jr., and Harry R. Rubenstein, *Design for Victory: World War II Posters on the American Home Front* (New York: Princeton Architectural Press, 1998).

3. Meg Jacobs, "'How about Some Meat?' The Office of Price Administration, Consumption Politics, and State Building from the Bottom Up, 1941–1946," *Journal of American History* 84 (December 1997): 910–947; on the failure of GM, Ford, and U.S. Steel to implement labor-management coordination throughout their respective plants, see Sanford M. Jacoby, "Union-Management Cooperation in the United

States during the Second World War," in *Technological Change and Workers' Movements*, ed. Melvyn Dubofsky (Beverly Hills, CA: Sage Publications, Inc., 1985), pp. 100–129.

4. For mention of the National Association of Manufacturers' "Soldiers of Production" campaign, see Fones-Wolf, *Selling Free Enterprise*, p. 27.

5. David Culbert, "'Why We Fight': Social Engineering for a Democratic Society at War," in *Film and Radio Propaganda in World War II*, ed. K. R. M. Short (Knoxville: University of Tennessee Press, 1983), pp. 173–191. From 1940 to V-J Day, the armed services created six times as much audiovisual material as had been created for civilian use in all the years before the war. The official output included the films of the U.S. Office of Education, the War Department, and the Office of War Information (OWI). OWI mobilized the 16 mm nontheatrical club and school circuit, and weekly theatrical exhibitions alternating officially produced and Hollywood-produced films through the Motion Picture Industry's War Activities Committee. See Association of National Advertisers, *New Horizons for Business Films* (New York: National Association of Advertisers, 1946), p. 48; and Richard Dyer MacCann, *The People's Films: A Political History of U.S. Government Motion Pictures* (New York: Hastings House, 1973), pp. 125–127, 129–130, 135–137, 153–159.

6. Slide, *Before Video*, p. 102.

7. "'A Fly on the Wheel,'" *Fortune* 35 (January 1947): 138, 140; "The Man Who Put Business in Show Biz," *Sales Meetings Magazine* (July 1970): 70–73, 134, 136–138, 140–143, 145–146.

8. Between 1939 and 1940 clients and films included General Motors (*To New Horizons, Leave It to Roll-Oh*), U.S. Steel (Technicolor "Prologue" to *Men Make Steel*), Household Finance Corporation (*Happily Ever After, Heap O'Livin': An "Evening with Edgar Guest"*), Anheuser-Busch (*Reflecting Our Confidence in the Future of America*), Coca-Cola (*Refreshment through the Years*), American Tobacco (*The Story of Lucky Strike*), the Chamber of Commerce of the United States (*Free Men Build a Nation*), and the Republican National Committee, for whom Handy equipped a motor coach with a projection and public address system for showings of a compilation film promoting Republican presidential candidate Wendell Willkie. *Catalog of Copyright Entries Cumulative Series: Motion Pictures, 1912–1939* (Washington, DC: Library of Congress, 1951) and *Motion Pictures, 1940–1949* (Washington, DC: Library of Congress, 1953). The Willkie coach is seen in a photograph in the Handy collection of Pierce Rafferty, Petrified Films, New York.

9. Richard Polenberg, *War and Society: The United States, 1941–1945* (Philadelphia: J. B. Lippincott Co., 1972), p. 11.

10. Dismissed by industry managers as unworkable, Reuther's plan envisioned the creation of an industry-wide production board drawn from management and labor, in effect a tangible symbol of labor's political clout. The "Reuther Plan" nevertheless fostered an image of labor prescience in the stead of managerial intransigence, an image that became all the more prescient after Pearl Harbor. Nelson Lichtenstein, *The Most Dangerous Man in Detroit: Walter Reuther and the Fate of American Labor* (New York: Basic Books, 1995), pp. 161–166, 169–171; Lichtenstein, *Labor's War at Home: The CIO in World War II* (New York: Cambridge University Press, 1982), pp. 41–42, 85–89; David Brody, "The New Deal in World War II," in *The New Deal*, ed. Braemen et al., pp. 281–286; George R. Clark, "Strange Story of the Reuther Plan," *Harper's* 184 (May 1942): 645–654.

11. Campbell-Ewald drew upon its experience in managing General Motors' wartime advertising to recommend similar steps that client DuMont Laboratories might take in 1950 "in case of general mobilization of industry for defense or all-out war." See "A Presentation to DuMont by Campbell-Ewald Company," 29 August 1950, with cover memorandum from W. H. Case to Dr. Allen B. DuMont, 22 December 1950, folder: Sales and Advertising, 1950, box 46 Sales and Advertising, Allen B. DuMont Laboratories papers, Manuscript Division, LC. For examples of GM's wartime ads, see Borden, *Advertising Text and Cases*, pp. 529–533.

12. A title card explained, "If this picture will serve to clarify some of the thinking on war production problems, it will have served its purpose." *Close Harmony* (1942), copyright deposit synopsis MU 13199, LC; print, PA.

13. *To Each Other*, copyright deposit synopsis MU 14069, LC; print, PA.

14. Roy Rosenzweig, "'United Action Means Victory': Militant Americanism on Film," *Labor History* 24 (spring 1983): 274–288. The film found an audience after the war, conveying what its distributor, Brandon Films, described as "an understanding of the problems and issues unions were confronted with in the building of their memberships." *United Action* "is an American story of American men and women in American industry. The cast consists of union members, wives, kids, cops, farmers and union leaders." See "Public Affairs Films for Labor Co-ops, Community, Farm and Veteran Groups" (n.d.), Frontier Films collection, Manuscript Division, LC.

15. Otto H. Coelln, "The UAW-CIO Pioneers' Use of Films among Labor Unions," *Business Screen* 6, no. 4 (1945): 46.

16. On the reconversion strike wave at GM and elsewhere, see George Lipsitz, *Rainbow at Midnight: Labor and Culture in the 1940s* (Chicago: University of Illinois Press, 1994), pp. 109–113.

17. Harry A. Millis and Emily Clark Brown, *From the Wagner Act to Taft-Hartley*, pp. 287–291; Robert Griffith, "Forging America's Postwar Order: Domestic Politics and Political Economy in the Age of Truman," and Nelson Lichtenstein, "Labor in the Truman Era: Origins of the 'Private Welfare State,'" both in *The*

Truman Presidency, ed. Michael J. Lacey (New York: Cambridge University Press, 1989), pp. 57–88, 128–155; for an overview, see Thomas A. Kochan, Harry C. Katz, and Robert B. McKersie, *The Transformation of American Industrial Relations* (New York: Basic Books, 1986), pp. 21–37, 45–46.

18. James A. Gross, *The Reshaping of the National Labor Relations Board* (Albany, NY: State University of New York Press, 1974, 1981), passim, cited in David Brody, "On the Labor Representation Election: Some History and a Modest Proposal," paper presented at the Ninth Symposium of the George Meany Archive, November 17–18, 1996, National Archives at College Park.

19. Fones-Wolf, *Selling Free Enterprise*, pp. 78–82; Harris, *The Right to Manage*, p. 123.

20. These included *Working on Air* (1944) telling the story of propeller development by the corporation's Aeroproducts Division, one of a series of "Little Journeys in General Motors," and *GM and Its People—An American Industrial Team* (n.d.), which explained the corporation's decentralized organization and the importance of people in its success or failure. Borden, *Advertising Text and Cases*, p. 550.

21. Borden, *Advertising Text and Cases*, p. 549; for films, see *We Drivers* (1937), copyright deposit file MU 7159, revised in 1950 by Jam Handy Organization for General Motors Corp., print, FCA 1577, LC; *On to Jupiter* (1939), Soundmasters, Inc., for General Motors Department of Public Relations, 20 mins, b/w, sd, no copyright deposit; print, Department of Public Relations, General Motors Corporation (hereafter GM); *To New Horizons* (1940), Jam Handy for General Motors, (MP 10402), LC; print, GM.

22. Memoranda, "New Sales Sample-Motion Picture, General Motors-*Experiment*," 28 August 1946, and *The Easier Way*, 20 September 1946, PA.

23. General Motors president Charles E. Wilson suggested that what foremen most needed was the same containment given the rank-and-file UAW. Nelson Lichtenstein, "'The Man in the Middle': A Social History of Automobile Industry Foremen," in *On the Line: Essays in the History of Auto Work*, ed. Lichtenstein and Stephen Meyer (Chicago: University of Chicago Press, 1989), pp. 153–189; see also Baritz, *The Servants of Power*, pp. 134, 182–185, 189–190; Graebner, *The Engineering of Consent*, pp. 81–85; Gillespie, *Manufacturing Knowledge*, pp. 229–230.

24. A disclaimer at the film's conclusion stated "Resemblance of characters in this picture to actual people is coincidental." *The Open Door* (1945), copyright deposit file, MU 16571, LC; reviewed in *Business Screen* 7, no. 6 (1946): 16, and 8, no. 8 (1947): 29; print, PA.

25. *Doctor in Industry* (1947), copyright deposit file MU 496, LC; reviewed in *Business Screen* 8, no. 8 (1947): 29; print, PA.

26. Graebner, *The Engineering of Consent*, p. 85.

27. Memorandum, "New Sales Sample, Motion Picture-G.M.-'Strange Interview,'" 7 January 1947 and 15 January 1948, PA; *Strange Interview* (1947), copyright deposit file, MU 1769, LC.

28. *Unfinished Business* (1948), copyright deposit file, MU 3225, LC; "U.S. Steel Makes a Progress Report," *Business Screen* 9, no. 4 (1948): 23; advertisement, Jam Handy Organization, "Human Steel," *Business Screen* 9, no. 6 (1948): back cover; print, PA.

29. In the interest of theatrical pacing, Finch applauded the deletion of statistics and the deemphasis of the veteran's home life: "The theatrical version confines itself to steel shortage and what is being done about it. Operating figures are removed, and the veteran and his family are reduced to a mere incident. This version is fast moving and interesting." Finch pronounced the nine-minute picture "good theatrical merchandise" and noted that Handy had placed it in 4,000 theaters nationally where it would play to more than 10 million people. Memo, George B. Finch to All Contract Men (10/48), subject: Unfinished Business Nontheatrical and Theatrical, Bulletin no. 45, PA.

30. "N.A.M. Public information Program, 1940 (for Discussion by Public Relations Advisory Group, Tuesday February 20, 1940)," pp. 6–7, folder 74 NAM-Public Information Program-1940, box 78, NBC/SHSW.

31. "We Use Films in Our Program: National Association of Manufacturers," *Film News* 10 (March 1950): 6, 11.

32. Pamphlet, "Four Film Classics!" folder: Now! Action by Management-Films, general, box 68, NAM series I, acc. 1411, NAM/HL; for trade comment see *Business Screen* 2, no. 3 (1940): 18.

33. Pamphlet, "Four Film Classics!" folder: Now! Action by Management-Films, general, box 68, NAM/HL.

34. Pamphlet, "Coming Soon! Postmark—U.S.A.," folder: NAM film: Postmark, U.S.A., 23 September 1943, box 113, NAM/HL.

35. Pamphlet, "Three to Be Served," folder: black looseleaf notebook, Three to Be Served, nontheatrical promotion, box 69, NAM/HL.

36. "A Presentation to DuMont by Campbell-Ewald Company," 29 August 1950, with cover memorandum from W. H. Case to Dr. Allen B. DuMont, 22 December 1950, folder: Sales and Advertising, 1950, box 46, Sales and Advertising, Allen B. DuMont Laboratories papers, Manuscript Division, LC.

37. Ibid.

38. Association of National Advertisers, *The Job Ahead for Business: Selling the Company behind the Product* (New York: Association of National Advertisers, 1946), pp. 2–3; Association of National Advertisers and American Association of Advertising Agencies, *Report of the Joint A.N.A.-A.A.A.A. Committee on Improvement of Public Understanding of Our Economic System* (New York: Association of National Advertisers and American Association of Advertising Agencies, 1947), later published as American Association of Advertising Agencies et al., *A Program for American Opportunity through Advertising: A Report of the Subcommittee on Advertising* (Washington, DC: Domestic Distribution Department, Chamber of Commerce of the United States, 1947).

39. Fones-Wolf, *Selling Free Enterprise*, pp. 7–8, 22–24, 28–29, 33; Harris, *The Right to Manage*, pp. 105–106, 181–184, 192–194; Richard S. Tedlow, *Keeping the Corporate Image: Public Relations and Business, 1900–1950* (Greenwich, CT: JAI Press, 1979), pp. 121–125, 140–141; V. O. Key, *Politics, Parties, and Pressure Groups*, pp. 99–101; Robert M. Collins, "American Corporatism: The Committee for Economic Development, 1942–1964," *Historian* 44 (February 1982): 151–173; Griffith, "Forging America's Postwar Order" and "The Selling of America."

40. Association of National Advertisers, *The Job Ahead for Business*, pp. 2–3, 6. On Young, see Harold B. Thomas, "The Background and Beginning of the Advertising Council," in *The Promise of Advertising*, ed. C. H. Sandage (Homewood, IL: Richard D. Irwin, 1961), p. 23.

41. Americans, Robinson concluded, most frequently used a "test of motive" to judge their leaders. "Is this leader a man of good motives? Is he trying to do the right thing? That was the secret of Franklin D. Roosevelt as a salesman of leadership. He was a pretty successful salesman, you recall. He convinced the people that his heart was in the right place, that he was trying to help the common man." Claude E. Robinson, "Shifting Public Attitudes and What They Mean to Business," in Association of National Advertisers, *The Job Ahead for Business*, pp. 15–17.

42. John Orr Young, "Stop Shouting 'Free Enterprise' Unless You Give the Term Meaning," *Printers' Ink* 207 (May 5, 1944): 17–18, 88–92, folder: Inadequacy of term, "Free Enterprise," box 843, NAM/HL.

43. H. Obermeyer to Barton, 17 December 1943, folder: National Association of Manufacturers, 1935–1944, box 122, BB/SHSW.

44. "Bull Session," *Fortune* 42 (September 1950): 80.

45. Robinson added, "The great advantage of the word 'capitalism' is that it places the issue in the people's minds of a privately owned economy vs. a government directed one. Ownership, obviously, is only one facet of our society. What we hope to do is link up other facets around this concept, with particular reference to moral and spiritual as well as economic values." Robinson to Barton, 11 November 1956, folder: Roa–Rof (Claude Robinson) 1924–1961, box 60, BB/SHSW; Robert H. Haddow, *Pavilions of Plenty: Exhibiting American Culture Abroad in the 1950s* (Washington, DC: Smithsonian Institution Press, 1997), pp. 47–59.

46. Measures opposed included the Securities Exchange Act, National Labor Relations Act, Agricultural Price Parity, Railroad Pension Act, Public Works, Social Security Act, Emergency Work Relief, Banking Act of 1935, Public Utilities Holding Company Act, Anti-Strike Breaking Act, 1936 Revenue Act (corporate tax section), Food and Drug Act, Fair Labor Standards Act (wages and hours), Agricultural Adjustment Act, Federal Work Relief Act, and the creation of the Federal Security Administration, National Youth Administration, and Public Works Administration. For a comprehensive list of measures opposed and approved, see Alfred S. Cleveland, "NAM: Spokesman for Industry?" *Harvard Business Review* 26 (May 1948): 353–371; "Renovation in N.A.M.," *Fortune* 38 (July 1948): 72–75, 165–169; R. W. Gable, "N.A.M.: Influential Lobby or Kiss of Death?" *Journal of Politics* 15 (May 1953): 253–273.

47. Parkes later acknowledged the members of the public relations policy committee who had effected the change: Cloud Wampler; Colby M. Chester, former NAM president and chairman of the board of General Mills; Walter D. Fuller, president of Curtis Publishing Company; John Holmes; Malcolm Muir, director of McGraw-Hill Publishing Company; H. W. Prentis, Jr., director of Armstrong Cork Company; J. Howard Pew, director of Sun Oil Company; Morris B. Sayre, NAM president and president of Corn Products Refining Company; Wayne Burnett; and publicist John W. Hill of Hill & Knowlton. Holcombe Parkes to Members of the public relations policy committee, 6 January 1947, folder: National Association of Manufacturers, 1947–1952, box 34, John W. Hill papers, SHSW. Between 1945 and 1947 the NAM divided its budget between legislative lobbying in Washington and publicity headquartered in New York. In 1945 the NAM reported a total income of $3,663,460. On the "disbursement side" the association spent $1,979,000 on the Washington-based "N.A.M. Program" and $1,736,809 on public relations. In 1947 the association reported a total income of $4,717,425, spending $2,258,865 for public relations, a sum that included $168,500 for committee counsel and opinion research. Cleveland, "NAM: Spokesman for Industry?"; "Renovation in N.A.M.," *Fortune* 38 (July 1948): 72–75, 165–169.

48. Robinson, "Shifting Public Attitudes and What They Mean to Business," in Association of National Advertisers, *The Job Ahead for Business*, pp. 15–17; "Renovation in N.A.M.," *Fortune* 38 (July 1948): 72–75, 165–169.

49. Editorial, "How to Minimize Debate and Maximize Results in Public Relations," *Railway Age* 121 (December 28, 1946): 1073–1074, copy, folder: National Association of Manufacturers, 1947–1952, box 34, Hill Papers, SHSW.

50. National Association of Manufacturers, *The Challenge and the Answer* (New York, September 1947), cited in Millis and Brown, *From the Wagner Act to Taft-Hartley*, pp. 288–289.

51. Editorial, "How to Minimize Debate and Maximize Results in Public Relations."

52. Harris, *The Right to Manage*, pp. 105–106, 119–120; Fones-Wolf, *Selling Free Enterprise*, pp. 42–44; Lipsitz, *Rainbow at Midnight*, pp. 157–181, esp. pp. 161, 175–177; Millis and Brown, *From the Wagner Act to Taft-Hartley*, pp. 290–291, 315; Gable, "N.A.M.: Influential Lobby or Kiss of Death?"; Arthur M. Johnson, "American Business in the Postwar Era" and John Barnard, "American Workers, the Labor Movement, and the Cold War, 1945–1969," both in *Reshaping America: Society and Institutions, 1945–1960*, ed. Robert H. Bremner and Gary W. Reichard (Columbus: Ohio State University Press, 1982), pp. 101–145; Christopher L. Tomlins, *The State and the Unions: Labor Relations, Law, and the Organized Labor Movement in America, 1880–1960* (New York: Cambridge University Press, 1985), pp. 252–316.

53. National Association of Manufacturers, *The Challenge and the Answer* (New York, September 1947); for advertisements see *New York Times*, 8 January 1947, 28 and 30 April 1947, 11 May 1947, 1 June 1947, excerpted in Millis and Brown, *From the Wagner Act to Taft-Hartley*, pp. 288–289.

54. "Renovation in N.A.M.," *Fortune* 38 (July 1948): 72–75, 165–169; Philip Ash, "The Periodical Press and the Taft-Hartley Act," *Public Opinion Quarterly* 12 (summer 1948): 266–271; Fones-Wolf, *Selling Free Enterprise*, pp. 43–44.

55. Don Chapman, "Nasty Atrocious Mischief Makers, In Other Words N.A.M.," *The Searchlight*, 8 May 1947, p. 7; "N.A.M. Wrote Taft-Hartley Bill," *The Searchlight*, 22 May 1947, p. 1, Chevrolet Local no. 659, UAW locals 1947, Walter Reuther Library, Wayne State University, Detroit, MI (hereafter RL).

56. Cleveland, "NAM: Spokesman for Industry?"

57. "Renovation in N.A.M.," *Fortune* 38 (July 1948): 72–75, 165–169.

58. Stuart J. Little, "The Freedom Train: Citizenship and Postwar Political Culture, 1946–1949," *American Studies* 34 (spring 1993): 35–67; James Gregory Bradsher, "Taking America's Heritage to the People: The Freedom Train Story," *Prologue* 17 (winter 1985): 228–245; William A. Coblenz, "The Freedom Train and the Story of Its Origin: Our Civil Liberties on Wheels," *Manuscripts* 10 (winter 1958): 30–34, 59; for a complete list of exhibit documents and their texts, see Frank Monaghan, *Heritage of Freedom: The History and Significance of the Basic Documents of American Liberty* (Princeton, NJ: Princeton University Press, 1948).

59. Commenting on American discord in the aftermath of the Jay Treaty with Great Britain, which was opposed by anti-Federalists and French sympathizers, John Jay wrote to John Trumbull: "I wish to see our people more Americanized, if I may use that expression; until we feel and act as an independent nation, we shall always suffer from foreign intrigues." Coblenz to Monaghan, 16 April 1947, folder 4, box 2, RG 64 Records of the National Archives and Records Service, Educational Programs Division, Freedom Train, National Archives Building, Washington, D.C. (hereafter FT/NA). The letter appeared in the exhibit and in Monaghan, *Heritage of Freedom*, pp. 111–112. Monaghan reviewed advertising and pamphlet copy, ghosted an article about the train and its contents for foundation chairman Winthrop W. Aldrich, and prepared document stories for the exhibit catalog *Heritage of Freedom*. Novins to Monaghan, 3 October 1947, folder: Releases-A.H.F.-Oct. thru Dec. 1947, box 218, RG 200 National Archives Gift Collection, American Heritage Foundation Papers, National Archives at College Park (hereafter AHF/NACP); Novins to Hamer, 3 December 1947 and endorsement sheet, EP (Hamer) to A (Buck), 3 December 1947, folder 9, box 2, FT/NA.

60. For examples of merchandising among school groups, see "The American Heritage Program for New York City," 1948, box 9, AHF/NACP; for labor groups, see *The First Two Years: A Progress Report to the Trustees of the American Heritage Foundation* (July 1, 1949), pp. 105–114, box 10, AHF/NACP; and "Highlights of the National Rededication Program of the American Heritage Foundation" (ca. July 26, 1948), folder 11, box 2, RG 64, FT/NA.

61. Replier to Brophy, 11 November 1947, folder: AHF General Sept.–Dec. 1947, box 212; "A Presentation to the American Heritage Foundation July 26, 1948 by the Joint ANA-AAAA Committee on Improvement of Public Understanding of Our Economic System," folder: economic campaign-A.H.F., box 210; James Webb Young to Louis Novins, 10 November 1948, folder: economic campaign-AHF, box 210, AHF/NACP. The differences between the American Heritage Foundation's Freedom Train campaign of "National Rededication" and the Joint Committee's campaign of "American Opportunity" were of degree, rather than in kind, and significant because of the rift between Advertising Council specialists responsible for each. Though deprived of a national symbol on the order of the Freedom Train, Joint Committee specialists proceeded with the "American Opportunity"/"Miracle of America" economic education campaign under the auspices of the Public Policy Committee of the Advertising Council and the U.S. Chamber of Commerce. See American Association of Advertising Agencies et al., *A Program for American Opportunity through Advertising*.

62. Henry C. Link, "How to Sell America to the Americans," *Business Screen* 9, no. 1 (February 1948): 20–21.

63. Chester E. Evans and LaVerne N. Laseau, *My Job Contest* (Washington, DC: Personnel Psychology, Inc., 1950), p. 3, cited in Baritz, *The Servants of Power*, p. 154, n. 28.

64. Evans and Laseau, *My Job Contest*, p. 4.

65. "Harry B. Coen," May 1947, Albert Sobey Papers, file: biographical information: GM Personnel 78-10.32, General Motors Institute Alumni Historical Collection, Flint, MI; General Motors Corporation, *The Worker Speaks: My Job and Why I Like It* (Detroit: General Motors, 1947), series 60 box 6, auto-GM, Warshaw Collection, Archives Center, National Museum of American History, Smithsonian Institution (hereafter NMAH/SI); Alan Raucher, "Employee Relations at General Motors: The 'My Job Contest,'" *Labor History* 28 (spring 1987): 221–232.

66. General Motors Corporation, background information, "Studies of 'My Job' Contest Letters," n.d., vertical file pre-1960s folder GMC 1940s, box 14, RL; General Motors Corporation, *The Worker Speaks*, p. 26.

67. "What I Like or What I Don't Like about My Job," *The Searchlight*, 25 September 1947, Chevrolet Local No. 659, UAW locals 1947, RL.

68. "In 1937," its anonymous author recalled, "the union steward told me we would shut the plant down and sit down and not work until the foreman stopped being so mean and promised not to fire me because he was mad at his wife or other silly reason (such as needing a job for his brother-in-law). We sat down and I liked it as it was the first time I ever sat down at Chevrolet. . . . Kermit Johnson and Gib Rose told me to help keep the scabs out. . . . Tom Klasey got hit on the head by one of your watchmen. Maybe this was a big mistake as we are a big happy family." "Some Letters by They Who Remember," *The Searchlight*, 25 September 1947, RL.

69. Jimmy Kiger, "GM Grand Strategy," *The Searchlight*, 9 October 1947, RL.

70. General Motors Corporation, *The Worker Speaks*, pp. 96, 113, 130.

71. Ibid., pp. 34, 128. In December 1957 GM announced a similar letter-writing contest in honor of the corporation's "Golden Milestone" fiftieth anniversary. Employees were asked to "write a letter on this subject: 'The Golden Milestone—What It Means to Me, My Family, and My Community.'" A point system awarded 5,000 prizes ranging from televisions, bicycles, boats, and appliances to cars, General Motors stock, and a "Golden Milestone Home" erected on a lot anywhere in the United States. A catalog of prizes and point values described the first-place prize; it was available in Colonial, Contemporary, or Cape Cod design, complete with a Frigidaire kitchen designed by the GM styling staff, Delco heating and air conditioning, and Delco-Matic garage doors. Louis G. Seaton to Men and Women of General Motors, 31 December 1957, series 60 box 6, auto-GM, Warshaw Collection, Archives Center, NMAH/SI.

72. Text taken from "Cutting Continuity," *Letter to a Rebel*, 23 July 1948, copyright deposit file MP 3189, LC; for trade comment, see "*Business Screen*'s Recommendation to the U.S. Chamber," *Business Screen* 9, no. 4 (1948): 22.

73. Wells to Brophy, 18 August 1948, folder: Films-Music-Pledges-Slogans-Contests, box 210, AHF/NACP.

74. Joseph A. McCartin, "'An American Feeling': Workers, Managers and the Struggle over Industrial Democracy in the World War I Era," in *Industrial Democracy in America: The Ambiguous Promise*, ed. Nelson Lichtenstein and Howell John Harris (New York: Cambridge University Press, 1993), pp. 67–86; Daniel Nelson, *American Rubber Workers and Organized Labor, 1900–1941* (Princeton, NJ: Princeton University Press, 1988), pp. 57–60, cited in *Industrial Democracy in America*, p. 84.

75. *A Letter from America* (1950), Wilding Picture Productions for Goodyear Tire & Rubber Company, American Archives of the Factual Film, Iowa State University, Ames, Iowa (hereafter AAFF); for trade comment, see "Time to Show the Facts," *Business Screen* 10, no. 2 (1949): 21–22.

76. *The Birthright* (1954), Parthenon Pictures, Viking Production Companies for Chrysler, print 16-0010, AAFF.

77. *The Great Swindle* (1948), copyright deposit file LP 1690; print, PA; see also "Labor Looks to the Screen," *Business Screen* 9, no. 4 (1948): 21–22.

78. *Albert in Blunderland* (1950), Loew's Inc. presented by MGM, catalog synopsis; script in copyright deposit file LP 347; 35 mm, sd, Technicolor print, Sutherland Collection, LC.

79. *Albert in Blunderland* (1950), script, copyright deposit file LP 347; print FEA 20, LC; *Inside Cackle Corners* (1951), copyright deposit file MP 1497, print, FEA 1346, LC; *Make Mine Freedom* (1950), in Richard Prelinger, *Our Secret Century*, vol. 10 (Irvington, NY: Voyager Press, 1996) [CD-ROM]; *Meet King Joe—The American Worker* (1950), Richard Prelinger, *You Can't Take It with You* (Los Angeles: Voyager Press, 1987) [Laserdisc]; on Harding College and the Sloan Foundation, see Robert Schacht, "Informal Education," in Film Council of America, *Sixty Years of 16 mm Film, 1923–1937: A Symposium* (Evanston, IL: Film Council of America, 1954), p. 85; for Sutherland's "Chiquita Banana" work for BBDO and client United Fruit, see copyright deposit file MU 3749, LC.

80. United Labor League of Ohio, *The Robert Alphonso Taft Story, "It's on the Record!"* Ralph E. Becker Collection cat. 227739.1950.K28, pamphlet file, Political History Collection, NMAH/SI; memorandum, Lou Gulay to Senator Taft, September 13, 1950, folder: L. Richard Gulay, box 296 political file 1950, Robert A. Taft Papers, Manuscript Division, LC.

81. "This Is General Electric," *Business Screen* 10, no. 4 (1949): 25–26.

82. "Business Is Still in Trouble," *Fortune* 39 (May 1949): 67–71, 196–200; "Public Relations for the Long Pull," *Fortune* 44 (October 1951): 108–113; Nicholas Lemann, *Out of the Forties* (Austin: Texas Monthly Press, 1983 reprint New York: Fireside/Simon & Schuster, 1985); Steven W. Plattner, "How the Other Half Lived: The Standard Oil Company (New Jersey) Photographic Project, 1943–1950" (M.A. thesis, George Washington University, 1981), p. 124, cited in Stange, *Symbols of Ideal Life*, pp. 141–146.

83. "What Should Esso Be Doing in the Field of Economic Education for Employees," 1 April 1950, p. 5, corporation file, Labor-Management Documentation Center, Cornell University, cited in Harris, *The Right to Manage*, p. 271, n. 26.

84. *The Price of Freedom* (1949), Apex Film Corp. for the NAM, copyright deposit file MP 4393; print FBA 1289, LC; pamphlet, "The Price of Freedom," folder: films, Price of Freedom, box 69, NAM/HL.

85. Holcombe Parkes, "Review Comment," *Business Screen* 10, no. 4 (1949): 22.

86. Continuity, *The Price of Freedom* (1949), copyright deposit file MP 4393; print FBA 1289, LC.

87. "The Price of Freedom," *Business Screen* 10, no. 4 (1949): 21–22.

88. Merrick Jackson to John W. Hill, 5 May 1949, folder: National Association of Manufacturers, 1947–1952, box 34, Hill Papers, SHSW.

89. *Industry on Parade* also appeared in thirteen foreign countries and via low-powered television transmission on U.S. Air Force bases in the United States and abroad. Pamphlet, National Association of Manufacturers, *Industry on Parade* and attached press release, 15 October 1955, finding aid file, Motion Picture and Television Reading Room, LC.

Chapter 8

1. American Association of Advertising Agencies et al., *A Program for American Opportunity through Advertising*; pamphlet, "American Heritage Program for Your Community," RG 64 folder 4, box 3, FT/NA; pamphlet, "How Our Business System Operates" (E. I. du Pont de Nemours and Co., Inc., ca. 1951); pamphlet, "How Our Business System Operates" (General Electric Company, ca. 1951). The GE version explained: "The program in which you have participated is a review of certain points that you may have let slip your mind." See also pamphlet, "Wanted: 1,500 GE Leaders to Sponsor Adult Economic Education Discussion Groups with Associates and Neighbors" (General Electric Company, ca. 1954); pamphlet, "Highlights of the General Electric Economic Education Program" (General Electric Company, ca. 1954), Labor-Management Documentation Center, Cornell University, Ithaca, NY.

2. Francis X. Sutton et al., *The American Business Creed* (Cambridge, MA: Harvard University Press, 1956); William H. Whyte, *Is Anybody Listening? How and Why U.S. Business Fumbles When It Talks with Human Beings* (New York: Simon & Schuster, 1952); C. W. McKee and H. G. Moulton, *A Survey of Economic Education* (Washington: Brookings Institution, 1951).

3. Kim McQuaid, *A Response to Industrialism: Liberal Businessmen and the Evolving Spectrum of Capitalist Reform, 1886–1960* (New York: Garland, 1986), pp. 189–253; Robert M. Collins, "American Corporatism."

4. Howell John Harris designates the phenomenon as the "Great Enterprise Campaign" and an offshoot "Communications in Industry" movement. Though a notable failure in its attempt to alter the public's attitudes and beliefs toward business leadership, the Great Enterprise Campaign is significant because "the media the campaign employed, together with its underlying premises, show how businessmen understood their own society, and hoped to act upon it." Harris, *The Right to Manage*, pp. 105–127, 177–179, 188–199 (quoted from p. 193); Fones-Wolf, *Selling Free Enterprise*, pp. 1–11, 32–63; Robert Griffith, "The Selling of America"; Frank Fox, *Madison Avenue Goes to War*, pp. 45–67.

5. Chester H. Lang, "Business Review Public Relations Services Division," 7 January 1954, folder: General Electric 1951–1957, box 76 client correspondence, BB/SHSW.

6. *Better Living* 6 (March–April 1952): 34.

7. Lang, "Business Review Public Relations Services Division."

8. F. L. Dewey, "How Company Advertising Helps the Sales Program," 22 September 1954, folder 9, box 13, acc. 1803, DuP/HL.

9. Advertisement, General Electric Company, "What Is Television?" *Forum and Century* 101 (February 1939): overleaf. For a later example in a domestic setting, see advertisement, General Electric Company, "'Look, Pop! It's a Homer!'" *Forum and Century* 102 (September 1939): overleaf.

10. Press release, Radio Corporation of America, 20 April 1939, box 549 CWC 142-323A, Clark Collection, NMAH/SI; press release, Radio Corporation of America, 11 April 1939, author's collection.

11. Press release, Radio Corporation of America, 15 May 1939, "RCA World's Fair Exhibit," folder 20: New York World's Fair 1939–1940, box 79, NBC/SHSW; photograph caption, "'Musicorner' section of 'America At Home' exhibition at the New York World's Fair, 1940," Museum of Modern Art.

12. Gardner Harding, "World's Fair 1939: A Preview," *Harper's* 176 (December 1937): 129–137; Walter Dorwin Teague, *Design This Day: The Technique of Order in the Machine Age* (New York: Harcourt, Brace & Company, 1940), pp. 1–2.

13. Press release, General Electric Co., "General Electric at the New York World's Fair in 1940," folder: General Electric, box 1005 printed material distributed by exhibitors, NYWF/NYPL; brochure, "The General Electric Building New York World's Fair 1940," author's collection.

14. Lynn Spigel, *Make Room for TV: Television and the Family Ideal in Postwar America* (Chicago: University of Chicago Press, 1992), pp. 37–45, 99–109, 136–144; Cecelia Tichi, *Electronic Hearth: Creating an American Television Culture* (New York: Oxford University Press, 1991), pp. 11–29.

15. A canvass of "corporate voice" advertisers made by General Electric in 1955 identified eight television sponsors: General Electric, the *General Electric Theater*; U.S. Steel, the *United States Steel Hour*; DuPont, *Cavalcade of America*; Aluminum Company of America, *See It Now*; Ford, *Producers Showcase*; The Electric Light and Power Companies of America, *You Are There*; Reynolds Metals, *Mr. Peepers*; and the Aluminum Company of Canada, *Omnibus*. "Memorandum of Advisory Council Regarding Sponsorship of G.E. Theater," DuP/HL.

16. Robert Griffith, "The Selling of America."

17. Barton J. Bernstein, "The Truman Administration and the Steel Strike of 1946," *Journal of American History* 52 (March 1966): 791–803; Robert H. Zeiger, *American Workers, American Unions, 1920–1985* (Baltimore: Johns Hopkins University Press, 1986), pp. 101, 154; H. J. Harris, *The Right to Manage*, pp. 112, 154.

18. Thomas O'Malley, "'Every Important Work of Art Has a Message,'" *Television Magazine* 11 (October 1954): 34–35, 68–69; "Theatre Guild Show," *Tide* (October 15, 1945): 124–128; "Steel Melts the Public," *Sponsor* (March 17, 1950): 24–25, 49–56; Norman Nadel, *A Pictorial History of the Theatre Guild* (New York: Crown Publishers, Inc., 1969), includes an appendix of radio and television productions; *The Theatre Guild Anthology* (New York: Random House, 1936); H. William Fitelson, ed., *Theatre Guild on the Air* (New York: Rinehart & Company, 1947).

19. Brochure, J. Carlisle MacDonald, "United States Steel's Radio Program," n.d., BBDO Dep'ts: Radio, BBDO.

20. Ibid.

21. Fitelson, ed., *Theatre Guild on the Air*, pp. xi, 336–337.

22. Newton to Duffy, 15 July 1949, folder: U.S. Steel 1948–1951, box 80 client correspondence, BB/SHSW. Noting that plays had proved an "unsuitable source of material," Newton proposed that Langner consider adaptations of screenplays, a popular format of proven value pioneered by the top-rated *Lux Radio Theater*. Newton to Duffy, 8 February 1950 and 28 April 1948, folder: U.S. Steel 1948–1951, box 80 client correspondence, BB/SHSW.

23. Newton to Duffy et al., 15 July 1949 and 24 October 1950, folder: U.S. Steel 1948–1949, box 80 client correspondence; and Newton to Dave Danforth, 7 October 1952, folder: U.S. Steel 1952–1958, box 81 client correspondence, BB/SHSW.

24. Fairless's association with the annual Churchman's Award Dinner prompted Newton's discussion of BBDO's "research set-up" with Olds. Newton to Bruce Barton, 9 February 1949, folder: U.S. Steel 1948–1951, box 80 client correspondence, BB/SHSW. In a lawsuit brought by radio personality John Henry Faulk against Laurence A. Johnson and Vincent Hartnett of the anti-Communist AWARE, Inc., in 1962, former BBDO employee Jack Wren described his duties as the head of BBDO's research department: "My duties, among other things, was [*sic*] to protect our clients against false charges made that we loaded our shows with Communists, by Vincent Hartnett, who made these charges against us, who wrote poison-pen letters behind our backs to our clients, wrote to our officers accusing us of loading our shows with Communists. . . . My [other] duties were to read television scripts to make sure that they were accurate, especially dealing with realism." Cited in John Henry Faulk, *Fear on Trial* (New York: Simon & Schuster, 1964), p. 363. Wren reported to *Theatre Guild on the Air* producer George Kondolf. See "BBDO Organization Chart for United States Steel," attached to Harry Veith to Barton, 27 September 1951, folder: U.S. Steel 1948–1951, box 80 client correspondence, BB/SHSW. On the prominence of BBDO's research setup, and Wren's reputation in the industry, see John Cogley, *Report on Blacklisting*, vol. 2: *Radio-Television* (New York: Fund for the Republic, 1956), pp. 115–118.

25. Merle Miller, *The Judges and the Judged* (Garden City, NY: Doubleday & Company, Inc., 1952), pp. 72–73.

26. Duffy to MacDonald, n.d., copy dated 11 December 1952, folder: U.S. Steel 1952–1958, box 81 client correspondence, BB/SHSW. Duffy, Newton, and others available to BBDO's research setup presumably had the confidence of immediate information. Of the artists named in *Red Channels*, a list of 151 artists and alleged Communist affiliations published by *Counterattack* in June 1950, however, only two had any ongoing public association with the program: actress and playwright Ruth Gordon, whose *Over 21* aired May 18, 1952; and actor Burgess Meredith, whose appearances included *The Sea Wolf* (27 April 1952) and concluded with *Hobson's Choice* (26 October 1952), the last *Theatre Guild on the Air* to feature a performer listed in American Business Consultants, *Red Channels: The Report of Communist Influence in Radio and Television* (New York: Counterattack, 1950). For a concise, alphabetized list of the "named," see Barnouw, *The Golden Web*, p. 266. For casts and writers of guild radio and television productions, see Nadel, *A Pictorial History of the Theatre Guild*, appendix.

27. As an added precaution, Newton recommended that *Theatre Guild on the Air* producer George Kondolf "make a trip to Syracuse, after further study of the subjects of that letter in order to discuss the matter with the [American] Legion people there in person." Newton to MacDonald, 3 November 1952, copy, 11 December 1952, folder: U.S. Steel 1952–1958, box 81 client correspondence, BB/SHSW. On supermarket owner Lawrence A. Johnson and the Veterans Action Committee of Syracuse Supermarkets, see Cogley, *Report on Blacklisting,* vol. 2, pp. 100–109.

28. Newton to Duffy et al., 15 July 1949, folder: U.S. Steel 1948–1949, box 80 client correspondence, BB/SHSW.

29. "Improvement of Public Opinion about United States Steel," 9 January 1950, pp. 5, 7, attached to Barton to Newton, 14 February 1950, folder: U.S. Steel 1948–1951, box 80 client correspondence, BB/SHSW.

30. *A Christmas Carol*, NBC (1951), print DD 143 (Arch Pos), Coe Collection, SHSW.

31. On the Cratchit's feast, whose modern emphasis historian Paul Davis attributes to the stimulation of consumption, see Davis, *The Life and Times of Ebenezer Scrooge* (New Haven: Yale University Press, 1990), pp. 141, 184.

32. *A Christmas Carol*, NBC (1951), SHSW.

33. "Guild on the Screen," *Newsweek* 42 (November 16, 1953): 70; Larry James Gianakos, *Television Drama Series Programming: A Comprehensive Chronicle, 1947–1959* (Metuchen, NJ: Scarecrow Press, 1980), pp. 380–382.

34. Barton added, "I think Mrs. Hood's comments are important because she has a lot of time to talk with her husband." Barton to Newton, 19 June 1954, folder: U.S. Steel 1952–1958, box 81 client correspondence, BB/SHSW .

35. Newton to Barton, 11 June 1954, folder: U.S. Steel 1952–1958, box 81 client correspondence, BB/SHSW.

36. Press release, "The Westerner Stars on U.S. Steel TV Hour," 28 April 1954, folder: U.S. Steel 1952–1958, box 81 client correspondence, BB/SHSW.

37. W. Hume Logan, Jr., to Lammot du Pont, 27 August 1946, folder: Advertising Department 1940–1952 (PSC), box 4, acc. 1662, DuP/HL. In a second letter Logan wrote: "A program of this nature going into the homes of the middle and lower income group of housewives can offset and nullify a very large part of the educational program which the National Association of Manufacturers and other good organizations are carrying on." Logan to Lammot du Pont, 9 October 1946. Responding to Lammot du Pont's inquiry on behalf of Logan about Procter & Gamble's dramatization of soap opera villains, P&G's R. R. Deupree explained that P&G "had been using certain types of people as villains, but I think I have to agree with you that it is a bit unfortunate that they picked on an industrialist for this very black character. Apparently in these shows we have to have heroes and villains and anywhere you strike where a villain is involved, whether it is doctor, lawyer, merchant, or thief, you probably will have some trouble." R. R. Deupree to Lammot du Pont, 26 September 1946, folder: Advertising Department 1940–1952 (PSC), box 4, acc. 1662, DuP/HL.

38. Lammot du Pont to F. Lyman Dewey, 21 August 1950, folder: Advertising Department 1940–1952 (PSC), box 4, acc. 1662, DuP/HL.

39. "The Man Who Took the Freedom Train," *Cavalcade of America* 563 (April 12, 1946), DuP/HL.

40. Erik Barnouw wrote the script. "The Voice of the Wizard," *Cavalcade of America* 510 (Februrary 10, 1947), DuP/HL.

41. William H. Hamilton, "Report on 'Cavalcade of America,'" 12–13 June 1947, folder 22, box 11, acc. 1803, DuP/HL.

42. Maurice Collette to Barton, 31 August 1949, folder: DuPont 1948–1949, box 75 client correspondence, BB/SHSW.

43. Arthur Pryor, Jr., to Harold Blackburn et al., 27 June 1949, folder 2, general correspondence 1937–1949, box 1, Kenyon Nicholson papers, SHSW (hereafter KN/SHSW).

44. John Zoller to Harold Blackburn et al., 20 June 1949, folder 2, general correspondence 1937–1949, box 1, KN/SHSW.

45. Bill Millard to Harold Blackburn et al., 23 June 1949, folder 2, general correspondence 1937–1949, box 1, KN/SHSW.

46. Kenyon Nicholson to Harold Blackburn et al., 21 June 1949, folder 2, general correspondence 1937–1949, box 1, KN/SHSW.

47. "Report on Radio and Television for 1952," September 1951, folder 19: Reports and Surveys-1951–1957, box 4; see also memorandum, Advertising Department to Executive Committee, "Report on Television Research," 29 September 1955, folder 9, box 13, acc. 1803, DuP/HL.

48. F. L. Dewey, "How Company Advertising Helps the Sales Program," 22 September 1954, folder 9, box 13, acc. 1803, DuP/HL.

49. Brochure, *Cavalcade of America*. "The Last Will of Daniel Webster," copyright deposit file MP 4854, Motion Picture, Broadcasting and Recorded Sound Division, LC.

50. Typescript, "Television," BBDO Departments: Television, BBDO; Harold Blackburn to Barton, 9 October 1950, folder: DuPont, 1950–1957, box 76 client correspondence, BB/SHSW.

51. Lyman Dewey, "Introductory Remarks for TV Preview," 23 September 1952, folder 3, box 12, acc. 1803, DuP/HL. Initially the program appeared on the twenty-two station NBC network and on eleven additional stations not available to the network. Press release, "'Cavalcade of America' Comes to Television," 25 September 1952, folder 2: Cavalcade of America, NBC Audience Participation, box 137, NBC/SHSW.

52. The DuPont Company donated the rights to 70 *Cavalcade* episodes to Teaching Film Custodians. Anthony Slide, *Before Video*, p. 96.

53. John Driscoll to Lyman Dewey, 5 March 1952, folder 19, box 13, story subjects under consideration 1951–1952, acc. 1803, DuP/HL; "Poor Richard," copyright synopsis, deposit file LP 4089, LC.

54. "The Man Who Took a Chance," *Cavalcade of America* (October 29, 1952), Screen Gems, LP 3969, FCA 0750, LC.

55. Elma H. Franklin to Publicity Department, 23 March 1954, folder 16: W. A. Hart-Board of Directors speech 19 April 1954, box 12, acc. 1803, DuP/HL.

56. Edward L. Johnson, 31 March 1953, folder 16: W. A. Hart-Board of Directors speech 19 April 1954, box 12, acc. 1803, DuP/HL.

57. "Telegram to Promotional Manager," 10 October 1952, folder 2: Cavalcade of America, NBC Audience Participation, box 137, NBC/SHSW.

58. Gianakos, *Television Drama Series Programming*, pp. 338–343; newsletter mockup, "Looking in on Cavalcade" 6, no. 1 (September 1955), folder 9, box 13, acc. 1803, DuP/HL.

59. Robb M. DeGraff to Jock Elliott, 11 May 1956, folder 22, story suggestions-1956, box 13, acc. 1803, DuP/HL.

60. In 1955 the DuPont Advertising Department proposed to spend a total of $108,500 for television research in 1956 contracting with the Nielsen Television Index, the Dollard Reward Scale, the Advertest Report Test, the Link Special Study, Gallup-Robinson Impact Studies, and others. "Report on Television Research," 29 September 1955, folder 9, box 13, acc. 1803, DuP/HL.

61. Judy Dupuy, *Television Show Business* (Schenectady, NY: General Electric, 1945), pp. 7–8, 121–130.

62. "Memorandum to Advisory Council Regarding Sponsorship of GE Theater March 15, 1955," folder 9, box 13, acc. 1803, DuP/HL.

63. Ibid.

64. "Memorandum to Advisory Council Regarding Sponsorship of GE Theater," DuP/HL; Ronald Reagan with Richard G. Hubler, *Where's the Rest of Me?* (New York: Duell, Sloan & Pearce, 1965), pp. 251, 257–261, 266–267; Gary Wills, *Reagan's America: Innocents at Home* (Garden City, NY: Doubleday, 1987), pp. 285–288; Lou Cannon, *President Reagan: The Role of a Lifetime* (New York: Simon & Schuster, 1991), pp. 88–90; Christopher J. Matthews, "Your Host, Ronald Reagan: From G.E. Theater to the Desk in the Oval Office," *New Republic* 190 (26 March 1984): 15–18; Patrick Owens, "The President from G.E.," *Nation* 232 (31 January 1981): 106–110.

65. *General Electric Theater* left the air in 1962 in a welter of controversy surrounding the U.S. Justice Department's anti-trust investigation of MCA and the Screen Actors' Guild talent waivers granted to MCA-Revue. The hint of scandal diminished Reagan's value as company spokesman and program host. As SAG president in the 1950s Reagan had, after all, signed the waivers, and he had later benefited from the arrangement as a *General Electric Theater* program producer. The suggestion of impropriety fueled Reagan's increasingly anti-government demeanor on tour, and his insistence upon producing and starring in episodes combating Communist subversion in the final season of *General Electric Theater.* Wills, *Reagan's America*, pp. 263–266, 284–285.

66. "Memorandum to Advisory Council Regarding Sponsorship of GE Theater," DuP/HL.

67. Ibid.

68. "Rider on a Pale Horse," *General Electric Theater* (November 4, 1956), Revue Productions, Inc., print FCA 509, LC.

69. "The Town with a Past," *General Electric Theater* (February 10, 1957), Revue Productions, Inc., print FCA 511, LC; Reagan, *Where's the Rest of Me?* pp. 273–274.

Epilogue

1. Barton to Newton, 27 October 1954, folder: U.S. Steel 1952–1958, box 81 client correspondence, BB/SHSW.

2. Barton to Duffy, 11 August 1952, folder: Duffy, box 18, BB/SHSW.

3. Barton to William A. Hart, 28 March 1951; memorandum, Barton to Maurice Collette, 20 March 1951; Barton to William A. Hart, 5 April 1951, folder: DuPont 1950–1957, box 76 client correspondence, BB/SHSW.

4. Luce replied, "I'll keep that thought of yours in mind—about the apples. Something may come of it." Barton to Henry Luce, 2 February 1951 and Luce to Barton, 6 February 1951, folder: Luce, H. R. and C. B., 1936–1959, box 40, BB/SHSW. This exchange of correspondence occurred a little short of ten years to the week that Luce's seminal editorial "The American Century" appeared in *Life* 10 (February 17, 1941): 61–65. See Robert Edwin Herzstein, *Henry R. Luce: A Political Portrait of the Man Who Created the American Century* (New York: C. Scribner's Sons, 1994), pp. 179–185; James L. Baughman, *Henry R. Luce and the Rise of the American News Media* (Boston: Twayne Publishers, 1987), pp. 129–157, passim. In his *Memoirs* published in 1952, Herbert Hoover noted that "Some Oregon or Washington apple growers' association shrewdly appraised the sympathy of the public for the unemployed. They set up a system of selling apples on the street corners in many cities, thus selling their crop and raising their prices. Many persons left their jobs for the more profitable one of selling apples. When any left-winger wishes to indulge in scathing oratory, he demands, 'Do you want to return to selling apples?'" Herbert Hoover, *The Memoirs of Herbert Hoover: The Great Depression 1929–1941* (New York: Macmillan, 1952), p. 195, cited in Kenneth S. Davis, *FDR: The New York Years, 1928–1933* (New York: Random House, 1985), p. 475.

5. The photograph first appeared in the DuPont Company employee magazine, *Better Living*, in November 1951. See Jon M. Williams and Daniel T. Muir, *Corporate Images: Photography and the DuPont Company, 1865–1972* (Wilmington, DE: Hagley Museum and Library, 1984), pp. 54–57.

6. Others have since noted Barton's earnest suggestion that every Russian be given a copy of the Sears catalog and the address of the nearest Sears outlet. In sociologist David Riesman's Cold War parody "The Nylon War," the United States bombards the Soviet Union with planeloads of surplus hosiery, cigarettes, wristwatches, radios, refrigerators, Jeeps, and Toni wave kits. Barton to Stanley C. Allyn, 19 June 1956, folder: Aa-Am, 1920s–1963, box 1, Barton papers, SHSW, cited in Warren Susman, "Culture Heroes: Ford, Barton, Ruth," in *Culture as History*, pp. 122–131; David Riesman, "The Nylon War," in Riesman, *Abundance for What? And Other Essays* (Garden City, NY: Doubleday, 1964), pp. 67–79.

7. Haddow, *Pavilions of Plenty*, pp. 216–217.

8. "What Americans Really Think of Business" and "The Disenchanted Campus," *Newsweek* 67 (May 2, 1966): 84–86, 88.

9. Audrey Allen, "Corporate Advertising: Its New Look," *Public Relations Journal* 27 (November 1971): 6–13, 68–73.

10. Former Mobil vice-president for public affairs Herbert Schmertz explained in 1991, "It's not the shows that are important. It's exploiting it with the American public that's important. I don't care whether anybody watches the shows. I want them to feel socially pressured so they have to lie and say they watch the shows. It's the cartoons in the *New Yorker* and all the ancillary stuff that are important." Laurence Jarvik, "PBS and the Politics of Quality"; Jarvik, *PBS: Behind the Screen,* pp. 237–258; Herb Schmertz with William Novak, *Good-bye to the Low Profile,* pp. 26–27, 133–175, 209–212, 221–230; Timothy Brennan, "Masterpiece Theatre and the Uses of Tradition," in *American Media and Mass Culture: Left Perspectives,* ed. Donald Lazere (Berkeley: University of California Press, 1987), pp. 373–383; William L. Bird, Jr., "Advertising, Company Voice," in *Encyclopedia of Television*, ed. Horace Newcomb (Chicago: Fitzroy Dearborn Publishers, 1997), pp. 22–26.

11. "Business Thinks TV Distorts Its Image," *Business Week* (October 18, 1982): 26.

12. Alan Wolfe, "The Rise of Logo America," *The Nation* 238 (May 26, 1984): 625, 640–643.

13. David Horowitz, "The Politics of Public Television," *Commentary* 92 (December 1991): 25–32.

14. Jay Rosen, "Giving Them the Business," *Channels* 7 (February 1987): 16.

15. Robin Toner, "Word for Word: Advice for Republicans: Attention! All Sales Reps for the Contract With America!" *New York Times*, 5 February 1995, sec. E, p. 8; Ceci Connolly, "Consultant Offers GOP a Language for the Future," *Washington Post*, 4 September 1997, sec. A, p. 1; Alison Mitchell, "Word for Word: Republican Remedies: Speak Less Loudly and Stop Calling the Speaker 'Newt,'" *New York Times,* 12 October 1997, sec. 1, p. 7.

16. Leonard I. Pearlin and Morris Rosenberg, "Propaganda Techniques in Institutional Advertising," *Public Opinion Quarterly* 16 (spring 1952): 5–26.

17. The lively public debate about containing the power of corporations turned into an equally lively debate about containing, developing, or privatizing the activities of government agencies. Joseph S. Nye, Jr., and Philip D. Zelikow, "Conclusion: Reflections, Conjectures, and Puzzles," in *Why People Don't Trust Government*, ed. Nye, Zelikow, and David C. King (Cambridge, MA: Harvard University Press, 1997), pp. 251–281; Judith Miller, "Selling the Government Like Soap: It Seems to Work," *New York Times,* 14 September 1997, sec. 4, p. 3.

18. *New York Times Magazine*, 7 January 1990, p. 21.

19. Robyn Meredith, "G.M. Sponsors a Maker of Documentaries and Reaches PBS Viewers 15 Seconds at a Time," *New York Times*, 3 November 1997, sec. D, p. 12.

20. Mark Crispin Miller, "Free the Media," *The Nation* 262 (June 3, 1996): 9–15; Thomas Frank, "The New Gilded Age," in *Commodify Your Dissent: Salvos from the Baffler*, ed. Thomas Frank and Matt Weiland (New York: W. W. Norton & Company, 1997), pp. 23–28.

21. *The Business World, The New York Times Magazine*, 11 June 1989, p. 5.

Books

Adams, James Truslow. *Our Business Civilization: Some Aspects of American Culture*. New York: A. & C. Boni, 1929.

Aitken, Hugh G. J. *The Continuous Wave: Technology and American Radio, 1900–1932*. Princeton, NJ: Princeton University Press, 1985.

Akin, William E. *Technocracy and the American Dream: The Technocrat Movement, 1900–1941*. Berkeley: University of California Press, 1977.

Alexander, William. *Film on the Left: American Documentary Film from 1931 to 1942*. Princeton, NJ: Princeton University Press, 1981.

Allen, Frederick Lewis. *Since Yesterday: The Nineteen-Thirties in America*. New York: Harper & Brothers, 1940.

Allyn, Stanley C. *My Half Century with NCR*. New York: McGraw-Hill, 1967.

American Association of Advertising Agencies, Association of National Advertisers, and the Subcommittee on Advertising, Domestic Distribution Department, Chamber of Commerce of the United States. *A Program for American Opportunity through Advertising: A Report on the Subcommittee on Advertising*. Washington, DC: Domestic Distribution Department, Chamber of Commerce of the United States, 1947.

American Business Consultants. *Red Channels: The Report of Communist Influence in Radio and Television*. New York: Counterattack, 1950.

American Institute of Public Opinion. *The New Science of Public Opinion Measurement*. Princeton, NJ: AIPO, 1938.

Appelbaum, Stanley. *The New York World's Fair, 1939/1940: In 155 Photographs by Richard Wurts and Others*. New York: Dover Publications, 1977.

Applegate, Edd. *Personalities and Products: A Historical Perspective on Advertising in America*. Westport, CT: Greenwood Press, 1998.

Association of National Advertisers. *The Job Ahead for Business: Selling the Company behind the Product*. New York: Association of National Advertisers, 1946.

———. *New Horizons for Business Films*. New York: Association of National Advertisers, 1947.

Badger, Anthony J. *The New Deal: The Depression Years, 1933–40*. Houndsmills, Baskingstoke, Hampshire: Macmillan, 1989.

Badger, R. Reid. *The Great American Fair: The World's Columbian Exposition and American Culture*. Chicago: Nelson Hall, 1979.

Baida, Peter. *Poor Richard's Legacy: American Business Values from Benjamin Franklin to Donald Trump*. New York: William Morrow & Company, 1990.

Baritz, Loren. *The Servants of Power: A History of the Use of Social Science in American Industry*. Middletown, CT: Wesleyan University Press, 1960.

Barnouw, Eric. *The Golden Web: A History of Broadcasting in the United States*. Vol. 2, *1933–1953*. New York: Oxford University Press, 1968.

———. *The Image Empire: A History of Broadcasting in the United States from 1953*. New York: Oxford University Press, 1970.

———. *Media Marathon: A Twentieth-Century Memoir*. Durham, NC: Duke University Press, 1996.

———. *A Tower in Babel: A History of Broadcasting in the United States*. Vol.1, *To 1933*. New York: Oxford University Press, 1966.

Barnouw, Eric, ed. *Radio Drama in Action: Twenty-Five Plays of a Changing World*. New York: Rinehart & Company, Inc., 1945.

Barton, Bruce. *A Parade of the States*. New York: Doubleday, Doran & Co. and Garden City Publishing, 1932.

Baughman, James L. *Henry R. Luce and the Rise of the American News Media*. Boston: Twayne Publishers, 1987.

———. *The Republic of Mass Culture: Journalism, Filmmaking and Broadcasting in America since 1941*. Baltimore: Johns Hopkins University Press, 1992.

———. *Television's Guardians: The FCC and the Politics of Programming, 1958–1967*. Knoxville: University of Tennessee Press, 1985.

Bendiner, Robert. *Just around the Corner: A Highly Selective History of the Thirties*. New York: E. P. Dutton & Co., 1968.

Benét, Stephen Vincent. *The Selected Works of Stephen Vincent Benét*. Vol. 1, *Poetry*. New York: Farrar & Rinehart, 1942.

Bennett, Tony, et al., eds. *Formations of Pleasure*. Boston: Routledge & Kegan Paul, 1983.

Bernays, Edward L. *Biography of an Idea: Memoirs of a Public Relations Counsel*. New York: Simon & Schuster, 1965.

———. *Propaganda*. Port Washington, NY: Kennikat Press, 1928, reprint ed., 1972.

Bernstein, Irving. *A Caring Society: The New Deal, the Worker, and the Great Depression*. Boston: Houghton Mifflin Company, 1985.

Biles, Roger. *A New Deal for the American People*. DeKalb: Northern Illinois University Press, 1991.

Bird, William L., Jr., and Harry R. Rubenstein. *Design for Victory: World War II Posters on the American Home Front*. New York: Princeton Architectural Press, 1998.

Blum, John Morton. *V Was for Victory: Politics and American Culture during World War II*. New York: Harcourt Brace Jovanovich, 1976.

Blumenthal, Sidney. *The Permanent Campaign*. New York: Simon & Schuster, 1982.

Boddy, William. *Fifties Television: The Industry and Its Critics*. Chicago: University of Illinois Press, 1990.

Borden, Neil H. *Advertising Text and Cases*. Chicago: Richard D. Irwin, 1950.

Borden, Neil H., and Martin V. Marshall. *Advertising Management Text and Cases*. Homewood, IL: Richard D. Irwin, 1959 rev. ed.

Boyle, Kevin. *The UAW and the Heyday of American Liberalism, 1945–1968*. Ithaca, NY: Cornell University Press, 1995.

Braeman, John, Robert H. Bremner, and David Brody, eds. *The New Deal: The National Level*. Columbus: Ohio State University Press, 1975.

Bremner, Robert H., and Gary W. Reichard, eds. *Reshaping America: Society and Institutions, 1945–1960*. Columbus: Ohio State University Press, 1982.

Briggs, Susan. *Those Radio Times*. London: Weidenfeld & Nicholson, 1981.

Brinkley, Alan. *Liberalism and Its Discontents*. Cambridge, MA: Harvard University Press, 1998.

———. *Voices of Protest: Huey Long, Father Coughlin, and the Great Depression*. New York: Knopf, 1982.

Bronner, Simon J., ed. *Consuming Visions: Accumulation and Display in America, 1880–1920*. New York: Norton, 1989.

Brooks, Robert R. R. *When Labor Organizes*. New Haven: Yale University Press, 1937.

Brown, Donaldson. *Some Reminiscences of an Industrialist*. Easton, PA: Hive Publishing Co., 1977.

Brown, Les. *Television: The Business behind the Box*. New York: Harcourt Brace Jovanovich, 1971.

Buhite, Russell D., and David W. Levy, eds. *FDR's Fireside Chats*. New York: Penguin, 1993.

Burk, Robert F. *The Corporate State and the Broker State: The DuPonts and American National Politics, 1925–1940*. Cambridge, MA: Harvard University Press, 1990.

Bush, Donald J. *The Streamlined Decade*. New York: George Braziller, 1975.

Butterfield, Herbert. *The Whig Interpretation of History*. 1931; reprinted New York: W. W. Norton, 1965.

Callahan, North. *Carl Sandburg: His Life and Works*. University Park: Pennsylvania State University Press, 1987.

Cameron, William J. *The Ford Sunday Evening Hour Talks*. Dearborn, MI: Ford Motor Company, 1936.

Campbell, Colin. *The Romantic Ethic and the Spirit of Modern Consumerism*. New York: Oxford University Press, 1987.

Campbell, Russell. *Cinema Strikes Back: Radical Filmmaking in the United States, 1930–1942*. Ann Arbor, MI: UMI Research Press, 1982.

Cannon, Lou. *President Reagan: The Role of a Lifetime*. New York: Simon & Schuster, 1991.

Cantril, Hadley, *The Human Dimension: Experiences in Policy Research*. New Brunswick, NJ: Rutgers University Press, 1967.

Cantril, Hadley, and Gordon W. Allport. *The Psychology of Radio*. New York: Harper & Brothers, 1935.

Carmer, Carl. *Cavalcade of America: The Deeds and Achievements of the Men and Women Who Made Our Country Great*. New York: Crown Publishers, Inc., 1956.

———. *The Hudson*. New York: Farrar & Rinehart, 1939.

Center for the Study of Democratic Institutions. *The Relation of the Writer to Television*. Santa Barbara, CA: The Center for the Study of Democratic Institutions, 1960.

Chandler, Alfred D., Jr. *Strategy and Structure: Chapters in the History of the Industrial Enterprise*. Cambridge, MA: MIT Press, 1962.

Chandler, Alfred D., Jr., ed. *Giant Enterprise: Ford, General Motors, and the Automobile Industry*. New York: Harcourt, Brace & World, 1964.

Chandler, Alfred D., Jr., and Stephen Salsbury. *Pierre S. du Pont and the Making of the Modern Corporation*. New York: Harper & Row, 1971.

Cheape, Charles W. *Strictly Business: Walter Carpenter at DuPont and General Motors*. Baltimore, MD: Johns Hopkins University Press, 1995.

Ciment, Michel. *Conversations with Losey*. New York: Methuen, 1985.

Cochrane, Ira Lee. *Display Animation, 1939–40: The Yearbook of Motion Displays*. New York: Reede & Morton, 1940.

Cogley, John. *Report on Blacklisting*. Vol. 2, *Radio–Television*. New York: The Fund for the Republic, 1956.

Cohen, Barbara, Steven Heller, and Seymour Chwast. *Trylon and Perisphere: The 1939 New York World's Fair*. New York: Harry N. Abrams, 1989.

Cohen, Lizabeth. *Making a New Deal: Industrial Workers in Chicago, 1919–1939*. New York: Cambridge University Press, 1990.

Colby, Gerard. *DuPont Dynasty*. Secaucus, NJ: L. Stuart, 1984; rev. ed. of: *DuPont*, 1974.

Collins, Robert M. *The Business Response to Keynes, 1929–1964*. New York: Columbia University Press, 1981.

Corn, Joseph J., ed. *Imagining Tomorrow: History, Technology, and the American Future*. Cambridge, MA: MIT Press, 1986.

Corn, Joseph J., and Brian Horrigan. *Yesterday's Tomorrows: Past Visions of the American Future*. New York: Summit Books, 1984.

Crafton, Donald. *Before Mickey: The Animated Film, 1898–1928*. Cambridge, MA: MIT Press, 1982

Craig, Douglas B. *After Wilson: The Struggle for the Democratic Party, 1920–1934*. Chapel Hill: University of North Carolina Press, 1992.

Cray, Ed. *Chrome Colossus: General Motors*. New York: McGraw-Hill, 1980.

Cross, Charles. *A Picture of America*. New York: Simon & Schuster, 1932.

Crowther, Samuel. *John H. Patterson: Pioneer in Industrial Welfare*. Garden City, NY: Doubleday, Page & Company, 1923.

Cutlip, Scott M. *The Unseen Power: Public Relations, a History*. Hillsdale, NJ: L. Erlbaum Associates, 1994.

Czitrom, Daniel J. *Media and the American Mind: From Morse to McLuhan*. Chapel Hill: University of North Carolina Press, 1982.

Daniel, Pete, Merry A. Foresta, Maren Stange, and Sally Stein. *Official Images: New Deal Photography*. Washington, DC: Smithsonian Institution Press, 1987.

Davis, Kenneth S. *FDR: The New York Years, 1928–1933*. New York: Random House, 1985.

———. *FDR: The New Deal Years, 1933–1937: A History*. New York: Random House, 1986.

———. *FDR: Into the Storm, 1937–1940: A History*. New York: Random House, 1993.

Davis, Paul. *The Life and Times of Ebenezer Scrooge*. New Haven: Yale University Press, 1990.

Day, James. *The Vanishing Vision: The Inside Story of Public Television*. Berkeley: University of California Press, 1995.

Dench, Ernest A. *Advertising by Motion Pictures*. Cincinnati, OH: Standard Publishing Co., 1916.

Denning, Michael. *The Cultural Front: The Laboring of American Culture in the Twentieth Century*. New York: Verso, 1966.

Diamond, Sigmund. *The Reputation of the American Businessman*. Cambridge, MA: Harvard University Press, 1955.

Doherty, Thomas. *Projections of War: Hollywood, American Culture, and World War II*. New York: Columbia University Press, 1993.

Dos Passos, John. *The Ground We Stand On: Some Examples from the History of a Political Creed*. New York: Harcourt, Brace, Jovanovich, 1941.

Douglas, Susan J. *Inventing American Broadcasting, 1899–1922*. Baltimore: Johns Hopkins University Press, 1987.

Dubofsky, Melvyn, ed. *Technological Change and Workers' Movements*. Beverly Hills, CA: Sage Publications, Inc., 1985.

Dupuy, Judy. *Television Show Business*. Schenectady, NY: General Electric, 1945.

Dutton, William S. *DuPont: One Hundred and Forty Years*. New York: C. Scribner's Sons, 1942.

E. I. du Pont de Nemours and Company. *DuPont: The Autobiography of an American Enterprise*. Wilmington, DE: E. I. du Pont de Nemours and Company, 1952.

Ellul, Jacques. *Propaganda: The Formation of Men's Attitudes*. New York: Knopf, 1965.

Engelbrecht, H. C., and F. C. Hanighen. *Merchants of Death*. Garden City, NY: Garden City Publishing Company, 1934.

Engelman, Ralph. *Public Radio and Television in America: A Political History*. Thousand Oaks, CA: Sage Publications, 1996.

Evans, Chester E., and La Verne N. Laseau. *My Job Contest*. Washington, DC: Personnel Psychology, Inc., 1950.

Ewen, Stuart. *PR! A Social History of Spin*. New York: Basic Books/Harper Collins, 1996.

Ewing, William A. *America Worked: The 1950s Photographs of Dan Weiner*. New York: Harry N. Abrams, 1989.

Faulk, John Henry. *Fear on Trial*. New York: Simon & Schuster, 1964.

Film Council. *Sixty Years of 16 mm Film, 1923–1983: A Symposium*. Des Plaines, IL: Practical Offset and Film Council of America, 1954.

Fine, Sidney. *Sit-Down: The General Motors Strike of 1936–1937*. Ann Arbor: University of Michigan Press, 1969.

Fisher, Douglas A. *Steel Serves the Nation, 1901–1951: The Fifty Year Story of United States Steel*. New York: United States Steel Corp., 1951.

Fitelson, H. William, ed. *Theatre Guild on the Air*. New York: Rinehart & Company, 1947.

Fleischhauer, Carl, and Beverly W. Brannan, eds. *Documenting America, 1935–1943*. Berkeley: University of California Press, 1988.

Flink, James J. *The Automobile Age*. Cambridge, MA: MIT Press, 1988.

Fones-Wolf, Elizabeth A. *Selling Free Enterprise: The Business Assault on Labor and Liberalism, 1945–1960*. Urbana and Chicago: University of Illinois Press, 1994.

Forty, Adrian. *Objects of Desire*. New York: Pantheon, 1986.

Fox, Dixon Ryan. *Ideas in Motion*. New York: D. Appleton-Century Company, 1935.

Fox, Dixon Ryan, and Arthur M. Schlesinger, eds. *The Cavalcade of America*. Springfield, MA: Milton Bradley, 1937.

———. *The Cavalcade of America*. Series 2. Springfield, MA: Milton Bradley, 1938.

Fox, Frank. *Madison Avenue Goes to War: The Strange Military Career of American Advertising, 1941–1945*. Provo, UT: Brigham Young University Press, 1975.

Fox, Richard Wrightman, and T. J. Jackson Lears, eds. *The Culture of Consumption: Critical Essays in American History, 1880–1980*. New York: Pantheon, 1983.

———. *The Power of Culture: Critical Essays in American History*. Chicago: University of Chicago Press, 1993.

Fox, Stephen. *The Mirror Makers: A History of American Advertising and Its Creators*. New York: William Morrow and Company, Inc., 1984.

Frank, Thomas, and Matt Weiland, eds. *Commodify Your Dissent: Salvos from The Baffler*. New York: W. W. Norton & Company, 1997.

Freidel, Frank. *Franklin D. Roosevelt: A Rendezvous with Destiny*. Boston: Little, Brown, 1990.

Frese, Joseph R., and Jacob Judd, eds. *Business and Government*. Tarrytown, NY: Sleepy Hollow Press and Rockefeller Archive Center, 1985.

Galambos, Louis, and Joseph Pratt. *The Rise of the Corporate Commonwealth: U.S. Business and Public Policy in the Twentieth Century*. New York: Basic Books, 1988.

Galbraith, John Kenneth. *The Great Crash, 1929*. Boston: Houghton Mifflin, 1955.

General Electric Company. *More Goods for More People at Less Cost: A Tribute to American Industry*. New York[?]: General Electric Co., 1940.

———. *Progress Is Our Most Important Product, Using the Slogan: Where, How, and When to Use the General Electric Slogan in Advertising, Displays, Sales Promotions, Motion Pictures and Publications*. New York[?] General Electric Co., ca. 1950.

General Motors Corporation. *American Battle for Abundance: A Story of Mass Production*. Detroit: General Motors, 1947.

———. *The Worker Speaks: My Job and Why I Like It*. Detroit: General Motors, 1947.

Gerstle, Gary, and Steve Fraser, eds. *The Rise and Fall of the New Deal Order, 1930–1980*. Princeton, NJ: Princeton University Press, 1989.

Gilbert, James. *Perfect Cities: Chicago's Utopias of 1893*. Chicago: University of Chicago Press, 1991.

Gillespie, Richard. *Manufacturing Knowledge: A History of the Hawthorne Experiments*. New York: Cambridge University Press, 1991.

Gipson, Henry Clay. *Films in Business and Industry*. New York: McGraw-Hill, 1947.

Glossberg, David. *American Historical Pageantry: The Uses of Tradition in the Early Twentieth Century*. Chapel Hill: University of North Carolina Press, 1990.

Golden, L. L. L. *Only by Public Consent: American Corporations Search for Favorable Opinion*. New York: Hawthorn Books, 1968.

Goldman, Eric. *Two Way Street: The Emergence of the Public Relations Counsel*. Boston: Bellman, 1948.

Goldman, Steven M., ed. *Science, Technology, and Social Progress*. Bethlehem, PA: Lehigh University Press, 1989.

Goode, Kenneth, and Zenn Kaufman. *Profitable Showmanship*. New York: Prentice-Hall, 1939.

Goodman, Paul. *Speaking and Language: Defence of Poetry*. New York: Random House, 1972.

Graebner, William. *The Engineering of Consent: Democracy and Authority in Twentieth-Century America*. Madison: University of Wisconsin Press, 1987.

Gray, James. *Business without Boundary: The Story of General Mills*. Minneapolis: University of Minnesota Press, 1954.

Greene, William N. *Strategies of the Major Oil Companies*. Ann Arbor, MI: UMI Research Press, 1982.

Grierson, John. *Grierson on Documentary*. Edited and compiled by Forsyth Hardy. New York: Harcourt, Brace & Co., 1947.

Gross, James A. *The Reshaping of the National Labor Relations Board*. Albany, NY: State University of New York Press, 1974, ca. 1981.

Gruening, Ernest. *The Public Pays: A Study of Power Propaganda*. New York: Vanguard Press, 1931.

Haddow, Robert H. *Pavilions of Plenty: Exhibiting American Culture Abroad in the 1950s*. Washington, DC: Smithsonian Institution Press, 1997.

Hall, Stuart, et al., eds. *Culture, Media, Language: Working Papers in Cultural Studies, 1972–79*. London: Hutchinson & Co. in association with the Centre for Contemporary Cultural Studies, University of Birmingham, 1980.

Halley, William C. *Employee Publications: Theory and Practice of Communications in the Modern Organization*. Philadelphia: Chilton Co. Book Division, 1959.

Harris, Howell John. *The Right to Manage: Industrial Relations Policies of American Business in the 1940s*. Madison: University of Wisconsin Press, 1982.

Harris, Neil. *Cultural Excursions: Marketing Appetites and Tastes in Modern America*. Chicago: University of Chicago Press, 1990.

Hawes, William. *American Television Drama: The Experimental Years*. University: University of Alabama Press, 1986.

Heibert, Ray Eldon. *Courtier to the Crowd: The Story of Ivy Lee and the Development of Public Relations*. Ames: Iowa State University Press, 1966.

Herzstein, Robert Edwin. *Henry R. Luce: A Political Portrait of the Man Who Created the American Century*. New York: C. Scribner's Sons, 1994.

High, Stanley. *Roosevelt—and Then?* New York: Harper & Brothers, 1937.

Hill, John W. *The Making of a Public Relations Man*. New York: David McKay Company, 1963.

Hilmes, Michele. *Hollywood and Broadcasting: From Radio to Cable*. Chicago: University of Illinois Press, 1990.

———. *Radio Voices: American Broadcasting, 1922–1952*. Minneapolis: University of Minnesota Press, 1997.

Hine, Thomas. *Populuxe*. New York: Knopf, 1986.

Hoover, Herbert. *The Memoirs of Herbert Hoover: The Great Depression 1929–1941*. New York: Macmillan, 1952.

Horowitz, Daniel. *The Morality of Spending: Attitudes toward the Consumer Society in America, 1875–1940*. Baltimore: Johns Hopkins University Press, 1985.

Horowitz, Joseph. *Understanding Toscanini: A Social History of American Concert Life*. Berkeley: University of California Press, 1994.

Hosmer, Charles B., Jr. *Preservation Comes of Age: From Williamsburg to the National Trust, 1926–1949*. Charlottesville: University of Virginia Press, 1981.

Hounshell, David A., and John Kenly Smith, Jr. *Science and Corporate Strategy: DuPont R&D, 1902–1980*. New York: Cambridge University Press, 1988.

Hoynes, William. *Public Television for Sale: Media, the Market, and the Public Sphere*. Boulder, CO: Westview Press, 1994.

Huber, Richard M. *The American Idea of Success*. New York: McGraw-Hill Book Company, 1976.

Hurley, F. Jack, ed. *Industry and the Photographic Image: 153 Great Prints from 1850 to the Present*. New York: Dover Publications, 1980.

———. *Portrait of a Decade*. Baton Rouge: Louisiana State University Press, 1972.

Ickes, Harold L. *The Secret Diary of Harold L. Ickes*. New York: Simon & Schuster, 1954.

Jaher, Frederic C., ed. *America in the Age of Industrialization: Essays in Social Structure and Social Values*. New York: Free Press, 1968.

Jakle, John A. *The Tourist: Travel in Twentieth-Century North America*. Lincoln: University of Nebraska Press, 1985.

Jarvik, Laurence. *PBS: Behind the Screen*. Rocklin, CA: Prima Publishing, 1996.

Jones, Alfred Haworth. *Roosevelt's Image Brokers: Poets, Playwrights, and the Use of the Lincoln Symbol*. Port Washington, NY: Kennikat Press, 1974.

Kahn, Douglas, and Gregory Whitehead, eds. *Wireless Imagination: Sound, Radio and the Avant-Garde*. Cambridge, MA: MIT Press, 1992.

Kammen, Michael. *In the Past Lane: Historical Perspectives on American Culture*. New York: Oxford University Press, 1997.

———. *Mystic Chords of Memory: The Transformation of Tradition in American Culture*. New York: Alfred A. Knopf, 1991.

Keaton, Diane, ed. *Mr. Salesman: A Book*. Santa Fe, NM: Twin Palms Publishers, 1993.

Kennedy, David M., and Michael E. Parrish. *Power and Responsibility: Case Studies in American Leadership*. New York: Harcourt Brace Jovanovich, 1986.

Kennedy, E. D. *The Automobile Industry: The Coming of Age of Capitalism's Favorite Child*. New York: Augustus M. Kelley, 1941.

Kettering, C. F. *Short Stories of Science and Invention*. Detroit: General Motors Corporation, 1945.

Key, V. O. *Politics, Parties, and Pressure Groups*. New York: Thomas F. Crowell Company, 1958.

Kirshenblatt-Gimblett, Barbara. *Destination Culture: Tourism, Museums and Heritage*. Berkeley: University of California Press, 1998.

Kisseloff, Jeff. *The Box: An Oral History of Television, 1920–1961*. New York: Viking, 1995.

Kochan, Thomas A., Harry C. Katz, and Robert McKersie. *The Transformation of American Industrial Relations*. New York: Basic Books, 1986.

Kuhn, Arthur J. *GM Passes Ford, 1918–1938: Designing the General Motors Performance-Control System*. University Park: Pennsylvania State University Press, 1986.

Kurtz, Howard. *Hot Air: All Talk, All the Time*. New York: Times Books, 1996.

Kuznick, Peter J. *Beyond the Laboratory: Scientists as Political Activists in 1930s America*. Chicago: University of Chicago Press, 1987.

Lacey, Michael, ed. *The Truman Presidency*. New York: Cambridge University Press, 1989.

Lazere, Donald, ed. *American Media and Mass Culture: Left Perspectives*. Berkeley: University of California Press, 1987.

Leach, Eugene E. *Tuning Out Education: The Cooperation Doctrine in Radio, 1922–38*. Washington, DC: Current, 1983.

Leach, William. *Land of Desire: Merchants, Power, and the Rise of a New American Culture*. New York: Pantheon Books, 1993.

Lears, Jackson. *Fables of Abundance: A Cultural History of Advertising in America*. New York: Basic Books, 1994.

Ledbetter, James. *Made Possible By ——: The Death of Public Broadcasting in the United States*. New York: Verso, 1997.

Leff, Mark H. *The Limits of Symbolic Reform: The New Deal and Taxation, 1933–1939*. New York: Cambridge University Press, 1984.

Leiss, William, Stephen Kline, and Sut Jhally. *Social Communication in Advertising: Persons, Products, and Images of Well-Being*. New York: Metheun, 1986.

Lemann, Nicholas. *Out of the Forties*. Austin: Texas Monthly Press, 1983; reprint New York: Fireside/Simon & Schuster, 1985.

Lerner, Michael. *The Politics of Meaning: Restoring Hope and Possibility in an Age of Cynicism*. Boston: Addison-Wesley, 1996, 1997.

Leslie, Stuart W. *Boss Kettering*. New York: Columbia University Press, 1983.

Leuchtenburg, William E. *Franklin D. Roosevelt and the New Deal, 1932–1940*. New York: Harper & Row, 1963.

———. *The FDR Years: On Roosevelt and His Legacy*. New York: Columbia University Press, 1995.

Lewis, David L. *The Public Image of Henry Ford: An American Folk Hero and His Company*. Detroit: Wayne State University Press, 1976.

Lichtenstein, Nelson. *Labor's War at Home: The CIO in World War II*. New York: Cambridge University Press, 1982.

———. *The Most Dangerous Man in Detroit: Walter Reuther and the Fate of American Labor*. New York: Basic Books, 1995.

Lichtenstein, Nelson, and Howell John Harris, eds. *Industrial Democracy in America: The Ambiguous Promise*. New York: Cambridge University Press, 1993.

Lichtenstein, Nelson, and Stephen Meyer, eds. *On The Line: Essays in the History of Auto Work*. Chicago: University of Chicago Press, 1989.

Linglebach, William E., ed. *Approaches to American Social History*. New York: Appleton-Century Company, 1937.

Link, Henry C. *The New Psychology of Selling and Advertising*. New York: Macmillan, 1932.

Lipsitz, George. *Rainbow at Midnight: Labor and Culture in the 1940s*. Chicago: University of Illinois Press, 1994.

Lorentz, Pare. *Lorentz on Film: Movies, 1927–1941*. Norman: University of Oklahoma Press, 1975; 1986.

Low, Rachael. *The History of the British Film, 1929–1939*. Vol. 3, *Films of Comment and Persuasion of the 1930s*. London: George Allen & Unwin, 1979.

Lundberg, Ferdinand. *America's 60 Families*. New York: The Vanguard Press, 1937.

———. *Who Controls Industry? And Other Questions Raised by Critics of America's 60 Families, with a Note on the Case of Richard Whitney*. New York: The Vanguard Press, 1938.

Lyons, Eugene. *The Red Decade: The Stalinist Penetration of America*. Indianapolis: Bobbs-Merrill Co., 1941.

MacCann, Richard Dyer. *The People's Films: A Political History of U.S. Government Motion Pictures*. New York: Hastings House, 1973.

MacDonald, J. Fred. *Don't Touch That Dial! Radio Programming in American Life from 1920 to 1960*. Chicago: Nelson-Hall, 1970.

———. *One Nation under Television: The Rise and Decline of Network T.V.* New York: Pantheon, 1990.

Maney, Patrick J. *The Roosevelt Presence: A Biography of Franklin Delano Roosevelt*. New York: Twayne Publishers, 1992.

Marc, David. *Demographic Vistas: Television in American Culture*. Philadelphia: University of Pennsylvania Press, 1984.

Marchand, Roland. *Advertising the American Dream: Making Way for Modernity, 1920–1940*. Berkeley: University of Californina Press, 1985.

———. *Creating the Corporate Soul: The Rise of Public Relations and Corporate Imagery in American Big Business*. Berkeley: University of California Press, 1998.

Marling, Karal Ann. *George Washington Slept Here: Colonial Revivals in American Culture, 1876–1986*. Cambridge, MA: MIT Press, 1986.

Marquis, Alice G. *Hopes and Ashes: The Birth of Modern Times, 1929–1939*. New York: Free Press, London: Collier Macmillan, 1986.

May, Lary. *Screening Out the Past: The Birth of Mass Culture and the Motion Picture Industry*. Chicago: University of Chicago Press, 1983.

———, ed. *Recasting America: Culture and Politics in the Age of Cold War*. Chicago: University of Chicago Press, 1989.

Mayer, Martin. *Madison Avenue, U.S.A.* New York: Harper, 1958.

McAllister, Matthew P. *The Commercialization of American Culture: New Advertising, Control and Democracy*. Thousand Oaks, CA: Sage Publications, 1996.

McCamy, James L. *Government Publicity: Its Practice in Federal Administration*. Chicago: University of Chicago Press, 1939.

McChesney, Robert M. *Telecommunications, Mass Media, and Democracy: The Battle for Control of U.S. Broadcasting, 1928–1935*. New York: Oxford University Press, 1993.

McCoy, Donald. *Landon of Kansas*. Lincoln: University of Nebraska Press, 1966.

McElvaine, Robert S. *The Great Depression: America, 1929–1941*. New York: Times Books, 1984, 1993.

McKee, C. W., and H. G. Moulton. *A Survey of Economic Education*. Washington, DC: Brookings Institution, 1951.

McQuaid, Kim. *Big Business and Presidential Power: From FDR to Reagan*. New York: Morrow, 1982.

———. *A Response to Industrialism: Liberal Businessmen and the Evolving Spectrum of Capitalist Reform, 1886–1960*. New York: Garland, 1986.

Meikle, Jeffrey L. *Twentieth Century Limited: Industrial Design in America, 1925–1939*. Philadelphia: Temple University Press, 1979.

Michelson, Charles. *The Ghost Talks*. New York: G. P. Putnam's Sons, 1944.

Michigan University Survey Research Center. *"Big Business" from the Viewpoint of the Public*. Ann Arbor, MI: Institute for Social Research, 1951.

Miller, Arthur. *Timebends: A Life*. New York: Grove Press, 1987.

Miller, Mark Crispin. *Boxed In: The Culture of TV*. Evanston, IL: Northwestern University Press, 1988.

Miller, Merle. *The Judges and the Judged*. Garden City, NY: Doubleday & Company, Inc., 1952.

Millis, Harry N., and Emily Clark Brown. *From the Wagner Act to Taft-Hartley: A Study of National Labor Policy and Labor Relations*. Chicago: University of Chicago Press, 1950.

Modleski, Tania. *Loving with a Vengeance: Mass-Produced Fantasies for Women*. Hamden, CT: Archon Books, 1982.

Molella, Arthur P. *FDR, The Intimate Presidency: Franklin Delano Roosevelt, Communication, and the Mass Media in the 1930s*. Washington, DC: National Museum of American History, Smithsonian Institution, 1982.

Moley, Raymond. *After Seven Years*. New York: Harper & Brothers, 1939.

Monaghan, Frank. *Heritage of Freedom: The History and Significance of the Basic Documents of American Liberty*. Princeton, NJ: Princeton University Press, 1948.

Mosely, Leonard. *Blood Relations: The Rise and Fall of the du Ponts of Delaware*. New York: Atheneum, 1980.

Musser, Charles. *Before the Nickelodeon: Edwin S. Porter and the Edison Manufacturing Company*. Berkeley: University of California Press, 1991.

Musser, Charles, in collaboration with Carol Nelson. *High-Class Moving Pictures: Lyman H. Howe and the Forgotten Era of Traveling Exhibition, 1880–1920*. Princeton, NJ: Princeton University Press, 1991.

Nadel, Norman. *A Pictorial History of the Theatre Guild*. New York: Crown Publishers, Inc., 1969.

Nelson, Cary, and Lawrence Grossberg, eds. *Marxism and the Interpretation of Culture*. Urbana and Chicago: University of Illinois Press, 1988.

Nelson, Daniel. *American Rubber Workers and Organized Labor, 1900–1941*. Princeton, NJ: Princeton University Press, 1988.

Newcomb, Horace, ed. *Television: The Critical View*. New York: Oxford University Press, 1994.

Newsom, Jon, ed. *Perspectives on John Philip Sousa*. Washington, DC: Library of Congress, 1983.

Niven, Penelope. *Carl Sandburg: A Biography*. New York: Charles Scribner's Sons, 1991.

Northrup, F. S. C., ed. *Ideological Differences and World Order*. New Haven: Yale University Press, 1949.

Novick, Peter. *That Noble Dream: The "Objectivity Question" and the American Historical Profession*. New York: Cambridge University Press, 1988.

Nye, David E. *Image Worlds: Corporate Identities at General Electric, 1890–1930*. Cambridge, MA: MIT Press, 1985.

Nye, David, and Carl Pedersen, eds. *Consumption and American Culture*. Amsterdam: VU University Press, 1991.

Nye, Joseph S., Philip D. Zelikow, and David C. King, eds. *Why People Don't Trust Government*. Cambridge, MA: Harvard University Press, 1997.

O'Connor, John, and Lorraine Brown, eds. *Free, Adult, Uncensored: The Living History of the Federal Theatre Project*. Washington, DC: New Republic Books, 1978.

Paletz, David L., Roberta E. Peterson, and Donald L. Willis. *Politics in Public Service Advertising on Television*. New York: Praeger, 1977.

Patterson, William D., ed. *America: Miracle at Work: The Best Public Interest Advertising of 1952 Based on the First Annual Saturday Review Awards for Distinguished Advertising in the Public Interest*. New York: Prentice-Hall, 1953.

Pease, Edward C., and Everette E. Dennis, eds. *Radio—the Forgotten Medium*. New Brunswick, NJ: Transaction Publishers, 1995.

Peiss, Kathy Lee. *Cheap Amusements: Working Women and Leisure in Turn-of-the-Century New York*. Philadelphia: Temple University Press, 1986.

Perkins, Francis. *The Roosevelt I Knew*. New York: Viking Press, 1946.

Phelan, James, and Robert Pozen. *The Company State: Ralph Nader's Study Group Report on DuPont in Delaware*. New York: Grossman Publishers, 1973.

Pimlott, J. A. R. *Public Relations and American Democracy*. Princeton, NJ: Princeton University Press, 1951, New York: Kennikat Press, 1972.

Plattner, Steven W. *Roy Stryker, U.S.A., 1943–1950: The Standard Oil (New Jersey) Photography Project*. Austin: University of Texas Press, 1983.

Polenberg, Richard. *War and Society: The United States, 1941–1945*. Philadelphia: J. B. Lippincott Co., 1972.

Postman, Neil. *Amusing Ourselves to Death: Public Discourse in the Age of Show Business*. New York: Viking, 1985.

Potter, David M. *People of Plenty: Economic Abundance and the American Character*. Chicago: University of Chicago Press, 1954.

Pound, Arthur. *Industrial America: Its Way of Work and Thought*. Boston: Little, Brown & Company, 1936.

———. *The Turning Wheel: The Story of General Motors through Twenty-Five Years, 1908–1933*. Garden City, NY: Doubleday, Doran & Company, 1934.

Psychological Corporation. *The Perils of Peace: A Study of Public Opinion and Morale*. New York: Psychological Corporation, 1941.

Qualter, Terrence H. *Opinion Control in the Democracies*. New York: St. Martin's Press, 1985.

The Queens Museum. *Dawn of a New Day: The New York World's Fair, 1939/40*. New York: Queens Museum and New York University Press, 1980.

Queeny, Edgar M. *The Spirit of Enterprise*. New York: Charles Scribner's Sons, 1943.

Radosh, Ronald, and Murray Rothbard, eds. *A New History of Leviathan: Essays on the Rise of the American Corporate State*. New York: E. P. Dutton & Co., 1972.

Rae, John B. *The American Automobile Industry*. Boston: Twayne Publishers, 1984.

Rath, Frederick L., Jr., et al. *Local History, National Heritage: Reflections on the History of the AASLH*. Nashville, TN: American Association for State and Local History, 1991.

Raucher, Alan R. *Public Relations and Business, 1900–1929*. Baltimore: Johns Hopkins University Press, 1968.

Reagan, Ronald, with Richard G. Hubler. *Where's the Rest of Me?* New York: Duell, Sloan & Pearce, 1965.

Reisman, David. *Abundance for What? And Other Essays*. Garden City, NY: Doubleday, 1964.

Robbins, Bruce, ed. *The Phantom Public Sphere*. Minneapolis: University of Minnesota Press, 1993.

Roeder, George H., Jr. *The Censored War: American Visual Experience during World War Two*. New Haven: Yale University Press, 1993.

Rorty, Richard. *Achieving Our Country: Leftist Thought in Twentieth Century America*. Cambridge, MA: Harvard University Press, 1998.

Rosen, Philip T. *The Modern Stentors: Radio Broadcasters and the Federal Government, 1920–1934*. Westport, CT: Greenwood Press, 1980.

Rosenman, Samuel I. *Working with Roosevelt*. New York: Harper & Brothers, 1952; New York: Da Capo Press, 1972.

Rosenzweig, Roy. *Eight Hours for What We Will: Workers and Leisure in an Industrial City, 1870–1920*. New York: Cambridge University Press, 1983.

Ross, Irwin. *The Image Merchants: The Fabulous World of Pubic Relations*. Garden City, NY: Doubleday, 1959.

Ross, Steven J. *Working-Class Hollywood: Silent Film and the Shaping of Class in America*. Princeton, NJ: Princeton University Press, 1998.

Rothel, David. *Who Was That Masked Man? The Story of the Lone Ranger*. South Brunswick, NJ: reprint ed., A. S. Barnes, 1976.

Routzahn, Mary Brayton. *Traveling Publicity Campaigns: Educational Tours of Railroad Trains and Motor Vehicles*. New York: Russell Sage Foundation, 1920.

Rubin, Joan Shelley. *The Making of Middlebrow Culture*. Chapel Hill: University of North Carolina Press, 1992.

Samuel, Raphael, Ewan MacColl, and Stuart Cosgrove, eds. *Theatres of the Left, 1880–1935: Workers' Theatre Movements in Britain and America*. Boston: Routledge & Kegan Paul, 1985.

Sandage, C. H., ed. *The Promise of Advertising*. Homewood, IL: Richard D. Irwin, 1961.

Sandburg, Carl. *The Complete Poems of Carl Sandburg*. New York: Harcourt Brace Jovanovich, 1976.

Sanders, Barry. *The Private Death of Public Discourse*. Boston: Beacon Press, 1998.

Sarjeant, Charles F., ed. *The First Forty: The Story of WCCO Radio*. Minneapolis: T. S. Denison & Co., 1964.

Schatz, Ronald W. *The Electrical Workers: A History of Labor at General Electric and Westinghouse, 1923–1960*. Urbana and Chicago: University of Illinois Press, 1983.

Schickel, Richard. *Intimate Strangers: The Culture of Celebrity*. Garden City, NY: Doubleday & Co., 1985.

Schiller, Dan. *Theorizing Communication: A History*. New York: Oxford University Press, 1996.

Schiller, Herbert I. *Culture, Inc.: The Corporate Takeover of Public Expression*. New York: Oxford University Press, 1989.

Schlesinger, Arthur M., Jr. *The Coming of the New Deal*. Boston: Houghton Mifflin, 1958.

———. *The Crisis of the Old Order, 1919–1933*. Boston: Houghton Mifflin, 1957.

———. *In Retrospect: The History of a Historian*. New York: Harcourt, Brace & World, 1963.

———. *The Politics of Upheaval*. Boston: Houghton Mifflin, 1960.

Schmertz, Herb, with William Novak. *Good-bye to the Low Profile: The Art of Creative Confrontation*. Boston: Little, Brown & Company, 1986.

Schroeder-Gudehus, Brigitte, ed. *Industrial Society and Its Museums, 1890–1990: Social Aspirations and Cultural Politics*. Langhorne, PA: Harwood Academic Publishers, 1993.

Schudson, Michael. *Advertising, the Uneasy Persuasion: Its Dubious Impact on American Society*. New York: Basic Books, 1984.

Schwartz, H. W. *Bands of America*. Garden City, NY: Doubleday, 1957.

Seldes, Gilbert. *The Great Audience*. New York: Viking Press, 1951.

Sherwood, Robert E. *Roosevelt and Hopkins: An Intimate History*. New York: Harper, 1948.

Short, K. R. M., ed. *Film and Radio Propaganda in World War II*. Knoxville: University of Tennessee Press, 1983.

Sizer, Theodore, Andrew C. McLaughlin, Dixon Ryan Fox, and Henry Sidel Canby. *Aspects of the Social History of America*. Chapel Hill: University of North Carolina Press, 1931.

Sklar, Robert, and Charles Musser, eds. *Resisting Images: Essays on Cinema and History*. Philadelphia: Temple University Press, 1990.

Slide, Anthony. *Before Video: A History of the Non-Theatrical Film*. New York: Greenwood Press, 1992.

Sloan, Alfred P., Jr. *Adventures of a White-Collar Man*. New York: Doubleday, Doran & Company, 1941.

———. *My Years with General Motors*. Garden City, NY: Doubleday & Company, 1963.

Sloan, Kay. *The Loud Silents: Origins of the Social Problem Film*. Chicago and Urbana: University of Illinois Press, 1988.

Smallwood, James, ed. *Will Rogers' Daily Telegrams*. Stillwater: Oklahoma State University Press, 1979.

Smith, Ira R. T., with Joe Alex Morris. *"Dear Mr. President . . .": The Story of Fifty Years in the White House Mail Room*. New York: Julian Messner, 1949.

Smulyan, Susan. *Selling Radio: The Commercialization of American Broadcasting, 1920–1934*. Washington, DC: Smithsonian Institution Press, 1994.

Spigel, Lynn. *Make Room for TV: Television and the Family Ideal in Postwar America*. Chicago: University of Chicago Press, 1992.

Spigel, Lynn, and Denise Mann, eds. *Private Screenings: Television and the Female Consumer*. Minneapolis: University of Minnesota Press, 1992.

Spitzer, Leo. *A Method of Interpreting Literature*. Northampton, MA: Smith College, 1949; reprint ed., New York: Russell and Russell, 1967.

Stange, Maren. *Symbols of Ideal Life: Social Documentary Photography in America, 1890–1950*. New York: Cambridge University Press, 1989.

Staudenmaier, John M. *Technology's Storytellers: Reweaving the Human Fabric*. Cambridge, MA: Society for the History of Technology and MIT Press, 1985.

Steele, Richard W. *Propaganda in an Open Society: The Roosevelt Administration and the Media, 1931–1941*. Westport, CT: Greenwood, 1985.

Sterling, Christopher H., and John M. Kitross. *Stay Tuned: A Concise History of American Broadcasting*. Belmont, CA: Wadsworth Publishing Co., 1990.

Stillinger, Elizabeth. *The Antiquers*. New York: Alfred A. Knopf, 1980.

Stott, William. *Documentary Expression and Thirties America*. With a new afterword. Chicago: University of Chicago Press, 1986.

Strasser, Susan. *Satisfaction Guaranteed: The Making of the American Mass Market*. New York: Pantheon Books, 1989.

Strasser, Susan, Charles McGovern, and Mathias Jutt, eds. *Getting and Spending: European and American Consumption in the Twentieth Century*. New York: Cambridge University Press, 1998.

Stryker, Roy Emerson. *In This Proud Land*. New York: Galahad Books, 1973.

Susman, Warren. *Culture as History: The Transformation of American Society in the Twentieth Century*. New York: Pantheon, 1984.

Susman, Warren, ed. *Culture and Commitment, 1929–1945*. New York: George Braziller, 1973.

Sussman, Leila A. *Dear FDR: A Study of Political Letter-Writing*. Totowa, NJ: Bedminster Press, 1963.

Sutton, Francis X., et al. *The American Business Creed*. Cambridge, MA: Harvard University Press, 1956.

Taylor, Graham D., and Patricia E. Sudnik. *DuPont and the International Chemical Industry*. Boston: Twayne Publishers, G. K. Hall & Company, 1984.

Teague, Walter Dorwin. *Design This Day: The Technique of Order in the Machine Age*. New York: Harcourt, Brace, 1949 rev.

Tedlow, Richard S. *Keeping the Corporate Image: Public Relations and Business, 1900–1950*. Greenwich, CT: JAI Press, 1979.

———. *New and Improved: The Story of Mass Marketing in America*. New York: Basic Books, 1990.

Theatre Guild. *The Theatre Guild Anthology*. New York: Random House, 1936.

Tichi, Cecelia. *Electronic Hearth: Creating an American Television Culture*. New York: Oxford University Press, 1991.

Tomlins, Christopher L. *The State and the Unions: Labor Relations, Law, and the Organized Labor Movement in America, 1880–1960*. New York: Cambridge University Press, 1985.

Tugwell, Rexford G. *The Democratic Roosevelt: A Biography of Franklin D. Roosevelt*. Garden City, NY: Doubleday & Company, 1957.

United States Congress. Senate. *Investigation of Lobbying Activities: Hearings before a special committee to investigate lobbying activities, 74th, 75th Congresses*. Washington, DC: United States Government Printing Office, 1935–1938.

———. *Violations of Free Speech and Rights of Labor. Hearings pursuant to resolution 266 before a Subcommittee of the Committee on Education and Labor, 75th, 76th Congresses*. Washington, DC: United States Government Printing Office, 1937–1939.

Upward, Geoffrey C. *A Home for Our Heritage: The Building and Growth of Greenfield Village and Henry Ford Museum, 1929–1979*. Dearborn, MI: Henry Ford Museum Press, 1979.

Useem, Michael. *The Inner Circle: Large Corporations and the Rise of Business Political Activity in the U.S. and U.K.* New York: Oxford University Press, 1984.

Walker, Strother Holland, and Paul Sklar. *Business Finds Its Voice: Management's Effort to Sell the Business Idea to the Public*. New York: Harper & Brothers, 1938.

Wall, Joseph Frazier. *Alfred I. du Pont: The Man and His Family*. New York: Oxford University Press, 1990.

Waples, Douglas. *Print, Radio and Film in a Democracy*. Chicago: University of Chicago Press, 1942.

Ward, Larry Wayne. *The Motion Picture Goes to War: The U.S. Government Film Effort during World War I*. Ann Arbor, MI: UMI Research Press, 1985.

Warren, Frank A. *Liberals and Communism: The "Red Decade" Revisited*. Bloomington: Indiana University Press, 1966.

Weible, Robert, and Francis R. Walsh, eds. *The Popular Perception of Industrial History*. Lanham, MD: University Publishing Associates, Inc., 1989.

Whisnant, David E. *All That Is Native and Fine: The Politics of Culture in an American Region*. Chapel Hill: University of North Carolina Press, 1983.

Whiteside, Thomas. *The Relaxed Sell*. New York: Oxford University Press, 1954.

Whyte, William H. *Is Anybody Listening? How and Why U.S. Business Fumbles When It Talks with Human Beings*. New York: Simon & Schuster, 1952.

Wilitz, John E. *In Search of Peace: The Senate Munitions Inquiry, 1934–36*. Baton Rouge: Louisiana State University Press, 1963.

Wilkinson, Norman B. *Lammot du Pont and the American Explosives Industry, 1850–1884*. Charlottesville: University Press of Virginia, 1984.

Williams, Jon M., and Daniel T. Muir. *Corporate Images: Photography and the DuPont Company, 1865–1972*. Wilmington, DE: Hagley Museum and Library, 1984.

Williams, Raymond. *Television: Technology and Cultural Form*. London: Fontana/Collins, 1974, New York: Schocken Books, 1975.

Wills, Gary. *Reagan's America: Innocents at Home*. Garden City, NY: Doubleday, 1987.

Winfield, Betty Houchin. *FDR and the News Media*. Urbana: University of Illinois Press, 1990.

Winkler, Allan M. *The Politics of Propaganda: The Office of War Information, 1942–1945*. New Haven: Yale University Press, 1978.

Wolfskill, George. *The Revolt of the Conservatives: A History of the American Liberty League, 1934–1940*. Boston: Houghton Mifflin Co., 1962; Westport, CT: Greenwood Press, 1974.

Wolfskill, George, and John A. Hudson. *All but the People: Franklin D. Roosevelt and His Critics, 1933–1939*. New York: Macmillan, 1969.

Yale University Press. *The Chronicles of America Photoplays*. New Haven: Yale University Press, n.d.

Zeiger, Robert H. *American Workers, American Unions, 1920–1985*. Baltimore: Johns Hopkins University Press, 1986.

Zim, Larry, Mel Lerner, and Herbert Rolfes. *The World of Tomorrow: The 1939 New York World's Fair*. New York: Harper & Row, 1988.

Articles

Achilles, Paul S. "A Reply to Dr. Doob's Comments Concerning the Psychological Corporation." *Psychological Bulletin* 35 (October 1938): 548–551.

Adams, James Truslow. "My Methods as a Historian." *Saturday Review of Literature* 10 (June 30, 1934): 777–778.

Ainsworth, Gardner. "The New York Fair: Adventure in Promotion." *Public Opinion Quarterly* 3 (October 1939): 694–704.

Allen, Audrey. "Corporate Advertising: Its New Look." *Public Relations Journal* 27 (November 1971): 6–13, 68–73.

American Film Center. "World's Fair—1940." *Film News* 1 (May 1940): 1–2.

———. "World's Fair Films." *Film News* 1 (July 1940): 1–8.

Angell, James Rowland. "A Bastard Democracy: The Danger and the Method of Avoidance." *Vital Speeches of the Day* 3 (July 15, 1937): 578–580.

———. "The Moral Crisis of Democracy." *Vital Speeches of the Day* 2 (August 1, 1936): 670–674.

———. "Second Thoughts after the Election." *Vital Speeches of the Day* 3 (December 1, 1936): 98–101.

Angly, Edward. "Both Sides Gird for New Battle in Auto Strike." *New York Herald Tribune,* 25 January 1937, p. 8.

Ash, Philip. "The Periodical Press and the Taft-Hartley Act." *Public Opinion Quarterly* 12 (summer 1948): 266–271.

Aufderheide, Patricia. "After the Fairness Doctrine: Controversial Broadcast Programming and the Public Interest." *Journal of Communication* 40 (summer 1990): 47–72.

———. "Are Private Interests Ruling Public Television?" *Business and Society Review* 69 (spring 1989): 16–19.

———. "The Coporatization of Public TV: Why Labor's Voice Is Seldom Heard on PBS." *Extra!* (November/December 1988): 12–14.

———. "Public Television and the Public Sphere." *Critical Studies in Mass Communication* 8 (June 1991): 168–183.

Barton, Bruce. "The Public." Delivered before the Congress of American Industry, in conjunction with the annual convention of the National Association of Manufacturers, December 4, 1935. *Vital Speeches of the Day* 2 (December 16, 1935): 174–177.

———. "This Magic Called Radio." *American Magazine* 93 (June 1922): 11–13.

Basso, Hamilton. "The Liberty League Writes." *New Republic* 87 (July 22, 1936): 319–321.

Baughman, James L. "Television in the 'Golden Age': An Entrepreneurial Experiment." *Historian* 47 (February 1985): 175–195.

Bendiner, Robert. "Vox Populi, Inc." *The Nation* 156 (March 27, 1943): 449–450.

Bernstein, Barton J. "The Truman Administration and the Steel Strike of 1946." *Journal of American History* 52 (March 1966): 791–803.

Better Living. Wilmington, DE: E. I. du Pont de Nemours and Company (1946–).

Better Living 4 (March–April 1950): 10–11. "Industry's Boss."

Bigelow, Burton. "Should Business Decentralize Its Counter-Propaganda?" *Public Opinion Quarterly* 1 (April 1938): 321–324.

Bradsher, James Gregory. "Taking America's Heritage to the People: The Freedom Train Story." *Prologue* 17 (winter 1985): 228–245.

Brennan, Timothy A. "The Fairness Doctrine as Public Policy." *Journal of Broadcasting and Electronic Media* 33 (fall 1989): 419–440.

Brinkley, Alan. "The Problem of American Conservatism." *American Historical Review* 99 (April 1994): 409–429.

Brooks, Van Wyck. "On Creating a Usable Past." *Dial* 64 (April 11, 1918): 337-341.

Burch, Philip H., Jr. "The NAM as an Interest Group." *Politics and Society* 4 (fall 1973): 97–130.

Business Screen 9, no. 4 (1948): 22. "*Business Screen*'s Recommendation to the U.S. Chamber."

——— 2, no. 6 (1940): 7, 31. "Camera Eye."

——— 2, no. 7 (1940): 14–15. "Films at the 1940 New York World's Fair."

——— 7, no. 8 (1946): 18. "How the UE–CIO Sees 'Big Business.'"

——— 9, no. 4 (1948): 21–22. "Labor Looks to the Screen."

——— 2, no. 5 (1940): 17–18. "The National Theme in Pictures."

——— 2, no. 3 (1940): 34. "New York Fair Films."

——— 10, no. 4 (1949): 21–22. "The Price of Freedom."

——— 1, no. 1 (1938): 19, 62. "Salesmen Get the Idea."

——— 2, no. 6 (1940): 10. "Steel's New York Fair Theatre."

——— 3, no. 1 (1940): 16–19. "Symphony in Dimension."

——— 10, no. 4 (1949): 25–26. "This is General Electric."

——— 10, no. 2 (1949): 21–22. "Time to Show the Facts."

——— 4, no. 6 (1945): 46. "The UAW-CIO Pioneers Use of Films among Labor Unions."

——— 9, no. 4 (1948): 23. "U.S. Steel Makes a Progress Report."

——— 9, no. 4 (1948): 22. "What Can Be Done: 'Letter to a Rebel' Points the Way."

Business Week (October 18, 1982): 26. "Business Thinks TV Distorts Its Image."

——— (May 27, 1939): 37–47. "Camera! Action! Sales!"

Casey, Ralph D. "Party Campaign Propaganda." *Annals of the American Academy of Political and Social Science* 179 (May 1935): 96–105.

———. "Republican Propaganda in the 1936 Campaign." *Public Opinion Quarterly* 2 (April 1937): 27–44.

Cattell, James McKeen. "The Psychological Corporation." *Annals of the American Academy of Political and Social Science* 110 (1923): 165–171.

Cawelti, John G. "Myth, Symbol and Formula." *Journal of Popular Culture* 8 (summer 1974): 1–9.

Charities and the Commons 21 (March 6, 1909): 1038–1039. "Theaters Second Only to Schools."

Chase, Stuart. "Ode to the Liberty League." *Nation* 141 (November 27, 1935): 613–614.

Chew, Fiona. "The Advertising Value of 'Making Possible' a Public Television Program." *Journal of Advertising Research* 32 (November/December 1992): 47–52.

Clark, George R. "The Strange Story of the Reuther Plan." *Harper's* 184 (May 1942): 645–654.

Clarke, Sally. "Consumers, Information, and Marketing Efficiency at GM, 1921–1940." *Business and Economic History* 25 (fall 1996): 186–195.

Cleveland, Alfred S. "NAM: Spokesman for Industry?" *Harvard Business Review* 26 (May 1948): 353–371.

Coblenz, William A. "The Freedom Train and the Story of Its Origin: Our Civil Liberties on Wheels." *Manuscripts* 10 (winter 1958): 30–34.

Coelln, Otto H. "Truth, Labor and Management Guts." *Business Screen* 7, no. 8 (1946): 17.

———. "The UAW-CIO Pioneers Use of Films among Labor Unions." *Business Screen* 6, no. 4 (1945): 46.

Collins, Robert M. "American Corporatism: The Committee for Economic Development, 1924–1964." *Historian* 44 (February 1982): 151–173.

Connolly, Ceci. "Consultant Offers GOP a Language for the Future." *Washington Post*, 4 September 1997, p. 1.

Corn, Joseph. "Selling Technology: Advertising Films and the American Corporation, 1900–1920." *Film and History* 11 (September 1981): 49–58.

Crossley, Archibald M. "Straw Polls in 1936." *Public Opinion Quarterly* 1 (January 1937): 24–35.

Crowther, Bosley. "Films for the Fair." *New York Times*, 5 March 1939, sect. 10, p. 5.

Current Opinion 74 (April 1923): 457. "Radio and the Theater."

Daniel, Hawthorne. "American History in Moving Pictures." *World's Work* 44 (September 1922): 540–547.

Denison, Merrill. "The Actor and Radio." *Theatre Arts* 17 (November 1933): 845–855.

———. "The Broadcast Play." *Theatre Arts* 15 (December 1931): 1008–1011.

———. "A Canadian Playwright Compares American and English Broadcasting." *Theatre Arts* 15 (October 1931): 868–869.

———. "Editorial Policies of Broadcasting Companies." *Public Opinion Quarterly* 1 (January 1937): 64–82.

DeVoto, Bernard. "Why Professors Are Suspicious of Business." *Fortune* 43 (April 1951): 114–115, 139–144.

Dixon, Peter. "Supplying Drama to Radio Audiences." *The Drama Magazine* 21 (October 1930): 7–8, 20.

Doob, Leonard W. "An 'Experimental' Study of the Psychological Corporation." *Psychological Bulletin* 35 (April 1938): 220–222.

Douglas, Susan J. "Notes toward a History of Mass Media Audiences." *Radical History Review* 54 (1992): 127–138.

Dudley, Drew. "Molding Public Opinion through Advertising." *Annals of the American Academy of Political and Social Science* 250 (March 1947): 105–112.

Durstine, Roy S. "The Future of Radio Advertising in the United States." *Annals of the American Academy of Political and Social Science* 177 (January 1935): 147–153.

———. "We're on the Air." *Scribner's* 83 (May 1928): 623–631.

Ermann, M. David. "The Operative Goals of Corporate Philanthropy: Contributions to the Public Broadcasting Service, 1972–1976." *Social Problems* 25 (June 1978): 504–514.

Fiddler, Fred H. "The Agency in Motion Pictures." *Business Screen* 2 (1940): 16.

———. "Today's Commercial Movies." *Advertising and Selling* 33 (October 1940): 21–23, 86.

Film News 10 (March 1950): 6, 11. "We Use Films in Our Program: National Association of Manufacturers."

——— 1 (May 1940): 1–3. "World's Fair—1940."

——— 1 (July 1940): 1–8. "World's Fair Supplement."

Foner, Philip. "A Martyr to His Cause: The Scenario of the First Labor Film in the United States." *Labor History* 24 (winter 1983): 103–111.

Fortune 17 (April 1938): 72–77, 110–114. "Alfred P. Sloan, Jr.: Chairman."

——— 9 (March 1934): 52–57, 113–126. "Arms and the Men."

——— 42 (September 1950): 80. "Bull Session."

——— 39 (May 1949): 67–71, 196–200. "Business Is Still in Trouble."

——— 44 (September 1951): 120–123. "Can Industry Use Television?"

——— 12 (December 1935): 102–107, 140. "The Case against Roosevelt."

——— 10 (November 1934): 65–75+. "DuPont."

——— 10 (December 1934): 80–89+. "DuPont II."

——— 35 (January 1947): 138, 140. "A Fly on the Wheel."

——— 44 (July 1951): 84–86, 122–128. "How Good Is 'Economic Education'?"

——— 11 (January 1935): 62–65+. "The Power and the Glory."

——— 44 (October 1951): 108–113. "Public Relations for the Long Pull."

——— 38 (July 1948): 72–75, 165–169. "Renovation in N.A.M."

——— 17 (January 1938): 62–68. "Toscanini on the Air."

Fox, Dixon Ryan. "The Synthetic Principle in American Social History." *American Historical Review* 35 (January 1930): 256–266.

Gable, R. W. "N.A.M.: Influential Lobby or Kiss of Death?" *Journal of Politics* 15 (May 1953): 253–273.

Galli, Anthony. "Corporate Advertising: More Than Just a Nice Warm Feeling All Over." *Journal of Public Relations* 27 (November 1971): 19–23, 75–76.

Gallup, George H. "A Scientific Method for Determining Reader-Interest." *Journalism Quarterly* 7 (March 1930): 1–13.

Gielgud, Val. "The Actor and the Broadcast Play." *Theatre Arts* 15 (February 1931): 119–122.

———. "The Broadcast Play." *Theatre Arts* 14 (November 1930): 456–462.

———. Side Lights on the Broadcast Play." *Theatre Arts* 15 (June 1931): 479–484.

———. "What Hope Radio Drama?" *Theatre Arts* 18 (April 1934): 307–309.

Gitlin, Todd. "Mass Media Sociology: The Dominant Paradigm." *Theory and Society* 6 (September 1978): 205–253.

Gladstone, Brooke, and Steve Behrens. "And That's Why I Underwrite PTV (Just between Us Corporations)." *Current* 2 (July 12, 1983): 5.

Goldman, Harry, and Mel Gordon. "Workers' Theatre in America: A Survey, 1913–1978." *Journal of American Culture* 6 (spring 1978): 169–181.

Goodman, Ezra. "Meet Pete–Roleum." *Sight and Sound* 8 (summer 1939): 62.

Grass, Robert C., David W. Bartges, and Jeffrey L. Piech. "Measuring Corporate Image Ad Effects." *Journal of Advertising Research* 12 (December 1972): 15–22.

Green, Thomas S., Jr. "Mr. Cameron and the Ford Hour." *Public Opinion Quarterly* 3 (October 1939): 669–675.

Griffith, Richard. "Films at the Fair." *Films: A Quarterly of Discussion and Analysis* 1 (November 1939): 61–75.

Griffith, Robert. "Dwight D. Eisenhower and the Corporate Commonwealth." *American Historical Review* 87 (February 1982): 87–122.

———. "The Selling of America: The Advertising Council and American Politics, 1942–1960." *Business History Review* 57 (autumn 1983): 388–412.

Hamilton, Clayton. "American History on the Screen." *World's Work* 48 (September 1924): 525–532.

Hanson, Elisha. "Official Propaganda and the New Deal." *Annals of the American Academy of Political and Social Science* 179 (May 1935): 176–187.

Harding, Gardner. "World's Fair, 1939: A Preview." *Harper's* 176 (December 1937): 129–137.

Harrison, S. L. "Prime Time Pablum: How Politics and Corporate Influence Keep Public TV Harmless." *Washington Monthly* 17 (January 1986): 33–39.

Hart, Joseph K. "Radiating Culture." *Survey* 47 (March 18, 1922): 948–949.

Havig, Alan. "Frederic Wakeman's *The Hucksters* and the Postwar Debate over Commercial Radio." *Journal of Broadcasting* 28 (spring 1984): 187–199.

Hazlett, Thomas W. "The Fairness Doctrine and the First Amendment." *Public Interest* 96 (summer 1989): 103–116.

Heald, Morrell. "Business Thought in the Twenties: Social Responsibility." *American Quarterly* 13 (summer 1961): 126–139.

Hearnshaw, F. J. C. "History on the Film." *Fortune* 145 (August 1933): 665–671.

Henderson, Carter. "Promotion Push: Electric Firms Plan Charged-Up Campaign to Boost Their Sales." *Wall Street Journal*, 8 February 1956, pp. 1, 10.

High, Stanley. "Radio Disarms Its Critics." *Literary Digest* 118 (August 11, 1934): 23.

———. "A Republican Takes a Walk." *Forum* 95 (May 1936): 261–267.

Hoffman, Paul G. "Will the *Talkies* Talk Their Way into Mass Selling?" *Magazine of Business* 56 (August 1929): 149–150, 194.

Hollitz, John E. "Eisenhower and the Admen: The Television 'Spot' Campaign of 1952." *Wisconsin Magazine of History* 66 (autumn 1982): 25–39.

Horowitz, David. "The Politics of Public Television." *Commentary* 92 (December 1991): 25–32.

Horten, Gerd. "'Propaganda Must Be Painless': Radio Entertainment and Government Propaganda During World War II." *Prospects* 21 (1995): 373–395.

Howlett, Robert Michael, and Rebecca Raglon. "Constructing the Environmental Spectacle: Green Advertisements and the Greening of the Corporate Image, 1910–1990." *Environmental History Review* 16 (winter 1992): 53–68.

Hughes, Lawrence M. "Jamison Handy: Master of 'Show 'Em.'" *Sales Management Magazine* 90 (March 15, 1963): 40–45.

Huntley, Charles H. "Plays By Radio." *Drama* 14 (November 1923): 52–53.

Hurwitz, Donald. "Broadcast Ratings: The Missing Dimension." *Critical Studies in Mass Communication* 1 (June 1984): 205–215.

Hynes, Terry. "Media Manipulation and Political Campaigns: Bruce Barton and the Presidential Elections of the Jazz Age." *Journalism History* 4 (autumn 1977): 93–98.

Institute for Propaganda Analysis. "The Movies and Propaganda." *Propaganda Analysis* 1 (March 1938): 1–4.

———. "Polls, Propaganda, and Democracy." *Propaganda Analysis* 4 (11 November 1940): 1–6.

The Iron Age 91 (April 10, 1913): 886–887. "Growing Use of Commercial Motion Pictures."

Jacobs, Meg. "'How about Some Meat?' The Office of Price Administration, Consumption Politics, and State Building from the Bottom Up, 1941–1946." *Journal of American History* 84 (December 1997): 910–941.

Jarvik, Laurence. "PBS and the Politics of Quality: Mobil Oil's 'Masterpiece Theatre.'" *Historical Journal of Film, Radio and Television* 12, no. 3 (1992): 253–274.

Jennings, Ralph M. "Dramatic License in Political Broadcasts." *Journal of Broadcasting* 12 (summer 1968): 229–246.

Johnston, Alva. "Profiles: Vaudeville to Television—I." *New Yorker* 22 (September 28, 1946): 32–43.

———. "Profiles: Vaudeville to Television—II." *New Yorker* 22 (October 5, 1946): 36–47.

———. "Profiles: Vaudeville to Television—III." *New Yorker* 22 (October 12, 1946): 36–46.

Jones, Alfred Haworth. "The Search for a Usable Past in the New Deal Era." *American Quarterly* 23 (December 1971): 710–724.

Jowett, Garth. "Dangling the Dream? The Presentation of Television to the American Public, 1928–1952." *Historical Journal of Film, Radio and Television* 14, no. 2 (1994): 121–145.

Kammen, Michael. "Business Leadership and the American Heritage." *Cornell Enterprise* 3 (1986): 21–28.

Kaplan, Wendy. "R. T. H. Halsey: An Ideology of Collecting American Decorative Arts." *Winterthur Portfolio* 17 (spring 1982): 43–53.

Kent, Frank B. "Charley Michelson." *Scribner's Magazine* 88 (September 1930): 290–296.

Klein, Julius. "What Are Motion Pictures Doing for Industry?" *Annals of the American Academy of Political and Social Science* 128 (November 1926): 79–83.

Kolodin, Irving. "Propaganda on the Air." *American Mercury* 35 (July 1935): 293–300.

Konisgberg, Eric. "Stocks, Bonds, and Barney: How Public Television Went Private." *Washington Monthly* 25 (September 1993): 12–15.

Krock, Arthur. "Scrooge and New Deal Ghosts Adorn a Christmas Tale." *New York Times,* 25 December 1934.

Krows, Arthur Edwin. "Motion Pictures—Not for Theaters." *Educational Screen* 19 (February 1940): 58–61.

Lapham, Jerrold H. "What Hope Radio Drama?" *Theatre Arts* 18 (January 1934): 44–50.

Lay, David. "Drawing the Crowds to Your Films." *System* 28 (September 1915): 327–332.

———. "Movies That Find Customers." *System* 28 (August 1915): 190–194.

———. "Putting 'Movies' on the Sales Force." *System* 28 (July 1915): 73–77.

Lazarsfeld, Paul F. "Remarks on Administrative and Critical Communications Research." *Studies in Philosophy and Social Science* 9 (1941): 2–16.

Leach, Eugene E. "Mastering the Crowd: Collective Behavior and Mass Society in American Social Thought, 1917–1939." *American Studies* 27 (spring 1986): 99–114.

Lears, T. J. Jackson. "The Concept of Cultural Hegemony: Problems and Possibilities." *American Historical Review* 90 (June 1985): 567–593.

Leff, Mark H. "The Politics of Sacrifice on the American Home Front in World War II." *Journal of American History* 77 (March 1991): 1296–1318.

Lessing, Lawrence P. "The Story of the Greatest Chemical Aggregation in the World: DuPont." *Fortune* 42 (October 1950): 86+.

Levine, Lawrence, Robin Kelley, Natalie Davis, and T. J. Jackson Lears. "AHR Forum: The Folklore of Industrial Society: Popular Culture and Its Audiences." *American Historical Review* 97 (December 1992): 1369–1430.

Lewis, David L. "Pioneering the Business Film." *Pubic Relations Journal* 27 (June 1971): 14–17.

Lichtenberg, Bernard. "Business Backs New York World Fair to Meet the New Deal Propaganda." *Public Opinion Quarterly* 2 (April 1938): 314–324.

Liebhold, Peter. "Seeking 'The One Best Way.'" *Labor's Heritage* 7 (fall 1995): 18–33, 56–61.

Link, Henry C. "How to Sell America to Americans." *Business Screen* 9, no. 1 (February 1948): 20–21.

———. "A New Method for Testing Advertising and a Psychological Sales Barometer." *Journal of Applied Psychology* 18 (February 1934): 1–26.

Lippmann, Walter. "The Radio Controversy." *New York Herald Tribune,* 18 January 1936, p. 15.

Lipsitz, George. "The Struggle for Hegemony." *Journal of American History* 75 (June 1988): 146–150.

Literary Digest 115 (January 28, 1933): 15. "'Cavalcade' as a Film Outshines the Play."

——— 65 (May 1, 1920): 36–37. "Fighting Waste with Movies."

——— 115 (January 21, 1933): 6. "The Machine's Friends Reply to the Technocrats."

Little, Stuart J. "The Freedom Train: Citizenship and Postwar Political Culture, 1946–1949." *American Studies* 34 (spring 1993): 35–67.

Living Age 320 (March 1924): 432. "Drama by Radio."

Los Angeles Times, 23 October 1936, p. 7. "Byrnes Accuses Vandenberg."

Lott, Margaret E. "The Showcase of an Industry." *DuPont Magazine* 30 (midsummer 1936): 6–7.

Lounsbury, Myron. "'Flashes of Lightning': The Moving Picture in the Progressive Era." *Journal of Popular Culture* 3 (spring 1970): 772–787.

Lovett, Robert Morss. "A G.M. Stockholder Visits Flint." *The Nation* 144 (January 30, 1937): 123–124.

Marchand, Roland. "The Corporation Nobody Knew: Bruce Barton, Alfred Sloan, and the Founding of the General Motors 'Family.'" *Business History Review* 65 (winter 1991): 825–875.

———. "The Fitful Career of Advocacy Advertising: Political Protection, Client Cultivation, and Corporate Morale." *California Management Review* 29 (winter 1987): 128–156.

———. "The Inward Thrust of Institutional Advertising: General Electric and General Motors in the 1920s." *Business and Economic History* 18 (1989): 188–196.

———."Part I—The Designers Go to the Fair: Walter Dorwin Teague and the Professionalization of Corporate Industrial Exhibits, 1933–1940." *Design Issues* 8 (fall 1991): 4–17.

———."Part II—The Designers Go to the Fair: Norman Bel Geddes, The General Motors 'Futurama,' and the Visit-to-the-Factory Transformed." *Design Issues* 8 (spring 1992): 22–40.

———."Where Lie the Boundaries of the Corporation? Explorations in 'Corporate Responsibility.'" *Business and Economic History* 26 (fall 1997): 80–100.

Mareth, Paul. "Public Visions: Private Voices." *Sight and Sound* 46 (winter 1976/77): 14–17.

Marling, Karal Ann. "A Note on New Deal Iconography: Futurology and the Historical Myth." In Jack Saltzman, ed., *Prospects: An Annual of American Cultural Studies,* vol. 4. New York: Burt Franklin & Company, 1979, pp. 421–440.

Matthews, Christopher J. "Your Host, Ronald Reagan: From G.E. Theater to the Desk in the Oval Office." *New Republic* 190 (March 26, 1984): 15–18.

May, Lary. "Making the American Way: Moderne Theatres, Audiences, and the Film Industry, 1929–1945." *Prospects* 12 (1987): 89–124.

McKee, Oliver, Jr. "Publicity Chiefs." *North American Review* 230 (October 1930): 411–413.

McKeown, M. R. "Detroit: The Commercial Hollywood." *Barron's* 16 (29 June 1936): 11–12.

McMahan, Harry W. "BBDO Is 'Best' Three out of Four Times—What Makes It Tick?" *Advertising Age* 35 (July 27, 1964): 71–74.

Melick, Weldon. "National Heckle Hour." *Reader's Digest* 28 (June 1936): 42–46.

Menken, Harriet. "Front Centre for Radio Drama." *Radio Digest* 26 (February 1931): 29, 96.

———. "The Play's the Thing." *Radio Digest* 28 (May 1931): 23, 106.

Meredith, Robyn. "G.M. Sponsors a Maker of Documentaries and Reaches PBS Viewers 15 Seconds at a Time." *New York Times*, 3 November 1997, sec. D, p. 12.

Miller, Judith. "Selling the Government Like Soap: It Seems to Work." *New York Times*, 14 September 1997, sec. D, p. 3.

Miller, Mark Crispin. "Free the Media." *The Nation* 262 (June 3, 1996): 9–15.

———. "TV: The Nature of the Beast." *The Nation* 266 (June 8, 1998): 11–13.

Mitchell, Alison. "Word for Word: Republican Remedies: Speak Less Loudly and Stop Calling the Speaker 'Newt.'" *New York Times,* 12 October 1997, p. 7.

Modern Industry 13 (February 15, 1947): 115–116, 118. "How Unions Pack Punch into 'Sales Films.'"

Montgomery, David. "Labor and the Political Leadership of New Deal America." *International Review of Social History* 39 (December 1994): 335–360.

Moores, Shaun. "'The Box on the Dresser': Memories of Radio and Everyday Life." *Media Culture and Society* 10 (January 1988): 23–40.

Murphy, M. J. "TV: Newest Way to Get Your Story into the Home." *Factory Management and Maintenance* 110 (May 1952): 110–112.

Nader, Ralph. "Challenging the Corporate Ad." *Advertising Age* 54 (January 24, 1983): M12–M14.

National Association of Manufacturers. "We Use Films in Our Program." *Film News* 10 (March 1950): 6–7, 11.

National Geographic 96 (October 1949): 529–542. "Freedom Train Tours America."

New York Herald Tribune, 19 October 1936, pp. 1, 6. "Rebroadcast Demanded on Vandenberg's Radio 'Debate.'"

——— 16 January 1936, p. 16. "Republicans' Skit Put on Air by News Coup."

New York Sun, 19 October 1936, pp. 1, 15. "Air Ban on Vandenberg Linked to Deal with James Roosevelt."

New York Times, 19 October 1936, pp. 1, 3. "Ask Rebroadcast for Vandenberg."

——— 16 November 1933, p. 29. "Corporation History Stressed at Dinner."

——— 23 February 1934, pp. 1, 10. "Leaders Deny Science Cuts Jobs; Warn against 'Research Holiday.'"

——— 9 January 1933, pp. 1, 3. "Leaders Put Faith in the Machine Age to End Depression."

——— 14 January 1936, pp. 1, 17. "Radio Chains Bar Republican Skit but Party Gets Chicago Outlet."

——— 14 January 1936, pp. 1, 13. "Republicans Give New Air Skits Here."

——— 22 January 1936, pp. 1, 14. "Republicans Give New Air Skits Here."

——— 15 January 1936, pp. 1, 13. "Republican Skit Assails Spending."

——— 12 December 1934, p. 6. "Sloan Sees Doom of Regimentation."

——— 21 October 1936, p. 20. "Will Press Attack, Says Vandenberg."

New Yorker 17 (September 6, 1941): 12. "Elder Statesman."

Newsweek 4 (October 20, 1934): 29–30. "Luxury Motors Pay to Keep Harmony on the Air."

——— 67 (May 2, 1966): 84–86, 88. "What Americans Really Think of Business" and "The Disenchanted Campus."

——— 70 (July 17, 1967): 78–79. "Word Man."

Nord, David Paul. "An Economic Perspective on Formula in Popular Culture." *Journal of American Culture* 3 (spring 1980): 17–28.

O'Malley, Thomas. "'Every Important Work of Art Has a Message.'—Lawrence Langner." *Television Magazine* 11 (October 1954): 34–35, 68–69.

O'Toole, John E. "Advocacy Advertising Shows the Flag." *Public Relations Journal* 31 (November 1975): 14–16.

Owens, Patrick. "The President from G.E." *The Nation* 232 (January 31, 1981): 106–110.

Parkes, Holcombe. "Review Comment." *Business Screen* 10, no. 4 (1949): 22.

Parry, Duke. "Hear America First! 'Parade of States' a Musical Pageant and Salutation to All Sections." *Radio Digest* 27 (November 1931): 2

0–21, 89–90.

Pearlin, Leonard I., and Morris Rosenberg. "Propaganda Techniques in Institution Advertising." *Public Opinion Quarterly* 16 (spring 1952): 5–26.

Perkins, Daniel J. "The Sponsored Film: A New Dimension in American Film Research?" *Historical Journal of Film, Radio and Television* 2, no. 2 (1982): 133–140.

Perschbacher, Gerald. "Auto Makers in Radio." *Old Car News and Marketplace* (November 12, 1992): 9.

Pimlott, J. A. R. "Public Service Advertising: The Advertising Council." *Public Opinion Quarterly* 12 (summer 1948): 209–219.

Pinney, Harvey. "The Radio Pastor of Dearborn." *The Nation* 145 (October 9, 1937): 374–375.

Powell, Harford. "Tiger Man." *Advertising and Selling* (January 19, 1933): 22–23, 28.

Printers' Ink 168 (August 9, 1934): 53–54. "Ford Rhapsody."

Pryor, Thomas M. "Tomorrow's Propaganda." *New York Times*, 18 June 1939, sec. 9, p. 4.

Radio Digest 18 (October 1, 1926): 2. "Important Fall and Winter Features Are Backed by Leading Broadcasters."

——— 25 (August 1930): 62. "Salute to Cities Continue."

Radio Fan-Fare (combining *Radio Digest*) 30 (June 1933): 8–9, 50. "Will Roosevelt Rule by Radio?"

Raff, Daniel. "Making Cars and Making Money in the Interwar Period." *Business History Review* 65 (winter 1991): 721–753.

Railway Age 121 (December 28, 1946): 1073–1074. "How to Minimize Debate and Maximize Results in Public Relations."

Raucher, Alan. "Employee Relations at General Motors: The 'My Job' Contest.'" *Labor History* 28 (spring 1987): 221–232.

Review of Reviews 67 (June 1923): 643–647. "'The Covered Wagon,' Epic of the Oregon Trail."

Rhoads, William B. "Roadside Colonial: Early American Design for the Automobile Age, 1900–1940." *Winterthur Portfolio* 21 (summer/autumn 1986): 133–152.

Ribuffo, Leo P. "Jesus Christ as Business Statesman: Bruce Barton and the Selling of Corporate Capitalism." *American Quarterly* 33 (summer 1981): 206–231.

———. "Why Is There So Much Conservatism in the United States and Why Do So Few Historians Know Anything about It?" *American Historical Review* 99 (April 1994): 438–449.

Robinson, Claude E. "Recent Developments in the Straw-Poll Field." *Public Opinion Quarterly* 1 (July 1937): 45–56 and (October 1937): 42–52.

Romer, Samuel. "Profile of General Motors." *The Nation* 144 (January 23, 1937): 96–98.

Rorty, James. "Advertising and the Depression." *The Nation* 137 (December 20, 1935): 703–704.

Rosen, Jay. "Chatter from the Right." *The Progressive* 52 (March 1988): 26–28.

———. "Giving Them the Business." *Channels* 7 (February 1987): 16.

Rosenzweig, Roy. "'United Action Means Victory': Militant Americanism on Film." *Labor History* 24 (spring 1983): 274–288.

Ross, Irwin. "Public Relations Isn't Kid-Glove Stuff at Mobil." *Fortune* 94 (September 1976): 106–111, 196–202.

Ross, Steven J. "Struggles for the Screen: Workers, Radicals, and the Political Uses of Silent Film." *American Historical Review* 96 (April 1991): 333–367.

Rowland, Willard D., Jr. "Continuing Crisis in Public Broadcasting: A History of Disenfranchisement." *Journal of Broadcasting and Electronic Media* (summer 1986): 251–274.

Rudge, Fred. "Strike Advertising Shows Lack of Know–How." *Printers' Ink* 214 (February 1, 1946): 21–22, 83–84.

Rudolph, Frederick. "The American Liberty League, 1934–1940." *American Historical Review* 56 (October 1950): 19–33.

Sales Management 37 (October 10, 1935): 400. "How Ford Uses Films on a Year-Around Basis."

——— 37 (October 10, 1935): 388+. "Leading Sales Films of 1934–35 and the Results Attained."

——— 37 (October 10, 1935): 383–385. "Sales Films Continue to Gain New Users."

——— 35 (August 15, 1934): 146–148. "World's Fair Reveals New Strength of Films as Advertising Media."

Sales Meetings Magazine (July 1970): 70–73+. "The Man Who Put Business in Show Biz."

Saveth, Edward N. "What Historians Teach about Business." *Fortune* 45 (April 1952): 118–119, 165–174.

Scholastic 28 (February 1936): 6–8. "A Washington's Birthday Broadcast."

School and Society 46 (July 3, 1937): 12–13. "Dr. Angell as Educational Counselor of the National Broadcasting Company."

Schumann, David W., Jan M. Hathcote, and Susan West. "Corporate Advertising in America: A Review of Published Studies on Use, Measurement, and Effectiveness." *Journal of Advertising* 20 (September 1991): 35–56.

Seldes, George. "Barton, Barton, Barton and Barton." *New Republic* 96 (October 26, 1938): 327–329.

Sethi, S. Prakash. "Issue-Oriented Corporate Advertising: Tax Treatment of Expenditures." *California Management Review* 19 (fall 1976): 5–13.

Seymour, Bob. "Jamison Handy—Founder of Business Audiovisuals." *Business Screen* 32 (February 1971): 33–35 and (March 1971): 23–35.

———. "World's Fair Letter." *Business Screen* 2, no. 6 (1940): 10.

———. "World's Fair Letter." *Business Screen* 2, no. 7 (1940): 8.

Shugrue, J. Edward. "Freedom Is Everybody's Business." *Business Screen* 9 (February 1948): 18–19

Simms, L. Moody, Jr. "Folk Music in America: John Powell and the 'National Musical Idiom.'" *Journal of Popular Culture* 7 (winter 1973): 510–517.

Sinclair, Upton. "Mobilizing the Movies." *National EPIC News* 2, no. 13 (August 19, 1935): 1.

Skinner, George A. "A Businessman Looks at Visual Education." *Education* 53 (February 1933): 324–328.

Smith, Fred. "Keeping Up with the March of Time." *Radio Digest* 28 (May 1931): 24–26.

Smith, Julian. "Transports of Delight: The Image of the Automobile in Early Films." *Film and History* 11 (summer 1981): 59–67.

Sokal, Michael M. "The Origins of the Psychological Corporation." *Journal of the History of the Behavioral Sciences* 7 (1981): 54–67.

Spalding, John W. "1928: Radio Becomes a Mass Advertising Medium." *Journal of Broadcasting* 8 (winter 1963–1964): 31–44.

Spaulding, Frank E. "America's History Vitalized." *Journal of the National Education Association* 14 (June 1925): 175–179.

Sponsor (March 17, 1950): 24–25+. "Steel Melts the Public."

Starr, Mark. "How One Union Uses Films." *American Federationist* 58 (March 1951): 23–24.

Stott, William M. "Hard Times and Happy Days: The Visual Iconography of Depression America." In Robert Weible, ed., *Essays from the Lowell Conference on Industrial History, 1982 and 1983*. North Andover, MA: Museum of American Textile History, 1985.

Survey 71 (August 1935): 238. "Town Meetings on the Air."

Tedlow, Richard S. "The National Association of Manufacturers and Public Relations during the New Deal." *Business History Review* 50 (spring 1976): 25–45.

Tide 22 (April 30, 1948): 24–38. "The Freedom Train."

——— 19 (October 15, 1945): 124–128. "Theatre Guild Show."

Time 30 (July 5, 1937): 52. "Angell to NBC."

——— 27 (June 1, 1936): 27. "Democrats' St. Paul."

——— 27 (January 27, 1936): 20. "Republican Drama."

Toner, Robin. "Attention! All Sales Reps for the Contract with America!" *New York Times*, 5 February 1995, sec. E, p. 7.

Variety 118 (May 1, 1935): 30. "A.T.&T.'s Celebration."

——— 120 (October 16, 1935): 44. "Cavalcade of America."

——— 118 (May 1, 1935): 38. "Horse Sense Philosophy."

——— 118 (June 5, 1935): 34. "Town Hall of the Air."

Varney, Harold Lord. "Autopsy on the Republican Party." *American Mercury* 40 (January 1937): 1–12.

Vogel, David. "Why Businessmen Distrust Their State: The Political Consciousness of American Corporate Executives." *British Journal of Political Science* 8 (January 1978): 45–78.

Waldman, Diane. "'Toward a Harmony of Interests': Rockefeller, the YMCA and the Company Movie Theater." *Wide Angle* 8, no. 1 (n.d.): 41–51.

Weil, Richard. "Says Business to Mr. DeVoto. . . ." *Fortune* 43 (June 1951): 99–10, 186–193.

Weinberg, Sydney. "What to Tell America: The Writers' Quarrel in the Office of War Information." *Journal of American History* 55 (June 1968): 73–89.

Westinghouse Magazine (February 1930): 11. "Radio Salute."

Williams, Raymond. "The Magic System." *New Left Review* no. 4 (July–August 1960): 27–32.

Williams, Thomas. "NBC Cuts a Five Candle Cake." *Radio Digest* 28 (December 1931): 30, 89–90.

Wilson, Charles E., as told to Beverly Smith. "Can We Save Free Enterprise?" *American Magazine* 132 (November 1941): 36–37, 64–65.

Winfield, Betty Houchin. "F.D.R.'s Pictorial Image, Rules and Boundaries." *Journalism History* 5 (winter 1978–1979): 110–114, 136.

Wolfe, Alan. "The Rise of Logo America." *The Nation* 238 (May 26, 1984): 625, 640–643.

Wood, Richardson. "The Corporation Goes into Politics." *Harvard Business Review* 21 (autumn 1942): 60–70.

Yore, J. J. "Enhanced Underwriting: A Corporate Perspective." *Current* 5 (March 11, 1986): 12–13.

Young, John Orr . "Stop Shouting 'Free Enterprise' Unless You Give the Term Meaning." *Printers' Ink* 207 (May 5, 1944): 17–18, 88–92.

Encyclopedias, Guides, Filmographies, and Bibliographies

Applegate, Edd, ed. *The Ad Men and Women: A Biographical Dictionary of Advertising*. Westport, CT: Greenwood Press, 1994.

Balkansky, Arlene. "Through the Electronic Looking Glass: Television Programs in the Library of Congress." *Quarterly Journal of the Library of Congress* 37 (summer–fall 1980): 458–475.

Barnouw, Erik, ed., *International Encyclopedia of Communications*. New York: Oxford University Press, 1989.

Bray, Mayfield. *Guide to the Ford Collection in the National Archives*. Washington, DC: National Archives and Records Service, 1970.

Brooks, Tim, and Earle Marsh. *The Complete Directory to Prime Time Network TV Shows, 1946–Present*. New York: Ballantine Books, 1979.

Castleman, Harry, and Walter J. Podrazik. *The TV Schedule Book: Four Decades of Network Programming from Sign-On to Sign-Off*. New York: McGraw-Hill, 1984.

Culbert, David. "Television Archives." *Critical Studies in Mass Communications* 1 (March 1984): 88–92.

Cutlip, Scott M. *A Public Relations Bibliography*. Madison and Milwaukee: University of Wisconsin Press, 1965.

Daniel, Pete, ed. *America in the Depression Years: Photographs from the Farm Security Administration and the Office of War Information Collections, 1935–1943, Master Guide*. Laurel, MD: Instructional Resources Corporation, 1979.

Dunning, John. *On the Air: The Encyclopedia of Old-Time Radio*. New York: Oxford University Press, 1997.

———. *Tune in Yesterday: The Ultimate Encyclopedia of Old-Time Radio, 1925–1976*. Englewood Cliffs, NJ: Prentice-Hall, 1976.

Fielding, Raymond. *A Bibliography of Theses and Dissertations on the Subject of Film: 1916–1979*. University Film Association Monograph no. 3. Houston, TX: School of Communication, University of Houston, 1979.

Film Library Quarterly 12, no. 2/3 (1979). American Labor Films. Double issue.

General Electric Company Publicity Department. *Motion Picture Films*. Schenectady, NY: General Electric Company, 1926.

Gianakos, Larry James. *Television Drama Series Programming: A Comprehensive Chronicle, 1947–1959*. Metuchen, NJ: Scarecrow Press, 1980.

Heintze, James R., ed. *Scholar's Guide to Washington, D.C., for Audio Resources*. Washington, DC: Smithsonian Institution Press, 1985.

Iowa State University Library. *Index to the Film Holdings of the American Archives of the Factual Film*. Ames: Iowa State University Library, 1983.

Library of Congress. *Catalog of Copyright Entries Cumulative Series: Motion Pictures 1912–1939*. Washington, DC: Library of Congress, 1951.

———. *Motion Pictures 1940–1949*. Washington, DC: Library of Congress, 1953.

May, George S., ed. *Encyclopedia of American Business History and Biography: The Automobile Industry, 1920–1980*. New York: Bruccoli Clark Layman, Inc., and Facts on File, Inc., 1989.

Murphy, William. "World War II Propaganda Films (Essay and Filmography)." In Anthony Rhodes, *Propaganda, the Art of Persuasion: World War II*. New York: Chelsea House, 1976, pp. 291–304.

Museum of Broadcasting. *Subject Guide to the Radio and Television Collection of the Museum of Broadcasting*. 2nd ed. New York: Museum of Broadcasting, 1979.

Museum of Modern Art. *The Film Catalogue: A List of Film Holdings in the Museum of Modern Art*. Boston: G. K. Hall, 1985.

Newcomb, Horace, ed. *Encyclopedia of Television*. Chicago: Fitzroy Dearborn Publishers, 1997.

Niver, Kemp R. *Early Motion Pictures. The Paper Print Collection in the Library of Congress*. Washington, DC: Library of Congress, 1985.

Perkins, Daniel J. "The American Archives of the Factual Film." *Historical Journal of Film, Radio, and Television* 10, no. 1 (1990): 71–80.

Prelinger, Richard, ed. *Footage 91: North American Film and Video Sources*. New York: Prelinger Associates, 1991.

Prelinger, Richard, and Celeste R. Hoffnar, eds. *Footage 89: North American Film and Video Sources*. New York: Prelinger Associates, 1989.

Rose, Brian G. *TV Genres: A Handbook and Reference Guide*. Westport, CT: Greenwood Press, 1985.

Rouse, Sarah, and Katharine Loughney. *Three Decades of Television*. Washington, DC: Library of Congress, 1989.

Rowan, Bonnie G., ed. *Scholars' Guide to Washington, D.C., Film and Video Collections*. Washington, DC: Smithsonian Institution Press, 1980.

Rowan, Bonnie G., and Cynthia G. Wood, eds. *Scholars' Guide to Washington, D.C., Media Collections*. Washington, DC: Woodrow Wilson Center Press; Baltimore: Johns Hopkins University Press, 1994.

Schatz, Thomas. "Film Archives." *Critical Studies in Mass Communications* 1 (March 1984): 83–88.

Smart, James R. *Radio Broadcasts in the Library of Congress, 1924–1941: A Catalog of Recordings*. Washington, DC: Library of Congress, 1982.

State Historical Society of Wisconsin. *Sources for Mass Communications, Film and Theater Research: A Guide*. Madison: State Historical Society of Wisconsin, 1982.

Summers, Harrison B. *A Thirty-Year History of Programs Carried on National Radio Networks in the United States, 1926–1956*. New York: Arno Press, 1971.

University of California–Los Angeles, Department of Theater Arts. *ATAS/UCLA Television Archives Catalog. Holdings in the Study Collection of the Academy of Television Arts and Sciences/University of California, Los Angeles Television Archives*. Pleasantville, NY: Redgrave Publishing Co., 1981.

Wid's Yearbook, 1920–21. "Important Industrial Films," pp. 167–177.

Advertisements

E. I. du Pont de Nemours and Company, Inc. "For Bill Demby, the Difference Means Getting Another Shot." *The Business World. The New York Times Magazine,* 11 June 1989, p. 5.

———. "It Started One Saturday Night." *Saturday Evening Post* 208 (October 5, 1935): 51.

Electrical Research Products, Inc. "Makes Personal Appearance in 10 Cities at Once." *Time* 15 (June 16, 1930): 65.

General Electric Company. "'Look, Pop! It's a Homer!'" *The Forum and Century* 102 (September 1939): overleaf.

———. "What Is Television?" *The Forum and Century* 101 (February 1939): overleaf.

General Motors. "General Motors Has Found a Way to Keep People in Their Seats without Using Seat Belts," *New York Times Magazine,* 7 January 1990, p. 21.

———. "The New General Motors Radio Program 'The Parade of the States.'" *Radio Digest* 28 (December 1931): 9.

J. Walter Thompson Company. "Pioneering in a New Audience of 85 Million." *Business Screen* 2, no. 6 (1940): 39.

Jam Handy Organization. "Human Steel." *Business Screen* 9, no. 6 (1948): back cover.

Modern Talking Picture Service, Inc. "A Report of Showings, Audiences and Total Costs of the Commercial Sound Motion Picture 'The Middleton Family' Prepared for Westinghouse Electrical & Mfg. Co. and Fuller & Smith & Ross Inc." *Business Screen* 3, no. 4 (1941): 18–19.

Pathe News, Inc. "Even Salesmanship Now Comes in Cans!" *Business Screen* 1, no. 2 (1938): 10.

Roland Reed Productions. "Reviewed Like A Hollywood 4 Star Feature." *Business Screen* 1, no. 1 (1938): 57.

Standard Oil Company of New York. "Come to New England! See Where History Was Made." *Saturday Evening Post* 200 (April 21, 1928): 120–121.

——— "Come to New England This Summer and See the Workshop of the Nation." *Saturday Evening Post* 200 (June 2, 1928): 106–107.

———. "Romance Calls You to the Genessee Country in Central New York: Explore the Land of Lore and Legend." *Saturday Evening Post* 200 (April 28, 1928): 171.

Westinghouse Electrical & Manufacturing. "Putting the Romance of Industry on the Air." *Radio Digest* 27 (June 1931): 3.

Dissertations and Theses

Banks, Mark James. "A History of Broadcast Audience Research in the United States, 1920–1980, with an Emphasis on the Rating Services." Ph.D., University of Tennessee, 1981.

Boddy, William Francis. "From the 'Golden Age' to the 'Vast Wasteland': The Struggles over Market Power and Dramatic Formats in 1950s Television." Ph.D., New York University, 1984.

Carlat, Louis E. "Sound Values: Radio Broadcasts of Classical Music and American Culture, 1922–1939." Ph.D., Johns Hopkins University, 1995.

Diskin, Marvin Newton. "A Descriptive and Historical Analysis of the Live Television Anthology Drama Program, The United States Steel Hour, 1953–1963." Ph.D., University of Michigan, 1963.

Jones, David. "The U.S. Office of War Information and Public Opinion during World War II, 1939–1945." Ph.D., State University of New York–Binghampton, 1976.

Jordan, John Matthew. "Technic and Ideology: The Engineering Ideal and American Political Culture, 1892–1934." Ph.D., University of Michigan, 1989.

Langston, Billie Joe. "A Historical Study of the UAW Television Program 'Telescope.'" Ph.D., University of Michigan, 1969.

Lopata, Roy Haywood. "John J. Raskob: A Conservative Businessman in the Age of Roosevelt." Ph.D., University of Delaware, 1975.

Mann, James G. "Engineer of Mass Education: Lenox R. Lohr and the Celebration of American Science and Industry." Ph.D., Rutgers University, 1988.

Mashon, Kenneth Michael. "NBC, J. Walter Thompson, and the Evolution of Prime-Time Television Programming and Sponsorship, 1946–1958." Ph.D., University of Maryland at College Park, 1996.

Mayerle, Judine. "The Development of the Television Variety Show as a Major Program Genre at the National Broadcasting Company, 1946–1956." Ph.D., Northwestern University, 1983.

McGinnis, John Vianney. "The Advertising Council and the Cold War." Ph.D., Syracuse University, 1991.

Nowlin, Eric Guy. "A Survey of the Development of the Business and Industrial Film." Ph.D., Northwestern University, 1976.

Rumm, John C. "Mutual Interests: Managers and Workers at the DuPont Company, 1802–1915." Ph.D., University of Delaware, 1989.

Schultz, Debra Lauren. "A History of the Television Interview Program in Network Broadcasting in the United States." Ph.D., New York University, 1985.

Shaw, Myron Berkley. "A Descriptive Analysis of the Documentary Television Program, the 'Armstrong Circle Theatre,' 1955–1961." Ph.D., University of Michigan, 1962.

Smith, David Dion. "The Jam Handy Organization and the Discussional Filmstrip." M.A., Wayne State University, 1975.

Stanton, Michael Joseph. "A History of the Research and Planning Department of the National Broadcasting Company, Incorporated (1931 to 1976)." Ph.D., Bowling Green State University, 1977.

Stewart, Robert Hammel. "The Development of Network Television Program Types to January 1953." Ph.D., Ohio State University, 1954.

Multimedia

Prelinger, Richard. *Our Secret Century: Archival Films from the Darker Side of the American Dream*, vols. 1–10. Irvington, NY: The Voyager Company, 1996 [CD-ROM].

Prelinger, Richard, and Robert Stein, producers. *To New Horizons: Ephemeral Films, 1931–1945*. Los Angeles: Voyager Press, 1989 [Laserdisc].

———. *You Can't Get There from Here: Ephemeral Films, 1946–1960*. Los Angeles: Voyager Press, 1988 [Laserdisc].

Albert in Blunderland (1950)
Loew's Inc. presented by MGM. Animated cartoon. Revised in 1961. Script (copyright deposit file LP 347). Print: sd technicolor 35 mm (print FEA 20). Sutherland collection, Library of Congress (hereafter LC).

All-American Soap Box Derby (1936)
Jam Handy Picture Service. Print: sd bw 16 mm. Prelinger Associates, New York (hereafter PA).

America and Sons, Unlimited (1948)
Chamber of Commerce of the United States. Critically review ed in "America and Sons, Strictly Limited," *Business Screen* 9, no. 4 (1948): 2. No copyright deposit. Print: American Archives of the Factual Film, Iowa State University, Ames, IA (hereafter AAFF).

American Portrait (ca. 1936)
Wilding Picture Productions, Inc., for the Institute of Life Insurance (n.d.). Director: Wallace Fox, story: John Eugene Hasty; starring Alan Ladd. The story of the progress of the life insurance industry, told through "Sam Smith" (Alan Ladd). Print: 42 min sd bw 16 mm (FBB 0844), LC.

The American Road (1953)
Ford Motor Co. The history and progress of automobile transportation in America, touching upon the contributions of Ford workers. Prints: PA; AAFF; (EL MP16-227) Dwight D. Eisenhower Library; (FC 4906) LC.

BBDO Presents 1954 DuPont Convention (1954)
Presentation by BBDO. Highlights the contributions made by BBDO to the DuPont Company's growth and the marketing of its products, as told in case histories of "packages to Wilmington"—BBDO ad proofs, films, and television commercials. Concludes with cameos of BBDO's DuPont account executives, and a testimonial to the close teamwork of agency and client. Print: sd color, Victoria Schuck Collection (16 RNC: 30), John F. Kennedy Library, Boston, MA.

Back to the Farm (1915)
Gaumont Co. for General Electric. Shot sequence (copyright deposit file LP 4302). Print: si bw, Museum of Modern Art (hereafter MoMA); (ca. 529) State Historical Society of Wisconsin (hereafter SHSW).

Behind Your Radio Dial (1949)
RKO Pathé for National Broadcasting Company. Pictures network sustaining programs and listener research activities. No copyright deposit file. Print: sd bw MoMA; (CA 259) SHSW.

The Benefactor (1918)
General Electric. No copyright deposit file. Print: sd bw MoMA.

Big Enterprise in the Competitive System (1954)
Brookings Institution. "Objective: To explain the economic background of big business. Treatment: Direct recording to establish Dr. Caplan using his voice-over to explain charts and animation describing the role of big business in the competitive system" (copyright deposit file MU 5631). Print: 4 reels sd Kodachrome, AAFF.

The Birthright (1954)
Parthenon Pictures, Viking Production Companies, for Chrysler Corporation. Print: 40 min sd color (16-0010), AAFF.

Caravan (1939)
Sound Masters and the members of the Parade of Progress for General Motors Department of Public Relations. Story, Wilford L. Nos; photography: Richard B. Smith; narrator, James F. Clemenger. "Millions of people visited the great world expositions of the past few years. Yet there were many more millions who were unable to make the journey to distant cities, and so they missed seeing the wonders of science and industry on display. So that all of us might realize the constant progress of science, Charles F. Kettering, General Motors vice president in charge of research, conceived the idea of an exposition on wheels, to transport the world of tomorrow to the very doorstep of the people of North America. Huge streamlined trucks were constructed. . . ." No copyright deposit. Print: 9 min sd bw, General Motors Film Library.

Cavalcade of America: "The Man Who Took a Chance" (10/29/52)
Screen Gems. Story of Eli Whitney's theory of serial production applied to muskets for the U.S. Army. The closing story of chemistry contrasts the spinning wheel with modern textile and dye making. (annotated script, copyright deposit file LP 3969). Print: sd bw 16 mm (FCA 0750), LC.

Close Harmony (1942)
Jam Handy. A photoplay "with a barber shop setting," in which "one of the customers successfully answers the questions of the other customers and the employees of the shop in regard to the conversion of American factories from peacetime to war production. He convinces the others that industry is doing a good job in the manufacture of military equipment." (copyright deposit file MU 13199). Print: sd bw, PA.

The Crime of Carelessness (1912)
Made by Thomas A. Edison in cooperation with the National Association of Manufacturers. By James Oppenheim. Released Dec. 30, 1912. An industrial safety film stressing the necessity for following safety instructions posted in factories. Smoking causes a damaging fire, bringing tragedy to two young people who were in love and planned to be married. "The splendid success which greeted 'The Workman's Lesson' which the Edison Company made in conjunction with the National Association of Manufacturers last Spring is sufficient guarantee of the worth of 'The Crime of Carelessness' which we are releasing under the same conditions" (*Kinetogram* [Dec. 15, 1912]: 15; copy in copyright deposit file LP 214, LC). Print: si bw 16 mm (FBA 195), LC.

Curiosity Shop (1948)
Alcoa's follow-up to *Unfinished Rainbows*. Director: Jean Yarborough. Screenplay: Leo S. Rosencrans. Cast: John Litel, Richard Hogan, June Lockhart. Reviewed in *Business Screen* 9, no. 3 (1948): 24–25. No copyright deposit. Print: sd color, AAFF.

The Dawn of Better Living (1945)
Walt Disney Productions for Westinghouse Electric Corp. Animated cartoon. Describes the need for more circuits in new homes with more appliances. Script (copyright deposit file MU 15998). Print: 17 min sd color 16 mm two copies (FBA 294/295), LC.

Doctor in Industry (1946)
Jam Handy for General Motors Employee Relations. Director, Haford Kerbawy; production supervisor, Esther Schrodel; scenario, Gordon H. Miller. Cast: Kenneth Randall, William Post, Jr.; Martha Randall, Nell O'Day; John Randall, Frank Thomas; Sgt. Brown, Thomas Hume; Sidney Duncan, Walter Greaza; Sam Gregg, Duke York. "The personification of those who saw the need for the advancement of industrial medicine." "The picture is climaxed with a pictorial review of the industrial medicine facilities, policies and practices as they exist throughout the divisions of the General Motors Corporation today" (copyright deposit file MU 496). Reviewed in *Business Screen* 7, no. 7 (1946): 25, and 8, no. 8 (1947): 29. Print: 5 reels sd bw, PA.

The DuPont Story (1951)
Jack Chertok, producer. Print: sd color, AAFF.

DuPont Theater: "The Man from St. Paul" (1/29/57)
Juvenile problem story starring Michael Landon. Features a "Story of Chemistry" commercial about the enterprising activities of Junior Achievement youth who sell Christmas corsages door to door and later custom-made yard markers—taking orders, controlling production, managing sales, and making a neat profit and dividend for stockholders—and return value to the people in their community who invested in the business. The JA youth overcome the same problems that DuPont encounters on a larger scale. Print: sd bw 16 mm (FCA 0741–0742), LC.

DuPont Theater: "The Man Who Asked No Favors" (3/5/57)
Hawthorne Productions, Inc. With Lew Ayers. The story of the discovery of an immunization for smallpox. The commercial points out that the country needs big leaguers and little leaguers, just like big and little business, and teamwork between the two. Print: 1 reel sd bw 16 mm (FCA 749), LC.

Electric Showcase: "World's Fair Entertainment Spectacular" (1965)
"Hosts Gordon and Sheila MacRae introduce performances at the 1965 World's Fair in New York City. . . . Includes commercials for Investor Owned Electric Light and Power Companies" (catalog card). Print: 2 reels sd bw 16 mm (DC 636–637). Gilbert Cates Collection, SHSW.

Electric Theatre: "Bundle at Wells Fargo" (3/23/52)
Screen Associates. A Screen Televideo Release. Produced by Gil Ralston. Minute animated spot on the expert management of local electric power and light businessmen and employees. Middle commercial opens on a portrait of Lenin, intoning, "His name was Vladimir Lenin. . . . [Soviet leaders have said], 'we must force the U.S. to spend itself into destruction'—and now to defend ourselves this nation is forced to spend and spend for defense—but not into destruction—not if we guard against wasteful and unnecessary government spending. For example, some groups in the government actually want to spend billions of dollars on needless federal power electric projects—many of these would only duplicate plants and lines already planned by America's business managed electric companies." A closing commercial asks, "What does electricity do for you?" Sponsored by "your business managed electric company. . . . Business management serves you best" (copyright deposit file LP 1665). Print: sd bw (FCA 0173), LC.

1104 Sutton Road (1958)
Wilding Picture Productions for Champion Paper and Fibre Company. "An industrial 'self-improvement' film which tells the story of Adam [Hathaway], a dissatisfied factory worker. Through the intervention of a magical alter-ego, he becomes foreman, then president of the company. His dissatisfaction follows him until he realizes: 'no matter what your station in life, if you want cooperation, affection, guidance or skill, you must produce it through your attitudes and working habits.' Panel discussion follows . . . led by one of the actors in the film" (catalog card). Print: sd color 16 mm (FE 255), SHSW, AAFF.

Ford People (1956)
Raphael G. Wolff Studios for Ford Motor Co. Kodachrome. "Discusses the role of automation in the automotive industry and the constant search for better products and improved techniques" (LC catalog card). Presents the modern automobile as a "living room on wheels"; dramatizes the American idea of continuous

progress, represented by a concept car, which in actuality later became the "Batmobile." Print: 22 min sd color 16 mm (FCA 481), LC.

Ford Theater: "First Born" (9/10/53)
Starring Ronald Reagan and Nancy Davis. Tape (T78:0046), Museum of Television and Radio, New York.

From Dawn to Sunset (1937)
Jam Handy for Chevrolet Motor Division, General Motors Sales Corp. "When morning comes to America thousands of men and women go to their work in the factories and offices of the automotive industry. They work, building the modern motorcar. On payday they crowd the stores and shops to buy with their pay checks the things that they need and want. At close of day they are home again with time for their home life, for play, and for rest. Picture, narration, and music tell the story of the daily history of the men and women who staff the factories and offices of the automotive industry." Synopsis (copyright deposit file MU 7768), LC; print: PA.

General Electric Theater: "The Town with a Past" (1957)
Revue Productions, Inc. 10 Feb 1957. With James Stewart. Commercial breaks mark the first anniversary of the electric utilities' "Live Better Electrically" program and "National Electric Week." Commercial opens on Nancy Reagan in her home's utility room as she moves to her "favorite room—the kitchen," where she is joined by Ronald Reagan, who suggests, "when you live better electrically, you lead a richer, fuller, more satisfying life. And it's something all of us in this modern age can have." Print: 27 min sd bw 16 mm (FCA 511), LC.

General Motors Institute (1944)
Jam Handy Organization for General Motors Corp. "A dramatized story of a boy who gets his training at General Motors Institute. The picture opens with the historical background of the training school" (copyright deposit file MU 15862). Print: 27 min sd bw 16 mm (FCA 512), LC.

The Great Swindle (1948)
Union Films. Director: Carl Marzani. "Harassed by shortages, Tom Grey votes for the removal of price controls after reading NAM propaganda. When prices rise, he views a union film, 'The Big Squeeze,' which places the blame for high prices on monopoly control of our economy, and points out the advantages of membership in the union." *Business Screen* 9, no. 4 (1948): 21–22. Synopsis (copyright deposit file LP 1690). Print: 36 min sd bw, PA.

The Honeymoon V-8 (1935)
Audio Productions, Inc., for Ford Motor Co. "'Honeymoon V-8' shows the trend in industrial movies to the Hollywood style of presentation. It makes use of a love story and contains a minimum of direct selling." A general advertising film for the 1935 Ford, shown by Ford dealers who arrange presentations in their showrooms (*Sales Management* 37 [October 10, 1935]: 394). Print: sd bw 35 mm (200FC 4406 and 4407), National Archives at College Park (hereafter NACP).

Industry on Parade (syndicated television series, 1950–)
Producer: George W. Johnstone. NAM file, "Fact Sheet," October 15, 1955, Motion Picture Broadcasting, and Recorded Sound Division, LC.

Inside Cackle Corners (1951)
Produced by John Sutherland Productions for Harding College. Animation. Cartoon characters invest their profits in research to develop machines and tools to turn out a new and better toaster (copyright deposit file MP 1497). Print: 9 min sd color 16 mm (FEA 1346), LC.

It's Everybody's Business (1954)
John Sutherland Productions for Chamber of Commerce of the U.S.A., in cooperation with E. I. du Pont de Nemours. Animation. "Explains that our business system, built on freedoms guaranteed by the Constitution, has enabled America to have a high standard of living" (LC catalog card). The theme, "freedom to go into business," is dramatized in the setting of the colonial economy, focusing on a hatter, who goes into business with investors, employees, taxes, competition, customers. Cut to the present, where wartime economic controls have been removed in peacetime, and business is beset with runaway taxation and waves of destructive forces (copyright deposit file LP 4670). Print: 22 min sd color 16 mm (FEA 667–668), LC.

It's Only the Beginning (1952)
John Sutherland Productions, Inc. Live action and animation. A modern story of young "Daniel Boone Smith." A discourse upon the democratic values of widespread stock ownership among six million small shareholders; explorers in research, creating new jobs and business in transportation, communication, entertainment, food, health, and shelter. Print: sd color 16 mm (FAA 4121), LC.

Joe Turner, American (1950)
Apex Film Corp. for the NAM. Producer, Jack Chertok; director, Sammy Lee; story and production, Holcombe Parkes. Cast: Don Beddoe, Robert Shayne, Douglas Dumbrille, Morris Ankrum, Art Baker. "A dramatization of the experience of a small-town businessman who is jolted from his antipathy toward politics by the death of his grandson from a contaminated city water supply" (LC catalog card). (copyright deposit file LP 218). Print: 27 min sd bw 16 mm (FCA 653), LC.

Key to Our Horizon (1953)
Jam Handy for General Motors. Opens with a filmic comparison between a street scene captured by da-

guerreotype and later by film. It infers that social benefits accrued from the advent of the motorcar and our individual system of transportation. File not located (MU 5500). Print: sd bw, PA.

Leave It to Roll-Oh (1940)
Jam Handy Picture Service for General Motors. "This picture opens on an imaginary scene in a home showing what life might be like if we had mechanical men as servants. Roll-oh, the chromium-plated butler, is a domestic paragon with vacuum cleaner feet, and many other useful attachments. Though robots in human form are still to come, the picture explains, even now we do have many small mechnical servants to make work easier for us—automatic toasters, door openers, safety devices and industrial machines. In our motorcars, for example. . . ." (copyright deposit file LU 9603). Print: sd bw, PA.

A Letter from America (1949)
Sponsored by Goodyear. Reviewed in "Time to Show the Facts," *Business Screen* 10, no. 2 (1949): 21–22. No copyright deposit. Print: (12-0053) 31 min sd bw, AAFF.

Letter to a Pilot (1950)
RKO Pathé. Director: Harry W. Smith. A detailed explanation of the operation of Trans World Airlines via a background story of a TWA pilot who answers a fan letter from a passenger. Short scenes of a pilot's family life. Print: 1 reel sd bw 16 mm (DC 410). Kleinerman Collection, SHSW.

Letter to a Rebel (1948)
RKO Pathé. "This Is America," no. 9. Produced by Jay Bonafield. "Free enterprise and the capitalistic system are defended by a smalltown newspaper editor in a letter to his son, a college student who fancies himself a rebel against the established order" (copyright file MP 3189; a revised, updated version for 1950–51 copyright MP 895). *Business Screen*'s recommendation to the U.S. Chamber of Commerce; see "What Can Be Done: 'Letter to a Rebel' Points the Way," *Business Screen* 9, no. 4 (1948): 22. Print: 17 min sd bw (FEA 740–741), LC.

The Lone Ranger's Triumph (1949)
Apex Film Corp. Based on the radio script "Frontier Town," by Frank Striker. Producer, Jack Chertok; director and author of screenplay, George B. Steitz, Jr.; editor, Alex Hubert (copyright deposit file LP 184). Print: sd bw 16 mm (FCA 720), LC.

Louisiana Story (1948)
Robert Flaherty Productions, Inc., for Standard Oil [New Jersey]. "Filmed in the Petit Anse bayou country of southern Louisiana, this documentary dramatization of the simple life of the Cajuns shows, from the point of view of a small boy, the natives' wonderment at the mechanical wizardry of an oil company's floating derrick" (copyright deposit file LP 2093). Print: 2 reels sd bw 16 mm reference print (FCA 9545–9546), LC.

Magic in the Air (1942)
Jam Handy for Chevrolet. "Explains the basic principles of television. Beginning with scenes taken in the television studios at Radio City, the construction of the iconoscope is shown and its theory of operation is explained. . . . Then using an automobile as an illustration, the part motion pictures play in television programs is demonstrated" (copyright deposit file MU 12054). Print: sd bw, PA.

The Man He Might Have Been (1913)
Thomas A. Edison in cooperation with the NAM. "A man who was forced by his father to go to work when he was a boy reflects on what his life could have been if he had been able to continue his education" (LC catalog card). Same cast as *The Crime of Carelessness*. Print: 25 min si bw 16 mm (FBA 1041), LC .

March of Time: "Public Relations—This Means You" (1948)
Vol. 14, issue 4. "This March of Time Forum Edition film brings to the public eye, often for the first time, many of the leaders in this newest profession and highlights some of its history—how it began and where it stands today" (copyright deposit files MP 3284 and MP 26046): Albin Dearing's promotion of Aspen, CO; Bernays, Ivy Lee, the National Safety Council; W. A. Irvin of Big Steel; the NAM in 1947; convention of PR executives; shots of children touring the Freedom Train. Fourth National Conference of Public Relations Executives (1947). The narrrator relates: "We've got to do a job. A job of selling our way of life to our kind of people. A job of keeping freedom alive in this world, so men may continue to hope, and to dream." On the Freedom Train: "Under democracy public responsibility and a well informed public opinion are basic safeguards of the hope for a brighter tomorrow." Print: sd color and bw 16 mm (FBA 3102), LC.

Men and Machines (1947)
20th Century–Fox Film Corp. for the NAM. Part of Fox Movietone series, "The World Today," produced by Edmund Reek. "In the end you have something to do your work in less time, for less money; you have something that makes your job easier, and gives you greater freedom; something to build a new kind of world" (script, copyright deposit file MP 3155). Uses out-takes of 20th Century-Fox features, along with documentary footage. Scenes from *General Motors Institute*. Print: 2 reels bw sd positive 16 mm (FBA 9102), LC. Apparently a remake of the 1937 version.

Men Make Steel, Technicolor Prologue (1940)
Jim Handy Organization for United States Steel. "A newly married couple . . . recognizes that U.S. Steel labels stand for highest quality. The picture ends with a display of U.S. Steel labels, which serves as a transition splice to the story behind the labels—Men Make Steel" (copyright deposit file MU 10685), LC. Print: sd color 35 mm, UCLA Film and Television Archives, Los Angeles, CA.

The Middleton Family at the World's Fair (1939)
Westinghouse. Director and screenplay, Robert R. Snoddy; from a story by G. R. Hunter and Reed Drummond. Cast: Harry Shannon, Marjorie Lord, Douglas Stark, George J. Lewis, Adora Andrews, James Lydon, Ruth Lee, Georgette Harvey. Originally entitled *Fair Weather*. (Script, Westinghouse History Center, Pittsburgh.) No copyright deposit. Print: sd color, Petrified Films, New York.

Millions of Us (1936)
American Labor Productions. "A down-and-out worker's dramatic resistance to the temptation of strike-breaking in the depression of the 30's. . . . Solidarity as the key ingredient in morale-building" (ILGWU catalog). "'Millions of Us,' the first out-and-out propaganda film, is in behalf of organized labor. It was shown amid considerable stealth the other day in a projection room far removed from Hollywood's traveled paths. It was admitted that the names on the screen were fictitious and the financial sponsors were shielded in mystery. It is known, however, that a number of liberal directors, writers and players provided the money and aided in its manufacture." Douglas W. Churchill, "A Stealthy Tread in Hollywood," *New York Times*, 23 August 1936, sec. 9, p. 3. "We want a man sized hunk of everything our hands made. And just think, buddy—that's the whole cockeyed country." No copyright deposit. Print: 20 min sd bw 16 mm (FAA 158), LC.

National Cash Register Company (ca. 1921)
An untitled short picturing safety features of NCR plants, NCR employee activities, and the amenities of NCR employment. Scenes include the employee lunchroom, which seats women, then men; a visit to the company "schoolhouse"; the company suggestion box; a demonstration of guards on flywheels and other safety cages; a tour of the Dayton community's swimming pools, baseball diamonds, and picnicking families. The film concludes with an NCR sales convention. On stage are represented "abnormal conditions," "high prices, large profits, shortage of help." A man operates a lever mechanism, entitled "readjustment period." A bridge appears, emblazoned: "new improvements, long line, service . . . thorough approach, better window displays, better repair department." In the keystone of the bridge arch is the motto, "I Will Not Fail." The audience, presumably comprised of NCR salesmen, rushes onto the stage, flags waving, and takes the bridge. Print: si bw 16 mm, PA.

On to Jupiter (1939)
Soundmasters, Inc., for General Motors Department of Public Relations. Inspired by C. F. Kettering. This film was likely produced for exhibition at the GM auditorium of the corporation's New York World's Fair exhibit. Opens with a pan to an office high atop Rockefeller Center, where a group of business executives are discussing prospects for future progress. One of the group remains unconvinced. After his guests depart, he is visited by a vision—the personification of "Change," portrayed as a young man in a business suit. Change takes the willing executive through the "doubt" that greeted Eli Whitney; the radiofacsimile machine; the discoveries of Louis Pasteur; and Kettering's automobile self-starter. Convinced of the possibilities for future progress, based upon the record of the past, the executive tenders his "sword." Change, in the same spirit, returns the sword and takes the executive on a tour of the future, climaxing with a visit to General Motors' World's Fair Futurama. "One day perhaps we may hear—On to Jupiter!" No copyright deposit. Print: 20 min sd bw, General Motors Film Library.

The Open Door (1945)
Subtitled: "The Story of Foreman Jim Baxter, His Family and His Job." Jam Handy for General Motors. Director, Haford Kerbawy; production supervisor, Esther Schrodel; scenario, Gordon H Miller. Cast: Jim Baxter, William Post, Jr.; Ruth Baxter, Betty Kelley; Monte, George Mathews; Vance, Harvey Stephens; Marshall, Loring Smith; Taylor, Kirk Brown. "Intended primarily for General Motors foremen. The picture is designed to prove beyond any doubt that a foreman in General Motors is on the management staff" (synopsis, copyright deposit file MU 16571). Reviewed in *Business Screen* 7, no. 6 (1946): 16, and 8, no. 8 (1947): 29. Print: 5 reels sd bw, PA.

Our American Heritage (1947)
RKO for the American Heritage Foundation's "National Rededication Week." Producer: Dore Schary. No copyright deposit. Prints: sd bw (FPB 0036 neg., FPB 0037 neg. track), LC; NACP.

Our Union— Local 91 (1950)
Promotional Films Co. The story of Local 91 of the International Ladies Garment Workers Union. "First of all, the union is a bread and butter question. The union is the answer to many questions that arise in the shop. The size of the pay envelope—out of which will come rent and the grocery bill, and milk for the kids. And maybe a movie on Sunday." Gift of the AFL-CIO Film Div. No copyright deposit. Print: 1 reel sd color 16 mm (FBB 1655), LC.

People, Products, and Progress: 1975 (1955)
Chamber of Commerce of the United States, made by Creative Arts Studios. "Describes possible living conditions in the United States in 1975" (LC catalog card). Opens with businessman-narrator seated at a desk with a "crystal ball" provided by industry. Expresses confidence in the future provided "we" keep the current economic system. Examples of future progress, seen in animated sequences, include a farm, food store, a home, gas industry, cement industry, a city of the future, steel industry, and an atomic-powered automobile (copyright deposit file MP 5673). Print: 28 min sd Anscocolor 16 mm (FCA 990), LC.

Politics and the Rigged Tax System (ca. 1957)
AFL and CIO Committee on Political Education. The film dollies in on a still photo of Daniel Chester French's sculpture of Abraham Lincoln, accompanied by "The Battle Hymn of the Republic." "Politics of, by and for

the people, brought to you by the members of organized labor who work and live in your community." Narrator/host narrates: "Hello there. This is the fifth of a series of programs whose purpose is to stimulate increased interest and political activity on the part of people who work for a living. Interest in politics. Interest in active citizenship. Earlier programs have pointed out that business, especially big business, has always been active and highly influential in American politics in pursuit of its own special interests. It's been demonstrated that historically, as at the present moment, the objectives of organized labor in our political life have been goals common to nearly all people." Print: 14 min sd bw 16 mm Kinescope (RG 200 AFL-CIO 6), NACP.

The Price of Freedom (1949)
Apex Film Corp. for the NAM. Producer, Jack Chertok; director, William Thiele; co-authors, David P. Sheppard and Thomas M. Wolff. Cast: Arthur Franz, Ray Collins, Michael Chekhov, Will Wright. "A dramatization of the awakening of a young newspaperman to the newspaper's social responsibility and to the dangers threatening American democracy" (LC catalog card). Script (copyright deposit file MP 4393). Print: 23 min sd bw 16 mm (FBA 1289), LC.

Productivity—Key to Plenty (1949)
Encyclopedia Britannica Films in collaboration with J. Frederic Dewhurst, the Twentieth Century Fund. "A topic of great current importance to every thinking person. Its theme is American production—how we in America have achieved a capacity to produce coupled with a standard of living unequalled anywhere else in the world." Script, continuity, and user guide (copyright deposit file MP 3990). Print: 2 reels 21 min sd bw 16 mm (FBA 1300), LC.

Progress Report—1943 (1943)
Jam Handy for GMC Public Relations, "to show the press of America, General Motors' progress in its war work" (copyright deposit file MU 14230). Print: sd bw 16 mm, PA.

Public Opinion (1946)
EB Films with Harold Lasswell. The film shows public opinion specialists plotting the number of times newspapers mention issues related to the floating of bonds for a new town water plant. It describes the American election as an opinion census, the widest measure of public opinion, and thus points out the need for competent witnesses and expert opinions (script, copyright deposit file MP 1383). Print: 11 min sd bw 16 mm (FAA 4486/4487), LC.

Public Opinion Polls (1947)
United Productions of America. The film "shows how public opinion polls are an attempt to determine broad trends of public thought. . . . Concludes with examples showing how the poll, properly used, can serve as a guide for action in a speeded up world" (copyright deposit file MP 2012). Print: 10 min sd bw animation 35 mm (FEA 1703), LC.

The Quarterback (1950)
Apex Film Corporation for the NAM. Producer, Jack Chertok; director, Sammy Lee; screenplay, David T. Sheppard; adviser, Holcombe Parks. Cast: Robert Sterling, Frank Conroy, Gail Davis, John Kellogg, Tom Harmon. "A college football hero who has become a real estate salesman learns through experience that success in life, as in studies and sports, depends on effort and planning, not on glamour and reputation alone" (LC catalog card). Copyright deposit MP 64. Print: 29 min sd bw 16 mm (FCA 1069), LC.

'Round & 'Round (1938)
Jam Handy for General Motors Department of Public Relations. "A half-reel picture done in special technique of dolls in motion. The scene of the picture is Widget-land. Against this background a major point in economics is explained" (copyright deposit file MU 9311). Print: sd bw 35 mm, PA.

Scenes from the NYWF for 1940 (1940)
Similar to *Scenes from the World of Tomorrow*. Apparently updated for 1940 exhibition. Changes include a new Ford Theater program likening women's fashions to automobiles, and a brief glimpse of a screening of *Symphony in "F."* Print: sd bw 35 mm, tape (200 FC-4319), NACP.

Scenes from the World of Tomorrow (1940)
Ford Motor Company. Print: sd bw 35 mm, tape (200 FC-4451), NACP.

Science in Business (1945)
Produced by the *March of Time* for the Association of National Advertisers. Print: (NARS Signal Corps 111 EF 221.1 and .2), tape, NACP.

Selling America (1939)
Jam Handy for GMC Dept. Public Relations. For training in automotive sales, service, and public relations. "Mr. Paul W. Garrett's *Public Relations: Industry's No. 1 Job* is shown to Ben Franklin. He reads a few sentences and then tells the service manager and the salesman that public relations—really personal relations grown up—are most important in modern business" (copyright deposit file LU 8657). Reviewed in "America's First Salesman," *Business Screen* 1, no. 2 (1938): 30, and "Salesmen Get the Idea," *Business Screen* 1, no. 1 (1938): 19, 62. Print: sd bw 16 mm, PA; AAFF.

Sightseeing at Home (1943)
Wilding Picture Productions for General Electric. "An educational two-reel motion picture in black and white on the subject of television." Focuses upon the GE station WRGB in Schenectady, NY. Production no. 1293. Complete shooting script (copyright deposit file MU 13145). Print: 15 min sd bw 16 mm (FAA 4612), LC.

Steel—a Symphony of Industry (1936)
Audio Productions in cooperation with the American Iron and Steel Institute. Cinematography, Don Malkames; script, William Laub; editing, Sol S. Feuerman; musical score, Edwin C. Ludwig. Opening panorama of steel yards, derricks, suspension bridges, and manufacturing. "Men and steel provide a nation with its comforts, its luxuries and its progress." In the final shot, an ingot in the form of the United States is made. Print: sd bw, PA.

The Sword and the Quill (1959)
CBS News and the Advertising Council. Narrator: Walter Cronkite. Begins December 7, 1941, with an account of Pearl Harbor destruction and the advertising industry's determination to help win the war. In the postwar period come new emergencies: the selling of the U.N.; the Smokey the Bear campaign; polio vaccinations; urban renewal; and the Better Schools campaign. Includes cameos of advertising executives Lee Bristol, Ted Repplier, and Time/Life's Roy Larsen. Print: sd bw (NARS 200 314), NACP.

Symphony in "F" (1940)
Audio Productions for Ford Motor Company. "Each time the 'Theme in F' is heard, we find ourselves observing on the screen the Ford idea as the constructive and impelling force towards progress and prosperity. . . . It is intended that *Symphony in F* will give every audience a happy and constructive picture of what is back of the symbolic characters at work on the Cycle of Production at the Ford Exhibit at the New York World's Fair. . . ." (*Business Screen* 2, no. 6 [1940]: 7, 31). No copyright deposit. Print: 15 min sd Technicolor (FC 4355, 4356), NACP.

T.V. Time (ca. 1955)
Republican National Committee. Campaign school. Carroll P. Newton, BBDO executive and adviser to the Republican campaign, gives a talk on television time buying. He notes that people are not as interested in "politics" as they are in "entertainment." To date, only one telecast has attracted a larger audience than the scheduled program it preempts—vice president Nixon's "Checkers" speech of September 23, 1952. Cites the necessity of successful pre-broadcast promotion in newspapers and paid advertising. Print: sd bw (16 RNC: 80), Victoria Schuck Collection, John F. Kennedy Library.

Televideo Theatre: "The Enchanted Well" (6/5/52)
Screen Associates. Produced by Gil Ralston. Middle commercial offers a testimonial from a man who has just become an American citizen. "I remember how it all started in my native country. . . . Railroads, electric light companies, the butcher, bakers, doctors, and then one night. . . . We believe that the socialistic trend toward government ownership of any industry, business or profession is everybody's problem because it concerns everybody's freedom" (copyright deposit file LP 1778). Print: sd bw (FCA 0396), LC.

Test Tube Tale (1941)
Jam Handy Picture Service, Inc. "This picture, for theatrical release, shows how industrial chemistry is responsible for the creation of new materials as well as the preserving of materials. Many articles in everyday use, the result of chemical experiments, are seen in an average American home. . . . As an example, the automobile body is treated for rust-resistance and covered with a finish that is the result of laboratory research. That industrial chemistry offers an alluring future to the young man is the closing note of the picture" (copyright deposit file MU 10950). Print: sd bw, PA.

To Each Other (1943)
Jam Handy for United States Steel. "An elderly man sits on the hillside where he used to come so often with his son, whose letter from somewhere overseas he now reads. The old man thinks aloud throughout the picture, telling his son of the stupendous achievement of his company, United States Steel, in war production. His story appears on the screen. As he talks, we are taken from one plant to another all over the United States. Finally, the old man, still sitting on the hillside, tells his son he is proud because he, too, is in the service of the nation, fighting for the day of victory—'the day when you'll be coming home.'" (copyright deposit file MU 14069). Print: sd bw 16 mm, PA.

To New Horizons (1940)
Jam Handy for General Motors. "Keeping abreast [of man's progress] is the development of industry in general, to the extent that greater comfort, wealth, and a fuller enjoyment of life are now available to more people." Film depicts GM's World's Fair Futurama, "where in color photography, a prophecy for future progress is unfolded" (copyright file MP 10402). Print: sd bw and color 16 mm, PA.

Unfinished Business (1948)
U.S. Steel. "A 10-minute version of 'Unfinished Business.' The film is narrated by George Hicks whose voice is familiar to millions of listeners of United States Steel's Sunday evening dramatic series, *The Theatre Guild on the Air.*" "It is the inspiring story of United States Steel's record-breaking peacetime production accomplishments, made possible by thousands of men like Jim Robbins" (copyright deposit file MU 3225). See also "U.S. Steel Makes a Progress Report," *Business Screen* 9, no. 4 (1948): 23; advertisement, Jam Handy Organization, "Human Steel," *Business Screen* 9, no. 6 (1948): back cover. Print: 10 min sd bw 16 mm, PA.

Unfinished Rainbows (1942)
Wilding Pictures for Alcoa. Director: Jean Yarborough. Story: Leo Rosencrans. Editor: Barney Rogan. Photography: Art Arling. Cast: John Maxwell, Albert Moran, Jean Del Val, John Dilson, Alan Ladd, Janet Shaw. No copyright deposit. A condensed version entitled *More Worlds to Conquer* is described in "Alcoa on the Screen," *Business Screen* 7, no. 6 (1946): 21–23. Print: sd bw, AAFF.

United Action Means Victory (1941)

In cooperation with Frontier Films. UAW-CIO and the 1939 GM tool and die strike. Print: sd bw 16 mm (200 FC 4924), tape, NACP.

United States Steel Hour: "A Christmas Carol" (1951)

Producer, Fred Coe; director, Gordon Duff; script, David Swift. Sir Ralph Richardson as Scrooge, Arthur Treacher as the ghost of Christmas Past, Melville Cooper as Present, Margaret Phillips as Mrs. Cratchet, Malcolm Keen as Marley's ghost, Alan Napier as Charles Dickens, Norman Barrs as Bob Cratchet, Robin Craven as Mr. Fezziwig, Robert Hay Smith as Tiny Tim, Roderick Walker as Fred. A bespectacled George Hicks introduces Irving S. Olds, chairman of the board of U.S. Steel. Print: sd bw 16 mm archival positive (DD 143), Coe Collection, SHSW.

——— "No Time for Sergeants" (3/15/55)

Starring Andy Griffith. Tape (T81:0169), Museum of Television and Radio, New York.

——— "A Wind from the South" (9/14/55)

Tape (T81:0139), Museum of Television and Radio, New York.

We Drivers (1950)

Jam Handy Organization for General Motors Corp. Revision of the 1938 film. "Animated cartoon characters whisper words of advice into the driver's ear" (LC catalog card). Print: 13 min sd color 16 mm (FCA 1577), LC.

With These Hands (1950)

Promotional Films for the International Ladies Garment Workers Union (ILGWU). "The life of an about-to-retire garment worker, applying for a union pension, recounted in flashbacks. Alexander Brody recalls joining the union in 1910, the trials of the sweatshop days—unemployment, organization strikes, tragedy like the Triangle Shirtwaist fire—as the formative years of the ILGWU are paralleled with his personal growth, the lives of his friends, and the establishment of his family. History and entertainment are subtly blended in this social commentary" (ILGWU catalog). No copyright deposit file. Print: 40 min sd bw 16 mm 2 copies (FDA 206/207), LC; tape (RG 174.20), NACP.

The Workman's Lesson (1912)

Thomas A. Edison. Made in cooperation with the National Association of Manufacturers. Cast: Bigelow Cooper, Gertrude McCoy. An industrial safety film. Demonstrates why factory workers should use the safety devices with which their machines are equipped. The first of three Edison-NAM collaborations. Print: si bw (FBA 1677 J 17092325), LC.

Index

Page numbers in *italics* refer to illustrations.

A

ABC (American Broadcasting Company), 116, 190
Abraham Lincoln (Sandburg), 104, 109, 110
Academy Awards. *See* Films, Hollywood
Achilles, Paul S., 6
Adams, James Truslow, 28, 97, 108
Adams, John Quincy, 76
Addams, Jane, 75, 78
Advertest Report Test, 243n60
Advertising: anti-labor, 46, 54; automobile, *see* Automobile industry; Barton's philosophy of, 19–23, 94–95; billboard, 46, *47;* "Bull Session" parody on, 159–60, *161;* cost of, (budget cuts) 25, 45, (conservative campaigns) 15–16, 51, (radio broadcasts) 15–16, 51, 65, 68; dinner plans as form of, 38, 95; "economic education" campaign, 163–81, 183–84; films sponsored by, 167; and free enterprise ideology, 183; institutional, 4, 19, 23, 31–32, 36–38, 68, 133; labor, 146; magazine, 23, 28–29, 32, 37, 69, 138, 212; by NAM, 162; 1936 campaign as test of, 94–95; op-ed, 210; peacetime, predictions about, 158; personal voice in, 11; World War II, 146–49, 157–58, 159. *See also* Radio broadcasts; Television
Advertising agencies, 5, 7, 16; American Association of, 158, 163; and films, 121; GM changes, 43; in 1936 campaign, 88; and personality of client/sponsor, 25; and radio, 26. *See also entries for individual agencies*
Advertising Council, 158, 160, 162, 163
AFL (American Federation of Labor), 54, 89; *Labor for Victory* radio program of, 116
Albert in Blunderland (Sloan Foundation film), 176
Aldrich, Winthrop W., 156, 238n59
Alfred I. du Pont: The Family Rebel (James), 106
Alfred P. Sloan Foundation, 176
Al Jolson Show (radio program), 31
Allen, Edward M., 223n6
Allen, Frank G., Gov., 29
Allen, George G., 223n6
Allen, Henry J., 61
All That Money Can Buy (Sherwood play), 110
Aluminum Company of America (Alcoa), 201, 202
Aluminum Company of Canada, 202
America Marching On (NAM film), 131
American Adventure (radio program), 65, 72
American Anniversary (NAM film), 156
"American Cavalcade" (program proposed by NBC), 35, 62–65, 74
American Family Robinson (NAM radio program), 25, 53, 54–59, 61, 90, 92
American Heritage Foundation, 9, 168
American Historical Association, 74
American Legion, 50, 192
American Liberty League, 3, 83, 100; attacks on, 84–85; backers of, 13, 67–68, 117; du Pont's association with, 66, 67, 81, 82, 195; and politics, 91, (opposes FDR) 12, 195; and radio time, 15–16, 49, 50; suspends operations, 94
American Rolling Mill Company, 53
American Telephone and Telegraph Company, 21, 74
American Tobacco Company, 235n8
American Viscose, 135
American Way, the, 103
America's Town Meeting of the Air (NBC radio), 102
America—Yesterday, Today and Tomorrow (NAM film), 131
Anderson, Maxwell, 189
Angell, James Rowland, 101–4, 106
Anheuser Busch, 235n8
Anthony, Susan B., 78
Anti-Communism. *See* Communist Party
Apex Productions (television films), 180, 181
Arent, Arthur, 116
Armstrong Circle Theater (TV series), 119, 200
Army, U.S., films sponsored by, 146, 149
Arnold, Edward, 110
Association Against the Prohibition Amendment, 67
Association of American Railroads, 160
Association of National Advertisers, 158, 159, 163
Atwater Kent Hour (radio program), 27
Audio Productions, Inc., 146
Automobile industry, 30–31, 36–37; advertising expenditures, 37, 221n38; auto shows, 37, 45; exhibits, *123*, 129; films, 25–26, 37, 121–32 passim, 137, 146–47; wartime, 146–47. *See also* Ford Motor Company; General Motors (GM); UAW (United Auto Workers)
AWARE, Inc. (anti-Communist organization), 241n24
Aylesworth, Merlin H., 17, 30, 32–33, 91; Sloan's correspondence with, 38, 39, 40, 42–43

B

Baker, George, 52
Bankhead, Tallulah, 194
Bard, F. N., 59, 60
Bardo, C. L., 53
Barnouw, Erik, 116
Barrymore, Ethel, 114
Barton, Bruce Fairchild, 4, *20*, *33*, 133, 159, 212, 224n19; background of, 18–19; and *Cavalcade of America*, 66, 68, 98–99; on DuPont, 68, 69; on New Deal, 12; and politics of better living, 5–6, 17–23; and radio, 27, 28, 30, 32, 33; on Roosevelt's re-election, 94–95; and television, 194–95, 207–8
Barton, Clara, 75, 81
Barton, William E., Rev., 18
Barton, Durstine & Osborn (BDO), 18, 27, 31
Baseball (TV film), 212
Batten, George, Agency, 18
Batten, Barton, Durstine & Osborn (BBDO), Inc., 5, 19, 28, 29, 106, 159; "better living" ad campaign, 9, 22–23, 69–76 (*see also Cavalcade of America*); clients of, 17, 27, (DuPont) 17, 69–70, 197, 200, (GE) 201; conservatism of, 115; and control of programs, 189, 191, 192, 197; founding of, 4, 17, 18; *March of Time*, 92, 115; and 1936 campaign, 92; radio department, 6, 8, 26, 116; switches from NBC to CBS, 66; and television, 9, 118, 188, 201, (blacklists) 191–92; and *Theatre Guild* radio program, 189, 190, 191
BBC (British Broadcasting Corporation), 26, 65, 230n22
Belasco, David, 129
Bel Geddes, Norman, *136*
Bell, James Ford, 51, 63
Benét, Stephen Vincent, 110, 113–15
Benny, Jack, 31, 204
Berlin, Irving, 80
Bernays, Edward L., 4, 37–38, 74
Best Years of Our Lives, The (film), 156
Bethlehem Steel, 6, 53
"Better living" campaigns, 4; BBDO and, 9, 22–23, 69–76; DuPont, 97–98, 99, 115–17, 189, 195 (*see also Cavalcade of America*)
Better Living (Du Pont magazine), 115, 184, 208
Betty and Bob (radio program), 52
Betty Crocker School of the Air (radio program), 52
Billboard advertising, 46, *47*
Bill of Rights (on Freedom Train), 163
Birthright, The (Chrysler film), 167, 171–73
Black, Hugo, 50
Blackburn, Harold, 198
Blackett, Hill, 88, 92
Blackett, Sample & Hummert advertising agency, 51–52, 88
Blacklisting of performers, 191–93; programs defended, 189
Blodgett, Thomas H., 223n6
Booth, Evangeline, 18
Boren, Wallace, 121
Borg-Warner, 53
Boyce, Burke, 35, 64, 65
Bradley, Preston, 51
Brandon Films, 235n14
Brass Hats (metal trades industrialists), 53
Bray Studios, Inc., 146
Brennan, Walter, 147
Bridges, Harry, 61
Briggs, Susan, 65
British Information Services, 149
Britten, Fred A., 223n4
Brooks, Robert R. R., 46
Brophy, Thomas D'Arcy, 168
Brown, "Hi," 198
Brown, Thad, 51, 52
Buick advertising, *Buick Concert* (radio program), 31
Bullis, Harry A., 54
Bunche, Ralph, 200
Bunting, Earl, 160
Burnett, Wayne, 237n47
Burns, Ken, 212
Burton Holmes Films, Inc., 146
Business: and administrative decentralization, 31, 131, 236n20; "better living" approach, *see* "Better living" campaigns; business talks broadcast 236n20; "better living" approach, *see* "Better living" campaigns; business talks broadcast, 15–16, 25, 27, 38, 40–46 passim; definition of, 3; FDR attacks, 84; -government relations (New Deal), 3, 12, 15, 36, 118, 183, (postwar) 158; -labor relations, *see* Labor; New Vocabulary of, *see* New Vocabulary; in 1936 campaign, 87–95; public image of, 115, 183, 210–11; response of, to Depression, 15, 36–38, 39; responsibility of, for Depression, 21, 36; sponsorship of media by, *see* Films, sponsored; Radio broadcasts; Television; story of, as story of America, 14; television seen as anti-business, 211; World War II and postwar, 183. *See also* Free enterprise; National Association of Manufacturers (NAM)
Business Screen magazine, 137, 163, 176, 177, 180
Butterfield, Herbert, 22
By Their Works (GE film), 176–77

C

Cadillac advertising, *Cadillac Symphony Concerts* (radio program), 31, 40
Cagney, James, 110
Cameron, William J., 25, 41–42

Campbell-Ewald advertising agency, 43, 45, 46, 146–47, 158
Cantril, Hadley, 61
Capp, Al, 176
Carlton, Henry Fisk, 90
Carmer, Carl, 106, *107*, 108
Carnegie Hall broadcast (1928), 27
Case, W. H., 158
Cattell, James McKeen, 6
Cavalcade anthology (1937), 81
Cavalcade (Coward play), 65
Cavalcade of America (radio program), 38, 68–85, 91, *105*, 189, 212; audience of, 199–201; BBDO and, 23, 27, 81, 85, 97, 104, 197, (change of venue) 66, (as long-term investment) 68, 82; and "better living," 23, 97, 189, 195; CBS and, 66, 83, 99, 101; client control of, 197; debut of, 66, 71; dramatic anthology formula, 8, 49, 81, 188, 195; free enterprise as subtext of, 196; historical advisers for, 72–73, 97, 106–8; ideal protagonists of, 108, 116; limitations of, 76; literary figures dramatized, 111–15, 117; music for, 79–81; NBC and, 65, 83, 101, 103–4, 109, 115; political stance of, 81, 109, (ambiguity) 115; programs reprised, 116–17; as "propaganda," 75, 81; PSC study of, 7, 100–1; and Sandburg, 110–13, 114–15; screenplays adapted for, 110; survival of, after 1936 election, 97–101, 118; tours the country, 104; women featured in episodes of, 75, 78–79; during World War II, 97, 108, 110, 118
Cavalcade of America (TV program), 9; begins, 66, 119, 181, 197–201; contemporary subjects introduced, 200
CBS (Columbia Broadcasting System), 8, 41, 85, 91, 109, 111; and *Cavalcade of America*, 66, 83, 99, 101; experimentation by (1930s), 26; news program first sponsored by, 52; in 1936 campaign, 90, 91, 92, 93; sustaining-time strategies, 15, 16, 50, 58; switch from NBC to, 65–66, 83
Celanese Corporation, 135
Century of Progress exposition (1933–39), 38–40, 41, 129, 135; sponsored films shown at, 122, *128*
Chalmers, Thomas, 109
Chamber of Commerce, St. Louis, 53
Chamber of Commerce, U.S., 158, 163, 183, 235n8
Chapman, Don, 162
Chappell, Matthew N., 6
Chechov, Michael, 180
Chertok, Jack, 178, 180, 181
Chester, Colby M., 14, 16, 22, 50, 223n6, 237n47
Chevrolet, 165, 166; advertising, 31, 39, (Soap Box Derby) 25–26, 167; assembly demonstrated at Chicago fair, 136; films made for, 25–26, 124–25, 127, 131; paper published by Local 659 (UAW-CIO), 162; sales convention musical, *125*. *See also* General Motors
Chicago, commemoration of settlement of. *See* Century of Progress exposition
Chicago Daily News, 111, 223n4
Chicago Tribune, 90, 223n4
Christian Herald, 60
Christian Science Monitor, 60
Christmas Carol, A (Dickens), TV production of, 193–94
Chrysler Corporation, 36, 53; films sponsored by, 122, *127*, 137, 167, 171–73; New York World's Fair exhibit, *123*
CIO (Congress of Industrial Organizations): radio dramas sponsored by, 116; and Taft election comic book, 176, *177*. *See also* UAW-CIO
Civilian Conservation Corps, 133
Civil War, The (TV film), 212
Civil War, U.S., 66, 104, 227n98
Clark, Fred G., 16, 49, 50, 51, 92
Close Harmony (GM film), 147
Coca-Cola, films produced for, 125, 235n8
Coen, Harry B., 165
Cold War consumerism, 208
Colgate, Bayard, 62
Collette, Maurice, 23, 207
Collier's magazine, 138
Colonial Revival, 28
Columbia University: Faculty Club, 38; History Department, 74
Comic book distributed by CIO, 176, *177*
Committee for Economic Development, 158
Committee on Public Information, 37
Common Sense (Paine), 163
Communications Act (1934), 60
Communist Party, 192; and anti-Communism, 50, 51, 191–92, 243n65
Congress, U.S.: elections, 14, 15, 18–19; FDR's message to (1936), 84; investigation of candidates, 50; NAM and, 162; "pressure groups" and, 103; Republican majority expected (1946), 160; Senate investigations, 50, 66, 68
Congress of American Industry, 22
Conkle, E. P., 116, 231n43
Connelly, Marc, 109
Conreid, Hans, 200
Conservatism: of BBDO, 115; Benét's parody of, 114; entrepreneurial right, 3, 12 (*see also* Business); 1930s as "seedtime" of, 9; in 1936 campaign, 87–95; principles of, 5; radio campaigns promoting, 15–16, 49–60, 103–19; and radio station ownership, 230n21; and "usable past," 13–14
Coolidge, Calvin, 18
Cooper, James Fenimore, 108

Corbett, Harvey Wiley, 221n55
Corcoran, Thomas, 83, 84
Cornhuskers (Sandburg), 111
Corn Is Green, The (Hollywood film), 178
Corwin, Norman, 111
Cotten, Joseph, 204
Coughlin, Charles E., Father, 16, 63
Counterattack (anti-Communist newsletter), 191–92
Country Gentleman magazine, 138
Court of King Duco, The (pilot radio program), 69
Coward, Noel, 65
Crawford, Joan, 204
Crooks, Richard, 41
Crosby, Bing, radio show, 184
Crosby, Enoch, 108
Crossley, Archibald M., 100
Crowley, Charles, *210*
Crusaders, Inc., 15, 16, 49–51, 53, 63, 91; *Voice of* (radio talks), 92

D

Dallas (TV series), 211
Damrosch, Walter, 102
Darragh, Lydia, 200
Davenport, Tom, 197
David, Donald K., 223n6
Davis, Donald D., 16, 51–53; as "Si Perkins," 52–53
Davis, Francis B., Jr., 223n6
Dayton Engineering Laboratories (Delco), 30
Deadline for Action (union film), 176
Declaration of Independence, manuscript draft of (on Freedom Train), 163
Demby, Bill, 212
Democratic National Committee, 67
Democratic National Convention (1936), 84
Democratic Party, 67, 83, 110; Jeffersonian (anti-Roosevelt) Democrats, 82; in 1936 campaign, 88, 89, 93; and radio time (vs. Republicans), 16, 60–61, 90; Speakers Bureau, 83. *See also* Roosevelt, Franklin D.
Dennis James Carnival (TV program), 201
Depression, the, 114, 208; and advertising budgets, 25–26; business response to, 15, 36–38, 39; business responsibility for, 21, 36; introspection fueled by, 73, 83; NAM membership during, 53, 162; as "psychological," 13; radio programs during, 25, 30, 36, 97; and sponsored films, 125–26; younger generation's ignorance of, 184, 210
Detroit Steel Castings Company, 13
Detroit Symphony broadcasts, 41
Deupree, R. R., 242n37
Dewey, F. Lyman, 184, 197, *210*
Dewey, John, 103
Dewey, Thomas E., 18

Dickens, Charles, 193
Dickinson, Emily, 117
Dictionary of American Biography, 106
Dinner plans. *See* Advertising
Dix, Dorothea, 81
Doctor in Industry (GM film), 153–55
Dollard Reward Scale, 243n60
"Dominant circle of ideas," 217n21
Doric Quartette, 69
Douglas, Lewis, 60
Driscoll, John, 115, 198
Dr. Lyons toothpowder, 52
Duffy, Ben, 192, 194, 207
DuMont Laboratories, 235n11
Du Pont, Alfred I., 66; biography of, 106
Du Pont, Coleman, 66
Du Pont, Eleuthère Irénée, 66, 99, 195
Du Pont, Henry B., 99
Du Pont, Irénée, 82, 83, 99, 117
Du Pont, Lammot, 62–68 passim, 81, 83, 98–103 passim, 106, 109, 196, 242n37
Du Pont, Pierre Samuel, 30, 32, 66, 67, 99
DuPont Cavalcade Theater (TV series), 200–1
DuPont de Nemours & Company, E. I., 3, 6; and American Liberty League, 66, 67, 81, 82, 195; anti-trust suit against, 196–97; as BBDO client, 17, 69–70, 200; "better living" campaign, 97–98, 99, 115–17, 184, 189, 195, 208, 212; changing leadership in, 97; and decentralization, 131; employee education campaign, 183; invests in General Motors, 30–31; magazine advertising by, 23, 212; and NAM, 53, 66, 82; New York World's Fair (1939/40) exhibits, 134–35, 186; and politics, (isolationism) 109, (1936 campaign), 91; and public relations, 66–72, 196; radio broadcasts sponsored by, 5, 7, 15, 23, 66, 68 (*see also Cavalcade of America* [radio program]); stock rises, 13; and television, 181, 184, 195-201, 202, 208, 212 (*see also Cavalcade of America* [TV program])
DuPont Decorators (radio program), 69
DuPont Magazine, 99
DuPont Story, The (TV program), 181
Durant, William C., 30
Durstine, Roy Sarles, 18, 26 27, 28, 30; and *Cavalcade of America*, 8, 66, 69, 74, 75, 76, 229n1; and "new vocabulary," 6; switches from NBC to CBS, 66
Dynasty (TV series), 211

E

Easier Way, The (GM film), 151
Eastman Kodak, 53, 135
"Economic education" campaign. *See* Advertising
Edgerton, John E., 13, 53

Edison, Thomas Alva, life dramatized, 196, 204
Elections. *See* Congress, U.S.; Presidential campaigns and elections
Electric Light and Power Companies of America, 202
Elgin Watch Company, 122
Elliott, Jock, 200
Emmett, Daniel Decatur, 80
Everett, Marshall, 27
Experiment (GM film), 151

F

Fair Deal–New Deal coalition. *See* New Deal
Fairless, Benjamin F., 191, 192, 195
Fairness Doctrine, 211
Falcon Crest (TV series), 211
Farley, James A., 67, 93
Farm Security Administration, 9
Fascism, attacks on, 50
Faulk, John Henry, 241n24
Federal Communications Commission, 91, 211
Federal Radio Commission, 51, 92
Federal Theater Project (FTP), 116, 189
Fickett, Homer, 115, 189
Fidler, Fred H., 121
Field, "Po," 158
Film News magazine, 137
Films, Hollywood, 109–10, 225n5; Academy Awards, 65, 178; business criticism of, 115
Films, sponsored, 8–9, 121–43; by advertising industry, 167; business leadership view of, 145; by industry, 25–26, 37, 121–32 passim, 137–38, 146–56, 167–73, 176–77, by labor, 149, 173–75, 176; by the Left, 9; by NAM, 9, 25, 124, 131, 133, 156–57, 178–81; at New York World's Fair (1939/40), 8, 121, 122, 127, 137, 146; by Sloan Foundation, 176; television, 180, 181; UAW-CIO film library, 149; during World War II, 8, 145–50
Finch, George B., 155–56
Fishbein, Morris, 221–22n55
Fisher, Charles T., 36
Fisher Body, 36, 39; strike at (1936–37), *see* General Motors (GM)
Fiske, C. P., 26
Flaherty, Robert, 177
Fleming, John, 201
Fletcher, Henry P., 89, 90–91, 92
Flynn, Errol, 110
Folk culture, 32
Fonda, Henry, 110
Fontanne, Lynn, 189, 190
Ford, Henry, 31, 149, 220n20; "philosophy" expounded, 42
Ford Motor Company, 6, 226n60; exhibits mounted by, 129, *130;* films sponsored by, 122, 124–29 passim, 137; GM as competitor, 36; and radio, 25, 41–42; and television, 202; and unions, 149
Ford Sunday Evening Hour (radio program), 25, 41–42
Fortune magazine, 66, 159; on FDR, 10, 12
Foster, Stephen, 32, 80
Fox, Dixon Ryan, 38, 72–74, 75–78 passim, 81–82, 97
Frank, Glenn, 221n55
Franklin, Benjamin, 35, 108, 116–17, 155, 198
Franklin, Elma H., 198–99
Fred Waring Show, The (TV series), 201
Freedom Train exhibit, 9, 160, 162–63, 167, 168, 196
Free enterprise: business and industry campaign for, 170, 177, 183; overuse of term, 159; revolt against system denied, 165; as subtext of *Cavalcade of America*, 196. *See also* Business
Freeman, Douglas Southall, 104
Frith, Simon, 26
From Dawn to Sunset (GM film), 131, *132*
Frontier Films, 149
Frontiers of the Future (NAM film), 131
Front Page, The (radio production), 190
Fuller, Walter D., 237n47
Fuller & Smith & Ross, Inc., 143

G

Gable, Clark, 115
Gallup, George H., and Gallup polls, 100, 159, 243n60
Galsworthy, James, 35
Gardiner, William Tudor, Gov., 29
Garrett, Paul Willard, 14, 23, 36–37, 40–45 passim
Garrison, William Lloyd, 78
General Electric (GE), 6, 21, 52, 184, 208; advertising by, 4, 7, 19–20, (BBDO and) 17, 19, 23, 133; employee education campaign, 183; exhibits mounted by, 187; films sponsored by, 124, 125, 176–77; and television, 9, 119, 181, 184–89 passim, 201–5, 207, 212
General Electric Theater (TV series), 9, 119, 181, 188, 189, 200–5, 207; leaves air, 243n65
General Federation of Women's Clubs, 104
General Foods, 14, 16, 50, 51
General Mills, 23, 53, 54; and the Crusaders, 16, 52, 63; films and TV sponsored by, 181; and first singing commercial, 52
General Motors (GM), 3, 6; company history published, 38, 74; competition with Ford and Chrysler, 36; decentralization at, 31, 131, 236n20; DuPont invests in, 30–31; exhibits mounted by, 25, 38, 39, 167 (World's Fair "Futurama") 136, 137, 150; employee magazine (*GM Folks*), 7, 167; employee "My Job" con-

test (MJC), 9, 165–67; films sponsored by, 122, 124–25, 131, *132*, 146–47, 150–55; foremen employed by, 151; founded, 30; institutional advertising (1920s, 1930s), 4, 19, 23, 31–32, 37–38, 133; and Liberty League, 67; and NAM, 53; public relations, 37, 38, 67, 100, 131, 157–58, 165-67; radio sponsorship by, 14, 15, 32–33, (dropped, 1938–41) 45, (*General Motors Family Party*) 27, 32; (*General Motors Symphony Concerts*) 14, 25, 40–46 passim, 49, 83, (and NBC) 35, 38, 40, 41–43, 45, 49, ("Voice of") 25, 40, 41, 43–44, 46 (*see also Parade of the States*); response of, to Depression, 36–38; stock rises, 13; strikes against, (1936–1937) 14, 44–45, 46, 131, 165, (1939) 149; television programming, 212; wartime advertising, 146–47; during World War II, 158

Gennett, Fred, 92

George Washington: The Forging of a Nation (TV series), 212

Gershwin, George, 189, 222n67

Gettysburg Address, Lincoln's reading copy (on Freedom Train), 163

Gianinni, A. P., 61

Girdler, Tom M., 53

GM Folks (employee magazine), 7, 167

"Good Neighbor League," 83

Goodrich, B. F., Company, 135

Goodyear Tire & Rubber, film sponsored by, 167, 168–71

Goossens, Eugene, 43

Gordon, Ruth, 241n26

Gordon, W. E., 201

Graham, Otto, 200

Grant, Richard H., *136*

Gray, Carl R., 221n55

"Great Enterprise Campaign," 240n4

Great Lakes Exposition (Cleveland, 1936), 226n60

Great Swindle, The (union film), 173–75

Green, William, 89

Greenstreet, Sidney, 115

Greve, William M., 223n6

Griffith, Richard, 138

Gulay, Lou, 176

Guthrie, Woodie, 109

Guyan, David, 80

H

Hackett, Charles M., *210*

Hall, Stuart, 15

Hall Johnson Choir, 109

Hamilton, John, 93

Hamilton, William H., 196

Hampden, Walter, 71, 72

Hancock, John, 156

Handful of Dust, A (Waugh), 204

Handy, Jamison, 124–25, 131, 146; and Jam Handy Organization, 138, 146, 147, 151–56 passim, 236nn21, 29

Hard, William, 92

Harding, Gardner, 186

Harding College (Arkansas), 176

Harding Sisters radio program, 69

Harper, Ann, 78

Harris, Louis, 210

Harris, Robert H., Rear Adm., 223n4

Harrison Radiator, 30

Hart, Lorenz, 189

Hart, William A., 23, 83, 100, 207

Hartnett, Vincent, 241n24

Haupt, Henry, 159

Hayes, Helen, 104, 190

Hedda Gabler (Ibsen), TV production, 194

Heinz, Howard, and H. J. Heinz Company, 51

Hell Bent for Election (UAW-CIO film), 149

Henry, O., 28, 117

Hepburn, Katharine, 190

Herbert, Don, 202, 204

Hess, Myra, 42

Hicks, George, 190, 193

High, Stanley Hoflund, 60–64, 72, 83–85, 101, 102, 231n43

Hill, George Washington, 115

Hill, John W., 180, 237n47

Hill & Knowlton advertising agency, 180

History of American Life, A (Fox and Schlesinger, eds.), 72

Hitler, Adolf, 26

Hodges, Rosco N., 166

Hollywood. *See* Films, Hollywood

Hollywood's Favorite Heavy: Businessmen on Prime TV (TV drama), 211

Holmes, E. Burton, 124, 146

Holmes, John, 237n47

Hood, Mrs. Clifford F., 194

Hook, Charles R., 53

Hooker, Elon H., 223n6

Hoover, Herbert, 4, 5, 18, 32, 60; administration of, 61, 67; as "villain," 208, 225n55

Hope for a Harvest (TV production), 194

Horning, Hugh, *210*

Horse Sense Philosophy (radio program), 52–53

Household Finance Corporation, 235n8

House of Representatives, U.S., 160. *See also* Congress, U.S.

Howard, Sidney, 189, 190

Howe, Lyman, 124

Howells, William Dean, 194

Hucksters, The (Hollywood film), 115

Hummert, Frank, 51–52

Hunt, Lawrence E., 167
Huston, Walter, 110, 116, 190
Hutton, Edward F., 50, 117, 215n10
Hyatt Roller Bearing Company, 30

I

Ibsen, Henrik, 194
Ickes, Harold, 11
I Married Joan (TV series), *204*
Industry on Parade (NAM TV series), 180–81
In Search of the Constitution (TV series), 212
Inside Cackle Corners (Sloan Foundation film), 176
Inter-American Affairs, U.S. Coordinator of, 149
In Tune with Tomorrow (Chrysler film), 127, 137
I Remember Mama (radio production), 190
Isolationism. *See* Politics

J

Jack Armstrong the All-American Boy (radio program), 52
Jack Benny Show (radio program), 31
Jackson, Merrick, 180
Jacobs-Bond, Carrie, 80
James, Marquis, 106, *107*, 108
Jam Handy organization. *See* Handy, Jamison
Jane Froman Show, The (TV series), 204
Japanese surrender documents (on Freedom Train), 163
Jay, John, 163
Jefferson, Thomas, 35, 99, 108, 163, 198
Jeffersonian Democrats, 82
Joe Turner, American (NAM film), 180
Johnson, Edward L., 199
Johnson, Laurence A., 192, 241n24
Johnston, Eric, 168
Johnstone, George W. "Johnny," 180
Jordan, Virgil, 223n4
Jowett, Frank A., 98
Juarez, Benito, 115
Justice Department, U.S., 243n65

K

Kansas City Star, 61
Kaplan, Eliot, 176
Kefauver show (TV) 208
Keith, B. F., vaudeville chain, 17
Kelley, Andrew, 52–53
Kelly, William Joseph, 166
Kent, Arthur Atwater, 27
Kent, Fred I., 223n6
Keppler, Victor, 69
Kettering, Charles F., 31, 37, 38, 39, *136*, 150, 189
Keynesian thesis, 14, 143
Khrushchev, Nikita, 208
Kiger, Jimmy, 166
Kingston, Douglas, 69
Kirtley, Lucille, 69
Klaxon, 30
Knights of Columbus, 18
Knox, Colonel Frank, 223n4
Knudsen, William S., *136*
Knute Rockne—All American (Hollywood film), 115
Kobak, Edgar, 62, 64, 82
Kondolf, George, 116, 189, 241nn24, 27
Kurenko, Maria, 27

L

Labor: advertising by, 146; anti-labor advertising, 46, 54; "collar line," 151; comic book distributed by, 176, *177;* films sponsored by, 149, 173–75, 176; -management relations, (change in) 129, (World War II and postwar) 146–47, 149–50, 162, 189; open shop, 53, 75; radio programs sponsored by, 116; and strikes, (1936–37) 14, 44–45, 46, 103, 131, 165, (1939) 149, (1949) 191; supports FDR, 149; and Truman administration, 189. *See also* Taft-Hartley Act (1947)
Labor Stage, Inc., 89
Ladd, Alan, 204
Ladies' Home Journal, 164
Lambert Pharmacal Company, 53
Landon, Alfred M., 8, 18, 61, 87–89, 92, 93–94
Lane, Rita, 69
Lang, Chester H., 184, 189
Langner, Lawrence, 189, 191, 192
Laphams of Boston, The (Howells), TV production, 194, 195
Lasker, Albert, 16, 51, 53
Laughton, Charles, 116–17
Law, F. M., 223n4
Lawrence, David, 60
Lee, Ivy, 59, 224n19
Left, the, films of, 9
LeHand, Margaret "Missy," 103
Lehman Brothers, 156
Letter from America, A (Goodyear film), 167, 168–71
Letter to a Rebel (RKO Pathé film), 167, 168
Lewis, Thomasene, 166
Lewis and Clark (TV film), 212
Liberalism: corporate, emergence of, 158, 183; New Deal–Fair Deal, attacks on, 160, 183 (*see also* New Deal)
Liberty at the Crossroads (NAM radio series), 89–90, 92
Liberty League. *See* American Liberty League
Liberty magazine, 138
Lichtenberg, Bernard, 122

Life magazine, 138, 208
Lincoln, Abraham, 13, 95, 163; biographical treatment of, 28, 108, 110, 113, 231n43
Link, Henry C., 6, 163–64, 165
Link Special Study, 243n60
Lippmann, Walter, 91, 106
Literary Digest, 60, 94
Living Newspaper (play), 122
Lohr, Lenox R., 90, 92, 102, 133–34
Lone Ranger, The (TV series), 181
Long, Huey, 16, 63
Lord & Thomas advertising agency, 16, 51
Lorentz, Pare, 122, 137–38
Louisiana Story (Standard Oil film), 177
Lucas, Eliza, 78–79
Luce, Henry, 208
Ludig, Edwin, 129
Ludlam, George, 65
Lund, Robert L., 53–54, 223n4
Lunt, Alfred, 189, 190
Lux Radio Theater, 241n22
Lyon, Peter, 115–16

M

McCall's magazine, 137
McCarthy, Charlie, 41
McChesney, Robert W., 16
McClellan, George B., 51, 52
McClure, S. S., 115
McCormick, Robert, Col., 90, 223n4
MacDonald, J. Carlisle, 190, 191, 192, 201
Macfadden Wage Earner's Forum, 159
McGuffey, William Holmes, and *McGuffey Readers*, 98
McInnerney, Thomas H., 223n6
McIntyre, Marvin H., 103
McKinley, William, 13
McLaughlin Group (TV series), 212
Madison Avenue. *See* Advertising agencies
Mahan, Syd, 138
Make Mine Freedom (Sloan Foundation film), 176
Making Advertisements and Making Them Pay (Durstine), 26
Man in Possession (TV production), 194
Man Nobody Knows, The (Barton), 19
March, Frederick, 190
March of Time (radio program), 92, 115, 116, 189
Marinovich, Tony, 149
Marion, Francis, Gen., 200
Martini, Michael, 149
Marx, Groucho vs. Karl, 184, *184*
Massey, Raymond, 104, 231n43
Maxwell, Lee W., 223n6
Meet King Joe—the American Working Man (Sloan Foundation film), 176
Meet the Press (TV series), 202
Melville, Herman, 117
Men and Machines (NAM film), 131, 133
Men Make Steel (U.S. Steel film), 137–38
Menuhin, Yehudi, 222n67
Men Who Made American Industry, The (radio program proposed by NAM), 62
Merchants of Death (Engelbrecht and Hanighen), 66
Meredith, Burgess, 111, *112*, 204, 241n26
Merivale, Philip, 104
Merki, Nancy, 200
Merrit, Hepzabeth, Merrit family, and Mesabi Iron Range story, 79, 115
Metropolitan Opera, 27, 111
Michelson, Charles, 67, 83
Middleton Family at the World's Fair, The (Westinghouse film), 8, 124, 138–43, 147, 156, 208
Milland, Ray, 190, 204
Millard, Bill, 197
Miller, Arthur, 115
Millikan, Robert A., 223n4
Minot, George R., 200
Miracle of America education campaign, 9
Mobil Corporation, 210, 211, 220n23
Modern Talking Picture Service, Inc., 143
Moffett, George Monroe, 223n6
Moley, Raymond, 110
Monaghan, Frank, 97, 106, 107, 108, 109
Monsanto Chemical, 14, 53, 135
Moore, Jos. A., 223n6
Morton, Alfred H., 62, 91
Motion Picture Association, 168
Motion pictures. *See* Films, Hollywood; Films, sponsored
Mott, Lucretia, 78
Moyers, Bill, 212
"Mr. Wealthy," 14
Muir, Malcolm, 237n47
Murrow, Edward R., 201
Museum of Science and Industry, 68, 98
Music, 102; for *Cavalcade of America*, 79–81; symphony concerts, 14, 25, 31, 40–46 passim, 83
Music Appreciation Hour (NBC radio), 102
Music Corporation of America (MCA), 202
Mussolini, Benito, 26
Mutual Network, 16, 50

N

National Advisory Council (business group), 51
National Archives (Education Staff), 163
National Association of Manufacturers (NAM), 3, 83; conventions of, 22, 135; corporate support of, 53, 117; diatribes of, 81; DuPont and, 53, 66, 82; films sponsored/distributed by, 9, 25, 124, 131, 133, 156–57, 178–81; and free

enterprise, 183; *Industrial Information Bulletin*, 54; membership during Depression, 53, 162; and open shop, 53; and politics, 158, (attacks on) 84–85, (1936 campaign) 91, (opposes FDR and New Deal) 12–14, 53–57, 160, 195, (and Wagner Act) 150, 160, 162; "propaganda" countered by unions, 173–75; publicity operations of (1930s), 54–60, (billboards) 46, *47;* and radio, 5, 15, 49, 118, (*American Family Robinson*), 25, 53, 54–59, 61, 90, 92, (NBC and) 16, 58–59, 60, 62–64, 65, (proposed program) 62; "renovation" of, 49, 53–54, 162; and "unit thinking and action," 13

National Cash Register Company, 124

National Committee on Education by Radio, 230n12

National Electric Light Association, 38

National Founders Association, 13

National Industrial Recovery Act (NIRA), 4, 15; NAM opposes, 53–54, 160, Sandburg's view of, 110

National Steel Company, 13, 53

National Woman Suffrage Association petition, 163

Nation magazine, 115

Nation's Business magazine, 225n59

Navy, U.S., films sponsored by, 146, 149

Nazi surrender documents (on Freedom Train), 163

NBC (National Broadcasting Company), 85; "American Cavalcade" proposal, 35, 62–65, 74; Blue Network, 29, 40, 51; business talks broadcast, 15–16; and *Cavalcade of America*, 65, 83, 101, 103–4, 109, 115; Columbia Network, 51; and DuPont programs, 69, 72, (switch to CBS) 65–66, 83; experimentation by (1930s), 26, 27, 28; and formula of choice, 49, 65; and General Motors, 35, 38, 40, 41–43, 45, 49; listener survey (1934), 6; and NAM, 16, 58–59, 60, 62–64, 65; news program refused by, 52; Pacific Coast Network, 69; political position, 60–61, (anti-administration) 8, 16–17, (and 1936 campaign) 90–91, (sustaining programs) 15–16, 50, 51, 58, 59 (*see also* Politics); public service programs, 102–3; Red Network, 40, 51, 223–24n12; television, 180, 201. *See also* Radio broadcasts

NBC News (TV), 180

Nell, Edwin, 69

New Deal, 4, 82, 84; business-government relationship, 3, 12, 15, 36, 103, 118, 183; cumulative effect of, 12; –Fair Deal coalition, 5, 160, 176, 183; opposition to/attacks on, 9, 17, 22, 50, 102, 103, (by entrepreneurial right) 3, 12–13, 18, 50–57 passim, 83, 160, 176, 183, (in 1936 campaign) 87, 88, 90, 93; public ambivalence toward, 7; sympathy for/support of, 12, 17, 74, 83, 103, 110

New Departure Manufacturing, 30

New Dimensions (Chrysler film), 127, 137

New Era, New Freedom, 4

New Masses magazine, 115

New Nationalism, 4

New Republic magazine, 13

Newton, Carroll P., 191–93, 194–95

New Vocabulary of business leadership, 140, 145; elaboration of concept, 4–7; lessons of, 15, 211; origin of, 4, 6; television and, 208, 212

New York *Evening Post*, 36

New York Historical Association, 73

New York Philharmonic Symphony orchestra, 40

New York Shipbuilding Company, 53, 59

New York *Sun*, 26

New York Times, 210

New York World's Fair (1939/40), 45, 68, 99, 106; exhibits, *123*, 129, *130*, *134*, 135–37, 138, 186, *187*, *188*; (GM "Futurama") 136, 137, 150; films shown at, 8, 121, 122, 127, 137, 146; television at, 133–34, 184, 186, 187–88

Nicholson, Kenyon, 197

Nielsen, A. C., Company surveys, 88, 159, 202, 243n60

Nixon, Richard M., 18, 208

Norr, Roy, 67

Northwestern Railroad, 122

Nye Committee (Senate, 1934–1936), 66

O

Oakland-Pontiac, 125

Obermeyer, Henry, 159

O'Brien, Pat, 115, 190

Odets, Clifford, 89

Office of Education, U.S., 235n5

Office of Price Administration (OPA), U.S., 160, 173, 175

Office of the U.S. Attorney General, 163

Office of War Information, U.S., 146, 149, 235n5

Olds, Irving S., 191–92, 193–94

Oldsmobile advertising, 31. *See also* General Motors

On Borrowed Time (radio production), 190

O'Neill, Eugene, 189

O'Neill, J., 90

On to Jupiter (GM film), 150

On Your Job (NBC radio), 102

Open Door, The (GM film), 151, *152*, 153, 155

Open shop. *See* Labor

Operation '46 (General Mills film), 181

Opinion Research Corporation, 159

Osborn, Alex F., 18

Owens-Corning, 135

Ozzie and Harriet (TV series), 204

P

Pageant of Art (NBC radio), 102
Paine, Thomas, 163
Paley, William S., 51, 52, 90, 92, 93
Panama Canal, 53
Parade of the States (GM radio program), 14, 27, 29, 30, 32–38 passim, 65
Paramount Pictures, 156, 157, 162
Parent Teacher Associations (PTA), 143
Parkes, Holcombe, 160, 178, 180
Partisan Review, 115
Pathescope Company of America, Inc., 146
Patterson, John, 61
Patterson, John C., 124
Patterson, Richard C., 59, 60
Paul Whiteman program (radio), 31
Payne, John Howard, 80
Pearl, Les, 23
Pechin, Charles, *210*
Perfect Fool, The (radio program), 21, 27
Perils of Peace, The (PSC report), 6–7
Perlman Rim, 30
Pew, J. Howard, 237n47
Philadelphia Orchestra, 41
Phillips Petroleum Company, 13
Pidgeon, Walter, 190
Pitikin, Walter B., 222n55
Poe, Edgar Allan, 117
Politics: of better living, *see* Better living campaigns; *Cavalcade of America* and, 81, 109, 115; disguised as fictional entertainment, 52–53, 58–59; DuPont and, 91, 109; entrepreneurial right and, *see* Conservatism; isolationism, 109; liberal, *see* Liberalism; and radio time, (anti-administration radio programs) 8, 16, 54–60, (Democrats vs. Republicans) 16, 60–61, 90, (facilities denied) 90–92, (sustaining time strategies and programs) 15–16, 49, 50, 51, 58, 59, 116. *See also* Congress, U.S.; Presidential campaigns and elections
Pollock, Channing, 69
Pontiac advertising, 31. *See also* General Motors
Popular Mechanics magazine, 19
Post, Emily, 69
Postmark—U.S.A.! (NAM-Paramount film), 156, *157*
Pound, Arthur, 38
Powell, John, 32
Pratt, Benjamin K., 92
Precisely So (Chevrolet film), 127
Prentis, H. W., Jr., 237n47
Presidential campaigns and elections: (1912) 26; (1928) 67; (1932) 27, 53; (1936) 8–15 passim, 81–84 passim, 87–95, 97, 101, 110, 149, (campaign expenses) 229n29; (1940) 114, 231n43, 235n8; (1944) 149
"Pressure groups," 101, 103
Preston, W. G., Jr., 101
Price of Freedom (NAM film), 9, 178–80
Procter & Gamble soap operas, 242n37
Prohibition, 49, 60, 67
Protestant ethos, 19, 216n1
Pryor, Arthur, 27, 80
Pryor, Arthur, Jr., 27, 30, 80, *107*, 197, 198
Psychological Brand Barometer, 6
Psychological Corporation (PSC), 6–7, 100–1, 163
Psychology of Radio, The (Cantril), 61
Public Broadcasting Service (PBS), 210–11
Public opinion polls, 6–7, 12, 100–1, 143, 159, 202, 243n60; image of U.S. business, 210; 1936 election, 88, 94
Purnell, Frank, 53
Putnam, George F., 129, 131

Q

Quaker Oats, 51
Quarterback, The (NAM film), 180
Queeny, Edgar M., 14

R

Radio broadcasts: business sponsorship of, 14, 25, 27, 41–42, 188–93, (cost of) 15–16, 51, 65, 68, (historical programs) 28 (*see also* DuPont de Nemours & Company, E. I.; General Motors [GM]); conservative, 15–16, 49–60, 103–19; during Depression, 25, 30, 36, 97; dramatic anthology program formula, 5, 8, 9, 35–36, 188, 189, 195, 211–12, (format established) 26, 49, (preference for) 118–19; and "economic education," 184; first singing commercial, 52; importance of, 23; labor sponsorship of, 116; and "magic of radio," 21; in 1936 campaign, 88–95; "no offense" premise, 211; public service, 102–3; sustaining strategies and programs, 15–16, 101–2 (*see also* Politics); symphony orchestra concerts, *see* Music. *See also* CBS; NBC
Rahmel, Henry H., 92
Railway Age magazine, 160
Rank, Arthur, 180
Rapee, Erno, 32
Raskob, John J., 13, 30–31, 67, 82, 117, 118
Ray Milland Show, The (TV series), 204
RCA (Radio Corporation of America), 66, 103; television, 133–34, 186
Reader's Digest magazine, 66
Reagan, Ronald, 115; as TV host, 119, 202, *203*, 204–5
Reagan, Ronald, Mrs. (Nancy Davis), 204–5
Red Channels (blacklist), 241n26

"Red Decade," 9
Red Thunder (Durstine), 26
R. E. Lee (Freeman), 104
Remy Electric, 30
Republican National Committee (RNC), 5, 15, 82, 87, 89–92, 93; films produced for, 235n8; radio division, 88, 118
Republican National Convention (1936), 88
Republican Party, 8, 10, 12, 18, 83, 223n4; Contract with America, 211; majority expected (1946), 160; in 1936 campaign, 87–94; and radio time (vs. Democrats), 16, 60–61, 90
Republic Steel Corporation, 53
Reuther, Walter, 146, 166
Revue Productions, 202, 204
Reynolds Metals Company, 202
Rhapsodie Negre (Powell), 32
Rhapsody in Steel (Ford film), 127, 128–29
Rice, Elmer, 189
Richardson, Sir Ralph, 193, 194
Riddle Me This (TV program), 201
Riesman, David, 244n6
Right, the. *See* Conservatism
Riis, Jacob, 76, 81
River, The (film), 121
RKO, 110, 231n43
RKO-Pathé, 167
Robert Alphonso Taft Story, The (CIO comic book), 176, *177*
Roberts, Roy, 61
Robinson, Claude E., and Robinson polls, 12, 100, 159, 160, 243n60
Rockefeller, John D., 115
Rockefeller, John D., Jr., 28
Rodgers, Richard, 189
Rogers, Will, 52, 59, 117–18
Roland Reed Productions, 137
Roosevelt, Franklin Delano, 63, 114; administration, 67, 122, 126; on Angell at NBC, 103; assassination feared, 227–28n108; elected, re-elected, (1932) 13, 53, (1936) 12, 15, 83–84, 93–95, 110, (1940) 114, (1944) 149; fireside chats, 7, 11, 26, 36; as governor of New York, 29; labor support of, 149; opposition to/attacks on, 8, 12, 17, 59, 82, 103, 126, 195, 225n55, (1936 campaign) 87, 88; popularity of, 4, 11–12, 237n41; radio style, 9, 10, 11–12, 93; speeches, 84, 89, 101, 102, 231n43; and Supreme Court, 102; Vandenberg "debate" with, 92–93. *See also* New Deal
Roosevelt, Theodore, 4, 26
Roosevelt (FDR) Library, 11
Roper, Elmo B., and Roper polls, 100, 159
Rosenman, Samuel I., 83, 84, 231n43
Ross, T. J., 68
Rothafel, S. L. "Roxy," 32
'Round & 'Round (GM film), 131, *132*
Royal, John F., 16–17, 44–45, 52, 58–62 passim; on 1936 campaign, 89, 230n11
Russell, Frank M., 16
Ruysdael, Basil, 99
Ryerson, Edward, 51

S

Sabin, Thomas G., 88, 89
Salvation Army, 18
Sample, Glenn, 51–52
Sandburg, Carl, 28, 97, 104, 109, 110–13, 114–15
Sarnoff, David, 44, 66, 103, 134
Saroyan, William, 189
Saturday Evening Post, 20, 28, 29, 37, 69, 138
Sayre, Morris B., 237n47
Schlesinger, Arthur M., 72–73, 74–77, 81, 97, 108
Schmertz, Herbert, 244n10
Schnabel, Artur, 42
Screen Actors' Guild (SAG), 202
Searchlight, The (UAW-CIO paper), 162, 166
Sears, Roebuck and Company, 122, 244n6
See It Now (TV series), 201
Selvage, James P., 54, 57–58, 59
Selznick International, 137
Senate, U.S. *See* Congress, U.S.
Senneff, Jonathan A., Jr., 14–15
Sentinels of the Republic, 50
Seth Parker (radio program), 82
Shakespeare, William, 28
Shaw, George Bernard, 189
Sherwood, Robert, 104, 110, 231n43
Shouse, Jouett, 94
Show of the Month (DuPont TV series), 208
Silver, Douglas, 59
Sinclair, Upton, 61, 126, 211
"Si Perkins," 52–53
Sklar, Paul, 13
Slabs of the Sunburnt West (Sandburg), 111
Sloan, Alfred P., Jr., 13, *33*, *136*, 212; and advertising campaigns, 31–32, 33, 37, (Century of Progress) 38–40, (radio) 30, 35, 36, 41, 42–43, 46; and "Futurama," 136; and GM's public relations, 67, 157; radio talks by, 27, 38; and Sloan Foundation, 176
Smith, Al, 67, 82
Smith, Everett, 159
Smith, J. Sanford, 201
Smith, John, Capt., 14
Snoddy, Robert R., 156
Soap Box Derby, 25–26, 167
Soap operas, 242n37
Socialism: and anti-Socialism, 50, 51; public view of, 7, 63
Socony, 220n23

Soconyland Sketches (radio program), 27, 28, 30, 36
Socony-Vacuum Oil, 53, 210
Sokolsky, George E., 54
Sousa, John Philip, 27, 80
Southern Committee to Uphold the Constitution, 50
Southern Railway System, 160
Souvaine, Henry, 41
Spy, The (Cooper), 108
Stalin, Joseph, 26, 121
Standard Oil of New Jersey, 53, 94; film sponsored by, 177
Standard Oil of New York, 27, 28
Stanton, Elizabeth Cady, 78
Stanton, Harry, 69
Starr Company, 92
Stein, Benjamin, 211
Stein, Charles M. A., 98
Stewart, Jimmy, 204
Stokowski, Leopold, 41, 43
Stoopnagle and Budd (radio program), 31
Strange Interview (GM film), 155
Stravinsky, Igor, 42
Strikes. *See* Labor
Stuart, Douglas, 51
Studebaker Company films, 122
Supreme Court, 102, 225n52
Susman, Warren, 19
Sussman, Leila A., 11
Sutherland, John, 176
Swift & Company, 53
Symphony concerts. *See* Music
Symphony in "F" (Ford film), 127–28, 129, 137

T

Tabloid journalism, 26
Taft, Robert Alphonso, 176
Taft-Hartley Act (1947), 9, 53, 145, 160, 167, 176; "free speech" provision of, 150
Talleyrand-Périgord, Charles-Maurice de, 19
Tallman, Robert, 116
Tariff protection, 4, 5, 13, 53
Teague, Walter Dorwin, 94, 186
Technocracy, 36, 37; Soviet workman's fear of, 121
Television: as "anti-business," 211; Barton's complaints about, 207; business involvement in, 9, 181, 208–13, (eight corporate sponsors, 1955) 241n15; business-sponsored films for, 180–81; commercials, 195, 204; cost of, 207; dawning of age of, 118–19, 121–22, 181, 191, 193–95, 208, (DuPont resists) 66, (1939/40 World's Fair and) 133–34, 184–88, (World War II delays) 143, 187; dramatic anthology format, 189, 195; experimental, during World War II, 201; "golden age" of, 197; historical programs, 198; performers blacklisted, 191–93; public, 210–11; shared sponsorship suggested, 201; soap operas, 242n37; theater format, 202
Texas Centennial (Dallas, 1935), 68, 81, 98
Texas Corporation, 53
Theatre Guild (New York), 188, 189, 191, 192
Theatre Guild on the Air (TV program), 119, 188–92
The People, Yes (Benét), 110, 111, 113
They Knew What They Wanted (Howard play), 190
This Advertising Business (Durstine), 26
This Is Nylon (DuPont film), 181
This Week with David Brinkley (TV program), 212
Thomas, Lowell, 133
Thomas, R. J., 149
Thompson, J. Walter, advertising agency, 121
Thorndike, Edward Lee, 6
Thorpe, Merle, 225n59
Three to Be Served (NAM-Paramount film), 157
Tide (advertising journal), 13
Tiger (Princeton magazine), 26
Tinney, Cal, 118
Tin Wedding (TV production), 194
Titterton, L. H., 58–59
Today magazine, 110
Today (TV series), 204
To Each Other (U.S. Steel film), 147, *148*, 156
To New Horizons (GM film), 150
Toscanini, Arturo, 45, 222n67
Town Hall of the Air, 65, 83
Townshend, Charles Francis, 61
Trammell, Niles, 51, 52
Treasury Department, U.S., 67
Triangle Club (Princeton), 26
Truman, Harry, administration, 189
Turning Wheel, The (Pound), 38, 74
"Two-step" communications effects, 37

U

UAW (United Auto Workers), 14, 45, 131, 146, 153, 166
UAW-CIO: films sponsored by and film library of, 149; paper published by, 162, 166; strike by (1936–1937), *see* Labor
Unemployment insurance, 14, 64
Unfinished Business (U.S. Steel film), 155–56
Union Carbide & Carbon, 122
United Action Means Victory (UAW-CIO film), 149
United Auto Workers. *See* UAW
United Electrical, Radio and Machine Workers, films sponsored by, 173–75, 176
United Motors Corporation, 30
United States Rubber, 6, 135
United States Steel, 6, 51, 53; defends blacklisted performers, 189, 191; films sponsored by, 137–38, 146, 147–49, 155–56; magazine advertising by, 193, 225n59; radio programs

sponsored by, 188–93; and steel strike (1949), 191; subsidiaries exhibit at New York World's Fair, 137, 138; and television, 191, 193–95, 201, 202, 207
United States Steel Hour (TV series), 9, 119, 188, 191, 194, 207
United Steel Workers of America, 189
United War Work Campaign, 18
Unit thinking, unit action, 13
University of Chicago Round Table (NBC radio), 102
Utley, S. Wells, 13–14

V

Vandenberg, Arthur H., 92–93
Van Patten, L. A., 50
Variety magazine, 65, 72
Vassos, John, 186
"Voice of General Motors," 25, 40, 41, 43–44, 46
Voice of the Crusaders radio talks, 92
Voorhees, Enders M., 192–93

W

Wagner Act (1935), 150, 160, 162
Wakeman, Frederic, 115
Walker, Mayor James "Jimmie," 29
Walker, Strother Holland, 13
Wampler, Cloud, 237n47
War Advertising Council, 159
Warburg, James P., 149
War Department, U.S., 235n5
Washburn Crosby Company, 51
Washington, Booker T., 81
Washington, George, 28, 35, 90, 106, 108, 198
Washington Post, 210
Watch Mr. Wizard (TV program), 202
Watts, Ridley, 223n6
Waugh, Evelyn, 204
WCCO Minneapolis, 51, 52
Webb, Kenneth, 72, 74, 75, 76, 81
Wedge, The (BBDO house organ), 6
We Drivers: GM film, 150; GM radio series, 43–44
Weisenberger, Walter B., 53, 54, 59, 64
Welles, Orson, 110, 115
Wells, H. G., 11
Western Electric Company, 21, 125, *126*
Western Union, 122
Westinghouse Electric and Manufacturing, 6, 21, 35, 53; exhibits at NY World's Fair, 134, 186; sponsors *Middleton Family* film, 8, 124, 138–43, 147, 156, 208
Westinghouse Salutes (radio program), 29–30, 35, 36
WGN Chicago, 90, 92
WGY Schenectady, 52
Wheaties Quartette, 52
Where's the Rest of Me? (Reagan), 205
"Whig theory" of history, 21–22, 73
Whig Interpretation of History, The (Butterfield), 22
White, R. H., 42
White, William Allen, 61, 215n10
Whiteman, Paul, 31, 222n67
White Top Folk Festival, 221n40
Whitman, Walt, 117
Whitney, Eli, 198
Whyte, William Allen, 159
Wier, E. T., 13
Williams, S. Clay, 223n6
Williamsburg, Virginia, 28
Williamson, A. R., 90
Willkie, Wendell, 18, 235n8
Willson, Meredith, 69
Wilshire, Joseph, 223n6
Wilson, Charles E. (General Electric), 176–77
Wilson, Charles E. (General Motors), 236n23
Wilson, Mark, 200
Wilson, Robert E., 221n55
Wilson, Woodrow, 4, 37, 90
Wisconsin, tribute to, *34*
Wise, Stephen, Rabbi, 103
Witmer, Roy C., 40, 45
WLAG Minneapolis, 51
WNBT, 171
Women's National Radio Committee, 72
Woodworth, Robert S., 6
Woollcott, Alexander, 109
Worker Speaks, The (GM pamphlet), 165, 167
Working on Air (GM film), 236n20
World Broadcasting System, 54, 58
World Court, 16
World's Columbian Exposition (1893), 30, 80
World's Fair, Chicago. *See* Century of Progress exposition (1933–1939)
World's Fair, New York (1939/40). *See* New York World's Fair
World War I, 18, 30–31, 37, 60, 66, 109
World War II, 14, 143; advertising during, 146–49, 157–58, 159; *Cavalcade of America* during, 97, 108, 110, 118; experimental television during, 201; films during, 8, 145–50; industrial mobilization in, 183; and labor relations, 146–47
Wren, John, 241n24
WRGB Schenectady (TV), 201
WTAM Cleveland, 17
Wyler, William, 156
Wynn, Ed, 21, 27

Y

Yale University, 101–2
Yankee Network, 16, 50
YMCA, 18

Yorktowne Sesquicentennial (1931), 32
Young, James Webb, 159
Young, John Orr, 159
Young, Owen D., 19–20, 52
Young & Rubicam advertising agency, 201
Youngstown Sheet & Tube Company, 53
Your Town—the Story of America (NAM film), 156
Youth Wants to Know (TV program), 202

Zoller, John, 197